DATE DUE

Developing vocabulary
Concepts for College Thinking

Second Edition

Sherrie L. Nist
University of Georgia

Michele L. Simpson
University of Georgia

Houghton Mifflin Company   **Boston   New York**

This book is dedicated to the pursuit of
Dixon Lane and the men who dream of living there.

Sponsoring Editor: Renée Deljon
Senior Associate Editor: Linda Bieze
Associate Project Editor: Gabrielle Stone
Associate Production/Design Coordinator: Jennifer Meyer
Senior Manufacturing Coordinator: Michael O'Dea
Marketing Manager: Nancy Lyman

Cover Designer: Cathy Hawkes

Both authors contributed equally to this textbook. Hence, the
determination was made to list their names in alphabetical order.

As part of Houghton Mifflin's ongoing commitment to the environment,
this text has been printed on recycled paper.

Printed in the U.S.A.

Library of Congress Catalog Card Number: 96-76940

Student Book ISBN: 0-669-41835-8
Instructor's Edition ISBN: 0-669-41850-1
Instructor's Resource Manual ISBN: 0-669-41851-X

1 2 3 4 5 6 7 8 9–QM–00 99 98 97 96

....

Preface

TO THE INSTRUCTOR

Developing Vocabulary Concepts for College Thinking, Second Edition, has received several improvements based on reviewers' comments, without changing the overall philosophy and goals of the text. Rather, we have tried to make the text more interesting and engaging by adding new readings, more activities, writing activities, and more options for instructors to use the text with their students. In addition, we hope we have made it clear that teaching vocabulary does not have to be a lock-step process. Instructors should feel free to modify any or all ideas from this text to meet the needs of their particular students and programs. Suggestions for modification are presented in greater detail in the *Instructor's Resource Manual.* Thus we suggest that you spend some time reading the *Instructor's Resource Manual* and examining the student text before you decide which approach or combination of approaches might work best with your students.

The philosophy behind *Developing Vocabulary Concepts for College Thinking,* Second Edition, remains consistent with that of the first edition. It is a structured approach to learning vocabulary that takes into consideration the importance of many different types of interactions with words. Based on current research in the field of vocabulary, the text teaches new words embedded in the context of reading activities. In addition, we stress that there is no one clean and perfect way to learn vocabulary. It certainly isn't as simple as **either** dictionary **or** context **or** word elements. Rather, *Developing Vocabulary Concepts,* Second Edition, stresses using a combination of all three approaches, pulling in students' prior knowledge whenever possible, and teaching a variety of generative vocabulary strategies that students will be able to apply on their own beyond the course for which they are using this book. As developmental reading instructors for many years, we have used these techniques and materials with our own students and have witnessed positive results. Not only have we watched students' knowledge of words grow, but students using the strategies and techniques described in *Developing Vocabulary Concepts,* Second Edition, have also improved comprehension and their reading and writing well beyond our classrooms.

The text is divided into two main parts. Part I, which includes the first four chapters, sets the stage for the activities in the four thematic chapters in Part II. Chapter 1, "Knowing a Word," focuses on what it means to know a word thoroughly. It presents the different stages of word knowledge and discusses why it is important to develop an extensive vocabulary. Chapter 2, "Generative Vocabulary Strategies," discusses numerous strategies that students can use as they learn words in this text and beyond. Chapter 3, "Dictionary Use," takes an unconventional approach to teaching students how and when to use a dictionary. Although we have a section in this chapter about how to "read" dictionary entries, the major focus is on how to judge definitions appropriately and how a dictionary can be used in conjunction with other generative strategies. Chapter 3 also introduces word etymologies. And Chapter 4, "Word Elements," discusses how to use prefixes, roots, and suffixes as another means of unlocking word meaning. In each of these four chapters, students also have an opportunity to learn numerous new words taken from text excerpts and short articles. These readings are tied to the themes presented in Part II. Students should read and carry out the activities in these first four chapters before beginning the thematic chapters.

The four chapters in Part II are organized around thematic topics—gender, education, health, and the environment. Each of these chapters contains three readings, two from magazines or other narrative text and one from a college-level textbook, so that students are introduced to both general and content-specific words. In addition, students engage in a variety of exercises and activities that provide multiple exposures to words and encourage conceptual thinking. These activities are described in the introduction to the thematic chapters. Students are encouraged to use the generative strategies outlined in Chapter 2 as ways of conceptually knowing rather than simply memorizing definitions for words. Each thematic chapter also includes writing activities and encourages metacognitive awareness as students engage in self-evaluating when they take the pretest and again before taking the chapter posttests.

In the first edition of *Developing Vocabulary Concepts for College Thinking,* posttests were included only at the end of each thematic chapter. But comments we received as we were planning the second edition led us to believe that many instructors used this text in combination with a reading or study skills text, thus not having time to complete all of the readings in a chapter. Consequently, in the second edition, we have tried to provide more flexibility in using the text by including two posttests, one that tests the words introduced in Readings A and B, and a second that tests the words from Readings A, B, and C. This gives you as an instructor several options. Students may do one of the following:

1. Take Posttest I over Readings A and B, then skip Reading C altogether and proceed to the next chapter.
2. Take Posttest I over Readings A and B, then proceed to Reading C and complete those activities. When students have finished Reading C, they can take Posttest II over Readings A, B, and C.
3. Complete the activities for Readings A and B and proceed to Reading C without taking Posttest I. Once they have completed all three readings, students can then take Posttest II, which covers all of the words presented in the chapter.

Certainly there are other combinations that you can try out. Our goal was simply to give instructors as many options as possible for their programs and students.

A final comment about the text. Although *Developing Vocabulary Concepts,* Second Edition, has vocabulary development as its goal, students also learn strategies that improve their overall comprehension. Such an approach encourages students to think beyond learning basic definitions to learning information in a more conceptual way. In addition, we also feel that discussion about words and concepts is important if students are to grow to their potentials. Therefore, throughout the text, we encourage talking about the readings and the words found in them, as well as the activities. We also recommend that students do some of the activities with a study partner or in a small group.

As teachers ourselves, we not only have enjoyed using this approach with our students, but also have found that our students have grown in their knowledge of words and concepts as a result. We hope that your experiences and the experiences of your students will be as positive as ours.

TO THE STUDENT

Knowledge of words influences every aspect of communication—speaking, writing, and understanding what others are saying or have written. Simply and straightforwardly put, individuals who possess limited vocabularies often are at a disadvantage. They may not be able to comprehend fully what others have written in the workplace, they may find some textbooks difficult, and they may have problems in communicating with peers and colleagues. It is for these reasons that we wrote this book.

You may have had previous experiences in vocabulary building in which you looked up words in a dictionary and had to memorize their definitions. What generally happens in situations like this one, however, is that as soon as you are tested over the words, you forget them. Learning vocabulary in this manner rarely leads to a conceptual understanding of words, which is the major focus of *Developing Vocabulary Concepts for College Thinking,* Second Edition. Our goal is to help you interact with words in such a way that you will know something about a word beyond a simple dictionary definition. The variety of activities provided in this text should enable you to understand words better. And if you can fully know a word's meaning (conceptualize words), you can feel comfortable using it in your own communication with others.

There are several aspects of *Developing Vocabulary Concepts* that differ from other vocabulary texts. First, all words are presented not only in the context of an actual reading, but also within the larger context of thematic chapters. We have selected four themes—gender, education, health-related issues, environment—and three readings within each theme to present the words. Words are not taught isolated from actual reading because without context, words alone actually have little or no meaning. Thus, in addition to learning new words, you will also learn information about the four themes in the book.

Second, the exercises provide exposure to a variety of activities, progressing from easier, more traditional activities, to those that are more difficult and conceptual. We encourage you to discuss the words with classmates and your instructor as additional ways to gain more conceptual word knowledge. And there are writing activities in which use of your newfound vocabulary is encouraged.

Third, *Developing Vocabulary Concepts* emphasizes the importance of generative strategies as a way of continuing to build vocabulary throughout life. Generative strategies are those you can develop and use with any reading task you have to do so that you require little assistance from others. All too often, readers simply skip over unknown words as they read, rather than making attempts at learning them. Related to the idea of generative strategies is the importance of using a dictionary as a tool rather than the answer. As we will point out, a dictionary alone rarely provides conceptual word knowledge. Consequently, *Developing Vocabulary Concepts,* will introduce you to a variety of approaches to learning new words on your own.

Finally, as you progress through this text, you will get the impression that learning vocabulary is not a particularly easy task, as it is often portrayed. But neither is it impossible. We outline and explain the steps to learning vocabulary in the introduction to the thematic chapters and encourage you to read it carefully before beginning the section. We also encourage you to try out the strategies and ideas suggested in *Developing Vocabulary Concepts.* Although all of them will not work for everyone, you will want to find those that help you most. As you work through the text, you will see your vocabulary grow, learn new strategies, and become more aware of words. But the biggest payoff will be in your overall reading comprehension.

S.L.N. and M.L.S.

Acknowledgments

Numerous individuals, who were either directly or indirectly involved with the completion and subsequent publication of this book, deserve thanks. The idea for writing *Developing Vocabulary Concepts for College Thinking* stemmed from the need we observed in our students. Hence, first and foremost, we owe a great deal of thanks and appreciation to them. During the past several years, they have validated our philosophical beliefs about teaching vocabulary, informed us emphatically about the kind of reading that interested them, and, perhaps most importantly, tried out a wide variety of activities important to our philosophical base. During this entire process, we have learned much about what encourages long-term vocabulary growth from them. In a sense, this text is a culmination of what they have taught us, as well as what we have taught them.

Second, our thanks to reviewers Naomi Barnett, Lorain County Community College; Gayle Hill, Virginia State University; Fred S. Kai, El Camino College; Robert W. Kopfstein, Saddleback College; Judith F. Kupersmith, St. Petersburg Junior College; Linda C. Lisman, SUNY-Binghamton; William J. McGreevey, Ocean County College; Maggi Miller, Austin Community College; Meritt Stark, Henderson State University; Barbara Travis, De Anza College; Sebastian J. Vasta, Camden County Community College; Paulette Vrett, McHenry County College; and Linda Wong, Lane Community College for their suggestions for the development of this text. We believe that incorporating these reviewers' suggestions has strengthened *Developing Vocabulary Concepts for College Thinking,* Second Edition, and made it useful for a large cross-section of college students.

Third, we thank our editors at Houghton Mifflin Company for their help with this new edition: Renée Deljon, Linda Bieze, and Gabrielle Stone.

Last, and certainly not least, we would like to thank our respective families for their support during our work on this edition. So, to our biggest fans—Steve, Kama, Mom, Dad, and Tom: we appreciated your patience and support.

S.L.N. and M.L.S.

Contents

Introduction to Chapters 1–4

The purpose of Part I of *Developing Vocabulary Concepts,* Second Edition, is to give you the tools to learn vocabulary in such a way that you can (a) learn new words on your own, and (b) learn words to the point that you will be able to remember them for future use. Chapter 1 addresses the importance of having a large vocabulary and what it means to truly know a word. Chapter 2 focuses on a variety of strategies that you can use to learn words for future use, while Chapter 3 takes a unique look at using a dictionary, including word etymologies (word origins). Finally, Chapter 4 targets word elements—prefixes, roots, and suffixes.

Although the primary purpose of the first four chapters is to give you the strategies you need to progress through the last four chapters, we have also introduced many words here. Each of these words is tied to a specific reading selection that represents one of the four major themes in *Developing Vocabulary Concepts,* Second Edition: gender issues, education, health-related issues, and the environment. Chapter 1 contains a selection describing Malcolm X's self-education while in prison. Chapter 2 contains three text readings entitled "Vats, Fats and Rats," "1962: The Court Bans Public-School Prayer," and "Instinct and Learning." The third chapter, "Dictionary Use," contains an article dealing with pollution, and the gender theme is represented in Chapter 4 with a text excerpt on the nonverbal communication that occurs between men and women. Words drawn from these articles are used as examples to demonstrate and reinforce the strategies taught. Each chapter presents a variety of activities that permit you to interact with words from the article or text excerpt. Note also that in this second edition, more readings and activities have been added to provide additional practice.

We encourage you to read these four chapters carefully. We also encourage you not only to do the activities in *Developing Vocabulary Concepts,* Second Edition, but also to discuss the words in class and to try to use them in your daily conversations and in your writing. Making a concerted effort to understand and try out the strategies presented in Part I will enable you to progress more efficiently and effectively through the last four chapters of this book.

1

Knowing a Word

Did You Know?
The word *boycott* originated from Captain Charles Boycott, a landlord who treated his tenants unfairly. To get even, the tenants refused to work and intercepted his food and mail. Today if you *boycott* a company you refuse to buy from that company.

Do you remember any of your past experiences with vocabulary improvement? If you are like most students, you were probably given 20 words a week that you had to look up in a dictionary so you could write a definition and sentence for each. Do you remember cramming madly for those Friday quizzes? Do you also remember immediately forgetting all those words the moment you escaped the classroom? If so, you are not alone. Those experiences in "expanding" your vocabulary may not have been effective or pleasant.

This textbook, however, will approach vocabulary expansion differently. More importantly, you will be able to remember the new words you learn for your own personal use. Before we discuss strategies that can increase vocabulary, however, we need to outline some basic notions that will underlie the rest of the text. Hence, the purpose of this chapter is to explain why vocabulary learning is important and what it means to know a word "conceptually."

In each chapter of this textbook there are one or more articles for you to read. The first one is "My Alma Mater" by Malcolm X. In this article Malcolm X describes how he educated himself while in prison. Before reading this article, think about and then respond to the following items:

1. Learning new words is important to me because

_____

_____

_____

_____

2. To increase my vocabulary I have done these things:

_____

_____

_____

_____

3. I know I really "understand" a new word when I can

_____

_____

_____

_____

_____

Now read the article, paying particular attention to the following list of words. In the article, these words are in bold print.

atheism	inevitable
dormant	quota
emulate	rehabilitation
engrossing	riffling
expounded	riveted
feigned	vistas

Reading

My Alma Mater
by Malcolm X

The first man I met in prison who made any positive impression on me whatever was a fellow inmate, "Bimbi." I met him in 1947, at Charlestown. He was a light, kind of red-complexioned Negro, as I was; about my height, and he had freckles. Bimbi, an old-time burglar, had been in many prisons. In the license plate shop where our gang worked, he operated the machine that stamped out the numbers. I was along the conveyor belt where the numbers were painted.

Bimbi was the first Negro convict I'd known who didn't respond to "What'cha know, Daddy?" Often, after we had done our day's license plate *quota,* we would sit around, perhaps fifteen of us, and listen to Bimbi. Normally, white prisoners wouldn't think of listening to Negro prisoners' opinions on anything, but guards, even, would wander over close to hear Bimbi on any subject.

He would have a cluster of people *riveted,* often on odd subjects you never would think of. He would prove to us, dipping into the science of human behavior, that the only difference between us and outside people was that we had been caught. He liked to talk about historical events and figures. When he talked about the history of Concord, where I was to be transferred later, you would have thought he was hired by the Chamber of Commerce, and I wasn't the first inmate who had never heard of Thoreau until Bimbi *expounded* upon him. Bimbi was known as the library's best customer. What fascinated me with him most of all was that he was the first man I had ever seen command total respect . . . with his words.

Bimbi seldom said much to me; he was gruff to individuals, but I sensed he liked me. What made me seek his friendship was when I heard him discuss religion. I considered myself beyond *atheism*—I was Satan. But Bimbi put the atheist philosophy in a framework, so to speak. That ended my vicious cursing attacks. My approach sounded so weak alongside his, and he never used a foul word.

Out of the blue one day, Bimbi told me flatly, as was his way, that I had some brains, if I'd use them. I had wanted his friendship, not that kind of advice. I might have cursed another convict, but nobody cursed Bimbi. He told me I should take advantage of the prison correspondence courses and the library.

When I had finished the eighth grade back in Mason, Michigan, that was the last time I'd thought of studying anything that didn't have some hustle purpose. And the streets had erased everything I'd ever learned in school; I didn't know a verb from a house. . . .

Many who today hear me somewhere in person, or on television, or those who read something I've said, will think I went to school far beyond the eighth grade. This impression is due entirely to my prison studies.

It had really begun back in the Charlestown Prison, when Bimbi first made me feel envy of his stock of knowledge. Bimbi had always taken charge of any conversation he was in, and I had tried to *emulate* him. But every book I picked up had few sentences which didn't contain anywhere from one to nearly all of the words that might as well have been in Chinese. When I just skipped those words, of course, I really ended up with little idea of what the book said. So I had come to the Norfolk Prison Colony still going through only book-reading motions. Pretty soon, I would have quit even these motions, unless I had received the motivation that I did.

I saw that the best thing I could do was get hold of a dictionary—to study, to learn some words. I was lucky enough to reason also that I should try to improve my penmanship. It was sad. I couldn't even write in a straight line. It was both ideas together that moved me to request a dictionary along with some tablets and pencils from the Norfolk Prison Colony school.

I spent two days just *riffling* uncertainly through the dictionary's pages. I'd never realized so many words existed! I didn't know which words I needed to learn. Finally, to start some kind of action, I began copying.

In my slow, painstaking, ragged handwriting, I copied into my tablet everything printed on that first page, down to the punctuation marks.

I believe it took me a day. Then, aloud, I read back, to myself, everything I'd written on the tablet. Over and over, aloud, to myself, I read my own handwriting.

I woke up the next morning, thinking about those words—immensely proud to realize that not only had I written so much at one time, but I'd written words that I never knew were in the world. Moreover, with a little effort, I also could remember what many of these words meant. I reviewed the words whose meanings I didn't remember. Funny thing, from the dictionary first page right now, that "aardvark" springs to my mind. The dictionary had a picture of it, a long-tailed, long-eared, burrowing African mammal, which lives off termites caught by sticking out its tongue as an anteater does for ants.

I was so fascinated that I went on—I copied the dictionary's next page. And the same experience came when I studied that. With every succeeding page, I also learned of people and places and events from history. Actually the dictionary is like a miniature encyclopedia. Finally the dictionary's A section had filled a whole tablet—and I went on into the B's. That was the way I started copying what eventually became the entire dictionary. It went a lot faster after so much practice helped me to pick up handwriting speed. Between what I wrote in my tablet, and writing letters, during the rest of my time in prison I would guess I wrote a million words.

I suppose it was *inevitable* that as my word-base broadened, I could for the first time pick up a book and read and now begin to understand what the book was saying. Anyone who has read a great deal can imagine the new world that opened. Let me tell you something; from then until I left that prison, in every free moment I had, if I was not reading in the library, I was reading on my bunk. You couldn't have gotten me out of books with a wedge. Between Mr. Muhammad's teachings, my correspondence, my visitors—usually Ella and Reginald—and my reading of books, months passed without my even thinking about being imprisoned. In fact, up to then, I never had been so truly free in my life. . . .

As you can imagine, especially in a prison where there was heavy emphasis on *rehabilitation,* an inmate was smiled upon if he demonstrated an unusually intense interest in books. There was a sizable number of well-read inmates, especially the popular debaters. Some were said by many to be practically walking encyclopedias. They were almost celebrities. No university would ask any student to devour literature as I did when this new world opened to me, of being able to read and *understand*.

I read more in my room than in the library itself. An inmate who was known to read a lot could check out more than the permitted maximum number of books. I preferred reading in the total isolation of my own room.

When I had progressed to really serious reading, every night at about ten P.M. I would be outraged with the "lights out." It always seemed to catch me right in the middle of something *engrossing*.

Fortunately, right outside my door was a corridor light that cast a glow into my room. The glow was enough to read by, once my eyes adjusted to it. So when "lights out" came, I would sit on the floor where I could continue reading in that glow.

At one-hour intervals the night guards paced past every room. Each time I heard the approaching footsteps, I jumped into bed and *feigned* sleep. And as soon as the guard passed, I got back out of bed onto the floor area of that light-glow, where I would read for another fifty-eight minutes—until the guard approached again. That went on until three or four every morning. Three or four hours of sleep a night was enough for me. Often in the years in the streets I had slept less than that.

I have often reflected upon the new *vistas* that reading opened to me. I knew right there in prison that reading had changed forever the course of my life. As I see it today, the ability to read awoke inside me some long *dormant* craving to be mentally alive. I certainly wasn't seeking any degree, the way a college confers a status symbol upon its students. My homemade education gave me, with every additional book that I read, a little bit more sensitivity to the deafness, dumbness, and blindness that was afflicting the black race in America. Not long ago, an English writer telephoned me from London, asking questions. One was, "What's your alma mater?" I told him, "Books." You will never catch me with a free fifteen minutes in which I'm not studying something I feel might be able to help the black man. . . .

Every time I catch a plane, I have with me a book that I want to read—and that's a lot of books these days. If I weren't out here every day battling the white man, I could spend the rest of my life reading, just satisfying my curiosity—because you can hardly mention anything I'm not curious about. I don't think anybody ever got more out of going to prison than I did.

In fact, prison enabled me to study far more intensively than I would have if my life had gone differently and I had attended some college. I imagine that one of the biggest troubles with colleges is there are too many distractions, too much panty-raiding, fraternities, and boola-boola and all of that. Where else but in prison could I have attacked my ignorance by being able to study intensely sometimes as much as fifteen hours a day? □

Based on your reading of "My Alma Mater," respond to the following items the way in which you think Malcolm X would have:

1. Learning new words was important to Malcolm X because

_____

_____

2. To increase his vocabulary, Malcolm X _____

_____

3. Malcolm X knew that he really "understood" a word when he

could _____

_____

WHY IS AN EXTENSIVE VOCABULARY IMPORTANT?

We know from research and personal experiences that an extensive vocabulary is essential for several reasons. Probably the best reason was expressed by Malcolm X in the article you just read. Malcolm X wanted to increase his vocabulary so he could read the books that his friend Bimbi had read. But an extensive vocabulary is also important to your academic career. To illustrate this point better, read the following paragraph, which was taken from a college-level psychology textbook. After reading, write a brief summary in the blank provided.

Freud conceived of humans as closed energy systems. He borrowed this theory from the principle of energy conservation. Entropy refers to the energy not available for work and, consequently, is cathected. In contrast is free energy which is available for other functions. If an individual is in homeostasis, then all energy is free and hedonism will accrue.

Key Idea _____

_____

You may have had a little difficulty in summarizing that paragraph. Even though you could correctly pronounce all the words, the number of difficult and unfamiliar words and concepts probably made the task of understanding more challenging. Students with extensive vocabularies are the readers who understand, with ease, what they have read. On the other hand, readers with limited vocabularies usually have difficulty reading and spend more energy and time on reading tasks. Therefore, if you improve your vocabulary, as Malcolm X did, you should see an improvement in your reading and listening comprehension.

If you had to read and reread the above paragraph in order to make some sense of it, you have experienced what it is like to read with a limited vocabulary. Readers with limited vocabulary knowledge are typically slow readers. They may need to reread and look up many words in a dictionary. Though rereading and dictionary usage are not negative behaviors, an overdependence on either could severely slow the reading process.

In contrast, readers with extensive vocabularies and background experiences are typically skilled readers who can easily make sense of what they read. Thus, a second reason why vocabulary knowledge is important is that it will increase reading rate and fluency.

A third reason why an extensive vocabulary is important concerns the power and precision you have at your command for expressing yourself in speaking and writing. To illustrate this point, carefully read the following pairs of sentences and check the one in each pair that communicates a more descriptive and vivid picture.

____ The movie starlet strolled seductively into the room and impishly mugged for the press.
____ The movie starlet walked into the room and posed for the press.

____ My energetic pooch adores frolicking in the yard.
____ My dog likes to play in the yard.

____ The tedium of my history class was due to my professor's loquaciousness.

_____ My history class was boring because my professor talked too much.

The first sentence of each pair contains the more powerful and descriptive vocabulary words. These words, in turn, communicate specific and precise images. The words in the second sentence of each pair, such as "walked," "posed," "likes," or "boring," are so ordinary that you probably received only a fuzzy or general sense of what the author intended. Dynamic and entertaining speakers and writers understand and use the power and richness of language. However, you need not be a professional writer or famous speaker to benefit from an extensive vocabulary. An extensive and rich vocabulary is essential for all the situations in college and in your career when you need to communicate effectively. The key to successful speaking and writing is to choose the most appropriate and precise word, not the most difficult.

Perhaps you are now convinced that there are many reasons to improve your vocabulary. With a greater understanding of words, you will be able to improve your

- reading and listening comprehension.
- reading rate and fluency.
- effectiveness in writing and speaking.

The next question that you need to ask yourself is what it means to understand or know a word. In the next section we will answer that question.

WHAT DOES IT MEAN TO KNOW A WORD?

Edgar Dale (1958) suggested that our word understanding probably exists on a gradual continuum much like the one in Figure 1.1. In other words, there are some vocabulary words that you have never seen or heard; some words that you have seen or heard, but feel uncomfortable or unsure in giving their definition; some words for which you can give a general classification; and some words that you recognize and for which you feel comfortable providing a precise definition.

Let's examine an example using *engrossing,* a word used in the Malcolm X article. If you have never seen or heard *engrossing,* your knowledge of this word exists at the first stage. Students who avoid reading unless it is required by a course or professor probably have quite a few other words that fit in this first stage. Remember—the more you read the larger your vocabulary.

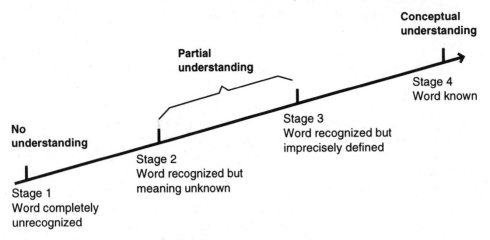

Figure 1.1 Dale's Stages

The second stage is reserved for the words that you have seen or heard somewhere, but do not know their meaning. For example, you may have heard a friend describe a book as **engrossing,** but did not know what she meant when she said that. This is a partial, although very limited, understanding of the word.

In the third stage are those words for which you have some general, yet fuzzy, notion of meaning. According to Dale, we have a large number of words in this "twilight zone"—words that fall between being known and being unknown. With the **engrossing** example, you might say, "Yes, I have heard of that word before—it describes someone or something in a positive manner, but I do not know the specifics." This fuzziness, also a partial understanding in word knowledge, can negatively affect your reading, listening, and understanding. For example, if you did not know the precise meaning of **engrossing,** you might conclude that your friend is describing the movie or book as **engrossing** because it was short and easy to read. This interpretation, of course, would be incorrect since an **engrossing** book is one that captures or occupies your attention.

Knowing precise and accurate definitions of words such as **engrossing** would occur in the fourth stage of vocabulary understanding. This stage comes the closest to capturing what is meant by conceptually knowing a word. That is, you understand a word upon recognition and can provide an appropriate and precise definition that fits the context. This is what you probably think of when you say that you "know a word."

Let's try out these four stages in knowing a word with some of the words from Malcolm X's article, "My Alma Mater." In Activity 1.1 you will determine what words from the article fit in each of the stages.

DIRECTIONS: Quickly search Malcolm X's article to find at least two words that could fit in each of the four stages. Remember to use your own word knowledge and to list the words in the blanks provided. You may wish to compare and contrast your lists with others in your class.

Stage One: I do not know these words at all (no understanding).

_____   _____

Stage Two: I recognize these words, but do not know what they mean (partial understanding).

_____   _____

Stage Three: I recognize these words, but cannot precisely define them (partial understanding).

_____ This word has something to do with _____

_____ This word has something to do with _____

Stage Four: I know these words because I can define them accurately and precisely (conceptual understanding).

engrossing This word means _____

_____

_____ This word means _____

_____

Although you were able to list definitions of several words in Activity 1.1, "conceptual knowledge" of a word involves more precision and detail than just a dictionary definition. In the next section we will explain conceptual word knowledge in more detail.

CONCEPTUALLY KNOWING A WORD

Knowing the definition of a word is important and may be sufficient in many situations. However, memorizing and connecting a definition to a targeted word is just a beginning point. A memorized definition is often the tip of the iceberg, the part mistakenly believed to be the total iceberg because it is so visible and obvious. Beneath the surface of the water is a much larger mass of ice which is far more important. Conceptual word knowledge is like the iceberg beneath the water in that it, too, is far more important than the obvious dictionary definition. Conceptual word knowledge assumes that you will begin with an appropriate definition and then add three layers beyond that definition. Just as there is much more to an iceberg than what appears floating above the water, so it is with knowing a word.

Figure 1.2 illustrates the three layers of conceptual knowledge, or the rest of the iceberg. Note that the tip of the iceberg starts with a dictionary definition of a word that fits the sentence in which you first discovered the word. Words, in themselves, have little or no meaning. The meaning of words comes from the author's message and surrounding words and sentences. These pieces, put together, are referred to as the *context*. Hence, you will always need to select the correct dictionary definition carefully. In Chapter 3 we will discuss this process in more detail.

SYNONYMS/ANTONYMS

As Figure 1.2 reveals, the first layer of conceptual word knowledge beneath the water requires you to think of appropriate synonyms, antonyms, examples, and nonexamples for a word. A thesaurus or some computer programs may help you with this, but the best source for synonyms (words with similar meanings) and antonyms (opposites) is frequently yourself. For example, if your dictionary did not list an antonym for the word **engrossing** and you knew that it described something that occupied or absorbed your attention, then all you need to do is to brainstorm some words in opposition to the definition. Possible antonyms for **engrossing** might include *boring* or *uninteresting*.

Closely related to synonym and antonym knowledge is the knowledge of examples and nonexamples for the words you are learning. Understanding examples that are discussed in the text and being able to think of others not discussed are both critical preparations for using words correctly in writing and speaking. To know that Malcolm X found books to be **engrossing** is an example from the text. But to be

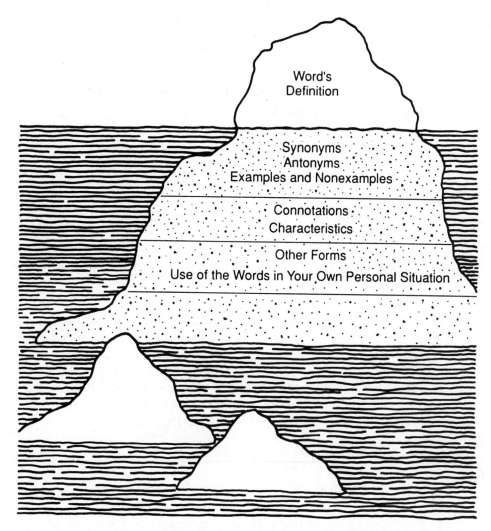

Figure 1.2 Conceptual Word Knowledge

able to apply the word ***engrossing*** to your own personal situation is even more important. If you could describe a book or movie such as *The Color Purple* as engrossing, then you are much closer to a conceptual knowledge of the word ***engrossing.***

ACTIVITY 1.2 _____

DIRECTIONS: Read each of the following words in the context provided in the article "My Alma Mater," by Malcolm X. Look up each word in the dictionary and, based on the way the word is used in the sentence, provide a synonym and antonym for each of the words in bold print.

1. He would have a cluster of people ***riveted,*** often on odd subjects you never would think of.

   Synonym _____

   Antonym _____

2. When he talked about the history of Concord, where I was to be transferred later, you would have thought he was hired by the Chamber of Commerce, and I wasn't the first inmate who had never heard of Thoreau until Bimbi ***expounded*** upon him.

   Synonym _____

   Antonym _____

3. I suppose it was ***inevitable*** that as my word-base broadened, I could for the first time pick up a book and read and now begin to understand what the book was saying.

   Synonym _____

   Antonym _____

4. Each time I heard the approaching footsteps, I jumped into bed and ***feigned*** sleep.

   Synonym _____

   Antonym _____

EXAMPLES/NONEXAMPLES

Being able to think of examples or situations that are not examples is also important to your word knowledge because it permits you to be more precise. This is especially true for courses such as sociology and psychology in which you are expected to learn massive lists of key ideas. Many times professors will devise test questions that ask you to apply a concept or key idea to a new situation. The example below, taken from a college-level psychology test, illustrates a test question asking for knowledge of a nonexample.

Which of the following would NOT be an example of hysteria?

  a. Not hearing anything although there is no physical cause for your deafness.
  b. Believing you are blind even if you can see.
  c. Experiencing strong labor pains although you are not pregnant.
  d. Walking although you are actually paralyzed.

In order to correctly answer this question, you would have to know that "d" is the nonexample since the other choices are good examples of hysteria.

According to Figure 1.2, the second layer of conceptual word knowledge requires you to understand the characteristics and connotations of a word. The characteristics and connotations for words are rarely stated directly in a dictionary. Instead, they come from experiences with other people, reading, listening, and attempting to try out words in writing and speaking. Consequently, this level of word knowledge is not learned quickly or immediately, but through repeated exposures to a word over a period of time.

To illustrate what it means to know the characteristics and connotations of a word, let's return to the word *engrossing.* After hearing and reading the word *engrossing,* you have probably determined that most people would like to be described in this manner. In other words, the word has a favorable connotation and you would react in a positive fashion if someone described you as an engrossing person or said that a speech you gave was engrossing. In contrast, the word *dull* has a negative connotation. You probably would be displeased if your best friend described you as having a dull personality. Thus, you can see that many words have either a positive and favorable or negative and unfavorable connotation and that these connotations may vary among individuals or across cultures.

ACTIVITY 1.3 ━━━━━━━━━━━━━━━

DIRECTIONS: In this activity, try your hand at generating some **nonexamples.** *The first one has been done for you to give you an idea of how to approach this activity.*

1. Give an example of someone you would NOT want to *emulate*.

    I would not want to *emulate* a person who was mean and rude

    because people would not like me very much.

2. Give an example of something an *atheist* would NOT believe.

    An *atheist* would not believe that _____

    _____

3. Give an example of when you might NOT need *rehabilitation*.

    You would not need *rehabilitation* if_____

    _____

4. Give an example of an animal that does NOT go into

    dormancy in the winter. An animal that does not go into

    dormancy in the winter would be _____

    _____

5. Give an example of a situation in which you would NOT want

    to *feign* sleep. You would not want to *feign* sleep _____

    _____

PERSONALIZING WORDS

The third and final layer of conceptual word knowledge requires you to be able to use a word in situations and forms different from your first encounter with the word. This means you can apply a new word to your own experiences. For example, when you read the word *emulate* in the selection about Malcolm X, you learned that Malcolm wanted to *emulate* or imitate Bimbi, a fellow convict. With this layer of word knowledge, you could apply *emulate* to your own life. Perhaps you have wanted to *emulate* your brother or sister because he or she has a successful job. Or perhaps your roommate likes to *emulate* or imitate the way you act in the morning after the alarm rings loudly. You probably have also asked your roommate not to *emulate* your grouchy morning behavior in front of your friends.

Understanding that many words can be used in different forms or functions is also part of the last level of conceptual knowledge. For example, *emulate* is the verb form, but it can also be used as a noun in the form of *emulation* and as an adjective in the form of *emulative.* Using another word from Malcolm X's article, the adjective *engrossing* can become a verb in the form of *engross* or a noun in the form of *engrossment.*

> Malcolm X was so *engrossed* in what he was reading that he was angry when the lights were turned out in the prison.

The word *atheism* can also function as a noun in the form of *atheist* or as an adjective in the form of *atheistic.* The noun *rehabilitation* comes from the verb *rehabilitate.* After learning a word in one form, with the third layer of word knowledge you have the flexibility to change forms and functions to make your own writing and speaking even more interesting and precise. These layers, like the part of the iceberg lurking beneath the water, are extremely important for many reasons, the most important of which is to provide a conceptual understanding so that you can use new words for your own speaking and writing situations.

ACTIVITY 1.4 _____

DIRECTIONS: All of the words below are taken from the article "My Alma Mater," but are not necessarily the targeted words in bold type. However, all of these words can become different parts of speech, thus having slightly different meanings. Change the word to the part of speech indicated and then write the definition of the new word.

   1. *impression* (noun), change to a verb _____

    Definition: _____

    _____

2. *opinions* (noun), change to an adjective _____

Definition: _____

_____

3. *correspondence* (adjective in this context), change to a

verb _____

Definition: _____

_____

4. *contained* (verb), change to a noun (there is more than one

possibility here) _____

Definition: _____

_____

5. *dormant* (adjective), change to a noun _____

Definition: _____

_____

ACTIVITY 1.5 _____

DIRECTIONS: Take two words from the list accompanying the article by Malcolm X and demonstrate your conceptual knowledge of these words. You may wish to work in pairs or groups on this activity.

The word: _____

Dictionary definition: _____

_____

Synonyms, example, nonexample, antonyms: _____

_____

Characteristics and connotations: _____

_____

Other forms: _____

_____

Sentence using the word or one of its forms: _____

_____

The word: _____

Dictionary definition: _____

_____

Synonyms, example, nonexample, antonyms: _____

_____

Characteristics and connotations: _____

_____

Other forms: _____

_____

Sentence using the word or one of its forms: _____

_____

As you were completing the activities in this chapter, you probably encountered several new words from Malcolm X's article. If you did not use all of the twelve general words while you were doing the activities, you should now look up the words in a dictionary. As you do this, remember to select the definitions that apply to the way each word was used in the article by Malcolm X. You may want to write your definitions on an index card so you can study and refer to them later. After doing this, you should complete Activities 1.6 and 1.7, which follow.

ACTIVITY 1.6

DIRECTIONS: Read each sentence carefully. If the boldfaced word is used correctly, mark C and go on to the next item. If the boldfaced word is used incorrectly, mark I and then make the sentence correct.

C   I   **1.** After the athlete went through a ***rehabilitation*** program, she was able to jump without hurting her knee.

C   I   **2.** Sam's ***atheistic*** beliefs were obvious when he volunteered to say grace at Thanksgiving dinner, thanking God for the food and company gathered at the table.

C   I   **3.** The car salesperson ***expounded*** on the advantages of buying a used car from this company.

C   I   **4.** The movie was so ***engrossing*** that I fell asleep after the first ten minutes.

C   I   **5.** The secretary who constantly ***feigned*** sickness was given a raise by her boss for her dedication to her work.

C   I   **6.** Professor Miller's lectures were always so ***riveting*** that most of the students chose to skip class.

C   I   **7.** Traveling to foreign countries opens new ***vistas*** to anyone who is open-minded and curious.

C   I   **8.** If you avoid reading, it is ***inevitable*** that you will have a wide and powerful vocabulary.

C   I   **9.** After ***riffling*** through the magazine in the drugstore, James decided to purchase it.

C I **10.** Most little boys try to *emulate* famous athletes such as Michael Jordan.

C I **11.** The hunters were able to reach their *quota* of deer very early in the week.

C I **12.** The quiet man's *dormant* temper exploded when he learned that his son had been killed by a drunken driver.

ACTIVITY 1.7

DIRECTIONS: Complete the following sentences, being as specific as possible in order to demonstrate your conceptual understanding of the boldfaced words.

1. The little girl who *feigned* illness_____

_____

2. After the gymnast received extensive *rehabilitation,* _____

_____

3. The book was so *engrossing* that _____

_____

4. The *vistas* gained from attending college include _____

_____

5. The student's *dormant* hunger was awakened when _____

_____

6. After *riffling* through the books on the shelf, _____

_____

7. People who are *atheists* believe _____

_____

8. After the insurance salesman reached his *quota* for the week,

_____

9. Parents often *expound* about the _____

_____

10. If you study hard and attend class, it is *inevitable* that _____

_____

11. The class became *riveted* to _____

_____

12. Many serious college students attempt to *emulate* _____

_____

SUMMARY

In this chapter we have discussed why learning vocabulary is important and what it means to know a word conceptually. As Malcolm X discovered in his homemade education, an extensive knowledge of words will improve your reading comprehension. A large vocabulary will also increase your listening comprehension, reading rate, and effectiveness in writing and speaking. However, memorizing definitions is not enough. That is why we also introduced the four stages by which word knowledge grows. A new word you encounter when you read or listen falls into one of these four stages:

    a. the word is completely unrecognized (no understanding).
    b. the word is recognized but the meaning is unknown (partial understanding).
    c. the word is recognized but imprecisely defined (partial understanding).
    d. the word is completely known (conceptual understanding).

We concluded the chapter by elaborating upon what it means to know a word accurately or conceptually. Conceptual knowledge includes the knowledge of synonyms, antonyms, examples or nonexamples, connotations or characteristics, and different forms of the word in new situations.

CHAPTER 2

Generative Vocabulary Strategies

Did You Know?
The word *prevaricate* originated from Latin and originally meant to
walk crookedly. Today, when you *prevaricate* you talk crookedly or bend
the truth.

Edgar Dale, in his article "How to Improve Your Vocabulary" (1958),
stated that "the best readers usually have the best vocabularies." Although his statement is certainly true, many—perhaps most—readers
skip over and ignore words that they do not know. Students tend to ignore unknown words for a variety of reasons, but the primary reason is
that they don't know any *generative* vocabulary strategies that might
help them determine a word's meaning and remember it for future
use. The purpose of this chapter, therefore, is to expose you to these
generative strategies—strategies that you will use independently to
increase your conceptual understanding of vocabulary.

In a sense, the vocabulary instruction that you are presently receiving in this text is an artificial situation. On initial examination, you
probably noticed that the majority of pages in this book are filled with
exercises designed to help you gain a more conceptual understanding of
words. The idea of what it means to know a word was fully explained in
Chapter 1. This approach to conceptual understanding will help you
learn new words for the course in which you are using this book, but in
the real world, you must also think about ways to increase conceptual
understanding of words in situations in which you receive little or no

instruction. That is what generative vocabulary strategies are all about. The purpose of this chapter, then, is to show you a variety of ways to learn and remember new words as you read on your own. As stated in Chapters 1 and 3, you will discover that although looking up words in a dictionary may be a beginning, it is not enough, particularly if you wish to increase understanding to the conceptual level.

Research suggests that those who have read a lot have a major advantage when it comes to vocabulary knowledge. As Malcolm X discovered, the best way to increase vocabulary, then, is not only by reading, but also through reading a variety of different types of material. Those who are well-read regularly read magazines, newspapers, texts, novels, and so on. Note that wide reading goes well beyond comic books, beauty magazines, and the sports page in the newspaper! It's not that reading these types of material is bad—we would consider any reading to be good reading—it's simply not enough in terms of both quantity and quality to have much effect in increasing your chances of meeting and learning new words. The message is that if you really do want to increase your vocabulary, and at the same time increase your knowledge, read! If you haven't been a reader in the past, it's never too late to start. In this chapter, and in those that follow, you will be reading a number of articles about a variety of topics. This diversity will serve as a vehicle for learning new words and concepts.

Now that you are ready to begin your new vocabulary-building program, you will need some tools in order to cope with the many new words you will encounter. The remainder of this chapter will explain some obvious and not-so-obvious ways of learning new words and building upon them.

Before continuing, however, read the article entitled "Vats, Fats and Rats," paying particular attention to the words in bold print. As generative strategies are introduced, you will apply them to the words and concepts presented. While reading this article, you will encounter the following words:

abundance	hormone
admonish	injects
ample	leptin
binge	mimics
bland	moderation
celebratory	obese
consistent	peptide
enhance	receptors
glucagon	voraciously

Reading

Vats, Fats and Rats

by Geoffrey Cowley and Adam Rogers

New alcohol and eating info may help set limits

Who would have thought that **abundance** could be such a curse? Nearly a third of U.S. adults are **obese,** and the associated illnesses claim 300,000 lives every year. Last week the federal government updated its official response to the crisis. Its new "Dietary Guidelines for Americans" offers the same **bland,** sensible advice as three earlier editions. But it also provides some small surprises.

Unlike past guidelines, the new ones specifically **admonish** consumers to limit fat-laden processed meats, such as sausage and salami. We're also warned to avoid heavily salted canned soups, frozen dinners and packaged snacks and dressings.

Vegetarianism was never mentioned before, but the government's experts now assure us that "vegetarian diets are **consistent** with the Dietary Guidelines." A meatless menu can provide **ample** protein and a full range of nutrients, the new pamphlet declares, "as long as the variety and amounts of foods consumed are adequate."

The biggest surprise involves alcohol. Whereas earlier guidelines denied that drinking holds any benefits, the new ones acknowledge that "alcoholic beverages have been used to **enhance** the enjoyment of meals by many societies" and cite recent studies suggesting that moderate drinkers have reduced rates of heart disease. "If you drink," the guidelines conclude, "do so in **moderation.**" The panel defined **moderation** as no more than one drink a day for women and no more than two for men.

If Americans lived by the new guidelines—or the old ones, for that matter—we would no doubt look better, feel better and live longer. Unfortunately, when it comes to food, knowing and doing are different.

Picture this: You're a lab rat, *voraciously* chowing down pellets after three days without food. Then someone *injects* a chemical into your brain and, hey, you're not hungry anymore! You simply can't eat another bite.

This is clearly something we could have used at Thanksgiving. And, as it turns out, this could be good news for humans as well as fat rats. Scientists reported that they have discovered a *protein* that tells mammals' brains it's time to stop eating. Called *glucagon*-like *peptide*-1, or GLP-1, the *protein* is known to help digest sugars in the human intestine. But the rat study showed that after a large meal, GLP-1 is also released in the brain to signal that the stomach is full, says Donald O'Shea, a researcher at London's Hammersmith Hospital. It is almost certain, O'Shea said, that GLP-1 is in the brains of humans too. O'Shea and his colleagues reported their findings in the journal *Nature*.

The discovery follows several recent ones involving obesity. Last summer scientists found a *hormone* called *leptin* that may help set body weight, and two weeks ago they found *receptors* for that protein in the brain. But GLP-1, whose production may be triggered by leptin, seems to be the most potent factor yet. A pill that *mimics* GLP-1 could help people lose weight more effectively. But unless you're a lab rat, we wouldn't suggest a *celebratory* eating *binge.* Weight control is devilishly complicated, and any possible pill is years away. ☐

As stated in Chapter 1, there are four stages of word knowledge, and it is important that you determine the level of word knowledge that will be satisfactory for your purpose. For example, if you are an art major enrolled in a biology course in order to satisfy a humanities requirement, it may not be important to have full conceptual understanding of words such as *glucagon, peptide,* and *leptin.* Although you would want to learn the definitions for your science course, it may not be terribly necessary to learn them conceptually. The situation would be quite different for someone majoring in science who would need to have a more conceptual understanding of these words for later use.

In addition to the several stages of word knowledge, there are also different word types. The words from science in the last paragraph, *glucagon, peptide,* and *leptin,* are often referred to as *content-specific* or course-related words. You would expect to encounter these words in biology or other science courses; you probably would not run into them on a regular basis in the course of reading a novel or a magazine. On the other hand, *general vocabulary* words are those that you might encounter in any or all materials you read. Other words from "Vats, Fats and Rats" such as **admonish**, **ample, voraciously,** and **moderation** are as common in newspapers and magazines as they are in novels and textbooks. You would want to have a conceptual understanding of these words regardless of what your major might be.

Before turning to specific generative vocabulary strategies, a word of caution is in order about the role of synonym/antonym books, thesauruses, or computer synonym/antonym programs. Most pocket computer dictionaries would also require this cautionary note. Tools such as these, although appropriate in some instances, are generally inappropriate for learning a more conceptual understanding of words. These devices probably work best in situations in which you already have a fair understanding of a word, but perhaps need another word to take its place or contrast with it. For example, if you were writing a paper and had used the word **ample** to describe the average salary of a CEO, then wanted to use another word with similar meaning later in the paper, you might refer to a thesaurus, synonym/antonym book, or a computerized dictionary. If, on the other hand, you thought that **ample** might be a good word to describe salaries and you were not sure of its exact meaning, you would want to consult a dictionary or perhaps use one of your generative vocabulary strategies in order to understand it better. The point that we want to stress here is that the tools you use to learn vocabulary should fit the situation in which you find yourself. For example, we have found that students often consult a thesaurus and then substitute one word that they don't understand very well with another word that they know even less well! In this situation, more often than not, the word is used incorrectly. What you should be able to do after learning about the different generative strategies for learning new words is to pick and choose the appropriate tools given your specific situation. Given that cautionary note, we now turn our discussion to generative vocabulary strategies: those strategies that you can study on your own as a way of enlarging and improving your current levels of vocabulary knowledge.

GENERATIVE STRATEGIES

Context Clues

Probably the most common strategy or approach recommended to students who have trouble determining the meaning of a word they meet during reading is to use context. Using context means using the words, sentences, or paragraph(s) surrounding the unknown word to help determine its meaning. Sometimes context provides a considerable amount of information about the meaning of an unknown word; at other times, context gives very little information. It is important for you to be able to determine just how much information you can get from the context so that you can decide whether you will need to use additional generative strategies in order to reach conceptual understanding.

Read each set of sentences below. The first sentence in each pair uses a word in a naturally occurring context. These sentences came directly from the article "Vats, Fats and Rats." The second sentence in each pair uses the word in an artificial context in which more information is provided about the word, but you probably would not encounter this kind of sentence very often in the course of your normal reading. In the past, teachers may even have given you practice determining context using sentences such as the second in each pair.

1A. Nearly a third of U.S. adults are *obese,* and the associated illnesses claim 300,000 lives every year.

1B. Because he had failed to exercise over the long, cold winter but continued to eat three large meals and snacks daily, James became *obese*—very overweight—weighing over 250 pounds, even though he was only 5 feet 5 inches tall.

2A. A meatless menu can provide *ample* protein and a full range of nutrients, the new pamphlet declares, "as long as the variety and amounts of foods consumed are adequate."

2B. Even though it was much more expensive, Emily liked to fly first class because the seats were more *ample* and uncramped, allowing her to have plenty of room to stretch out or to get some sleep.

3A. But unless you are a lab rat, we wouldn't suggest a *celebratory* eating *binge.*

3B. Everyone was in a *celebratory* mood after winning the regional championship. It was a big change from the sadness and depression everyone felt in the previous year, when the team lost in the first round.

3C. One type of eating disorder occurs when individuals *binge* eat. Bingers can eat entire cakes, a half-gallon of ice cream, and whatever else they can put their hands on, often consuming thousands of calories in one sitting.

4A. A pill that *mimics* GLP-1 could help people lose weight more effectively.

4B. When a child *mimics,* or copies, what her older sister does, the older sister serves as a role model whether she wants to or not.

5A. "If you drink," the guidelines conclude, "do so in *moderation.*" The panel defined *moderation* as no more than one drink a day for women and no more than two for men.

5B. Anthony believed that he drank in *moderation.* He never drank alcoholic beverages during the week, and kept his drinking to having two or three glasses of wine with dinner over the weekends.

The problem with trying to use context exclusively in the first sentence of each pair is that it fails to give much help. The problem with the second sentence in each pair is that the context is too rich, providing information that would not occur in a natural setting. Although the second sentence in each pair is not very realistic in terms of what you might expect to find in actual reading situations, each one does serve to provide some clues to look for to determine whether context might help.

Synonyms are the most common form of context clues. Sentences **1B** and **4B** are examples of the use of synonyms to help define troublesome words. Remember that synonyms are words that have the same or similar meanings, such as fast and speedy. Sentence **1B** gives an example in which *very overweight* means the same as *obese.* In this example, the punctuation—the dashes—also cues you that you might be getting additional information about the meaning of the word *obese.* Other punctuation, such as adjoining words or phrases set off by commas, may also provide cues. In sentence **4B,** once again you are provided with a synonym for *mimics* because the word *copies* follows it. Note that in this example the word *or* cues you that a definition will follow. Thus, we are aware that both punctuation and words such as *or* can cue you that the writer is going to provide more information about a word.

Antonyms, or opposites, are also common context clues. In sentence **3B,** the words *big change* and *from* indicate that there was a difference between how people felt last year and how they feel this year. Because in the previous year they felt sad and depressed after losing in the first round, *celebratory* must have something to do with being happy and feeling uplifted.

More realistic context clues would include those instances in which examples are used. In fact sometimes, such as in the sentences in **5A,** the examples given actually define the word for you as it is used in one particular context. In the second sentence, *moderation* is defined for you as "no more than one drink a day for women and no more than two for men." In this instance, *moderation* is defined differently for men and women. Sentence **5B** shows a different type of example, one in which a precise definition is not given, but the word is characterized. Note here that Anthony's *moderate* drinking habits were defined as no alcohol during the week and wine with dinner on weekends. These two examples also indicate the importance of understanding the context of how the word is used. The Dietary Guidelines' definition of *moderation* and Anthony's definition are different. Which is more moderate? Why?

Although you occasionally may encounter the types of context clues provided in **1B–5B** above, you are much more likely to encounter examples such as those in **1A–5A.** The precise meanings of these words are not provided, and if you have no knowledge of a word, you may have a difficult time figuring out its meaning, particularly a conceptual meaning, from the information provided. However, because the meaning of a word always depends on the context in which it is used, as examples **5A** and **5B** clearly demonstrate, it is important to note the context, particularly if you need to pursue the meaning of a word by checking the dictionary or other sources.

Let us look at another example from "Vats, Fats and Rats," this time focusing on words that would be considered more content-specific in nature. Reread the following excerpt taken from the article, noting the words in bold print:

> Scientists reported that they had discovered a *protein* that tells mammals' brains it's time to stop eating. Called *glucagon-like peptide-1,* or *GLP-1,* the *protein* is known to help digest sugars in the human intestine. But the rat study showed that after a large meal, *GLP-1* is also released in the brain to signal that the stomach is full. . . . It is almost certain, O'Shea said, that *GLP-1* is in the brains of humans too.

In this portion of the article, there are several terms that you might not understand, at least not at a conceptual level or what they mean in this particular context. For example, all of you probably know a definition for *protein.* What do you think of when you think of protein? Perhaps the most common response would be "a big juicy steak," or "some cheese." But do you think this is what the authors mean by *protein?* Probably not. They are discussing *protein* more from a scientific definition, which is from its chemical makeup.

Other terms here also may be unfamiliar to you—*glucagon, peptide,* and certainly *GLP-1.* But in this case, it is not that important to have a scientific understanding of these terms in order to understand the article. The author provides you with the important characteristics of *GLP-1,* most importantly that "it tells mammals' brains it's time to stop eating." Thus it is not that important to know the scientific definition of **glucagon** or **peptide** in order to understand this article. However, if you were reading this article as an assignment in a biology or chemistry course, your instructor would expect you to have not only a conceptual but also a scientific context understanding of these words.

"Vats, Fats and Rats" is fairly typical of what you can expect to encounter in your everyday reading, as is the following paragraph. Read it with an awareness of how context clues may or may not help to determine the meaning of the italicized words.

> After the mad scientist **conjured** up the **opaque** liquid, he cautiously poured it into a **vial.** He knew that the substance was quite **volatile** so he was extremely careful. Since he had worked so **arduously** on this project, he did not want it to blow up in his face before he had time to carry out his **dastardly** plan.

Before proceeding, complete the following activities.

ACTIVITY 2.1

DIRECTIONS: For each of the words from the above passage, first indicate whether or not context helps you. Second, indicate which of the four stages would describe your current level of understanding of the word. If you have forgotten these stages, refer to Chapter 1.

		Context		
	Word	**Yes**	**No**	**Stage**
1.	conjured	_____	_____	_____
2.	opaque	_____	_____	_____
3.	vial	_____	_____	_____
4.	volatile	_____	_____	_____
5.	arduously	_____	_____	_____
6.	dastardly	_____	_____	_____

How many of the **boldfaced** words did you already know? For the ones that you didn't know, in which situations did context help? At what stage was your understanding? Let's look at each situation and explain better when context might help and when it might not.

In the case of **conjured,** context provides some clues to the meaning. We know that it has something to do with "coming up with" or "making up" the liquid. We can tell it is an action in which the mad scientist is engaging. The fact that the scientist in question is "mad" (in this case, of course, *mad* means "crazy") also adds a slightly evil or mysterious element to the word **conjure.** In other words, through context, we get the general idea that what the scientist is doing probably isn't for the betterment of humanity!

For the word **opaque,** context is virtually useless. Unless you already know what *opaque* means, the surrounding words or sentences are no help at all. About the only thing that you can determine is that *opaque* can be a characteristic of a liquid. But since many adjectives can characterize liquids, that information provides little assistance.

Context clues for **vial** are also in short supply. It could have something to do with a place for safekeeping or perhaps some sort of container, but as for **opaque,** there is no direct definition stated or even implied. Without some prior knowledge of the meaning of **vial,** you strike out again!

Your luck changes somewhat when you get to **volatile.** Context tells you that when something is **volatile,** there must be some element of danger since it states that "he was extremely careful." In the next sentence, you gain information about what that danger might entail. *Volatile* must have something to do with the liquid being explosive since the mad scientist "did not want it to blow up in his face. . . ."

For the final two words, **arduously** and **dastardly,** the clues are just not there. Does **arduously** mean "carefully"? How about "a long period of time"? How about "hard"? **Dastardly** could mean anything from "well thought out" to "terrible" to "complex."

The point of this example is twofold. Most obvious is that sometimes context is of little help, and alone it rarely provides enough information about a word to gain a conceptual understanding. This is particularly true if you have no prior knowledge of the word. If you have some knowledge of the word (e.g., perhaps Stage 3 knowledge in which "I know **dastardly** has a negative connotation, but I am unable to provide a definition or write a sentence using it"), context may provide you with new examples and perhaps add slightly to your knowledge of the word.

The second point of this example is to show the importance of looking at the word in a context larger than a phrase or even one sentence. Often, information that comes several sentences or even several paragraphs before or after the unknown word may give you more information. Context is certainly important and should not be disregarded, but it is best used in conjunction with other generative strategies.

ACTIVITY 2.2 _____

DIRECTIONS: Read each of the following sentences and see how much you learn about each boldfaced word from context. In the space provided, give as much information about the word as you gained from the context and then make brief notes about the cues that helped you figure out what the word means. If you have no idea what the word means by the way it is used in the sentence, say so. The first one has been completed for you.

Example: Because Lorraine kept *vacillating* about which of the two jobs to take, she lost both of them and had to begin her job search all over again. *Vacillating* means not being able to decide or maybe switching back and forth.

Cues? There were two jobs in question; she lost both job

prospects._____

1. Quintin **abhors** writing and tries to avoid courses that require

   him to take essay exams. **Abhors** means _____

   _____

   Cues? _____

   _____

2. The organization **zealously** guards its records. Outsiders—

   including reporters—are not allowed access. **Zealously**

   means _____

   Cues? _____

   _____

3. When Antonio was a student, he had a knack for working at *mundane* jobs. He stuffed envelopes, was a bus boy, and, for a short period, counted traffic on country roads. *Mundane* means _____

_____

Cues? _____

_____

4. The politician's *chicanery* caused him to not be elected for a second term. *Chicanery* means _____

_____

Cues? _____

_____

5. Although Carla realized that it was totally *quixotic,* she daydreamed about running away to live on a desert island where she would live on the beach, wouldn't have to work, and could do exactly what she wanted to do. *Quixotic* means _____

_____

Cues? _____

_____

6. It is common to feel *lethargic* on a hot summer day.

Lethargic means _____

Cues? _____

_____

7. Although Jana was *taciturn* when she was with people she
didn't know very well, her brother Tate was *loquacious* and
would carry on a conversation with anyone at the drop of a
hat. *Taciturn* means _____

Cues? _____

_____

Loquacious means _____

Cues? _____

_____

8. Once the child *exacerbated* the wound by getting dirt in it,
his mother had no choice but to take him to the doctor's so it
would not get infected. *Exacerbated* means _____

_____

Cues? _____

_____

9. Although the idea was *inane,* or as his friends said, "just plain stupid," Cal worked hard on his new invention, hoping it would make him a millionaire. *Inane* means _____

_____

Cues? _____

_____

10. The dog's *incessant* barking angered everyone who lived in the small apartment building. *Incessant* means _____

_____

Cues? _____

_____

In this section we have examined the importance of context clues. When you encounter a word in your reading that you don't know, the first thing to do is to see how much the context can help you. Sometimes context is very helpful, so helpful that the word is defined for you well enough that you get a fairly clear meaning of the word. Other times, however, context will not offer enough information. In cases such as these, it is important to use additional generative strategies. The dictionary is perhaps the best step.

Dictionary

In this chapter we are not going to discuss how to use a dictionary; that is the purpose of Chapter 3. Mentioning dictionary use at this point is primarily to alert you to the fact that a good dictionary must be an integral part of vocabulary development. As we have just discussed, context often provides only a few precise clues to the meanings of unknown words. Therefore, being comfortable with using a dictionary, and being able to use it efficiently, effectively, and in conjunction with context, is an important aspect of generative vocabulary strategies.

Since Chapter 3 will focus on dictionary use, our purpose in this chapter is to show you how to create a personal dictionary that might help you incorporate new words into your existing vocabulary. Included in your personal dictionary should be those words, encountered in either pleasurable reading or in course-related reading, that you want to be able to remember and use at some time.

To start a personal dictionary, purchase a small three-ring notebook that will allow you to insert new pages. Start with one page in each section for each letter of the alphabet. Divide the notebook in half, using the first part for general vocabulary words and the second half for course-related or content-specific words. You might even want to divide the content-specific section into subsections, related to the courses you are taking. After dividing the notebook into the appropriate sections, divide each sheet of paper by drawing a line lengthwise beginning about one-third of the way across the page, as shown in Figure 2.1.

Once you have drawn lines down several sheets of paper, begin reading. As you come across unfamiliar words, write them down in the left-hand column. In the right-hand column, jot down any information about the word that you might pick up from context. Look up the word in a dictionary following the procedures outlined in Chapter 3. Reread the sentence and select the most appropriate definition based on the

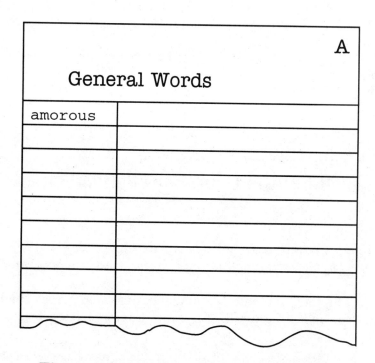

Figure 2.1 Page from a Personal Dictionary

way it is used in the sentence. Try to generate several synonyms and write those down as well. Then, using context clues and the appropriate dictionary definition, in your own words try to state what the word means.

A couple of cautions are in order that will be discussed in greater detail in Chapter 3. First, when you are writing down the meaning of a word, be careful not to define the new word using another word with which you are unfamiliar. For example, writing down a definition for *indigenous* as "intrinsic or innate" would be of little help. Second, avoid using a form of the word to define the unknown word. For example, if you looked up the word *emersion* and wrote down "the act of *emerging*" as your definition, you would be gaining little information. What does *emerging* mean? Finally, be sure that you are writing down the correct definition of the word as it is used in context. As we have already mentioned, many words have multiple meanings depending on the context in which they are used.

In order to practice making a personal dictionary and another generative strategy that follows it, vocabulary cards, read the following article entitled "1962: The Court Bans Public-School Prayer." Although this article was written in 1962, it is still relevant to the controversy of school prayer that goes on currently. As you read this article, pay particular attention to the words in bold print. In addition, as you are using generative strategies to learn as much as you can about the words, don't forget to think about the context in which the words are used.

Reading

1962: The Court Bans Public-School Prayer

Almighty God, we acknowledge our dependence upon Thee, and we beg Thy blessing upon us, our parents, our teachers, and our country.

A thunderclap of outrage and shock cracked across the land last week following a U.S. Supreme Court decision forbidding the *recital* in New York public schools of this 22-word prayer to a *nondenominational* God. For pure *tumult,* the reaction was inequaled since the Court's 1954 ruling on school desegregation. It gave fresh evidence that nothing jolts many Americans more strongly than a challenge to the religious feelings which are still bound up with their sense of national identity. "Somebody," *orated* West Virginia's Sen. Robert C. Byrd, "is tampering with America's soul."

In ruling 6 to 1 that the prayer trespassed against constitutional guarantees of religious freedom, the Court dealt only with a particular form of public worship local to New York State. However, many *fervent* observers read into the decision a *stringent* new view of church-state separation that seriously challenged their *conception* of the role of religion in a God-fearing society. As Georgia's Methodist Bishop John Owen Smith *portentously* put it: "It's like taking a star or stripe off the flag."

Offense: The prayer which caused the clash dates back to 1951, when the New York State Board of Regents, the highest educational authority in the state, recommended that the schools, at their option, adopt an act of *reverence.* "We didn't have the slightest idea the prayer we wrote would prove so controversial," says John F. Brosnan, former Chancellor of the Regents. "At the time, one rabbi said he didn't see how anybody could take offense."

The school board in suburban New Hyde Park, N.Y., found the prayer equally acceptable and in August 1958 sent out a notice that as of September, the Regents' prayer would be used in local schools. There was immediate opposition from a singularly determined man. Lawrence Roth, father of two sons, one in the community's elementary school and one in high school, was disturbed by the idea that the state could *impose* any prayer on his children. "We believe religious training is the *prerogative* of the parent," he said, "and not the duty of the government." When a group of *disgruntled* taxpayers confronted the president of the school board, however, the official reportedly told them, "the board has voted on this. If we say it's in, it's in."

At this, Roth, who is vice president of a small New York plastics manufacturing firm, sought the support of the New York Civil Liberties Union, which was to spend more than $6,000 on the case. "A number of people had called us about the prayer," says George Rundquist, head of the state group, "but none wanted to serve as *plaintiff.* No on wants to get involved in a religious conflict." Roth, although not a *martyr* by nature

("I never felt I was standing alone, like Atlas holding up the world"), was willing to go to court.

Suit: Roth advertised in a local weekly for other parents to join him in the suit, but of the 50 who originally agreed to do so, only five remained by the time the trial started in January 1959. "It's foolish to get mixed up in an unpopular cause," suggested the employer of one dropout. Lower state courts maintained the prayer was constitutional so long as schools did not *compel* any pupil to join in over his parents' objection. A year ago the New York Court of Appeals sustained the order. . . .

The majority opinion, which put the Roths in the glare of national publicity, was written by 76-year-old Justice Hugo L. Black, who last week marked his 25th year on the High Court. □

As you read "1962: The Court Bans Public-School Prayer," you probably came across several unknown words. For example:

> However, many *fervent* observers read into the decision a *stringent* new view of church-state separation that seriously challenged their *conception* of the role of religion in a God-fearing society. As Georgia's Methodist Bishop John Owen Smith *portentously* put it: "It's like taking a star or stripe off the flag."

There are at least four words in this brief section that may be troublesome: *fervent, stringent, conception,* and *portentously.* Write all four words down in your personal dictionary in the general vocabulary section. Then go to work on gathering as much information about the words as possible. Two of the words are used as adjectives (*fervent* and *stringent*) and one is used as an adverb (*portentously*), so it is difficult to gain much contextual information. We can tell, however, by the larger context of the article that many religion-oriented people were not pleased with the Supreme Court's ruling to remove this particular brief prayer from the schools. Another small context clue that might help is the word *However* at the beginning of the sentence. This leads you to believe that the Court ruled one way, *however* people may have interpreted the ruling somewhat differently. What would be the difference between "observers" and "*fervent* observers"? What about the difference between "a new view of church-state separation" and a "*stringent* new view of church-state separation"? Using the model provided in Figure 2.2, write any information you can generate about these words in the right-hand column of your personal dictionary. Use context and any knowledge you might already have about the words.

Now look up *fervent, stringent, conception,* and *portentously* in your dictionary and add the definitions to the information you already

	F
General Words	
fervent	Context: describes observers; DEF: having or showing great emotion or zeal.

	S
General Words	
stringent	Context: describes the new view; perhaps a negative word. DEF: imposing rigorous standards of performance; severe.

Figure 2.2 Specific Entries in a Personal Dictionary

have written. Be particularly careful to write down the definition based on the way the word is used in context. This is especially true for the word **conception.**

Once you get used to using your personal dictionary during reading, it will be difficult to read without it. In fact, eventually it will bother you to come across unknown words and simply skip over them. As your dictionary grows, it will also be useful in your own writing, or, in the case of the content-specific portion, when preparing for tests. When you read, you can either look up words if you have forgotten their precise meaning or you can add more unknown words as you encounter them.

ACTIVITY 2.3 _____

*DIRECTIONS: Now do the following activities to help you gain a more conceptual understanding of **fervent, stringent, conception,** and **portentously**. After looking up the words in the dictionary, answer the following questions about the words.*

1. Why do you think the author used the word **fervent** to

   describe the observers? _____

   _____

2. Can you think of someone or something else that could be

   described as **fervent?** _____

   Why? _____

3. Use **fervent** in a sentence so that someone reading your

   sentence would have a good understanding of what it means.

   _____

   _____

4. Why do you think that some people held a *stringent* as opposed to a nonstringent view of the decision?_____

_____

5. Can you think of a rule or regulation that would be considered *stringent?* _____

_____

Why?_____

6. Use *stringent* in a sentence so that someone reading your sentence would have a good understanding of what it means._____

_____

7. What would be a synonym for *conception* as it is used in this context? _____

8. What might cause one's *conception* of a problem to change?

_____

_____

9. Use *conception* in a sentence so that someone reading your sentence would have a good understanding of what it means when used in this particular context._____

_____

10. Why do you think that the author used *portentously* to describe Bishop Smith's statement? _____

_____

11. Name another situation when you might say something

portentously. _____

_____

12. Use the word *portentously* (or *portentous*) in a sentence so

that someone reading your sentence would have a good

understanding of what it means. _____

_____

ACTIVITY 2.4 _____

DIRECTIONS: Listed below are the other words from "1962: The Court Bans Public-School Prayer" that might give you some difficulty. Check the words for which you have only a Level 1 or Level 2 understanding. Put context information about each of these words in your personal dictionary.

___ recital

___ nondenominational

___ tumult

___ orated

___ reverence

___ impose

___ prerogative

___ disgruntled

___ plaintiff

___ martyr

___ compel

Vocabulary Cards

Some students prefer to make vocabulary cards instead of using a personal dictionary. Vocabulary cards are similar to the personal dictionary except that you use 3 x 5 index cards instead of a notebook. You may, like many students, prefer using cards because the words can be easily alphabetized for more efficient use, and they can be tucked conveniently into a pocket or carried in a purse or bookbag. In addition, you can group similar words together for easier learning, or you can mix up the cards to make sure you are not learning words in a specific order. Cards work particularly well if you want to make a concerted effort to increase your vocabulary and plan to collect words for an extended period of time.

When making vocabulary cards, follow some of the same procedures outlined for the personal dictionary. The first rule, however, is always to read with a stack of blank cards beside you. When you encounter an unknown word, whether in personal/pleasurable reading or in course-related reading, write the unknown word on the front of the card. After writing down the word, complete the card either immediately or when you have finished reading. There is support for both approaches. If you make cards as you read, it interrupts the flow and can affect comprehension. On the other hand, waiting until you have completed reading to find out the meanings of unfamiliar words can also cut down on your comprehension. Try it both ways and see which feels more comfortable. A compromise might be to wait until you have finished reading to look up words that do not hinder comprehension of what you are reading, but to stop and look up words that do influence comprehension.

Once you have decided on an approach, complete your cards in the following manner. First, if you have absolutely no understanding of the word (Stage 1), you may want to write the sentence in which the word was found on the front of the card so that you have the context in which to begin thinking about it. Then go to a dictionary. Because many words can be used as several different parts of speech, find the part of speech, based on context, and write it in the upper right-hand corner. Flip the card over. Read the dictionary definitions and find the one that best suits this context. Based on that definition, write a synonym in the lower left corner and an antonym in the lower right corner. More than likely, a dictionary will not give you a synonym or antonym. You will need to generate your own based on the word's definition. At the top of the card, write the dictionary definition based on the way the word is used in the sentence. Finally, if you can, generate a sentence based on the way the word was used in context. Remember, as discussed in Chapter 1, one way to tell if you are understanding the higher-level meaning of a word is by sentence writing. Figure 2.3 presents an example of a vocabulary card that could have been generated for **tumult** in the article "1962: The Court Bans Public-School Prayer."

If you are reading course-related texts containing many content-specific words, you might want to modify the cards somewhat. Figure 2.4 presents an example of a vocabulary card drawn from the first reading in this chapter. On the front, put the term in the center, on what page the definition can be found in the upper right, and a mnemonic to help you remember the meaning of the term in the lower right. (Mnemonics are memory devices that will be presented when we

Front

> noun
>
>
> tumult
>
> Sent: For pure tumult, the reaction was
> unequaled since the court's 1954 ruling on
> school desegregation.

Back

> DEF—The din and commotion of a great crowd;
> disorderly
>
> Tumult from all parts of the country was
> evident when the president announced a
> major tax increase.
>
> SYN—disturbance   ANT—calmness

Figure 2.3 A General Vocabulary Card

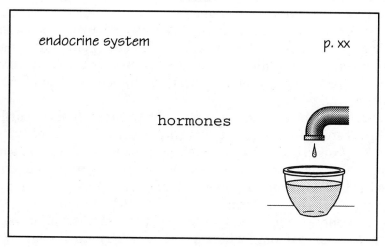

endocrine system   p. xx

hormones

DEF° An organic molecule secreted, usually in small amounts, in one part of an organism that regulates the function of another tissue or organ; produced by a variety of different cell-types.

EXS thyroxin, estrogen, insulin, somatotropin, glucagon

Figure 2.4 A Content-Specific Vocabulary Card

discuss imagery later in the chapter.) In the upper left-hand corner, include a piece of information that will help you group this card for future studying. This information can be a broad descriptor, as used in this example, or a date or event. Then flip the card over, and put on the back the meaning of the term as presented by your text. If the term is not clearly defined in the text chapter, check to see if there is a glossary in the text that defines terms. If there is no glossary, then consult a dictionary, but be sure to ask your professor about the term if it is still unclear to you. When you might need to know examples, include at least one on your card. For **hormones,** note that it is important to include examples of a variety of hormones. Often, however, no examples are given, even though you may be expected to know this information for a test. In a case such as this one, generate your own example, consulting with your professor and other classmates if necessary. Working through the examples encourages further thinking about the term and helps you gain a more conceptual understanding of what the word means.

You can alphabetize, add to, and refer to these general cards during future reading, writing, and learning, much like your personal dictionary. You can use the content-specific cards to self-test text concepts in preparation for exams. You can also group together like concept-specific cards. For example, you could make many cards related to different aspects of the endocrine system and then group them. In both instances, when studying, simply look at the target term on the front of the card. Then, without looking at the back, say aloud what the term means and give an example, if appropriate. Check the back to ensure that you were correct. If you were, go on to the next card. If you were incorrect, say the correct answer several times before going on to the next term. Always make sure that you say the answer out loud and that you can say the answer without looking before going on to the next term. In addition, once you know the cards from front to back, reverse the process. Read a definition and then supply the word that goes with it. Making and using course-related cards for study is especially good for classes in which many new terms are presented rapidly. Such courses might include biology, psychology, sociology, chemistry, and even art history.

ACTIVITY 2.5 _____

DIRECTIONS: Go back and look at the words you checked in Activity 2.4 on page 48. Make vocabulary cards for each of the words you checked, as well as for any other words from the article with which you are unfamiliar. As you make your vocabulary cards, follow the example in Figure 2.3.

_____

ACTIVITY 2.6 _____

DIRECTIONS: Practice making and studying 10 content-specific vocabulary cards for any course in which you are currently enrolled. If you can, try this generative strategy with a course in which you are required to learn many new terms. Try to group like terms together for studying.

ACTIVITY 2.7 ———————————

DIRECTIONS: Which generative strategy do you prefer: keeping a personal dictionary or creating vocabulary cards? Write a one-page explanation of why you prefer the strategy and what the advantages and disadvantages of each strategy might be.

ACTIVITY 2.8 ———————————

DIRECTIONS: By now you should have a Level 3 or Level 4 knowledge of each of the targeted words in "1962: The Court Bans Public-School Prayer." Study your personal dictionary entries or your cards and then answer the following questions about the words. If you have difficulty doing this activity without referring to your dictionary or cards, you might want to think about your level of understanding for the troublesome word(s).

1. When you *impose* your values on someone else you ————

   ————————————————

2. A student might become *disgruntled* if —————

   ————————————————

3. The *recital* of a speech might cause you to be nervous

   because————————————————

   ————————————————

4. In order to *compel* their children to study, parents could ——

   ————————————————

5. If you are the *plaintiff* in a trial you_____

_____

6. In a *nondenominational* church _____

_____

7. *Martyrs* are those who _____

_____

8. One should show *reverence* in church because_____

_____

9. Wars are considered times of *tumult* because_____

_____

10. It is one's *prerogative* to select his/her own religion because

_____

_____

11. It is often said that politicians are masters of *oration*

because they _____

_____

Mnemonics, Imagery, and Keywords

Although you may make an effort to improve your vocabulary using a personal dictionary or a set of vocabulary cards, there may be some words that you have a difficult time learning and remembering. Often, using an alternative memory device will help. *Mnemonics* is the overall term given to a variety of memory aids. *Mnemonic* comes from the Greek *mnemonikos,* meaning "mindful." We will discuss *imagery* and *keywords,* which are more specific types of mnemonics.

Imagery is probably the most widely used memory aid. Put simplistically, images are pictures in your head. Rather than remembering something through words as you might normally do, you remember through images or pictures. Imagery is best used when learning more concrete words. Often, concrete words are nouns, since most nouns are objects that can be seen or touched. Some words, regardless of what part of speech they are, are more easily imaginable than others. For example, because the word **recital** is more concrete, it would be more easily imaged than **prerogative.**

Because imagery benefits some students more than others, try this experiment. Close your eyes and listen while your instructor, roommate, or friend reads the following passage. Try to imagine, or picture in your head, what you would see and feel.

It is an extremely hot summer day. You decide that an ice cream cone might be in order. You walk into the cool, air-conditioned store and decide that sherbet may be more soothing and cooling on this hottest of all summer days. Because it is so hot and you are so ravenous, you decide to have three scoops, each a different flavor. First, the server puts a large scoop of orange sherbet into the cone. Then he puts the lime on top of the orange. Finally comes the pale yellow pineapple. Your mouth waters! You pay for your cone, and once again venture out into the dastardly heat. Your sherbet immediately begins to melt. No matter how fast you eat it, the sherbet, in rainbows of orange, green, and yellow, streams down the side of the cone, all over your clean white shirt, and onto the ground. You are a sticky mess, but it was well worth it!

How much of this scene could you image? Could you see the different colors of sherbet melting over the side of the cone? Could you feel the cool of the air-conditioning and the heat of the day? If you could, imagery is a technique that you should try as a way of learning and remembering new vocabulary.

In addition to devising images for words, you might also try using *keywords*. When using keywords, you think of a catchy sentence or phrase that is related to the word in some way. In addition, you can associate the word to you personally in some way. Personalizing keywords, as well as images, helps memory. For example, if you were having trouble remembering **obese,** which means "extremely fat or grossly overweight," you might think of the word as "O+BEES," which sounds like obese. Then think of an image that is associated with o-bees, perhaps seven very fat bees flying around. The bodies of the bees might be shaped like fat O's as shown in Figure 2.5. This method helps create verbal or visual images to help you remember what obese

Figure 2.5 An Image for Obese

means. Both examples use mnemonics and imagery. Also keep in mind that your mnemonics and images need to make sense only to you. In fact, the more they are personalized, the easier they are to retrieve from your memory.

Let's look at another example using the word *tumult.* Remember that *tumult* means "a commotion or disturbance." If you wanted to try to remember the meaning of this word using the keyword method, you might try thinking of *tumult* as "two malts." For those of you who might not know what a malt is, it is a thick, creamy drink, usually chocolate, that is very similar to a milkshake. Malts tend to be very rich, so you can't drink very much of them before feeling full. Thus, you could think of a sentence such as "two malts caused my stomach to feel as if it were in *tumult.*" Relating "two malts" to *tumult* might help you remember the meaning of the word using the keyword method without using any visualization.

ACTIVITY 2.9

DIRECTIONS: Now that you have some idea about what imagery involves, let's think about some of the words from the two readings used so far in this chapter. Do the following activities as a way of seeing how imagery might help you better remember the meanings of some words.

1. Which article, "Vats, Fats and Rats" or "1962: The Court Bans Public-School Prayer," is easier, overall, to image?

   _____

   Why? _____

   _____

2. On a scale of 1 to 5 (with 1 being not imaginable at all and 5 being very imaginable) rate the following words:

   _____ obese   _____ consistent

   _____ admonish   _____ ample

   _____ tumult   _____ fervent

   _____ prerogative   _____ plaintiff

3. For the words that you gave a high imagery score (4 or 5), what kind of images did you get in your head? You can either draw the image or write out what you visualized.

   Word _____

   Image _____

   _____

   Word _____

   Image _____

   _____

   Word _____

   Image _____

   _____

DIRECTIONS: In the space provided, create images, keywords, and/or mnemonics for two of the following terms taken from the first two readings used in this chapter: **bland, ample, reverence,** *and* **fervent.** *Remember that your image should help you call up the meaning of the word easily.*

Image for _____. Image for _____.

Relations Among Concepts

In Chapter 1, we presented the idea that complete word knowledge involves more than simply memorizing dictionary definitions, or merely learning words in isolation. These activities often do not get at the connotation of words, which is important if you are to understand the conceptual meaning of words. (Connotation will be discussed fully in Chapter 3.) At times, then, it is important to learn and remember how concepts are related to each other. In addition, it is often easier to remember words if they are *grouped and labeled* before learning them.

Let's say that you had to learn the following list of words taken from "Vats, Fats and Rats" and "1962: The Court Bans Public-School Prayer":

abundance	fervent
admonish	moderation
ample	obese
binge	stringent
disgruntled	

You could arrange these words into different groups and then give each group a label. For example, **abundance, ample,** and **obese** all have something to do with being oversized or having a larger amount of something than normal. Another way to categorize some of the words might be to group them according to having something to do with foods or eating habits. In this instance, you might group *abundance,* as in an *abundance* of food to eat; *binge,* as in an eating *binge; moderation,* as in always eat and drink in *moderation;* and *obese,* as in *binge* eating may cause you to become *obese.* Another way to group some of the words would be according to negative or positive connotation. What words could be grouped in this way? Can you think of other ways these words could be grouped? Keep in mind that the goal is to categorize words in ways that will help you remember them. Therefore, your groupings may be different from those of classmates.

After grouping similar words together, you can then use other generative strategies, such as vocabulary cards. Put your definitions on cards, as described earlier in the chapter, clip them together, and learn them as a group, rather than in isolation. Once the words are grouped, it is also easier to begin to think about their connotative elements. That is, although *ample* and *obese* both have to do with excessiveness, each means something a little different. You might think of someone who is just a little overweight as *ample.* But *ample* individuals are not necessarily *obese.* Those who are *obese* have taken "*ampleness*" too far, since their weight may be harmful to their health.

Another way to see relations among words is to create *conceptual maps.* Before discussing conceptual maps, however, read the text excerpt entitled "Behavior and Natural Selection" that begins on page 61. Mapping presents visually how words, ideas, and concepts are related. Maps are useful not only for learning definitions, but also for organizing and remembering lists. As such, concept maps can be used to see the relations between words or concepts; thus they are useful generative strategies to use in some of your courses.

If you had read the text excerpt as part of your reading assignment in biology and knew that you would be responsible for understanding both innate and learned behavior, you might construct a concept map. Look at the map in Figure 2.6. The portion of the map on innate behavior has been filled in for you. Notice that first the characteristics of innate behavior are given as well as an example of how the digger wasp's life cycle is actually totally innate behavior. Another part of innate behavior is instincts. Note that in this instance as well, the definition (or characteristics) of instincts is given, along with several examples and explanations of instinctive behaviors.

Finally, notice that a map would probably be more effective for learning interrelated concepts than would other generative strategies mentioned in this chapter, such as the personal dictionary or vocabulary cards. By looking at this map, it is easy to see at a glance the contrast between innate and learned behaviors. Such relations might be

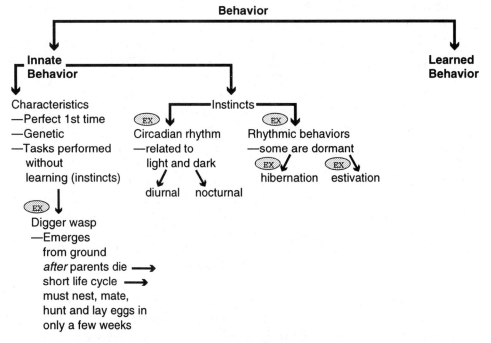

Figure 2.6 Mapping for Behavior and Natural Selection

more difficult to observe with other strategies. This example also serves the purpose of showing the importance of selecting the most effective strategy for the task at hand.

Reading

INSTINCT AND LEARNING

People sometimes say a good athlete was born knowing how to play ball. Of course, no one is born with such highly developed skills. Playing ball is a behavior that must be learned. Yet some behaviors are present at birth. What are some of these inherited behaviors? How do they differ from learned behaviors?

McLaren, Rotundo, and Gurley-Dilger, "Instinct and Learning," from *Biology*, D. C. Heath and Company, 1991, pp. 771–773. Copyright © 1991 by D. C. Heath and Company. Reprinted by permission of Houghton Mifflin Company.

Behavior and Natural Selection

... Genes provide the blueprint for an organism's physical makeup. These physical traits are acted on by the forces of natural selection. Beneficial traits will be preserved in a population; harmful traits will not be preserved.

Like physical traits, *behavior,* or what an animal does, contributes to its survival and reproductive success. There are three main ways by which natural selection acts on behavior.

1. An animal's behavior must allow it to survive. For example, it must be able to find food when it is hungry. It also must be able to escape or hide from predators.
2. An animal's behavior must allow it to reproduce. It must be able to find a mate and prepare a nesting site. In many species, successful reproductive behavior also involves care of offspring while they are young.
3. An animal's behavior must allow it to determine which stimuli are important for survival and reproduction. There are many sights, sounds, and smells in the environment. It is not necessary, nor is it possible, to respond to everything.

Innate Behavior

Animal behavior falls into two broad categories: innate behavior and learning. ***Innate behavior*** is behavior that is done perfectly the first time it occurs. It is genetically programmed. The organism is born knowing how to do it.

Consider, for example, the digger wasp. By the time a female digger wasp emerges from her underground pupa, her parents have been dead for several months. The newly emerged wasp will live for only a few weeks. During this brief time, she must dig a hole for a nest, construct the nest, mate, hunt prey to place in the nest to nourish her young, and lay her eggs. There is little time for her to learn these tasks. Furthermore, there is no one to teach her. She is born knowing how to complete the tasks. Such complex behaviors that are performed perfectly without learning are called ***instincts.***

Instinctive behavior patterns are often repeated in response to changes in the environment. Behavior that is based on a 24-hour cycle is called a ***circadian rhythm.*** Circadian rhythms are related to the lengths of daylight and darkness. Some animals, such as bluejays and ground squirrels, are active during the day. These organisms are said to be ***diurnal.*** Other animals, such as flying squirrels and bats, are active at night. They are *nocturnal.*

Rhythmic behaviors also occur over long periods of time. ***Hibernation,*** a period of dormancy, occurs in some animals in response to cold winter temperatures and limited food supplies. During hibernation, an animal's metabolism slows down dramatically. Its body temperature drops to near that of its surroundings and its breathing rate is greatly reduced.

Many animals in hot, arid environments also become dormant when conditions are harsh. This is usually during the hottest, driest months. ***Estivation,*** like hibernation, is a period of dormancy in which an animal's metabolism slows down greatly. Can you think of a reason why this behavior is advantageous?

Dormancy does not occur in all animals. Many birds and mammals, for example, move to new locations as the seasons change. This behavior, called ***migration,*** enables animals to find new breeding and feeding grounds. Migrating animals usually follow the same routes year after year.

Learning

In contrast to instinctive behaviors, certain behaviors are obviously learned. No one is born knowing how to solve algebra problems. *Learning* occurs when an animal's experience results in a change of behavior. Learned behavior is not determined by an organism's genes. Because it permits behavior that is flexible, learning allows an animal to adapt to changes in its environment.

Learned behavior is characteristic of organisms with complex nervous systems. In general, the more advanced the brain, the more elaborate the patterns of learned behavior.

Learning is also related to the amount of time a developing animal spends with its parents. In animals that develop without parental care, behaviors are more likely to be innate. The longer the ***developmental period,*** the more learning (and less innate behavior) there is. Humans, who have the longest period of parent–young attachment, have the highest level of learning and the fewest innate behaviors of all animals. The reason is that the human brain takes several years to develop completely. During the entire period of brain development, a baby depends on its parents to provide it with food, shelter, protection, and anything else it needs. But during this time of dependence, an enormous amount of learning takes place. By the time the baby becomes an adult, he or she is capable of complex behavior.

Learning, unlike instinct, offers great potential for changing behaviors as conditions in the environment change. For example, if an animal innately knows how to build a certain type of nest, it is at a loss if the specific building materials are not available. However, if nest building is a learned behavior and a new building material becomes available, an animal can learn a new type of nest building. Learning ability is related to the life span of an animal. If an animal lives for only a few weeks, as the digger wasp does, the ability to meet a changing environment may not be necessary. On the other hand, in animals that live for many years, such as primates, the ability to change behavior as the environment changes is extremely valuable.

ACTIVITY 2.11

DIRECTIONS: Complete the portion of the concept map for learned behavior in Figure 2.6. Try to organize the map so that you can see the difference between innate and learned behaviors.

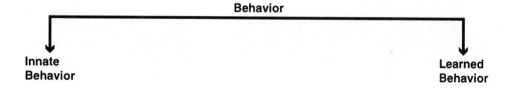

ACTIVITY 2.12

DIRECTIONS: Below you will find a list of words that are associated with either innate or learned behavior. Group each of the words accordingly. You should be able to use your map to help you.

adaptation	estivation
genetic	parental attachment
instinctual	hibernation
circadian rhythm	diurnal
migration	environmental influence
developmental period	digger wasp

Innate	*Learned*
_____	_____
_____	_____
_____	_____
_____	_____
_____	_____
_____	_____

ACTIVITY 2.13

DIRECTIONS: To practice mapping, go back to Chapter 1 and skim the article entitled "My Alma Mater" by Malcolm X. Pull out and list below the characteristics of Malcolm X before and after Bimbi introduced him to the world of books.

Malcolm X

Before Bimbi	After Bimbi
hustler	persistent
_____	_____
_____	_____
_____	_____
_____	_____
_____	_____
_____	_____

Charting is another format for organizing new terms, not only to learn definitions but also to see relations among concepts. Charting works especially well when you are comparing or contrasting concepts. For example, you could use charting if you wanted to see at a glance how innate behavior contrasts with learned behavior. As shown in Figure 2.7, put the key terms across the top of the chart. Next decide which factors would be important to know in order to gain a good conceptual understanding of each of the terms. Put these down the left-hand side. Then proceed by filling in the chart.

To study the chart, cover everything except characteristics and the two key terms, innate behavior and learned behavior. Then talk through the information, saying it out loud and, if possible, visualizing it mentally. If you forget something important, say it again several times, making sure that you can talk through and/or visualize all of the information without looking at the chart.

It is important to note that mapping and charting serve almost the same purpose. It simply comes down to personal preference. Both generative strategies help you sell relations between and among concepts and are especially helpful when you know you have to compare and contrast. Try out both of the strategies and see which one you prefer.

	Innate Behavior	**Learned Behavior**
Role of genetics		
Types of organisms		
Role of environment		
Role of experience		
Example		

Figure 2.7 Charting for Innate and Learned Behavior

ACTIVITY 2.14 _____

DIRECTIONS: Using the article "Vats, Fats and Rats" that you read at the beginning of the chapter, complete the following chart and map (on a separate page if necessary). The chart focuses on the changes in eating guidelines and the map focuses on new research in controlling obesity.

	Old Guidelines	New Guidelines
Meat		
Fat		
Vegetables		
Alcohol		

```
                        ┌─────────── Controlling Obesity ───────┐
                        │                                       │
Experiment                                          Transfer to humans
```

RECITING AND REVIEWING

One of the advantages to all of the generative strategies presented in this chapter is that you can easily test yourself if you construct the strategy correctly. Sometimes students make the big mistake of "thinking they will recognize information when they see it." Those who fall into this trap generally do so because they have opted for a short-term solution to learning terms and definitions, and thus do not have a real understanding of the words. Memorization without understanding cannot stand the test of time, and students who memorize without understanding find themselves confused during exams and mix up words and their definitions. If you have ever experienced this dreadful situation, you have also experienced firsthand the pitfalls of using a short-term solution. In addition, those who use this method do not self-test in a blind fashion (saying the definitions, characteristics, examples, and so on without looking at the vocabulary card) and often come away from studying vocabulary, as well as other materials from their courses, with the false assumption that they really understand and know the information when in fact they do not.

The long-term solution for learning word meanings is to stretch your understanding across the three layers of word knowledge. Multiple exposures to a word in different situations and in different forms, much like those you will experience in this text, will help you learn and remember new words. The long-term solution also relies heavily on recitation, rather than "looking at," and blind self-testing. In self-testing, it is important to cover up the information that contains the "answer." In other words, rather than simply reading over your vocabulary cards or maps, you reveal only the keyword and then say the definition and any other pertinent information without looking at it. If you are unable to follow this procedure, then read the card or portion of the map several times to yourself. Try again, saying it "blindly" (without looking at it), and then check to see if you are correct.

Reciting helps get the information into your long-term memory, and reviewing helps to keep it there. In a sense, then, reviewing is an extension of reciting. Once you have learned the words, the trick is to review them to the point of automaticity. Automaticity refers to the ability to recall something very fast—to the point where it is automatic. When you do something automatically, you don't have to think about it, like writing your address or telephone number. If you are learning vocabulary for the sake of learning it, rather than simply to do well in a testing situation, reciting should enable you to know the words so well that you can recognize them in your reading and use them in your writing or speaking.

In this book you will practice recitation, self-testing, and reviewing. These strategies work well if you remember the following guidelines:

1. Speak out loud, not in your head.
2. When speaking, pretend you are giving a lecture to someone else. Try looking in the mirror or taping yourself for motivation.
3. When writing, imagine an audience. Pretend that you are writing to someone about the new words you have learned.
4. Conduct your reciting, self-testing, and reviewing over a period of time. Rather than spending an hour practicing 40 psychology terms, try five or six sessions lasting 10 minutes each over a period of two days.
5. Group similar words together to make learning easier.

ACTIVITY 2.15 _____

DIRECTIONS: *Answer each of the following questions so that it is clear that you have an understanding of the words in bold print. Each of the words was presented in one of the first two readings in this chapter.*

1. When might you state your ideas *portentously?*

   _____

2. What might happen if you go on too many eating *binges?*

   _____

3. What might cause students to become *disgruntled?*

   _____

4. When might the doctor suggest that you follow a *bland* diet?

   _____

5. What might cause someone to become a *martyr?*

   _____

6. Why might you *admonish* your dog?

   _____

7. What might cause you to eat *voraciously?*

   _____

8. When might it be inappropriate to *mimic* someone?

   _____

ACTIVITY 2.16

DIRECTIONS: Answer the following questions based on the third reading in this chapter on innate and learned behaviors.

1. Define *innate behavior.*

2. Why is the digger wasp an example of an organism that engages in *innate behavior?*

3. Give an example of a *diurnal* animal.

4. Give an example of a *nocturnal* animal.

5. List and define two *rhythmic behaviors* in which animals are *dormant*.

6. What causes *learning* to happen?

7. Explain the three factors to show whether organisms are capable of *learned behavior*.

SUMMARY

In this chapter we have discussed the importance of not only learning new words but also knowing and using generative vocabulary strategies. Generative strategies are those that you can do on your own as you work at enlarging and improving your vocabulary. Several strategies were suggested to help you with both general and content-specific terms. These strategies included:

1. Making the most of context clues.
2. Introducing dictionary use.
3. Constructing personal dictionaries.
4. Making vocabulary cards for general and content-specific words.
5. Using mnemonics, imaging, and keywords.
6. Learning relations among concepts using categorizing, mapping, and charting.

We ended the chapter with some suggestions about how to recite and review using the generative strategies outlined.

3

Dictionary Use

Did You Know?
The word *pariah* originated from India's caste system. The lowest caste, or group, was hired to beat drums or **parai** at certain festivals. Today the word *pariah* means any despised person or outcast.

Every vocabulary book offers advice about how to use a dictionary. Although this book is obviously not an exception to the rule, we do offer a less traditional approach to many aspects of dictionary use. We assume, for example, that since you are in college, you have had a considerable amount of previous experience looking up words in a dictionary. Therefore, we will spend only a small amount of time discussing dictionary entries, guide words, and the like. Rather, most of the chapter will offer suggestions that might help you realize the strengths of dictionary use, and help you use a dictionary more as a learning tool than as a single source for learning all unknown words. This chapter, then, will discuss five main issues relating to the dictionary: (1) identifying effective definitions, or word denotation; (2) interpreting dictionary entries; (3) describing word etymologies and word origins; (4) understanding word connotations, or the more experiential part of learning words; and (5) combining both context and dictionary use to learn new words.

It may come as a surprise to learn that, at best, dictionaries often offer limited assistance in learning unknown words. Elements of practicality must be taken into consideration when compiling a dictionary. One element is that lexicographers (individuals who compile dictionaries) are obviously limited by space. Current standard dictionaries have over 200,000 entries. If lexicographers wrote explicit and strong definitions for all 200,000 entries, such a dictionary would be so large that few people would be able to lift it, and so expensive that few could afford to buy it. As a result, some dictionary entries are fairly strong and useful, while others tend to be less helpful.

In order to make this chapter as practical as possible, we have included a magazine excerpt entitled "A Bigger Hole in the Ozone." This reading contains numerous words that we will discuss as we present information about the denotation and connotation of words. Before proceeding with the remainder of the chapter, read the article. The boldfaced words that have been targeted for further study are included here for your convenience.

anchors	forecast
benign	graver
chlorofluorocarbons	incidence
conservative	intensify
cripple	regulators
endangered	solvents
fatality	stratosphere

Reading

. . . .

A Bigger Hole in the Ozone
EPA Predicts 200,000 More Skin-cancer Deaths

by Sharon Begley

The nations of the world have never agreed on how to halt the destruction of rain forests or save **endangered** species. But when it came to saving the ozone layer, which screens out the sun's harmful ultraviolet rays, they knew just what to do. Or so it seemed. In 1987, 24 nations meeting in Montreal pledged that, by the year 2000, they would halve their production of **chlorofluorocarbons** (CFCs), chemicals that destroy ozone. That was when the only ozone hole that had been noticed was over Antarctica. But soon after, satellite data showed that ozone above the United States had dropped 1.5 percent. That persuaded more than 90 countries last June to agree to ban CFCs entirely by 2000. Developing nations were given until 2010 to stop producing ozone-damaging chemicals; wealthier countries promised them up to $240 million to help make the switch.

Now it seems that the problem is far **graver** than anyone thought. Environmental Protection Agency chief William Reilly announced that ozone loss over the United States since 1978 has amounted to a "stunning" 4 to 5 percent. The preliminary satellite data, which scientists have been analyzing since last autumn, show that Europe, the Soviet Union and northern Asia experienced similar losses, while areas at the latitude of Sweden and Hudson Bay saw losses of 8 percent. "Past studies had shown about half that amount," said Reilly. "As a result, there could be 200,000 deaths from skin cancer in the United States over the next 50 years" in addition to the 400,000 otherwise expected over that period. The **fatality** estimate was 21 times what the EPA had **forecast** earlier. Ultraviolet radiation can also cause cataracts, weaken the immune system, damage crops and disrupt the reproduction of plankton that **anchors** the marine food chain.

Danger: Sunlight

• Every 1 percent drop in ozone allows 2 percent more ultraviolet light to reach Earth's surface.

• Every 1 percent reduction in ozone raises the **incidence** of skin cancer by 5 to 7 percent.

• The 5 percent loss of ozone over the U.S. is expected to cause 4,000 more skin-cancer deaths a year.

• The ozone loss is greater at higher latitudes. Over Leningrad, it is as much as 8 percent.

And the ozone loss is almost certain to get worse. CFCs stay in the atmosphere for decades. The EPA's Eileen Claussen told

Newsweek that the agency's models show ozone loss of 10 to 12 percent over the next 20 years—"and we've already thrown out those estimates because they are far too **conservative.**"

Reilly vowed that the EPA would **intensify** its efforts to find substitutes for ozone-eating substances. Researchers have made progress in finding **benign** chemicals that do the job of chlorine-based **solvents,** but they have been less successful in replacing the CFCs used in refrigerators and air conditioners. If substitute chemicals can be found, developing nations might be persuaded to phase out CFCs by 2000 rather than 2010. Right now, countries such as China and India believe that abandoning CFCs too quickly would **cripple** their economies. Eliminating CFCs before 2000, though, would not make much difference, because so many of the chemicals are already on their way to the **stratosphere.** In effect, **regulators** are running out of ideas. "Because such aggressive steps have already been taken," Claussen says, "it's hard to come up with anything more that can make a difference." □

DENOTATION: EFFECTIVE AND LESS EFFECTIVE DICTIONARY DEFINITIONS

Although dictionaries can be used for many purposes, their main function is to provide denotations, or definitions, of words. But not all definitions are created equal. To get an idea of the difference between strong and weak dictionary entries, we'll look at several examples. The following sentence came from the article you just read:

> The nations of the world have never agreed on how to halt the destruction of rain forests or save **endangered** species.

In this sentence, unless you already know the meaning of **endangered,** the context fails to provide much assistance as to its meaning. So, as a conscientious student, you next proceed to a dictionary for a definition. But the entry for **endangered** reads in the following manner:

en•dan•gered (ĕn-dān′jərd) *adj.* Faced with extinction.

The dictionary definition provides little help unless you know the meaning of **extinction,** and so you are left in a frustrating situation in which neither context nor the dictionary gives enough assistance to gain even partial word knowledge.

Let's examine another example from the same passage for which the dictionary may be somewhat more friendly and effective. Read the following sentence:

Every 1 percent reduction in ozone raises the *incidence* of skin cancer by 5 to 7 percent.

In this example, you get a vague idea of the meaning of *incidence* through context, but you still may feel the need for a clear and precise dictionary definition. When you look up the target word, this time you are given the following definitions:

> in•ci•dence (ĭn′sĭ-dəns) *n*. **1.** the act or an instance of happening; occurrence. **2.** Extent or frequency of occurrence: *high incidence of malaria.* **3.** *Phys.* **a.** The arrival of radiation or a projectile at a surface. **b.** Angle of incidence.

This entry is much clearer, and as such, is easier to understand, but you still must be able to select the definition that suits the context. It is easy to eliminate definition 3 since the point of the sentence has nothing to do with physics. The example in definition 2 is directly related to how the word *incidence* is used in the article. This example talks about the "high *incidence* of malaria" or the frequency of malaria, and the article talks about the "*incidence* of skin cancer" or the frequency of skin cancer. These two very different examples of dictionary entries show that some definitions are better and stronger than others.

ACTIVITY 3.1

DIRECTIONS: Read the section from "A Bigger Hole in the Ozone" for each of the words listed to see how they are used in context. Then read the four dictionary definitions. Rate each definition on a continuum from 1 to 5 according to your view of the definition's effectiveness. Rate the definition "1" if you think that it gives very little information about the word; rate it "5" it you think the definition is effective and useful. Rate the definition "2," "3," or "4" if it is somewhere between. Be as careful as possible since you will use your decision as the basis for another activity later in the chapter.

> grave¹ (grāv) *n.* **1.a.** An excavation for the interment of a corpse. **b.** A place of burial. **2.** Death or extinction [ME < OE *græf. See* **ghrebh-²*.**]
> grave² (grāv) *adj.* **grav•er, grav•est. 1.** Requiring serious thought; momentous. **2.** Fraught with danger or harm. **3.** Dignified and somber in conduct

or character. See synonym **serious. 4.** Somber or dark in hue. **5.** (*also* grāv). *Lang.* **a.** Written with or modified by the mark (ˋ), as the è in Sèvres. **b.** Of or referring to a phonetic feature that distinguishes sounds made at the periphery of the vocal tract, as in labial consonants and back vowels. [Fr. < OFr. < Lat. *gravis* See **gʷerə⁻¹*** .]—**grave′ly** *adv.*—**grave′ness** *n.*

grave³ (grāv) *tr.v.* **graved, grav•en** (grā′vən) or **graved, graving, graves. 1.** To sculpt or carve; engrave. **2.** To stamp or impress deeply; fix permanently. [ME *graven* < OE *grafan* See **ghrebh⁻²*** .]

grave⁴ (grāv) *tr.v.* **graved, grav•ing, graves.** To clean and coat (the bottom of a wooden ship) with pitch. [ME *graven.*]

gra•ve⁵ (grä′vā) *adv. & adj. Mus.* In a slow and solemn manner. [Ital. < Lat. *gravis,* heavy. See GRAVE².]

in•ten•si•fy (ĭn-tĕn′sə-fī′) *v.* **-fied, -fy•ing, -fies.** — *tr.* **1.** To make intense or more intense. **2.** To increase the contrast of (a photographic image). — *intr.* To become intense or more intense. — **in•ten′si•fi•ca′tion** (-fĭ-kā′shən) *n.*

crip•ple (krĭp′əl) *n.* **1.** One that is partially disabled or unable to use a limb or limbs. **2.** A damaged or defective object or device. — *tr.v.* **-pled, -pling, -ples. 1.** To cause to lose the use of a limb or limbs. **2.** To disable, damage, or impair the functioning of. [ME *crepel* < OE *crypel.*] — **crip′pler** *n.*

fore•cast (fôr′kăst′, fōr′-) *v.* **-cast** or **-cast•ed, -cast•ing, -casts.** — *tr.* **1.** To estimate or calculate in advance, esp. to predict (weather conditions) by analysis of meteorological data. **2.** To serve as an advance indication of; foreshadow. — *intr.* To calculate or estimate something in advance; predict the future. — *n.* A prediction, as of coming events. [ME *forecasten,* to plan beforehand : *fore-* fore- + *casten,* to throw, calculate, prepare; see CAST.] — **fore•cast′a•ble** *adj.* — **fore′cast′er** *n.*

1. graver   1 2 3 4 5

2. intensify   1 2 3 4 5

3. crippled   1 2 3 4 5

4. forecast   1 2 3 4 5

Characteristics of Effective Definitions

In order to use a dictionary to its fullest extent, you need to understand that some definitions will be clearer and better than others, thus enhancing denotative word knowledge. An extremely effective dictionary definition has the following five characteristics (adapted from McKeown, 1990):

1. The definition does not use another form of the same word in the definition. For example, defining a **regulator** as "one that regulates" gives virtually no information about the meaning of the unknown word. A definition such as this would be considered very ineffective.

2. The definition uses precise language that has a high degree of explaining power. Vague language often fails to represent the word. The first definition of **incidence** offers a good example of vague language. *Act, instance,* and *happening* are all vague words.

3. The definition should be written in such a way that readers are not likely to substitute an incorrect synonym for the target word. A good example of this can be seen in the word adamant. **Adamant** is defined as "a legendary stone believed to be impenetrable" or "an extremely hard substance." The definition provides no information about what can or cannot be **adamant.** In fact, this definition actually encourages the reader to substitute the word "hard" for **adamant** and write a sentence such as the following:

> Automobiles are made of **adamant** substances that are not easily damaged.

Since **adamant,** when used as an adjective, actually means unyielding or firm and usually has to do with abstractions such as beliefs or opinions, the following sentence uses the word correctly:

> Although most of her friends disagreed, June was **adamant** in her beliefs on certain environmental issues.

4. Definitions that provide multiple pieces of information should also offer some guidance about the way these pieces of information should be integrated. For the word **chronic,** the following entry is provided:

chron•ic (krŏn′ĭk) *adj.* **1.** Of long duration; continuing: *chronic problems.* **2.** Lasting for a long period of time or marked by frequent recurrence: *chronic colitis.* **3.** Subject to a habit or pattern of behavior for a long time. [Fr. *chronique* < Lat. *chronicus* < Gk. *khronikos,* of time < *khronos,* time. — **chron′i•cal•ly** *adv.* — **chro•nic′i•ty** (krŏ-nĭs′ĭ-tē) *n.*

Note that although several pieces of information are given, the entry does provide guidance concerning when they might be appropriate. The entry states that something *chronic* can be "of long duration; continuing," and also offers *"chronic problems"* to indicate something that can be *chronic.*

5. Definitions should provide examples, when necessary, so that readers can see proper usage of the word, particularly in situations in which it may be easy to misinterpret the stated definition. The word *chronic* above illustrates examples of correct context that are usually very helpful. *"Chronic colitis,"* and *"chronic problems"* are useful examples to extend dictionary understanding.

ACTIVITY 3.2 _____

DIRECTIONS: Return to Activity 3.1 and reread the dictionary entries for the four words you rated. On the lines provided below, write which of the five characteristics each definition provides. Then rate the words again on the continuum provided. How accurate were your initial ratings?

1. graver	_____	1 2 3 4 5
2. intensify	_____	1 2 3 4 5
3. crippled	_____	1 2 3 4 5
4. forecast	_____	1 2 3 4 5

It would be only in rare instances that a definition would possess all five characteristics. An effective definition might have two or three characteristics, while a less effective definition might have only one, or in some cases, none, of the five characteristics.

As you have seen, dictionaries provide a wide range of definition levels. But they also provide additional information beyond the meaning of the word. Now that you have an idea about the characteristics of effective and less effective definitions, let's progress a step further and examine the other information that dictionary entries supply.

MAKING SENSE OF DICTIONARY ENTRIES

Although dictionary definitions are not perfect, they can be an excellent starting point for understanding a word. You must, however, know how to interpret an entry effectively so that you will be able to select the most appropriate definition. As mentioned in Chapter 1, words rarely exist and have meaning in isolation, but instead they gather meaning from surrounding words and sentences. Consequently, the first listed dictionary definition might not be the most appropriate one. You will have to read all the entries before making a judgment. In this section, we will help you in the selection process by explaining the typical entry pattern for one dictionary, *The American Heritage College Dictionary, Third Edition.* In fact, we will be using the dictionary throughout the entire book as our guide to words and their definitions.

Rather than practice dictionary entry skills in a series of drills, you will work with some targeted words from "A Bigger Hole in the Ozone." If some time has passed since you read this article, you might want to review it to refresh your memory before going on to the next section.

Interpreting a Typical Entry

Dictionary entries for *fatality, conservative,* and *benign,* taken from the article, have been isolated below. Imagine for a moment that you feel a bit unsure about the conceptual meaning of these words. One of the first things to do is check the definitions in your dictionary. Begin with the word *fatality.* What do you see immediately after the word? Your entry should be similar to the one below.

> **fa•tal** (fāt'l) *adj.* **1.** Causing or capable of causing death. **2.** Causing ruin or destruction; disastrous. **3.** Of decisive importance; fateful. **4.** Concerned with or determining destiny. **5.** *Obsolete.* Having been destined; fated. [ME, ⑤ fateful < OFr. < Lat. *fātālis* < *fātum,* prophecy, doom. See FATE.]
>
> ① ② ③ ④
> **fa•tal•i•ty** (fā-tăl'ĭ-tē, fə-) *n., pl.* **-ties. 1.a.** A death resulting from an accident or a disaster. **b.** One killed in such an occurrence. **2.** The ability to cause death or disaster. **3.** The reality of being determined by fate. **4.** A decree made by fate; destiny. **5.** The quality of being doomed to disaster.

The information presented in parentheses (*1*) is the phonetic spelling of the word to aid pronunciation. If you are unsure of how to pronounce a word, this can be helpful. Remember, learning the meaning of a word without being able to pronounce it in your own conversations is somewhat useless. You learn words so you can use them in communication.

The second item of information typically found is the part of speech of the word (*2*). In the *fatality* entry, "n" stands for noun. Because some words can also be used as adjectives (adj), adverbs (adv), or verbs (v), it is important to scan the entire entry quickly for the part of speech that matches how the word is used in the context you are reading. If you forget the abbreviations used in your dictionary, there should be a key, usually located somewhere either at the beginning or near the end of the book.

The third item of information given for *fatality* is another abbreviation (*3*). What does "pl" stand for? Check your key to see. Generally, the third piece of information in a dictionary entry provides the inflected forms, that is, how words can be changed to express different relationships within sentences. Hence, the word *fatality* can also occur as *fatalities,* a plural of the noun *fatality.*

Now you finally get to the definitions (*4*)! A word of advice before you read the possibilities. Each dictionary has its own system or hierarchy for arranging definitions. The definitions in *The American Heritage College Dictionary* are listed analytically. That is, they are listed "according to central meaning clusters." Other dictionaries list definitions in order of historical usage, thus making their last definition the most current or widely used. Still others list the most current or widely used definition first. When using a dictionary, always check the policy for arrangement by reading the user's guide or introduction. If you are not using *The American Heritage College Dictionary,* check to see how your dictionary orders definitions.

Definition 1a for *fatality* is "a death resulting from an accident or a disaster." Does that fit the sentence from the article? Try it out.

> The deaths resulting from disasters estimate was 21 times what the EPA had forecast earlier.

The definition appears to fit, makes sense in the paragraph, and communicates meaningful information. Check to see how many characteristics of strong definitions the entry for *fatality* has.

One other piece of information that is often included in dictionary entries is a summary of the word's etymology, or history. Note that for the word *fatality* no etymology is given. But if you looked at the entry for the root word *fatal,* you would find this etymological information. We have pointed out this information to you as indicated by number *5*. Using etymological information will be discussed later in this chapter.

The *fatality* entry was rather basic, so let's try another word that is a bit more difficult. Look up the word ***conservative*** and quickly scan the entire entry. It should be similar to the entry below.

> **con•ser•va•tive** (kən-sûr′ve-tĭv) *adj.* **1.** Favoring traditional views and values; tending to oppose change. **2.** Traditional; restrained in style: *a conser-*

vative suit. **3.** Moderate; cautious. **4.a.** Of or relating to the political philosophy of conservatism. **b.** Belonging to a conservative party, group, or movement. **5. Conservative.** Of or belonging to the Conservative Party or the Progressive Conservative Party. **6. Conservative.** Of or adhering to Conservative Judaism. **7.** Tending to conserve; preservative. — *n.* **1.** One favoring traditional views and values. **2.** A supporter of political conservatism. **3. Conservative.** A member or supporter of the Conservative Party. **4.** *Archaic.* A preservative agent or principle. — **con•ser´va•tive•ly** *adv.* **con•ser´va•tiveness** *n.*

Notice that the entry is longer and has more definitions than does *fatality.* Notice that *conservative* can be used as an adjective and a noun. The other distinguishing feature is that the word *conservative* can be a proper noun or adjective, and thus is sometimes capitalized. This meaning of *conservative* refers to a specific political party in the United Kingdom. The capitalized version does not apply in the context of this chapter's reading because we are discussing estimates of ozone loss in the atmosphere, not political parties. Consequently, we will focus only on the uncapitalized definitions. Remember that many words in dictionaries can define a specific people or group. Sometimes you will be looking for these definitions, but most of the time you will be searching for the uncapitalized versions.

How is the word *conservative* used in the article? Is it an adjective or a noun? As used in this sentence, *conservative* is an adjective. Now select the most appropriate definition. Carefully examine definitions 1, 2, and 3, noting the example in italics in 2: *"a conservative suit."* In this dictionary, examples are often provided and are signaled as examples through the use of a colon followed by the example in italics. Now examine definition 3. Which definition is the most appropriate? Does "cautious" or "moderate" fit the sentence?

Were any of our estimates of ozone layer loss too cautious?

This definition seems appropriate for the word *conservative* in this context. We will practice these guidelines of interpreting dictionary entries in Activity 3.3, which follows.

ACTIVITY 3.3 _____

DIRECTIONS: Using the dictionary entries from the preceding pages, answer the following questions about the words taken from the article.

---

graver (page 75)

The sentence: Now it seems that the problem is far **graver** than anyone thought.

1. Note that the entry for **grave,** the root word for **graver,** is rather lengthy. What is the significance of the superscript preceding each of the entries? _____

    _____

2. Which of the five entries is the most pertinent to how the word **graver** is used in this article? _____

    _____

3. How many definitions in this entry are pertinent to the word **graver** as an adjective? _____

    _____

4. How is **grave** used in the fifth definition?_____

    _____

intensify (page 76)

The sentence: Reilly vowed that the EPA would **intensify** its efforts to find substitutes for ozone-eating substances.

5. According to this entry, in what ways can the word **intensify** be used? _____

    _____

6. Of the two definitions, which appears to be the most

appropriate for the context of the article? _____

_____

7. If you could not make sense of the first definition because you did not understand the word *intense,* what should you do?____

_____

8. What is a good definition for the word *intensify?* Make sure you do not define the word by using another form of the word.

_____

cripple (page 76)

The sentence: Right now, countries such as China and India believe that abandoning CFCs too quickly would *cripple* their economies.

9. In what ways can the word *cripple* be used?_____

_____

10. Which way is more appropriate for the context of this reading?

_____

11. What is a good definition for *cripple* in this sentence?

_____

forecast (page 76)

The sentence: The fatality estimate was 21 times what the EPA had *forecast* earlier.

12. According to this entry, as what parts of speech can the word

forecast be used? _____

_____

13. What do *tr.* and *intr.* mean? How could you find their meanings?

_____

_____

14. Which definition is the most appropriate for the context of this

article? _____

_____

Understanding Etymological Information in a Typical Entry

When you analyze the *etymology,* or history, of a word, you can often find information that is interesting and useful in helping you understand and remember new words encountered in reading. Etymological information usually occurs between square brackets [ ] and, in *The American Heritage College Dictionary,* follows all the definitions for a given root word. For example, if you examine the entry for *fatal* on page 79, you will see these brackets after the last definition. Some dictionaries, however, place this information at the beginning of the entry. Check your dictionary to find where the etymological information is presented.

Use the glossary of abbreviations in the front of the dictionary to interpret the symbols within the brackets and to determine where the word originated. Return to the *fatal* entry. Inside the brackets you see the following:

[ME, fateful < OFr. < Lat. *fātālis* < *fātum,* prophecy, doom. See FATE.]

In *The American Heritage College Dictionary,* the most recent known pre–Modern English stage is given first, with each earlier stage following in sequence. In the example above, Middle English (ME), Old French (OFr.), and Latin forms have the same basic definition as shown by both the "<" mark as well as the two Latin examples given—*fatalis* and *fatum*. You may already know one of the more common meanings of *fatal:* "causing or capable of causing death" as in a *fatal* automobile accident. One of the most important things to observe about etymological entries is that most words have origins in other languages and have been evolving for long periods of time.

Let's examine a dictionary entry and etymology for the word **be-nign.** Remember that the first step in determining meaning is to check the context to determine the word's part of speech and to see what information you can gather about the word. As used in the article, **benign** is an adjective. The dictionary entry reads as follows:

> **be•nign** (bǐ-nīn′) *adj.* **1.** Of a kind and gentle disposition. **2.** Showing gentleness and mildness. **3.** Tending to exert a beneficial influence; favorable. See Syns at **favorable. 4.** *Medic.* Of no danger to health; not recurrent or progressive; not malignant. [ME *benigne* < OFr. < Lat. *benignus.* See **genə-*.**]
> — **be•nign′ly** *adv.*

The above entry has four definitions. The last entry refers to something "not malignant," such as a benign tumor. Since this definition pertains to diseases and the author is describing chemicals that are not chlorine-based, this definition can be eliminated. An examination of the three remaining definitions reveals that definition 3 seems most appropriate to this context—tending to promote well-being; beneficial.

By checking the etymological entry we can learn more information about **benign.** The word originated from Middle English, Old French, and the Latin root *benignus.* Since *benignus* means well, there appears to be a relationship between definition 3 and the word's etymology. If you were to check your own dictionary for words such as *benefactor, beneficial,* and *benediction* you would discover that these words are cognates of **benign** since they too originate from *benignus.*

The final step is to substitute definition 3 to determine whether it makes sense. Does this make sense?

> Chemicals that promote well-being can do the job of other solvents that contain chlorine.

Interpreting dictionary entries is a matter of understanding the format of your dictionary and taking the time to interpret the symbols and abbreviations provided in the etymological entry. Because your understanding of a new word can be enhanced by the interpretion of etymological entries, practice is provided in Activity 3.4, which follows.

DIRECTIONS: Using the dictionary entries from the pages that precede and follow Activity 3.4, answer these questions about the words taken from the article.

1. Explain the origin of the word ***grave*** (see pages 75–76).

   _____

2. Explain the origin of the word ***cripple*** (see page 76). How are the original word and meaning related to the present usage of the word ***cripple?***

   _____

   _____

3. Explain the origin of the word ***fatality*** (see page 79).

   _____

4. Explain the origin of the word ***anchor*** (see page 92).

   _____

5. Explain the origin of the word ***stratosphere*** (see page 94). What are the two parts to this word?

   _____

   _____

We should point out that some words have extremely fascinating histories and etymological entries. Some of these histories are so intriguing that you will be able to place the word's meaning in your long-term memory and retrieve it forever. In the next section, some of these words and their entries will be discussed.

Unusual Word Origins in Etymological Entries

Although many of the more difficult English words do originate from languages no longer spoken, there are many other sources for English words besides Latin and Greek. A considerable number of words that we use daily originate from modern languages such as French, Spanish, and German. For example, the words *elite, naive,* and *gourmet* all come from French words and expressions. Other words can trace their history to stories of interesting people and places. *Maverick* owes its beginnings to a man named Sam Maverick who was a Texas rancher in the 1800s. Mr. Maverick had such a soft heart that he refused to brand his cattle. Cattle rustlers called his unmarked cattle *mavericks.* The label has been applied to people who are independent or rebellious because they do not follow the crowd or general trends. When you check the etymology of *maverick* you will see that Samuel Maverick is listed as the source of the word.

Hence, when you read an etymological entry, make sure you look for the following sources of a vocabulary word:

1. **Places** — Examples: marathon, meander
2. **Mythology** — Examples: mentor, lunatic
3. **Acronyms**, or the abbreviation of a series of words by using the first letters — Example: *laser* stands for Light Amplification by Simulated Emission of Radiation
4. **Inventions** — Examples: modem, boom box
5. **Clips**, or the shortening of a word — Example: *fax* as a clip of *facsimile* or *perks* as a clip of *perquisites*
6. **Blends**, or the blends of sounds and meanings of two words — Examples: *Medicaid* is a blend of medic(al) and aid; *telecast* is a blend of tele(vision) and (broad)cast
7. **Names of people** — Examples: Maverick, Gerrymander
8. **Foreign languages** — Examples: gourmet, cigar

Depending on your dictionary, these other sources for a word's origin may be noted in the etymological information with brackets. If your dictionary does not fully explain the stories behind the words and you are interested in this, consider the following books as sources:

1. *Word Origins and Their Romantic Stories* by Wilfred Funk (New York: Funk and Wagnalls, 1950)
2. *Name into Word* by Eric Partridge (London: Secker and Warburg, 1949)
3. *Hog on Ice* by Charles Funk (New York: Paperback Library, 1973)

4. *Words from the Myths* by Isaac Asimov (Boston: Houghton Mifflin Company, 1961)
5. *Origins: A Short Etymological Dictionary of Modern English* by Eric Partridge (New York: Macmillan, 1962)
6. *The Oxford English Dictionary, Second Edition,* by J. A. Simpson and Edmund S. Weiner (Oxford: Oxford University Press, 1989)

The following activity provides an additional opportunity to analyze the intriguing stories behind our language.

ACTIVITY 3.5 ───────────────────────────

DIRECTIONS: Using your dictionary, determine the origins of the following words. You may wish to do this in small groups.

1. What is the origin of the word *mentor?* Who has been your

   mentor? _____

2. What is the origin of the word *narcissism?* Whom do you

   know who could be described as a *narcissist?* _____

   _____

3. What is the origin of the words *faux pas?* What has been your

   most embarrassing *faux pas?* _____

   _____

4. What is the origin of the word *meander?* When have you

   meandered? _____

   _____

5. What is the origin of the word *malapropism?* Give an example

   of a *malapropism.* (Hint: see *malapropos.*) _____

   _____

6. What is the origin of the word *chortle?* Would you be pleased if someone *chortled* at one of your jokes? Is this word a blend or a clip?_____

_____

7. What is the origin of the word *curio?* Have you ever received a *curio?* _____

_____

8. What is the origin of the word *quixotic?* _____

_____

9. What is the origin of the word *nemesis?* What is an example of one of your *nemeses?* _____

_____

10. What is the origin of the word *snafu?* _____

_____

CONNOTATION: LINKS TO EXPERIENCE

Now that you have a good idea about denotative, or dictionary, word knowledge, let's examine word *connotation*—a more abstract part of word knowledge that also leads to conceptual understanding. Connotation refers to the knowledge about words gained from experiences.

It should be apparent by now that a dictionary alone rarely provides conceptual knowledge. Stage 4 word knowledge generally comes from extensive reading and numerous encounters with words used in different contexts. Evidence for this claim stems from what is known in the study of words as the *Sapir-Whorf Hypothesis*. Simply, this hypothesis states that you can think only about ideas that your language system can explain or understand. For example, if you are from a state with a tropical climate, such as Florida or some portions of California, you would see palm trees daily. People who live in these areas don't see just palm trees; they see many different kinds of palms—coconut palms, date palms, royal palms, fishtail palms, and the like. Individuals who visit these climates generally see only "palm trees" and do not differentiate among palms because the specific kinds are not part of their language system. It is this sort of differentiation that helps develop your connotative knowledge about words. As previously stated, what you read in a dictionary provides the denotative knowledge of words; what you add to the knowledge of words through your own experiences are the connotative elements. In order for you to know a word conceptually, both elements must be present.

To illustrate the difference between denotation and connotation, we'll start with an easy example. If you look up **dog** in *The American Heritage College Dictionary,* the entry reads as follows:

> **dog** (dôg, dŏg) *n.* **1.** A domesticated canid (*Canis familiaris*) related to foxes and wolves and raised in many breeds. **2.** Any of various members of the family Canidae, such as the dingo. **3.** A male animal of the family Canidae, esp. of the domesticated breed. **4.** Any of various other animals; the prairie dog. **5.** *Informal.* **a.** A person: *you lucky dog!* **b.** A contemptible person: *You stole my watch, you dog.* **6.** *Slang.* **a.** An unattractive or uninteresting person; **b.** An inferior product or creation. **7. dogs.** *Slang.* The feet. **8. andiron. 9.** *Slang.* A hot dog; a wiener. **10.** Any hooked or U-shaped metallic devices used for gripping or holding heavy objects. **11.** *Astron.* A sun dog. —*adv.* Totally; completely. Often used in combination: *dog-tired.* —*tr.v.* **dogged, dog•ging, dogs. 1.** To track or trail persistently. **2.** To hold or fasten with a dog. — *idioms.* **dog it.** *Slang.* To fail to expend the effort to accomplish something. **go to the dogs.** To go to ruin; degenerate. **put on the dog.** *Informal.* To make an ostentatious display. [ME *dogge* < OE *docga*.]

If someone had told you as a young child to look up the meaning of the word **dog** because you were expected to learn what **dog** means from a dictionary, you probably would have had little idea what a dog is after seeing this definition. In fact, if someone gave you the above definition without telling you that it is the definition of the word **dog,** you might assume that it is a cat or some other animal. Just how could you define **dog** so that a reader would be sure of what you were talking about? Would it be possible to construct an effective definition of **dog** that meets all five of the criteria mentioned earlier in this chapter? For this example, it is probably not particularly important to have an effective definition because most people have had a variety of experiences with dogs. Unless you have been isolated, you not only can distinguish a dog from a cat, but you also can distinguish among different breeds of dogs. If your brother calls and tells you that he has just bought a Great Dane puppy, you would have a much different mental picture than if he told you that he had just bought a poodle. Your knowledge of dogs has not resulted from any dictionary, but from the variety of experiences you have had.

Other connotations that you might have about dogs probably occur as a result of your experiences. If you grew up with dogs, always had one or more dogs as pets, and they slept in your bed or shared cookies with you, your reaction when you see a dog, or even when you hear the word, will be a positive one. However, if you never had a dog because your mother thought they were nasty, dirty creatures with fleas, or if you had been bitten by a dog, your reaction when you see a dog or hear the word might be one of disgust or fear. These elements of words cannot be written in a dictionary. Rather, we learn these connotations through everyday experiences—reading widely, interactions with others, and the media.

A second example might illustrate the role that *connotation* plays in a more realistic reading situation. You encounter the following sentence during reading:

> The senator's *gaffe* caused the audience to laugh out loud, but the senator continued his speech without pause.

Context does not provide much information. **Gaffe** could be a joke or some sort of action. You really can't tell what. When you look up the word you find the following definition:

> **gaffe** also **gaff** (găf) *n.* **1.** A clumsy social error. **2.** A blatant mistake or misjudgment. [Fr. < OFr., hook. See GAFF¹.]

If you go back and reread the characteristics of a good definition, you will find that the definition for **gaffe** is ineffective. Just what is "a clumsy social error"? And "blatant" in the second definition may be another unfamiliar word. Asked to generate a sentence for **gaffe**, having never seen the word before, you would be faced with a difficult task. You might write something like "My friend made a **gaffe** when he dripped strawberry sauce all over his shirt in the expensive French restaurant." Neither dictionary nor context gives you any information about which "social errors" constitute **gaffes** and which do not.

If you possessed more connotative knowledge of **gaffe,** however, you might know that a **gaffe,** as indicated in the original context, is usually something spoken and is generally a mistake that an individual does not realize he or she has committed. Understanding such connotative elements suggests that although dripping strawberry sauce on your shirt may not be considered socially acceptable, it would also not be considered a **gaffe.** Hence, the connotative elements of a word, although not revealed in a dictionary, are as important as a dictionary's denotative entries.

USING CONTEXT AND A DICTIONARY

As mentioned earlier, words by themselves have no meaning; it is only when they are put into some context that meaning is effectively communicated. This is why it is crucial to know how a word is used before you look it up in a dictionary. There are three key situations when it is particularly crucial to use a combination of both context and a dictionary:

1. when words can be used as more than one part of speech;
2. when the word is used as only one part of speech but can take on either slightly or dramatically different meanings; and most importantly,
3. when you are dealing with content-specific terms.

Words as Different Parts of Speech

Many words can be used as different parts of speech. Sometimes the part of speech changes the meaning of the word only slightly, but on other occasions, meanings change more dramatically.

There are several examples of such words in "A Bigger Hole in the Ozone." As an example, let's look at the word ***anchors. Anchors*** is found in the following context:

> Ultraviolet radiation can also cause cataracts, weaken the immune system, damage crops and disrupt the reproduction of plankton that ***anchors*** the marine food chain.

Although you might be familiar with one of the noun forms of ***anchor,*** in this context, ***anchor*** is used as a verb. When you look up the word in the dictionary, you find the following entry:

an•chor (ăng′kər) *n.* **1.** *Naut.* A heavy object attached to a vessel and lowered overboard to keep the vessel in place either by its weight or by its flukes, which grip the bottom. **2.** A rigid point of support, as for securing a rope. **3.** A source of security or stability. **4.** *Sports.* **a.** An athlete who performs the last stage of a competition. **b.** The end of a tug-of-war team. **5.** An anchor-person. — *v.* **-chored, -chor•ing, -chors.** — *tr.* **1.** To hold fast by or as if by an anchor. **2.** *Sports.* To serve as anchor for (a team or competition). **3.** To narrate or coordinate (a newscast). — *intr. Naut.* To drop anchor or lie at anchor. [ME *anker, ancher* < OE *ancor* < Lat. *ancora, anchora* < Gk. *ankura.*]

In this situation, even with several verb definitions given, it still is not totally apparent which one would be best, so it's important to think through the three transitive verb definitions. The third, "to narrate or coordinate," really fails to fit this context. The context states that plankton *anchors* the food chain, but here it does not mean that it coodinates it. Similarly, the second definition, "to serve as anchor for," does not fit, especially given the two sample phrases.

There is only one choice left. *Anchor* in this context must have something to do with holding fast or fixing, as suggested in the first definition. If you think of someone or something that secures or fixes as making something firm or stable, then, yes, plankton can hold fast or fix. What the author is trying to communicate by using *anchor* in this context is that plankton makes the food chain stable. Without plankton, the food chain would not function as nature intended.

Words That Have Meaning Changes

In addition to making sure that you know what part of speech a word is used as, there is a second reason why using context in combination with a dictionary becomes important. Sometimes the part of speech remains the same, but the meaning changes, sometimes dramatically, other times only slightly. An example of a dramatic change comes to mind with the term *CD*. Out of context, how do you know what kind of *CD* we are referring to? Is it the music kind—the abbreviation that comes from a *compact disc*—or is it a *certificate of deposit* that you might purchase as a way of saving money for the future?

A similar, although certainly not as dramatic, example occurs with the word *regulators* from "A Bigger Hole in the Ozone." It reads:

> Eliminating CFCs before 2000, though, would not make much difference, because so many of the chemicals are already on their way to the stratosphere. In effect, *regulators* are running out of ideas.

The American Heritage College Dictionary indicates two major different definitions of *regulator,* both of which are nouns.

> **reg•u•la•tor** (rĕg′yə-lā′tər) *n.* **1.** One that regulates, as: **a.** The mechanism in a watch by which its speed is governed. **b.** A clock used as a standard for timing other clocks. **c.** A device used to maintain uniform speed in a machine; a governor. **d.** A device used to control the flow of gases, liquids, or electric current. **2.** One that ensures compliance with laws and regulations.

In this instance, the correct definition is relatively easy to select, since in context it is obvious that the *regulator* in question is a person, not some device. The only definition that could refer to a person would be the second one. But "one that ensures compliance with regulations" tells us little. At this point you would look up the words *ensure, compliance,* and *regulations* to determine that the definition means one who makes sure that others obey rules or laws. Now you are ready to put the two pieces of information together to conclude that the ***regulators*** are individuals who direct how much and what kind of CFCs are allowed to be released into the stratosphere.

Words Used as Content-Specific Terms

Perhaps the most important situation in which to use context, as well as a dictionary, is when you encounter difficult content-specific terms. Content-specific terms are those words unique to a specialized field or course of study. You will encounter numerous content-specific words in courses such as psychology, sociology, and biology, and these words often appear on exams. Consequently, you will need an organized approach to determine their meaning. As discussed in Chapter 2, there are several generative strategies that can provide significant assistance in learning content-specific words. A dictionary may not be as helpful as some of these generative strategies, but it still can be used if certain modifications are made. Let's examine these modifications with the word ***stratosphere,*** taken from "A Bigger Hole in the Ozone." The context reads as follows:

> Eliminating CFCs before 2000, though, would not make much difference, because so many of the chemicals are already on their way to the ***stratosphere.***

As with general vocabulary words, the first step should be to check the surrounding words and sentences for definitional hints. In this situation, context does not provide much information. We do know that ***stratosphere*** is a noun in this sentence. Hence, the second step is to check a dictionary or a glossary for more information. Rather than using a general dictionary, it is usually better, if possible, to check a specialized dictionary for the meaning of content-specific words. Check your library's reference section for a listing of these specialized dictionaries, as there is one for almost every content area. Some of the more common ones are Taber's *Cyclopedic Medical Dictionary,* the *Harvard Dictionary of Music, A Dictionary of Economics,* and *A Dictionary of Anthropology.* You should also check the back of your textbook, because many have their own specialized glossaries.

To illustrate the difference between a glossary entry and a dictionary entry when looking at content-specific words, carefully read the following two entries, the first taken from a dictionary and the second taken from a text glossary:

strat•o•sphere (străt′ə-sfîr′) *n.* **1.** The region of the atmosphere above the troposphere and below the mesosphere. **2.** An extremely high or the highest point or degree on a ranked scale. [Fr. *stratosphère* : Lat. *strātus*, a spreading out; see STRATUS + *-sphère,* sphere (< OFr. *espere;* see SPHERE).]

> **Stratosphere**—a region of the atmosphere based on temperature between approximately 10 to 35 miles in altitude.

The dictionary entry is confusing, but the textbook glossary definition is superior and useful because it is precise and meaningful to someone who is not an environmental expert or science major.

The final step is to check the glossary definition to make sure it fits the original context. Does the following make sense?

> Chemicals are on their way up to a region approximately 10 to 35 miles high in altitude.

In the ***stratosphere*** example, the glossary was more useful than the dictionary entry and surrounding words and sentences. In the next example, we will examine another content-specific word, ***chlorofluorocarbons,*** for which context is more helpful in determining the meaning. The word is first encountered in the following sentence:

> In 1987, 24 nations meeting in Montreal pledged that, by the year 2000, they would halve their production of ***chlorofluorocarbons*** (CFCs), chemicals that destroy ozone.

Notice that an initial explanation of CFCs is provided in this sentence. That is, CFCs are chemicals that destroy ozone. Obviously, this is a partial definition, but a start toward conceptual understanding of the word. The next step is to check a dictionary or a glossary for further details. You gain a bit more information from the dictionary entry below.

chlo•ro•fluor•o•car•bon (klôr′ō-flŏŏr′ō-kär′bən,-flôr′-, -flōr′-, klōr′-) *n.* Any of various halocarbon compounds consisting of carbon, hydrogen, chlorine, and fluorine, once used widely as aerosol propellants and refrigerants and now believed to cause depletion of the atmospheric ozone layer.

You now know that CFCs are compounds that contain carbon, hydrogen, chlorine, and fluorine, but an analysis of the word itself might have told you this. You also learn from the dictionary entry that CFCs were once widely used as refrigerants and in aerosol cans.

To add further to the information given in the dictionary definition and the initial sentence, you can check the rest of the article for additional explanations or characteristics of CFCs. By scanning the rest of the article, you learn the following information about CFCs:

1. They will be banned in the year 2000 by 90 countries. Hence, they seem to be dangerous.
2. CFCs stay in the atmosphere for decades. Therefore, they are potent and long-lasting.
3. The Environmental Protection Agency (EPA) is looking for substitutes for CFCs, but this task has been difficult. This is especially true for refrigerators and air conditioners.
4. Some scientists believe that eliminating CFCs would not make much difference, since so many CFCs are already in the stratosphere.

With this information from the article and the dictionary you should be able to write a precise and useful definition for *chlorofluorocarbons.* Take some time and write your definition below:

My definition for CFCs: _____

_____

_____

Your definition should be similar to this one: "CFCs are compounds of carbon, hydrogen, chlorine, and fluorine that appear to have long-lasting and dangerous effects on the ozone layer since they can last in the atmosphere for decades. CFCs are used in refrigerators, air-conditioners, and aerosol propellants. Presently, 90 developed nations have agreed to ban CFCs by the year 2000, but other countries have yet to do likewise." This definition illustrates the detail necessary for conceptual understanding of a word and the precision necessary for success in content-area courses.

ACTIVITY 3.6 _____

DIRECTIONS: Read and answer each of the following questions, all of which focus on the word **solvents,** *which you found in "A Bigger Hole in the Ozone."*

1. Find the word *solvents* in the last paragraph of "A Bigger Hole in the Ozone." Read carefully how it is used in context and explain what you know about the word by the way it is used. Use the space below to write out your explanation.

_____

_____

_____

_____

_____

2. What part of speech is *solvents* in this context? _____

3. Now look up *solvent* in a dictionary. Which definition best suits the context? Write this definition in the space below and explain your choice.

_____

_____

_____

_____

ACTIVITY 3.7 _____

DIRECTIONS: You will need your own dictionary to complete the following activity. The sentences that follow are taken from selections in Part II of this book.

THE SENTENCE: Sex was never about equality but about *difference,* and sexual equality implied the phasing-out of male-female differences—in the *jargon* of the time, *androgyny.*

1. How many definitions of the word *jargon* does your dictionary

have? _____

2. Write the dictionary definition of *jargon* that fits this

sentence. _____

_____

3. What are some other forms of the word *jargon?*

_____

4. How many definitions of the word *androgyny* does your
dictionary have? See the word *androgynous.*

_____

5. Explain the origin of the word *androgyny.*

_____

6. Write the dictionary definition of *androgyny* that fits this
sentence.

_____

THE SENTENCE: I am your basic do-gooder, and prior to teaching
this class I blamed the poor academic skills our kids have today on
drugs, divorce and other *impediments* to concentration necessary
for doing well in school.

7. How many definitions of *impediment* does your dictionary
have?

_____

8. Explain the origin of the word *impediment.*

_____

9. Does your dictionary have a legal definition for the word
impediment? Does that definition fit the sentence above?
Why or why not?

_____

10. Write the definition for *impediment* that fits the sentence above.

_____

THE SENTENCE: The few birds seen anywhere were *moribund;* they trembled violently and could not fly.

11. Before you look up this word in your dictionary, make a guess as to its meaning by using clues in the sentence. What is your educated guess as to the meaning of *moribund?* What clues did you use?

_____

12. What part of speech is *moribund* as it is used in the sentence?

_____

13. Explain the origin of the word *moribund.*

_____

14. Can you think of other words that have originated from the same source and mean approximately the same thing? Give one example.

_____

15. Write the meaning of *moribund* as it is used in the above sentence.

_____

ACTIVITY 3.8 _____

DIRECTIONS: You have learned several content-specific and general words from the article "A Bigger Hole in the Ozone." You may wish to return to the dictionary entries and activities in this chapter so you can make vocabulary cards for each of the targeted words. (See Chapter 2 for a review of vocabulary cards.) There are 14 words from this selection:

anchors	forecast
benign	graver
chlorofluorocarbons	incidence
conservative	intensify
cripple	regulators
endangered	solvents
fatality	stratosphere

ACTIVITY 3.9

DIRECTIONS: Answer each of the following questions, demonstrating that you have a clear understanding of the boldfaced words. Each of the words was presented in "A Bigger Hole in the Ozone."

1. What have 90 countries agreed to do to help reduce the problem of ***chlorofluorocarbons?***

   _____

2. Give some examples to illustrate how the ozone problem is ***graver*** than most people ever imagined.

   _____

3. What is the estimated ***fatality*** count for people dying from skin cancer in the United States? How does this ***forecast*** differ from the one provided earlier by the EPA?

   _____

4. Why would abandoning CFCs in some countries ***cripple*** their economies?

   _____

5. How has the EPA ***intensified*** its efforts in finding solutions to the problems of our ozone layer?

   _____

6. Are *regulators* optimistic in their attempts to find a solution? Why or why not?

_____

Before completing the final activity for Chapter 3, you should recite your vocabulary cards using the suggestions in Chapter 2. The directions for the activity are below.

ACTIVITY 3.10 _____

DIRECTIONS: Read eac.
used correctly, circle C and go
faced word is used incorrectly, circ.
correct.

C   I   **1.** The Olympic athlete's chances for winning a
were ***crippled*** when it was discovered that he .
been taking steroids.

C   I   **2.** After failing the accounting midterm, the business
major decided to ***intensify*** his efforts by avoiding
class and skipping the daily assignments.

C   I   **3.** The television announcer had ***forecast*** snow, but th
weather turned warm and we had only rain.

C   I   **4.** After learning that the damage to her car was
graver than she expected, Louise felt a sense of
relief and happiness.

C   I   **5.** Chris was extremely depressed when the doctor told
her that her tumor was ***benign.***

C   I   **6.** Many zoos and corporations are attempting to
preserve ***endangered*** animals with special
educational programs.

C   I   **7.** In the United States, the ***incidence*** of measles and
smallpox has significantly decreased.

C   I   **8.** The bus driver, who had caused several passenger *fatalities*, was rewarded with a bonus and a letter of appreciation.

C   I   **9.** When estimating how much pizza and how many beverages are needed for a party of hungry college students, it is always wise to be *conservative*.

C   I   **10.** The chairperson of our club, an organized and dedicated worker, *anchors* the goals and projects we have established.

C   I   **11.** *Regulators* trained in airline safety turned out to investigate the procedures used by the pilots and stewardesses prior to the crash.

C   I   **12.** Anthony flew his kite through the *stratosphere*.

C   I   **13.** The United States and Britian are encouraging underdeveloped nations to use more *chlorofluorocarbons*.

C   I   **14.** Martin used the *solvent* to strip the paint from the cupboards.

SUMMARY

This chapter focused on several aspects of using a dictionary. Although dictionary definitions are an important tool for vocabulary development, they must be used wisely. Because the quality of dictionary entries may vary, it is important to use a variety of sources to gain conceptual word knowledge. It is also important to know the information contained in a dictionary entry and how to interpret it. This chapter explained how to use the entry and how to find out interesting and often helpful information about a word by focusing on the etymological entry. In addition to discussing the denotative meanings to words, how word connotations help the reader to know a word at the conceptual level was also discussed. This chapter concluded by discussing how to combine dictionary use with context in order to maximize word understanding.

CHAPTER 4

Word Elements

Did You Know?
The word *precipitate* originated from the Latin prefix *pre*, before, and the root *caput*, head. Visualize a person dashing headlong into something. Today one definition for *precipitate* is moving rapidly, recklessly, or unexpectedly.

ROOTS, PREFIXES, AND SUFFIXES

Many individuals believe that a knowledge of word elements can significantly increase your vocabulary because unknown words can be figured out by examining a prefix, suffix, or root. For example, for the word *incredible*, if you knew that the root *cred* means *belief* or *believe* and that the prefix *in* means *not*, you could estimate the word *incredible* to mean *not believable*. In this situation, understanding the meanings of a root and a prefix were important steps for independently determining the meaning of an unknown word. But learning word elements is not a cure-all, either. It is simply another piece of the puzzle, which, when put together with context and the dictionary, gives you many options for understanding words in a generative fashion.

When we use the term *word elements*, three different key words come to mind: *roots*, *prefixes*, and *suffixes*. Before proceeding, it is important to have a clear understanding of each word element.

Roots

The most important word element is a word's *root*. The root is the word element from which most of the meaning is derived, and thus the root carries the majority of the denotative or dictionary meaning. Word elements cannot be broken down any further than a root and still carry meaning. However, two roots can be put together to form a word, such as in the word *cinematography,* which is formed by combining two roots, *cinema* and *graph.*

Another alternative is that a root can be combined with either a prefix or suffix, as in the case of *consensus* (the prefix *con-,* meaning together + the root *sentire,* meaning to feel). In addition, some roots, such as *ego,* can stand alone, while others are called *combining roots* because they must be combined with prefixes, other roots, or suffixes in order to communicate meaning. *Vert-, fac-,* and *cede-* are three examples of combining roots.

The following is a list of some common roots, taken from Latin and Greek, that you will see in your reading. Keep in mind that this list, and the others that will follow, are not all-inclusive. We have included those that are high-utility. How many of these common roots do you already know? Look over the list and the example words in the right-hand column.

Root	Meaning	Example
acer-, acr	sharp, bitter	acerbic
amor-	love	amorous
arch-	chief, to rule	hierarchy
aud-	hear	audio (signal processor)
auto-	self	autocrat
bell(e)-	beautiful	embellishing
bio-	life	biosphere
cap-	take, hold	captivate
carn-	flesh	carnal
cede-	to go	preceded
cinema-	to move	cinematography
cogn-	to learn	cognitive
cosm-	universe, order	cosmopolitan
cred-	believe	credibility
dem-	people	demography
dict-	say, speak	dictated
ego-	I, self	egomania
fac-	make	facilitate
graph-	write	graphic simulator
hier-	high	hierarchy

Root	Meaning	Example
hydro-	water	dehydration
idio-	one's own peculiar style	idiosyncrasies
jur-	to swear	conjures
man-, manu-	hand	manipulate
mania-	madness	egomania
mis-, mit-	send	emits
mort-	death	moribund
neur-	nerve	neurotic
ped-, pod-	foot	pedometer
photo-	light	photochemical
phys-	nature	physiological
plac-, placa-	please	placate
polis-	city, state	cosmopolitan
press-	to press	oppression
sen-	old	senile
sol-	alone	solace
son-	sound	sonority
spec-	to look, see	specter
sym-, syn-	same, together	sympathy
vert-	turn	averted, convert
virtus-	goodness	virtuosity
viv-	live	vivacious
voc-	call	evocative

Prefixes

The next most important word elements are *prefixes*. Although prefixes do not add as much information to words as do roots, they do bring more meaning than suffixes. Prefixes are those elements added to roots at the beginning of a word. Sometimes they can be removed from the root and what is left can stand on its own and make sense. Such is the case with the word *interrelated*. When the prefix *inter-* is removed, what remains, *related*, is a word that has meaning even without the prefix attached. If, however, the prefix *re-* is removed from *reciprocated*, we are left with *-ciprocated*, which makes no sense by itself. Another important quality of prefixes to note is that they change the meaning of the root word.

The following is a list of some common prefixes. Look over the list and determine the ones that you already know. Also, read the example word for each prefix.

Prefix	Meaning	Example
a-	from, down, away	aberration, abolition
anti-	opposing, against	antiestablishment
bi-	two	binary
com-, con-	with, together	components, consolation
counter-	against	counterculture
de-	from, down	deterioration
di-	two	diatonic, dimension
dis-	not, apart	disintegrate, dispersed
e-, ec-	out	eccentric
em-, en-	not, into, very	embodied, enhance
epi-	under	epicenter
equi-	just, equal, fair	equivalency
ex-	out, former	extensive, exclusively
hyper-	exceedingly	hyperactive
im-, in-	not	impediments
il-, ir-	not	irrelevant
inter-	between	interfaith
mal-	harmful	maladjusted
mis-	wrongly, badly	mistreat
non-	not	nonlove
pro-	favoring, for	prolife
pre-	before	pretest, precede
post-	after	postmodernism
pseudo-	false	pseudoscience
psych-	mind, mental	psychic
re-	back, again	reassemble, respondents
semi-	half	semiliterate
socio-	social, society	sociology
sub-	below, under	submerge
trans-	across	transition
un-	not, reversed	unparalleled

Suffixes

The final word elements are *suffixes*. Suffixes carry the least amount of meaning. Their primary function is either to change the part of speech, as in *propose* to *proposition,* or to change the word to its plural form or to its past tense, as in the words *dimensions* and *circulated.* A few suffixes, such as *-logy,* which means "the study of," extend the meaning of the root, as in the case of *psychology.*

Read the list of common suffixes below. Notice that they have been divided by parts of speech.

Suffixes That Form Nouns	Suffixes That Form Adjectives
-ac	-able, -ible
-ance, -ancy	-ac, -ic
-dom	-al
-ence	-ant
-er	-ary
-ion, -tion	-dom
-ism	-en
-ist	-ful
-ment	-ive
-ness	-like
-ology	-ous, -ious
-ure	-some
	-y

Suffixes That Form Verbs	Suffixes That Form Adverbs
-ate	-ly
-ify	
-ize	

ADVANTAGES OF LEARNING WORD ELEMENTS

As mentioned above, learning a variety of word elements is not the only way to build your vocabulary, but when used along with other context and dictionary generative strategies, word elements can be helpful. Perhaps the biggest advantage in learning word elements is that learning one root can help you determine the meanings of more than one unfamiliar word which you encounter in your reading. And while you may not be able to gain full conceptual knowledge of the word through knowing its root, when this is combined with context, you probably will be able to determine a global meaning of the word. For example, for the root *trans-,* meaning "across," an unabridged dictionary lists numerous words derived from it. Thus, learning a root such as this becomes a real bargain. (Most dictionaries list far fewer derived words, however.) Knowing the meaning of *trans-* can help you determine the meanings of words like *transatlantic* and *transcontinental,* especially if you also use context. As mentioned in Chapter 3, these words are *cognates,* or related to each other. The following activity asks you to combine word elements and the use of context to determine word meanings.

ACTIVITY 4.1 _____

DIRECTIONS: Determine the meanings of the three boldfaced words based on your knowledge of the root word and the context.

Brian was such a ***pseudointellectual,*** always bragging at school about the recent piece of literature he had just finished, or the new classical CD he had just purchased. His friends, however, told a different story. The only things Brian read were comic books and detective magazines, and the closest he got to classical music was walking by Symphony Hall!

1. Based on the meaning of ***pseudo-*** and context, ***pseudointel-***

    lectual means _____

    _____

    _____

    _____

2. Now look up ***pseudointellectual*** in a dictionary. Give the dic-

    tionary definition. Were you correct in your guess? _____

    _____

    _____

    _____

Authors and entertainers often use a ***pseudonym*** for a variety of reasons. Authors may not want readers to know who wrote books which differ from their usual writing, while entertainers may use a ***pseudonym*** because they dislike their given names or because their agents believe other names will gain them greater recognition.

3. Based on the meaning of *pseudo-* and context, *pseudonym*

means _____

_____

_____

_____

4. Now look up *pseudonym* in a dictionary. Give the dictionary

definition. Were you correct in your guess?_____

_____

_____

_____

When Tameka began her summer job as a waitress at the expensive resort, she immediately noticed that there was a certain *hierarchy* among the employees at the restaurant. The busboys and dishwashers seemed to be at the bottom in importance among the workers. In contrast, the hostess and bartenders were at the top of the *hierarchy.* Tameka, a pre-law major, wondered if there would be a *hierarchy* among the lawyers in a law firm.

5. Based on the meaning of *hier-* in the list and the context,

hierarchy means _____

_____

_____

_____

6. Now look up *hierarchy* in a dictionary. Give the dictionary definition. Were you correct in your guess?_____

_____

_____

_____

Learning word elements has a tremendous payoff for those students taking certain courses. Although you may not encounter many affixed words in your history courses, you will come across numerous words that use prefixes, roots, and suffixes in psychology and in the hard sciences, such as biology, chemistry, and physics. For example, imagine that your introductory psychology class is studying a variety of mental disorders. One group of disorders discussed is *phobias.* *Phobia* is a root word that can stand alone and make sense, or it can be combined with other roots, prefixes, or suffixes to form new words. *Phobia* means an intense and abnormal or unnatural fear. All of you probably know someone who is at least slightly *phobic.* Your psychology book lists and defines a variety of phobias, each of which is a combination of either two roots or a prefix and a root.

ACTIVITY 4.2 _____

DIRECTIONS: Complete the following exercise based on the definition of each of the phobias.

    1. *Acrophobia:* fear of heights. *Acro-* means

    _____

    2. *Aquaphobia:* fear of water. *Aqua-* means

    _____

    3. *Dementophobia:* fear of insanity. *Dementi-* means

    _____

4. Herpetophobia: fear of reptiles. **Herpeto-** means

_____

5. Phonophobia: fear of speaking aloud. **Phono-** means

_____

6. Pyrophobia: fear of fire. **Pyro-** means

_____

7. Xenophobia: fear of strangers. **Xeno-** means

_____

Before proceeding, note that unless you know the meaning of both roots, little is gained. Simply knowing that _phobia_ means "fear" will only let you know that these phobias are fear of something, which would certainly not be precise enough to improve your score on a psychology quiz.

ACTIVITY 4.3

DIRECTIONS: For each of the roots below, find another word in a dictionary that contains the same root. Write the word and its meaning in the space provided.

1. **Acro-**_____

2. **Aqua-**_____

3. **Dementi-**_____

4. **Herpeto-** _____

5. **Phono-** _____

6. **Pyro-**_____

7. **Xeno-** _____

DIRECTIONS: Use one of the phobias above to respond to each of the following statements.

1. An individual with this phobia might not show up in class on the day she had to give a speech about the environment.

   _____

2. An individual with this phobia would have a difficult time attending a party where the only person he knew was the host.

   _____

3. An individual with this phobia would not be able to experience the beauty of taking a hot-air balloon ride.

   _____

4. An individual with this phobia probably would not want to roast marshmallows over a campfire.

   _____

5. An individual with this phobia would not elect to take swimming to fulfill her college physical education requirements.

   _____

6. An individual with this phobia would not have a snake for a pet.

   _____

7. An individual with this phobia might feel she has to spend a lot of money at a psychiatrist's office to prevent her from going crazy.

   _____

USING WORDS ELEMENTS IN A GENERATIVE MANNER

In order to use word elements as a generative strategy for vocabulary enrichment, you should remember two guidelines.

1. Try not to memorize the definitions of prefixes or roots in isolation. Attempting to learn definitions in this manner will often cause you to know a word at a superficial level rather than at a conceptual level.
2. When in doubt about your "guess" as to the meaning of a word that contains a root or prefix, use the dictionary or context to verify your hunch. Sometimes word elements, like content, communicate only a vague definition, so this extra step may be necessary and helpful to you in your quest to understand a word and a sentence.

The following text excerpt, entitled "Body Language: Nonverbal Communication," deals with communication, especially between women and men, that occurs without speaking. As you read the article, pay particular attention to the boldfaced words, since they all contain word elements (either prefixes, roots, or suffixes). When you have completed reading the excerpt, continue reading the text, and then do the activities that follow.

Vocabulary words from "Body Language: Nonverbal Communication" are listed here for your convenience.

assertive	neutral
asymmetrical	nonreciprocal
concept	nonverbal
confirmation	presumptuous
considerably	psychologist
conveys	reciprocate
demonstrated	replication
dimensions	socioeconomic
dominance	solidarity
egalitarian	subordinate
elaboration	verify
interactions	

Body Language: Nonverbal Communication

by Janet S. Hyde

The popularizers of the "body language" *concept* have pointed out the fact that we often communicate far more with our body than with the words we speak. For example, suppose you say the sentence "How nice to see you" while standing only six inches from another person or while actually brushing up against them. Then imagine, in contrast, that you say the sentence while standing three feet from the person. The sentence conveys a much different meaning in the two instances. In the first, it will probably convey warmth and possibly sexiness. In the second case, the meaning will seem formal and cold. As another example, a sentence coming from a smiling face conveys a much different meaning than the same sentence coming from a stern or frowning face.

Here I shall present what evidence there is on whether there are differences between women and men in *nonverbal* styles of communication, and what those differences mean (for a good, detailed discussion, see Mayo and Henley, 1981).

The politics of touch Studies consistently show that men touch women *considerably* more frequently than women touch men (Henley, 1973; Jourard, 1966). Having *demonstrated* the existence of a gender difference, we must now proceed to an interpretation of its significance.

Feminist scientists have interpreted this particular gender difference as a reflection of *dominance* relations between men and women, with men expressing dominance by touching women, which in turn reinforces women's **subordinate** status (Henley, 1973, 1975). Below follows some of the theorizing and data that lead to and support that interpretation.

In his essay "The Nature of Deference and Demeanor," Erving Goffman (1967) argued that, between a superior and a subordinate, relations will be **asymmetrical.** That is, the superior will have the right to certain familiarities with the subordinate that the subordinate is not allowed to **reciprocate.** Goffman further argued that touch by one person to another operates in this way. As an example, he considered the status system in a hospital, where doctors (the superiors) touch patients (the subordinates), but the reverse would seem unreasonable and **presumptuous.** Certainly there are many other examples. The boss puts his hand on the secretary's shoulder while giving her instructions, but she scarcely puts her hand on his shoulder when she returns the typed letters. Age, too, is a status dimension, with adults having status over children. We see adults walk up to a baby and stroke its cheek or tickle its sides, liberties they would scarcely take with another adult.

Psychologist Nancy Henley (1973; see **replication** by Major and Williams, 1980, cited in Major, 1981) did the original research and theorizing suggesting that these principles apply to relations between women and men—namely, that touch is a means by which men express dominance over women. In her original study, an observer spent 60 hours recording instances of touching in places such as a shopping center, a bank, and a college campus. For each instance, the gender, age, and approximate **socioeconomic** status of the two persons involved were recorded. Of the 28 instances of touch between people of approximately equal age and socioeconomic status, 23 involved a man touching a woman, but only five involved a woman touching a man. Thus men do touch women considerably more than women touch men. To **verify** the dominance interpretation of this result, Henley examined the touch relationships along the other dimensions—both of which are status indicators—namely, socioeconomic status (SES) and age. Regarding SES, there were fourteen cases in which the toucher was of higher status than the person being touched, while there were only five cases in which the toucher was judged to be of lower status. The results were similar for age. In 36 cases the toucher was judged to be at least ten years older than the person being touched, while there were only seven cases in which the toucher was at least ten years younger than the person being touched. From Henley's study it would be reasonable to conclude that

(1) there is a gender difference in touching, with men touching women more than the reverse, and (2) higher-status, dominant individuals tend to touch lower-status, subordinate individuals more than the reverse.

A recent study provides further **confirmation** and **elaboration** of Henley's conclusions (Summerhayes and Suchner, 1978). Subjects were shown photographs of female-male **interactions** and were asked to rate the extent to which each person dominated the interaction. The photographs varied along two **dimensions:** the status differences between the two people as indicated by their age and dress (female higher, versus equal, versus male higher), and who was touching whom (female toucher, versus no touching, versus male toucher). They found that when either a man or a woman touches another person, the effect is to reduce the perceived dominance of the person being touched. They even found that lower-status women could reduce the status of higher-status men by touching them. Other studies also confirm the belief that touching **conveys** dominance (Forden, 1981).

Of course, a touch does not always convey the meaning of dominance. A touch can also convey feelings of sexuality or of **solidarity** and friendship, or love (Major, 1981). Which of these meanings is conveyed depends on the situation. Friendship tends to be conveyed if the touch is between persons of approximately the same status and the touch is reciprocal, such as a handshake or a mutual hug (the prior discussion has been concerned with **nonreciprocal** touch, that is, one person touches another but the touch is not returned). While it is fairly easy for a man to convey dominance by a touch, it is probably more difficult for a woman to do so, and she is likely to have the touch interpreted as having a sexual meaning.

What are the practical implications of this research and theorizing? First, men who are concerned about establishing **egalitarian** relationships with women need to become aware of their use of touch. It can signal dominance and unequal roles even though one is not aware of doing so and does not intend to do so. Second, women who are concerned with trying to be more **assertive** and dominant in their interpersonal relations may want to consider increasing their use of touch. The risk in this approach is that the touch will be mistaken for a sexual message. One is therefore advised to aim for sexually **neutral** areas of the body, such as the shoulder or forearm. □

There are numerous words in the article that contain word elements. You are probably already familiar with some of these words, such as **nonverbal.** Even if you have never heard of **nonverbal** communication, you can easily get a general idea of what it means. Most students know that the prefix **non-** means not and that **verbal** has to do with talking. From these two pieces of information, you can conclude that **nonverbal communication** has to do with communicating with someone in a way other than talking. You might even go a step further and think about what kinds of communication this would include. Would a smile or a frown be **nonverbal communication?** Would shaking hands or touching someone's hand? What about shouting an obscenity at someone? Can you name two forms of **nonverbal communication?** If you want to gain additional information about the term, certainly the reading and context provide numerous examples.

ACTIVITY 4.5 _____

DIRECTIONS: List three different examples of **nonverbal communication** *given in the article.*

1. _____

2. _____

3. _____

Let's examine some of the other words from the article that contain prefixes.

ACTIVITY 4.6 _____

DIRECTIONS: Review the list of vocabulary words from "Body Language: Nonverbal Communication" on page 113. Then list below the six words that contain prefixes, underline the prefix for each, and write the meaning of the prefix. (You need not list **nonverbal** *again).*

	Word	**Meaning of the Prefix**
1.	_____	_____
2.	_____	_____
3.	_____	_____
4.	_____	_____
5.	_____	_____
6.	_____	_____

Now look over the 6 words. One of the words listed above contains a prefix, root, and suffix. Write that word below and then answer the questions that follow:

7. _____

8. What is the suffix in that word? _____

9. One word looks as if it begins with a prefix, but that is not the case. Which word fits in this situation? _____

ACTIVITY 4.7 _____

DIRECTIONS: Return to the article and underline the sentences that contain these 6 words with prefixes. Then complete the following activity to demonstrate your understanding of each word's definition. In some cases, the underlined sentence should provide you additional information about the targeted word and prefix. In other situations, the prefix and underlined sentence will provide you a possible hunch, but not the definitive meaning.

1. What word means "belonging to a lower or inferior class"?

_____

2. What word means "one who studies the mind or mental issues"?_____

3. What word means "a process in which two or more people come together to act or think between themselves"?_____

4. What word means that there is not an exchange between two or more persons or things? _____

5. What word means that the person or object lacks a state of balance or a sense of equivalence? _____

6. What word means "the involvement of both social and economic factors"? _____

ACTIVITY 4.8 _____

DIRECTIONS: **Sociology** and **psychology** contain prefixes (**socio-** and **psych-**) and both are courses that most college students take. There are many other prefixes and roots that appear in the names of college courses and even college majors. Listed below are some of those word elements and their meanings. Write in the blank the name of the college course or major. If you have difficulty with this, check either the dictionary or your college's catalog of courses.

Word Element	Meaning	Name of College Course/Major
1. anthro-	humankind, man	_____
2. archae-	ancient, earlier	_____
3. bio-	life	_____
4. geo-	earth	_____
5. gyneco-	women	_____

6. neuro-	nerve	_____
7. patho-	disease, suffering	_____
8. theo-	God	_____

The role of suffixes and prefixes is particularly important when you are looking up words in a dictionary. If you are using an abridged or condensed dictionary, words like **_dominance_** or **_nonreciprocal_** might not be listed as entries. However, you could probably find the words **_dominate_** or **_reciprocal_** in the dictionary and use your knowledge of suffixes and prefixes to determine the exact meanings of the two words. In the next activity you will have the opportunity to practice some typical suffixes.

ACTIVITY 4.9 _____

DIRECTIONS: Underline the suffix for each of the words listed below. Then in the blank provided write the part of speech for the word containing the suffix. Finally, write in the last blank the original form of the word. The first one has been done for you. You may wish to refer to the list of suffixes on page 107 to help you with these tasks.

Word	Part of Speech	Original Form of the Word
1. assert<u>ive</u>	adjective	assert (verb)
2. confirmation	_____	_____
3. considerably	_____	_____
4. dominance	_____	_____
5. elaboration	_____	_____
6. solidarity	_____	_____
7. replication	_____	_____

DIRECTIONS: Return to the article and underline the sentences that contain these seven words (Activity 4.9) with suffixes. In some cases you may already know the word. Use your prior knowledge, the suffixes, and the surrounding words in the sentences to help you determine the meaning of these seven words. Then, using that information, complete the activity below by filling in the blank with the correct word.

1. What noun means a copy or reproduction? _____

2. What noun means a work or product or task that is done with great detail and effort?_____

3. What noun means an act or piece of work that supports and establishes the certainty of something someone else has said or written?_____

4. What noun means that two or more individuals have mutual interests or fellowship among themselves?_____

5. What adjective describes individuals or efforts to be bold, confident, and self-assured? _____

6. What noun means a situation in which one individual or institution demonstrates control or power over the other? _____

7. What adverb means significantly or occurring in a large amount, extent, or degree? _____

ACTIVITY 4.11

DIRECTIONS: Find at least three other words from the reading that contain word parts. (Look at the word list on page 113 if you need some assistance.) Write them on the lines below. Then using word elements, context, and a dictionary, make vocabulary cards for each of the words you select. If you need to refresh your memory about what information goes on the cards, see Chapter 2.

1. _____

2. _____

3. _____

ACTIVITY 4.12

DIRECTIONS: Complete each of the following sentences, paying particular attention to the boldfaced words, each of which comes from the article "Body Language: Nonverbal Communication." Be sure that your completed sentence shows a conceptual understanding of the bold-faced word.

1. A scientist might ***replicate*** an experiment because_____

   _____

2. It would be ***presumptuous*** to think that _____

   _____

3. When you make a reservation at a hotel, you are given a

   confirmation number because_____

   _____

4. It would be important to be ***assertive*** when _____

   _____

5. If your professor asked you to *elaborate* your ideas, you would _____

_____

6. If a country remained *neutral* during a war, it would _____

_____

7. If you wanted to *verify* a claim that someone made, you might _____

_____

8. Someone who is your *subordinate* _____

_____

ACTIVITY 4.13 _____

DIRECTIONS: Answer the following questions, paying particular attention to the boldfaced words. The answers can be found in the article "Body Language: Nonverbal Communication."

1. Name two ways that males *convey dominance* toward women. _____

_____

2. Why are relations between a superior and a *subordinate* viewed as *asymmetrical?* _____

_____

3. What is the difference between touch that is *reciprocal* and touch that is *nonreciprocal?* _____

_____

4. Define *nonverbal communication.* _____

_____

5. How do *socioeconomic status* and gender *interact?* _____

_____

6. How might an individual indicate a *solidarity* of friendship?

_____

7. How have *psychologists* studied the *concept* of *nonverbal communication?* _____

_____

8. What would be the *dimensions* of an *egalitarian* relationship between a man and a woman?_____

_____

ACTIVITY 4.14 _____

DIRECTIONS: Turn to the index of vocabulary words at the back of this textbook. Scan the list of words, looking for three words that have prefixes, three words that contain roots, and three words that have suffixes. Select words that you do not know conceptually. Place those words in the lists below.

Words with Prefixes	Words with Roots	Words with Suffixes
1. _____	1. _____	1. _____
2. _____	2. _____	2. _____
3. _____	3. _____	3. _____

ACTIVITY 4.15

DIRECTIONS: Words do not have meanings in isolation—their meanings emerge from the context—the writer's sentences and ideas. However, you could make some educated guesses about the words you listed above in Activity 4.14 by using your knowledge of word elements, especially roots and prefixes. Select three words from Activity 4.14, make educated guesses for each, and then explain your reasoning. An example has been done for you.

Example: semiliterate: **Semi-** is a prefix meaning "half." **Literate** means that you can read and write. So **semiliterate** must mean that you can halfway, or partially, read and write.

1. _____

_____

_____

2. _____

_____

_____

3. _____

_____

_____

SUMMARY

In this chapter we have presented the advantages of using word elements as you learn vocabulary generatively. Prefixes, suffixes, and roots can be quite beneficial in adding to the information you need to know about vocabulary words. A knowledge of word elements can also be useful to you as you search for words in your dictionaries. We would recommend that your understanding of word elements be supported by the dictionary and by the context provided by the writer/author of what you are reading. When these three pieces of the puzzle are placed together, you will be well on your way to broadening and improving your conceptual vocabulary knowledge.

The first four chapters of *Developing Vocabulary Concepts for College Thinking* have introduced you to numerous strategies you can use to learn new words. These chapters have also introduced you to a number of new words within the context of different readings. Now it is time to apply what you have learned to the four thematic chapters that follow. Before beginning Chapter 5, however, be sure to read the "Introduction to Chapters 5–8."

PART II

Introduction to Chapters 5–8

There are four thematic chapters in this section of the textbook: 5, *Readings Concerning Gender Issues;* 6, *Readings Concerning Education Issues;* 7, *Readings Concerning Health-Related Issues;* and 8, *Readings Concerning the Environment.* Each chapter contains three reading selections that present a variety of topics related to the theme. The first two reading selections of each chapter have been taken from newspaper or magazine articles. For these selections general words have been targeted for study. General words, if you recall from Chapter 2, are those words that you could encounter in any communication situation. The third selection in each thematic chapter is an excerpt from a college-level textbook. In these selections, both general words and content-specific words have been targeted for study. Content-specific words, you will recall, are those words unique to a special area of study. For example, you would expect to study content-specific words like *rationalization* and *free association* in a psychology chapter.

Each thematic chapter in *Developing Vocabulary Concepts for College Thinking, Second Edition,* employs the same steps and procedures for learning the targeted general and content-specific vocabulary words. This introduction explains these steps.

STEPS FOR LEARNING GENERAL WORDS

As mentioned in Chapter 1, to "know" or conceptually understand a word involves more than being able to provide a brief definition or synonym. Hence, the activities in this text have been carefully developed to move you gradually through levels and layers of word knowledge. Instead of answering multiple-choice questions about the targeted vocabulary words, you will do considerable writing and thinking about each word in a variety of exercise formats. You will also discuss and share your definitions, sentences, and answers to the exercises with a classmate, a small group, or your instructor.

In the four thematic chapters you will complete eight steps for each set of targeted general words:

1. Pretest
2. Determining Meaning
3. Trying Out Meaning
4. Applying Meaning
5. Reciting and Reviewing
6. Conceptualizing Meaning
7. Self-Evaluating
8. Posttest

These steps are explained in more detail below. In addition, note that each section is accompanied by a picture cue.

 Pretest

In the pretest, you will first meet the targeted general vocabulary words. Before reading the designated selection, you will first select the best definition for each word. Then you will rate your level of understanding of each word with a 1, 2, or 3. Use the following guidelines when you rate your understanding:

1. I do not know this word at all (no understanding). I have never seen or heard this word before.
2. I recognize this word, but I do not know exactly what it means (partial understanding). I might be able to give some characteristics of the word, but I could not provide an exact meaning, nor could I use it in a sentence.

3. I know this word because I can define it accurately and precisely (conceptual understanding). I not only know and understand what the word means when I see or hear it, but I can also use it in a sentence.

The second part of the pretest is extremely important since it is very possible that you could guess and select the correct definition for a word but still not "know" the word, or be able to use the word correctly. Be honest with yourself as you do these ratings on the pretest.

After completing the pretest, you will check with your instructor for the correct answers and record your score. Then you will read the selection carefully, paying particular attention to the targeted words that you missed and for which your level of understanding was low (that is, a 1 or 2). You will also be asked to select two words from each reading that were not targeted in the pretest but that you would like to learn independently. You will list these two words following the other targeted words.

 Determining Meaning

After reading the selection, the next step is to determine the meaning of the targeted words and any other words you may have selected. Using a dictionary, you will select the most appropriate definition on the basis of how each word was used in the selection. We have used *The American Heritage College Dictionary, Third Edition,* as our reference, but most current dictionaries should be sufficient for the exercises and activities. As mentioned in Chapter 3, the appropriate definition may or may not be the first one listed in the dictionary entry. Be careful not only to select the most appropriate definition, but also to select the definition that matches the part of speech of the targeted word in the original sentence. For example, the word *institute* can be a noun or a verb, and this difference in the part of speech makes a large difference in your definition selection.

You will also create vocabulary cards for each targeted vocabulary word. The directions for this generative strategy are in Chapter 2. In this step we will also offer some imagery, keyword, and mnemonic strategies for learning the words that can be added to your cards. Once you have finished your vocabulary cards, you should share and discuss them with a classmate or your instructor to make sure that everything is accurate and correct. Do not skip this part of the process, or the remaining activities will be more difficult.

 **Trying Out Meaning**

You will be doing a variety of activities as part of this step, so it is important to follow the directions carefully. When you have finished the exercises for this step and all subsequent steps, check with your instructor for the correct answers. Be sure to correct any items that you have missed as you work toward conceptual understanding of the words.

 Applying Meaning

Here you will apply the meanings of the targeted words to situations slightly different from those in the reading selection. You will complete sentences, write your own sentences, or answer questions about the targeted words. If you have difficulty with this step, do not proceed any further. Rather, you should meet with your instructor for extra assistance until you feel comfortable with the exercises and targeted words.

 Reciting and Reviewing

This is perhaps the most important step in the entire process of learning a new word. This is the time to review what you have already learned. You may wish to add new sentences, definitions, synonyms, or antonyms to your vocabulary cards. For the words giving you some difficulty, you may wish to use some of the mnemonics discussed in Chapter 2 or meet with a classmate.

This fifth step is also the time for you to recite, using the ideas presented in Chapter 2. Recitation, as you may recall, is an active method of storing the word in long-term memory in order to use it in future situations. You will be expected to do the Recite and Review step on your own. The only reminder in the textbook will be the placement of the words RECITING AND REVIEWING and the picture cue. When you see these words, you should take the time to recite and review several times before attempting the next step, Conceptualizing Meaning.

Conceptualizing Meaning

Next, you will be expected to demonstrate that you "know" the targeted vocabulary words. You will complete activities, without the use of your vocabulary cards or previous activities, in which you must generate appropriate synonyms, antonyms, examples, nonexamples, and characteristics for each word. You will also be expected to know whether each word has a positive or a negative connotation and why. Finally, you will use each word in situations different from the original use of the word.

 ## Self-Evaluating

At the end of each reading selection, you will evaluate your level of conceptual understanding for each word studied and practiced. More specifically, you will determine which words you conceptually understand and which need additional study and review. In completing this step, it is extremely important to judge your present level of understanding honestly.

 ## Posttest

For each thematic unit (Chapters 5–8), there are two posttests. The first posttest after Readings A and B tests all the words presented in both of those readings. Posttest II, which follows Reading C, tests the words from Readings A, B, and C. Thus you will have three options as you prepare for the posttests. You can choose to:

1. Take Posttest I over Readings A and B. Then skip Reading C altogether and proceed to the next chapter.
2. Take Posttest I over Readings A and B. Then proceed to Reading C and complete those activities. When you have finished, take Posttest II over Readings A, B, and C.
3. After you have completed the activities for Readings A and B, proceed to Reading C without taking Posttest I. Once you have completed all three readings, take Posttest II, which covers all of the words presented in the chapter.

Be sure to check with your instructor about which option you should follow. Before taking the posttest, you should review all activities, study your vocabulary cards, review other generative strategies, and recite several times with a classmate or by yourself. As much as possible, you should also carry out the eight steps described here with the words you chose to study and learn independently.

STEPS FOR LEARNING CONTENT-SPECIFIC WORDS

In each thematic chapter, the steps for learning content-specific words will be similar to those for learning general words. The main difference, however, will be the addition of a few steps, since both content-specific and general words will be targeted for study. The steps for learning content-specific words are explained below.

 Pretest

The main difference in this step is that there will be a second pretest for the content-specific words presented in Reading C of each chapter. Although the pretests are included in your text, you will need to see your instructor for an answer key in order to check your work.

 Determining Meaning

In this second step, you will be determining the meaning and making vocabulary cards for the content-specific words.

 Organizing Concepts

The third step, Organizing Concepts, has been added in order to provide an opportunity to visualize how the content-specific and general words are interrelated. Furthermore, this step allows you to see how all the targeted words relate to the chapter's key concepts. To organize concepts, you will be practicing the generative strategies of charting, mapping, and grouping/labeling.

Beginning Conceptual Understanding

This step is similar to the third step for learning general words, Trying Out Meaning. Hence, you will be doing many of the same activities, but with a larger number of targeted words.

 Using Concepts

The fifth step, Using Concepts, is similar to Applying Meaning, the fourth step in learning general words. As mentioned earlier, if you have difficulty with the activities in Using Concepts, you should meet with your instructor for help before you move on to the additional activities.

 Reciting and Reviewing

This sixth step is the same as the sixth step in learning general words.

 Comprehending Concepts

Comprehending Concepts has been added in order to help you determine how well you have understood the key ideas presented in the chapter excerpt. Thus, you will engage in writing activities such as answering short-answer and essay questions containing the targeted content-specific and general words. You are urged to answer these questions without looking back at the excerpt and without using any of your generative strategies or activities (that is, vocabulary cards, charts, or maps).

 Self-Evaluating

This step is the same as in learning general words.

 **Posttest**

As mentioned in the steps for learning general words, you have three options from which to choose. Check with your instructor concerning which option you will take.

AN ADDITIONAL ACTIVITY FOR LEARNING THE TARGETED WORDS

In addition to the steps for each thematic chapter, there is another activity designed to help increase your conceptual understanding of the targeted words. This is explained below.

 Extending and Challenging

These activities provide an opportunity to explore the connotative elements of the targeted words or to examine what happens when different suffixes or prefixes are added to the targeted general words. Extending and Challenging activities are especially appropriate for students who learn the targeted words quickly and desire additional activities to challenge themselves.

 Writing Activities

The writing activities included in each thematic unit are designed to help you analyze and synthesize the concepts presented. In some activities, you will be asked to give and support your opinion about a topic that has been presented. In other activities, you will demonstrate your understanding of those concepts by answering essay-type questions. You many also be asked to use the new vocabulary words you have learned by writing a journal entry that asks you to think about the articles and text excerpts you have read.

SUMMARY

As you complete the activities in each thematic chapter, refer to this section as needed. Although the steps outlined may appear initially complex, they will soon become a meaningful routine. This routine will assure you that your efforts in learning the words will pay off. That is, you will be able to remember the words and store them for future use. More importantly, these steps will provide the mechanism to expand your conceptual understanding of words beyond this textbook.

Readings Concerning Gender Issues

Did You Know?
The word *chauvinism* originated from Nicolas Chauvin, a Frenchman,
who was an extreme believer in Napoleon and his causes. Today the word
applies to anyone who is unreasonably prejudiced about a cause.

In this thematic chapter you will be reading three different selections
that deal with gender issues. In the first selection, "When Harry
Called Sally . . . ," you will be reading about why men and women have
difficulty communicating. Many of the ideas in this article are based
on a recent book by Deborah Tannen. The second selection, "Confessions of a Former Chauvinist Pig," presents the male point of view in a
very humorous fashion. David Bouchier, the author, is a writer and
teacher. In the third selection, "Forms of Love," the authors define the
issue that is often the most debated one between males and females—
love. This selection is an excerpt from a college textbook that might be
used in a sociology or human sexuality course.

There are 61 targeted vocabulary words in this thematic chapter.
Most of the content-specific words could be found in sociology, psychology, or human sexuality courses. You will learn words like *infatuate*,

137

cognitive component, and *platonic love.* The general words you will learn should be an excellent addition for your reading and writing vocabulary. Some of these words are *acute, intrusive, disparate, averted, jargon,* and *déjà vu.*

In the first selection (Reading A), there are 13 targeted general words. As you read the first selection about the communication problems between men and women, see if the author has described a situation that has happened to you at some time. After you have finished the reading, you might ask yourself if Deborah Tannen's book favors the female point by her choice of words and phrases or whether the book is fair to both genders.

The second selection (Reading B) contains 19 targeted general words. Many of the words you will learn from this newspaper article are directly related to gender issues. For example, you will study *androgyny, egalitarian, liberation,* and of course, *chauvinism.* As you read this selection, be prepared to chuckle while you think. The author, David Bouchier, discusses the changing roles of females and the effect of these changes on males. You might ask yourself whether you agree with the author or feel that he has stretched the situation to make his case.

The last selection (Reading C) presents Robert Sternberg's definition and analyses of love. Before reading this textbook excerpt, you might wish to write your own definition of love and discuss with your male and female classmates their ideas on love. Then compare these to Sternberg's definition to see if you overlap in any way. As you read, please note that Sternberg presents three components of love and then explains two types of love—friendship and infatuation. Actually, Sternberg outlines eight forms of love, but this excerpt discusses only two. You might wish to find the textbook and finish the chapter. In Reading C there are 15 general words and 14 content-specific words.

Your instructor will probably remind you that you have three options with each unit in this text. After you have finished the activities in Reading A and Reading B, you can choose to:

1. Take **Posttest I** over Readings A and B. Then skip Reading C and turn to Chapter 6.
2. Take **Posttest I** over Readings A and B. Then turn to Reading C and complete those activities. When you have finished, take **Posttest II** over Readings A, B, and C.
3. Turn to Reading C and complete those activities, skipping **Posttest I** altogether. When you have finished, take **Posttest II** over Readings A, B, and C.

Reading A

When Harry Called Sally . . .

by Jerry Adler

 Targeted Words

averted

condescension

consolation

decipher

disparate

distinctions

dominance

endowed

enhance

inclined

inferiority

instinctively

phenomenon

 Pretest

DIRECTIONS: The words in this pretest will be introduced in the reading selection entitled "When Harry Called Sally. . . ." Before reading the selection, however, take the pretest by answering the questions about each boldfaced vocabulary word. Use the sentence to help you decide the correct answer, and circle that letter. Then rate your present knowledge of the word by circling 1, 2, or 3, depending on how familiar you are with the word. (Check pages 128–129 to review the scoring procedures.)

1. Men! Or, to put it another way, women! The only two creatures on God's good earth **endowed** with the miracle of speech. **Endowed** means
   a. burdened.
   b. explained.
   c. equipped or supplied.
   d. freed.

   Level of Understanding   1   2   3

2. By what mishap of evolution did they end up putting it [i.e., speech] to such *disparate,* indeed, conflicting, uses? *Disparate* means
   a. abusive.
   b. frightening.
   c. interesting.
   d. not similar.

   Level of Understanding   1   2   3

3. Sylvia was using language to *enhance* intimacy, by sharing her feelings about pregnancy with her mother. *Enhance* means
   a. reduce.
   b. increase.
   c. describe.
   d. learn.

   Level of Understanding   1   2   3

4. If only Sylvia and Marvin had understood these universal *distinctions,* Sylvia might never have moved back to her parents' house and Marvin's subsequent alcohol and legal problems might well have been *averted.* *Distinctions* mean
   a. truths.
   b. abilities.
   c. differences.
   d. friendships.

   Level of Understanding   1   2   3

5. *Averted* (see the above sentence) means
   a. revealed.
   b. discussed.
   c. increased.
   d. prevented.

   Level of Understanding   1   2   3

6. So strong is the urge to ***dominance*** in American men that they will drive right past a policeman rather than stop and ask for directions, because to ask for help is to put oneself in a position of ***inferiority.***
Dominance means a
a. condition of being in control or influencing.
b. state of being angry or upset.
c. condition of being confused.
d. state of being embarrassed.
Level of Understanding   1   2   3

7. ***Inferiority*** (see the above sentence) means a sense of
a. feeling afraid of authority.
b. feeling low in quality or value.
c. being friendly.
d. being dependent.
Level of Understanding   1   2   3

8. American marriages may never be the same, once spouses learn to ***decipher*** the "metamessages" men and women send to one another.
Decipher means
a. destroy.
b. interpret or read.
c. delay.
d. bargain or plead.
Level of Understanding   1   2   3

9. Tannen's research has led her to the discovery that men hate to be told to do anything. She uses this principle to explain the ***phenomenon*** known as nagging.
Phenomenon means
a. a recurring mystery.
b. an occurrence that you can sense.
c. a bad habit.
d. a secret that no one knows.
Level of Understanding   1   2   3

10. "A woman," she writes, "will be *inclined* to repeat a request that doesn't get a response because she is convinced that her husband would do what she asks if he only understood that she really wants him to do it."
Inclined means having
a. a tendency or preference.
b. a relaxed attitude.
c. a steep hill.
d. a difficulty.

Level of Understanding   1   2   3

11. But a man who wants to avoid feeling that he is following orders may *instinctively* wait before doing what she asked, in order to imagine that he is doing it of his own free will.
Instinctively means
a. stubbornly.
b. quickly.
c. naturally without thinking.
d. gradually with effort.

Level of Understanding   1   2   3

12. In this case, Edna's effort to get her husband to talk about his bleeding was interpreted by him as a kind of *condescension,* implying that he is incapable of dealing with the situation himself.
Condescension means an act where an individual
a. talks angrily with another.
b. deals with another in a superior manner.
c. tries to persuade another.
d. surrenders to another.

Level of Understanding   1   2   3

13. For the same reason that they refuse to ask for directions, men resist the intimacy of discussing their feelings, because it implies a need for help, advice, or *consolation.*
Consolation means an act of
a. financial support.
b. losing.
c. medical attention.
d. comfort.

Level of Understanding   1   2   3

PRETEST SCORING DIRECTIONS: Check with your instructor for the answers. Give yourself one point for each item that was correct, and record the number of 1s, 2s, and 3s you marked.

Number Correct _____

Level of Understanding

1 _____

2 _____

3 _____

Now read the article "When Harry Called Sally . . . ," paying attention to the targeted words, particularly those that you missed on the pretest or those for which your level of understanding was low.

. . . .

When Harry Called Sally . . .
Why Men and Women Can't Communicate

by Jerry Adler

When Sylvia found out she was pregnant, she couldn't wait to call her mother and spend hours on the phone planning for the new baby. Her husband, Marvin, on the other hand, put off calling his own parents until the weekend, when it was cheaper, and then spent 25 minutes talking to his father about a problem he was having with his gun. Finally his father asked what else was new.

"Nothing much with me," he replied, "but Sylvia's pregnant."

Men! Or, to put it another way, women! The only two creatures on God's good earth **endowed** with the miracle of speech—by what mishap of evolution did they end up putting it to such **disparate,** indeed, conflicting, uses? This is a question for "sociolinguists," whatever they are, and Deborah Tannen, who is one, explores it in her bestseller, "You Just Don't Understand: Women and Men in Conversation" *(330 pages. Morrow. $18.95).* Sylvia was using language to **enhance** *intimacy,* by sharing her feelings about pregnancy with her mother. Marvin, on the other hand, was defending his *independence* by distancing himself from the pregnancy, avoiding any discussion of his feelings. If only Sylvia and Marvin had understood these universal **distinctions.** Sylvia might never have moved back to her parents' house and Marvin's subsequent alcohol and legal problems might well have been **averted.***

Alberta and Murray are driving from Teaneck, N.J., to her cousin's wedding in Connecticut. They have been lost in the Bronx for half an hour, and Murray has just turned onto the Cross Bronx Expressway.

Alberta: I think we're headed back to New Jersey.

Murray: No, this is right.

Alberta: We seem to be going west.

Murray: Don't be ridiculous. What makes you think we're going west?

Alberta: Well, the sun is going down in front of us.

Murray (slams on the brakes): Well, if you don't care for the way I'm driving, you can try walking to your fat cousin's stupid wedding!

Who is right in this situation?

Alberta, focused on the goal of getting to the wedding, failed to consider that Murray would take her remark about the sun as a criticism of his ability to find the Merritt Parkway. The problem, in Tannen's theory, is that men and women use language differently. Women take the attitude that the purpose of a conversation is to explore cooperative solutions to common problems, while men regard speech as an extension of fighting by other means. So strong is the urge to **dominance** in American men that they will drive right past a policeman rather than stop and ask for directions, because to ask for help is to put one-

---

*The anecdotes in this article are not drawn from Tannen's book.

self in a position of *inferiority.* By contrast, according to Tannen, American women are so accustomed to asking for help that they have been known to ask strangers for directions *even when they know perfectly well where they are going.*

All over America, couples are waking up to insights such as these. American marriages may never be the same, once spouses learn to *decipher* the "metamessages" men and women send to one another. Tannen's research has led her to the discovery that men hate to be told to do anything. She uses this principle to explain the *phenomenon* known to sociolinguists as *nagging.* "A woman," she writes, "will be *inclined* to repeat a request that doesn't get a response because she is convinced that her husband would do what she asks if he only understood that she really wants him to do it. But a man who wants to avoid feeling that he is following orders may *instinctively* wait before doing what she asked, in order to imagine that he is doing it of his own free will. Nagging is the result, because each time she repeats the request, he again puts off fulfilling it."

> Edna: What's bothering you, honey?
> George: Nothin'.
> Edna: Something's bothering you, I can tell.
> George: Nothin's bothering me.
> Edna: Yes, it is.
> George: Why do you think something's bothering me?
> Edna: Well, for one thing, you're bleeding all over your shirt.
> George: It doesn't bother me.
> Edna: WELL, IT BOTHERS THE HELL OUT OF ME!
> George: I'll go change my shirt.

In this case, Edna's effort to get her husband to talk about his bleeding was interpreted by him as a kind of *condescension,* implying that he is incapable of dealing with the situation himself. For the same reason that they refuse to ask for directions, men resist the intimacy of discussing their feelings, because it implies a need for help, advice, or *consolation.* offering to change his shirt, George could present himself as meeting his wife's literal demand ("get that bloody thing out of my sight") without responding to her deeper need for a discussion of why he was bleeding in the first place, and how he felt about it.

Men! Or, to look at it from the opposite point of view, women! Whatever gave them the idea of living together? ☐

 **Determining Meaning**

PART I DIRECTIONS: Using the generative strategy of the vocabulary card, write a definition, synonym, antonym, and part of speech for each word below. Remember to select the most appropriate definition based on how the word is used in this reading. Be sure to pay particular attention to the words that you missed on the pretest. In addition, find a minimum of two more words from "When Harry Called Sally . . ." with which you are unfamiliar. Make vocabulary cards for those words also.

1. averted
2. condescension
3. consolation
4. decipher
5. disparate
6. distinctions
7. dominance
8. endowed
9. enhance
10. inclined
11. inferiority
12. instinctively
13. phenomenon
14.
15.

*PART II DIRECTIONS: As mentioned in Chapter 2, one way to learn the meanings of words that are difficult for you is to use the keyword strategy. If you are having trouble remembering the meaning of the word **disparate,** you might try this:*

In the word **disparate** you can see the small word **par,** a word familiar to a golfer. Imagine that you are a golfer and you never can achieve **par** on any hole. You would obviously become **discouraged.** The letters **dis-** begin the word **disparate.** So you can imagine a golfer who never receives a **par** who becomes **discouraged** because his game is so distinct and dissimilar from his friends who score lower and better. The meaning of **disparate** is distinct and dissimilar.

Try developing a keyword strategy for any of the other targeted words that you are having difficulty in learning. For example, the word **phenomenon** may be initially troublesome. What smaller words do you see in this word that could create a story similar to the golfing story?

Put your keyword strategies on the front of your vocabulary cards.

PART III DIRECTIONS: As mentioned in Chapter 4, word elements can often help you determine the meaning of a word. In addition, word elements can also help you remember the definition, especially if the etymology is interesting. Using the information about prefixes and roots listed in Chapter 4, answer the following questions.

1. What is the root of the word **avert?** What does this root mean?

   _____

2. What is the prefix used in the word **avert?** What does this

   prefix mean? _____

   _____

3. Using this information, what is the definition of **avert?**

   Does this definition match your dictionary definition? _____

   _____

4. The word **revert** is related to the word **avert.** Explain the

   meaning of the word using prefixes and suffixes. _____

   _____

5. What is the dictionary meaning of **revert?** _____

   _____

6. Can you think of any other words that use the same root as

   avert and **revert?** Use your dictionary and the etymological

   entry to check your ideas. _____

   _____

 Trying Out Meaning

DIRECTIONS: Read each sentence carefully. If the boldfaced word is used correctly, circle C and go on to the next item. If, however, the bold-faced word is used incorrectly, circle I and then correct the sentence.

C I **1.** The eager student tried to *enhance* his worldly knowledge by reading the *New York Times* and several magazines on a weekly basis.

C I **2.** The elderly woman *averted* financial disaster when she invested her life savings with the con artist.

C I **3.** The large male gorilla had gained *dominance* over the females and younger gorillas who inhabited the forest with him.

C I **4.** The dropout who had not learned how to read quickly *deciphered* the letter from his lawyer.

C I **5.** The proud and hardworking couple found it easy to accept the *condescension* of their wealthy landlord who inherited his fortune from his grandfather.

C I **6.** The husband and wife were so *disparate;* he liked to spend his spare time reading while she sought out parties and crowds of people for socializing.

C I **7.** Her feelings of *inferiority* caused her to feel comfortable seeking out new friends and unfamiliar situations.

C I **8.** The English professor praised the student on his term paper because he had overlooked the *distinction* between paraphrasing and copying someone's ideas as if they were his own.

C I **9.** The *consolation* offered by the minister helped the young widow who had lost her husband in the war.

C I **10.** The experienced schoolteacher was *inclined* to be stricter with his rules at the beginning of the school year.

C I **11.** The young baseball player was *endowed* with good eye-hand coordination and excellent speed.

C I **12.** When the school year began, all the American students in Beginning Russian knew how to speak and write the language *instinctively.*

C   I   **13.** Some companies, such as Nike, have benefited from the ***phenomenon*** of marking clothes, hats, and shoes with labels or specific color designs.

 Applying Meaning

DIRECTIONS: Respond to each of the following statements or questions. Your answer should reflect your understanding of the boldfaced word.

1. Would it be easy to ***decipher*** a letter that had been written by a two-year-old? Why or why not? _____

_____

2. Is it easy to like a person who consistently acts in a ***condescending*** manner? Why or why not? _____

_____

3. What abilities or skills would a professional baseball player need to be ***endowed*** with? _____

_____

4. Describe how someone who suffered from feelings of ***inferiority*** would act at a social occasion such as a party. _____

_____

5. Describe how young adults might ***enhance*** their opportunities to obtain a secure, well-paying job. _____

_____

6. Describe how a wise college student might *avert* academic failure or probation. _____

_____

7. Give an example of an individual who might offer *consolation* to a homeless family. _____

_____

8. Would the usual clothing of a lawyer be *disparate* from the clothing of a heavy metal rock star? Why or why not? _____

_____

9. Would yawning be an *instinctive* behavior? Why or why not? _____

_____

10. Describe one *distinction* between football and hockey. _____

_____

11. Would a professor wish to maintain *dominance* in the classroom? Why or why not? _____

_____

12. Would someone *inclined* toward physical activities such as jogging and biking choose to take the elevator or walk the stairs? Why? _____

_____

13. Give an example of a recent medical, scientific, or technological **phenomenon** that has improved your quality of life. _____

_____

Reciting and Reviewing

Conceptualizing Meaning

*DIRECTIONS: Write a meaningful sentence for each of the following words. Your sentence should indicate that you have a conceptual knowledge of the word. You can change the form of the word; for example, **condescension** could be changed to **condescending**. The example below should help you see the difference between what is acceptable and what is not. When you have finished, place these sentences on the backs of your vocabulary cards.*

Examples Using Words:
Weak: He was filled with feelings of *inferiority*.
Good: He was filled with feelings of *inferiority* because his parents kept telling him he was not as smart as his sister.

1. averted _____

2. condescension _____

3. consolation _____

4. decipher _____

5. disparate _____

6. distinction _____

7. dominance _____

8. enhance _____

9. endowed _____

10. inclined _____

11. instinctively _____

12. phenomenon _____

 Self-Evaluating

DIRECTIONS: Think about the words that you have studied in this reading. List in Column A those for which you have a conceptual understanding. In Column B, list the words for which you have just a partial understanding. In Column C, list the words for which you have no understanding or just a definitional understanding. You should study and review the words listed in Columns B and C before beginning the next reading.

Column A	Column B	Column C
_____	_____	_____
_____	_____	_____
_____	_____	_____
_____	_____	_____
_____	_____	_____
_____	_____	_____
_____	_____	_____
_____	_____	_____
_____	_____	_____
_____	_____	_____

Confessions of a Former Chauvinist Pig

by David Bouchier

 Targeted Words

abolition	intriguing
androgyny	jargon
baffled	liberation
chauvinism	nostalgic
déjà vu	oppressed
deviousness	passive
domestic	proposition
egalitarian	provisional
entrepreneur	tedious
indicted	

 Pretest

DIRECTIONS: The words in this pretest will be introduced in the reading selection "Confessions of a Former Chauvinist Pig." Before reading the selection, however, take the pretest by answering the questions about each boldfaced word. Use the sentence to help you decide the correct answer, and circle that letter. Then rate your present knowledge of the word by circling 1, 2, or 3, depending on how familiar you are with the word.

1. Young men today take their *egalitarian* relationships with women for granted.
   Egalitarian means a belief or principle stressing
   a. romance.
   b. equal rights for all humans.
   c. work.
   d. self-centered behavior.
   Level of Understanding   1   2   3

2. Raised in *chauvinism, indicted* by feminism and bypassed by the sexual revolution, some of us have spent half our lives coming to terms with the slippery idea of women's equality.
   Chauvinism means a
   a. belief that self-comfort is the most important goal.
   b. statement freeing yourself from outside responsibilities.
   c. prejudiced belief in the superiority of one's own group.
   d. statement supporting the equal rights of all individuals.
   Level of Understanding   1   2   3

3. *Indicted* (see the above sentence) means
   a. accused or charged.
   b. supported or helped.
   c. confused.
   d. explained.
   Level of Understanding   1   2   3

4. It had never occurred to us that women were *oppressed.*
   Oppressed means
   a. eager to be free.
   b. treated unjustly.
   c. sad about their workloads.
   d. hungry and tired.
   Level of Understanding   1   2   3

5. Women were declared the equals of men, and no longer to be treated as *passive* wives and sex objects.
   Passive means
   a. skilled in home economics.
   b. lacking common sense.
   c. attractive without trying.
   d. quietly accepting with no objections.
   Level of Understanding   1   2   3

6. But there was something *intriguing* about the prospect of sexual equality at last.
Intriguing means
a. causing fear.
b. arousing interest.
c. boring.
d. comforting.
Level of Understanding   1   2   3

7. A few men, myself included, decided the *liberation* of women and the *liberation* of men were part of the same problem.
Liberation means the act of
a. releasing or freeing from.
b. trying to achieve superiority.
c. trying to achieve equal rights and status.
d. fighting for liberal causes.
Level of Understanding   1   2   3

8. Women had always complained that housework and child care were *tedious* and exhausting.
Tedious means
a. boring and uninteresting.
b. difficult and demanding.
c. exciting and fun-filled.
d. rewarding and unique.
Level of Understanding   1   2   3

9. The men who took on an equal share of *domestic* work discovered that they had bought into a zero-sum *proposition*—one less boring job for her was one more boring job for him.
Domestic means pertaining to
a. business or occupations.
b. household or home.
c. personal finances.
d. relatives or friends.
Level of Understanding   1   2   3

10. *Proposition* (see the above sentence) means a/an
a. distribution.
b. investment.
c. offer of marriage.
d. plan or statement.
Level of Understanding   1   2   3

11. Exit those *nostalgic* family stories of grandma the apple pie wizard and grandpa the successful *entrepreneur.*
Nostalgic means
a. humorous.
b. longing for the past.
c. long-winded and never-ending.
d. unbelievable.
Level of Understanding   1   2   3

12. *Entrepreneur* (see the above sentence) means one who
a. organizes and takes responsibility for a business deal.
b. takes joy in repairing and fixing things around the house.
c. tells stories in an interesting manner.
d. spends time growing rare and beautiful flowers.
Level of Understanding   1   2   3

13. But the *abolition* of the traditional family was nothing compared to the *abolition* of sex.
Abolition means an act of
a. complete destruction.
b. complete support.
c. strong questioning.
d. strong growth.
Level of Understanding   1   2   3

14. Sex was never about equality but difference, and sexual equality implied the phasing-out of male-female differences—in the *jargon* of the times, *androgyny.*
Jargon means a/an
a. angry battle.
b. similarity.
c. comforting understanding.
d. specialized language.
Level of Understanding   1   2   3

15. *Androgyny* (see the above sentence) means
a. being totally against females gaining equality.
b. emphasizing the differences between the sexes.
c. being neither clearly male nor female in appearance.
d. supporting women's right to work outside of the home.
Level of Understanding   1   2   3

16. Women who looked and acted like men *baffled* the impulse to desire and to love.
Baffled means
a. encouraged.
b. frustrated, blocked.
c. raised, increased.
d. met.

                Level of Understanding   1   2   3

17. On good days, I can proclaim (to myself) a *provisional* victory.
Provisional means
a. complete and absolute.
b. surprising and exciting.
c. temporary, pending permanent arrangements.
d. rewarding, both financially and personally.

                Level of Understanding   1   2   3

18. Teaching and talking to teenagers, I get a dizzying sense of *déjà vu*, as though peering down a long funnel into the '50s.
Déjà vu means a/an
a. feeling that you have already experienced something actually being experienced for the first time.
b. feeling that causes great fear in large groups of people.
c. religious experience causing someone to repent their previous sins.
d. experience causing you to become frustrated and tired.

                Level of Understanding   1   2   3

19. Men still accuse women of *deviousness* and emotionality.
Deviousness means being
a. weak, not independent.
b. beautiful and desirable.
c. cruel and unreasonable.
d. tricky, not honest.

                Level of Understanding   1   2   3

PRETEST SCORING DIRECTIONS: Check with your instructor for the answers. Give yourself one point for each item that was correct, and record the number of 1s, 2s, and 3s you marked.

Number Correct _____

Level of Understanding

1 _____

2 _____

3 _____

Now read the article "Confessions of a Former Chauvinist Pig," paying attention to the targeted words, particularly those that you missed on the pretest or those for which your level of understanding was low.

· ·

Confessions of a Former Chauvinist Pig

by David Bouchier

Young men today take their **egalitarian** relationships with women for granted. They think it was *always* OK for men to express their feelings, change diapers and go all the way on a first date. Nobody remembers the casualties, the men who went to the wall for equality when the wall was a million miles high.

We male veterans of the sex war are past middle age now, and still repent of our past sins and present failings. Raised in **chauvinism, indicted** by feminism and bypassed by the sexual revolution, some of us have spent half our lives coming to terms with the slippery idea of women's equality.

Most men were stunned when a militant feminist movement appeared in the late '60s. It had never occurred to us that women were **oppressed.** They seemed to do extraordinarily

D. Bouchier, "Confessions of a Former Chauvinist Pig," *Atlanta Journal Constitution,* March 18, 1990. Reprinted by permission of David Bouchier.

well, sexually and economically, out of the games we all played. After all, who was setting the rules?

The rules of courtship, for example—the chaste dates, the first kiss, the gifts, the first meeting with her parents—were things that young men had to learn the way rats learn their way through laboratory mazes. The game made no sense to us, but we ran the maze out of training and habit.

Having played the game, we collected the prize—marriage and suburban life. About three days later, or so it seemed, along came feminism and the sexual revolution. All the rules changed. Women were declared the equals of men, and no longer to be treated as *passive* wives and sex objects. The New Woman would be sexually and economically free, just like a man.

"I wouldn't mind being a sex object for just one day," muttered a confused male friend of mine, almost weeping into his beer.

But there was something *intriguing* about the prospect of sexual equality at last. A few men, myself included, decided that the liberation of women and the *liberation* of men were part of the same problem. We came to see sexual liberation as a total, revolutionary thing, one that would abolish male responsibility for women and children and equalize the sexual game. So we set out to remake our lives in the feminist mold.

Our first surprise was the discovery that sexual equality, in the ordinary, everyday sense, was a terrible bore. Women had always complained that housework and child care were *tedious* and exhausting. Now we knew the truth of it. The men who took on an equal share of domestic work discovered that they had bought into a zero-sum *proposition*—one less boring job for her was one more boring job for him. Large chunks of our free time vanished into *domestic* tedium, and we got little in exchange but the cold comfort of self-righteousness.

"I'm doing the right thing," I would boast to my friends; but in my heart I knew they would be hanging out in a bar while I was cooking, or watching the game while I was shopping.

Things weren't much better at work. The flood of highly qualified women into every business and profession simply made life tougher for men, as more people competed for the same number of jobs and promotions. The war between the sexes expanded out of the home and into the office.

And, of course, the family changed. The family is our storehouse of dreams, but the new, two-career egalitarian family felt different, more businesslike, less homelike than the families we grew up in. Exit those **nostalgic** family stories of grandma the apple pie wizard and grandpa the successful **entrepreneur.** Welcome to the new post-feminist nostalgia: how grandma became a mid-level IBM executive with the support of grandpa, the busy househusband. It was all a bit depressing.

But the **abolition** of the traditional family was nothing compared to the abolition of sex. We early male enthusiasts for feminism had misunderstood the sexual consequences of equality. Sex was never about equality but about *difference,* and sexual equality implied the phasing-out of male-female differences—in the *jargon* of the times, **androgyny.**

Yet the appearance of women as different and beautiful and sexually exciting turned out to be more fundamental than we had imagined. Women who looked and acted like men **baffled** the impulse to desire and to love. Superwoman, with her business suit and busy schedule and stuffed briefcase, was simply unattractive—too much like the guy at the next desk. And Superwomen soon began to say out loud that the domesticated, emotional male was pretty unattractive too; the term "wimp" was freely used.

Many men of my generation tasted the sour grapes of equality and gave up. But some of us kept working at it. In the long run, we made some big gains, but not the ones we expected. We didn't get real sexual equality, but we did escape the breadwinner trap, and all the guilt and anxiety that went with it. We really did build better partnerships with our wives, who became more interesting as they moved out of the house and into the world. We did learn a lot about ourselves as men, most of it bad.

The struggle with the Old Adam continues. Male chauvinists, like recovering alcoholics, are never completely cured. I've been trying to make myself over into an egalitarian male for almost a quarter century. On good days, I can proclaim (to myself) a **provisional** victory. I am lucky to have a truly egalitarian marriage, and I've learned to like and trust and admire women for their personalities and accomplishments, not just for their looks. On good days, I can feel that the feminist revolution is over and that both sexes won.

Yet so many of my friends have slipped or crawled back into traditional marriages, and the younger generation looks strangely familiar. Teaching and talking to teenagers, I get a dizzying sense of **déjà vu,** as though peering down a long funnel into the '50s.

There they are, lined up in the college classroom—row after row of Barbies and Kens. The gulf of misunderstanding between these young women and men seems as great as it was 30 years ago, and they still play the games I remember so well. Women still accuse men of coldness and faithlessness. Men still accuse women of *deviousness* and emotionality. Men still pursue, women still look away with giggles and secret smiles.

What keeps me awake some nights is this: Suppose I have finally changed, and everyone else has remained the same? □

 Determining Meaning

PART I DIRECTIONS: Using the generative strategy of the vocabulary card, write a definition, synonym, antonym, and part of speech for each word below. Remember to select the most appropriate definition on the basis of how the word is used in this reading. Be sure to pay particular attention to the words that you missed on the pretest. In addition, find a minimum of two more words from "Confessions of a Former Chauvinist Pig" with which you are unfamiliar. Make vocabulary cards for those words also.

1. abolition
2. androgyny
3. baffled
4. chauvinism
5. déjà vu
6. deviousness
7. domestic
8. egalitarian
9. entrepreneur
10. indicted
11. intriguing

12. jargon
13. liberation
14. nostalgic
15. oppressed
16. passive
17. proposition
18. provisional
19. tedious
20.
21.

*PART II DIRECTIONS: As mentioned in Chapter 2, one way to learn the meanings of words that are difficult for you is to use the keyword strategy. An example is provided below for the word **androgyny**.*

The meaning of *androgyny*—being neither female nor male in appearance—may be difficult to learn. In the word *androgyny* you can see the letters *drog*. Imagine that a *drog* is a rare breed of dog that looks like both a male and a female and no one, not even the vet, can tell the difference! Put this keyword strategy on the front of your vocabulary card. You may wish to develop a keyword strategy for words such as *egalitarian* or *entrepreneur* since they are complicated and both begin with the letter *e.*

PART III DIRECTIONS: As mentioned in Chapter 3, many of our words come from the French language. There are several words from this selection that are either directly taken from French or that owe their history indirectly to the French language. Can you list four of them below? If you have difficulty, check the etymological entries in your dictionary.

1. _____

2. _____

3. _____

4. _____

 Trying Out Meaning

DIRECTIONS: Select the word from the target list that best answers each of the questions below.

1. Which word means a prejudiced belief that one group is superior to another group?

   _____

2. Which word describes the household tasks of ironing, cleaning the bathroom, and washing windows?

   _____

3. Imagine that you passed someone in the mall who looked and behaved like both a male and female and whose appearance and behavior did not give you a clue as to sex. Which word means this condition?

   _____

4. Which word describes a homework assignment that was uninteresting and tiresome?

   _____

5. Which word describes an individual who is not active and prefers to do nothing?

   _____

6. What is another word for the feeling or illusion that you have experienced some situation previously?

   _____

7. What word is another word for an individual who likes to organize, operate, and assume the risks for a business deal?

   _____

8. What word describes an individual who feels frustrated or blocked at some job or task?

   _____

9. What word means the act of destroying or completely getting rid of something?

   _____

10. What noun describes the condition of being shifty, tricky, and dishonest?

    _____

11. Which adjective describes a situation that is satisfactory for the time being but will eventually change with some permanent arrangement?

    _____

12. Which adjective describes the belief or doctrine that equal rights for all individuals is a must?

_____

13. Which word means a plan or statement?

_____

14. Which noun means a specialized language or talk of a particular trade, such as might be used by baseball players or computer specialists?

_____

15. Which adjective describes a situation that might arouse your curiosity or interest?

_____

16. Which noun means the action of trying to free a group from confinement and control by another group?

_____

17. Which adjective describes the feelings you have when you long or desire for the things, persons, or situations of your past?

_____

18. Which verb means accused or charged, as in a crime?

_____

19. Which adjective describes a group that might feel overwhelmed or crushed and bothered unjustly through the use of force or an authority?

_____

 **Applying Meaning**

DIRECTIONS: Complete each of the following sentences, being as specific as possible in order to demonstrate your thorough understanding of the boldfaced word.

1. A **baffled** student in a math class might _____

    _____

2. Most adults feel **nostalgic** about _____

    _____

3. When you find someone to be **intriguing** you want to _____

    _____

4. After being assigned numerous **domestic** tasks, the adolescent

    _____

5. Her **deviousness** was obvious when she _____

    _____

6. If you had an experience of **déjà vu,** you would _____

    _____

7. The older man demonstrated his **chauvinism** when he_____

    _____

8. You know you have observed an example of **androgyny** when

    you _____

    _____

9. Because the employer granted the new employee *provisional*

   status, the worker _____

   _____

10. The group supporting the *abolition* of the law _____

    _____

11. Most people try to avoid *tedious* jobs such as _____

    _____

12. When we say that the businessman offered his client a

    proposition, we mean _____

    _____

13. If you felt *oppressed,* you might _____

    _____

14. A *passive* football fan would _____

    _____

15. Her *egalitarian* attitudes and beliefs were obvious when she

    _____

16. After hearing that they would be *indicted* for the theft, they

    _____

17. If your psychology instructor uses a lot of *jargon,* you should

    _____

18. *Entrepreneurs* are individuals who enjoy _____

    _____

19. Groups searching or demanding *liberation* have included ____

_____

Reciting and Reviewing

Conceptualizing Meaning

PART I DIRECTIONS: Choose the word or phrase that does not relate to the other two, and write it in the blank after "Exclude." In the blank labeled "General Concept" write the concept that describes the remaining words.

EXAMPLE:

funny
serious
humorous

a. **Exclude:** serious

b. **General concept:**
   characteristics of comedians

1. egalitarian
    liberation
    chauvinism

a. **Exclude** _____

b. **General concept** _____

_____

2. tedious
    intriguing
    exciting

a. **Exclude** _____

b. **General concept** _____

_____

3. oppressive
    devious
    honest

a. **Exclude** _____

b. **General concept** _____

_____

PART II DIRECTIONS: When you can provide an example of something, you generally have a good conceptual knowledge of the word. Follow the instructions below and, if necessary, explain your choices.

1. Give an example of **androgynous** (the adjective form of androgyny) clothing. _____

   _____

2. Give an example of a rule that you believe should be **abolished** (verb form of abolition). Then explain why you believe **abolition** is necessary. _____

   _____

3. Give an example of a time you have been **baffled** and explain why. _____

   _____

4. Give an example of a time you have experienced **déjà vu.** ____

   _____

5. Give two examples of **domestic** tasks that you do not mind doing. Then explain why you find them acceptable. _____

   _____

6. Give an example of something for which someone could receive an **indictment** (noun form of indicted)._____

   _____

7. Give two examples of *jargon* that you use that your friends probably do not understand. From what field or area of interest do these words come? _____

_____

8. Give an example of a *passive* behavior in the classroom. _____

_____

9. Describe an example when you or your relatives have been *nostalgic.* _____

_____

10. Give an example of a *proposition* that has been extended to you at some time. _____

_____

11. Give an example of a time when *provisional* approval would be satisfactory and one example when *provisional* approval might be annoying. _____

_____

12. Give an example of a famous *entrepreneur* who has made a fortune from his/her deals. _____

_____

 Extending and Challenging

PART I DIRECTIONS: The following words are taken from the two previous reading selections. Place the words you feel have a positive

connotation in the left column and the words you feel have a negative connotation in the right column. Then add your own four words (that is, two words from each reading) to the columns. Some words may not have a positive or negative connotation for you, so omit those. Be prepared to justify your decisions in groups or with a classmate.

condescension	deviousness	oppressed
inferiority	domestic	tedious
enhance	egalitarian	liberation
distinction	entrepreneur	chauvinism
consolation	passive	indicted

Positive   **Negative**

_____   _____

_____   _____

_____   _____

_____   _____

_____   _____

_____   _____

_____   _____

_____   _____

PART II DIRECTIONS: Below are several targeted words that can be changed or transformed in function and slightly changed in meaning with the addition or deletion of a suffix. You may wish to check the list of suffixes in Chapter 4 and use a dictionary as a reference. Make sure you write a meaningful sentence for each word.

1. What suffix would you add to the noun ***androgyny*** to make it an adjective describing a certain look that some people have?

   The suffix _____

   The transformed word _____

   A sentence using that transformed word _____

   _____

2. What suffix could you add to the adjective **passive** to make it a noun? (There are several options.)

The suffix _____

The transformed word _____

A sentence using that transformed word _____

_____

3. What suffix could you add to the adjective **oppressed** to make it a noun? (There are several options.)

The suffix _____

The transformed word _____

A sentence using that transformed word _____

_____

PART III WRITING ACTIVITIES DIRECTIONS: Writing is an extremely effective way of mastering new vocabulary words. The following are short answer questions and journal entry questions to which you may wish to respond. Share your responses either with a classmate or with your instructor.

1. The authors of Reading Selections A and B, both males, explain problems that make communication and existence between the sexes challenging and sometimes impossible. Discuss some of their key points.

_____

_____

_____

_____

_____

2. What do the authors see as possible solutions to the problems that exist between males and females? Do you agree with the authors? Why or why not?

_____

_____

_____

_____

_____

3. In a journal entry, describe either a situation in which you had difficulties interacting with a member of the opposite sex or a situation in which everything seemed "to click." Why do you think your situation was different from the ones described by the two authors? Try to use as many of the new words as possible.

_____

_____

_____

_____

_____

 Self-Evaluating

DIRECTIONS: Think about the words that you have studied in this reading. List those for which you have a conceptual understanding in Column A. In Column B, list the words for which you have just a partial understanding. In Column C, list the words for which you have no understanding or just a definitional understanding. You should study and review words listed in Columns B and C before beginning the next reading.

Column A	Column B	Column C
_____	_____	_____
_____	_____	_____
_____	_____	_____
_____	_____	_____
_____	_____	_____
_____	_____	_____
_____	_____	_____
_____	_____	_____
_____	_____	_____
_____	_____	_____

See your instructor for Posttest I.

Reading C

Forms of Love

by Elizabeth Rice Allgeier and Albert Richard Allgeier

 **Targeted Words**

General	Content-Specific
acute	cognitive components
calculated	components
continuation	consummate love

devastating	crystallization
encompass	emotional component
exclusivity	erotic love
fantasizing	infatuate
intrusive	intimacy
preceded	limerence
preoccupation	motivational component
profound	nonlove
reciprocated	passion
respondents	physiological arousal
sustain	platonic love
tantalizing	

 Pretest—General Words

DIRECTIONS: The following words will be introduced in the chapter excerpt "Forms of Love." Before reading the selection, however, take the pretest by answering the questions about each boldfaced vocabulary word. Use the sentence to help you decide the correct answer, and circle that letter. Then rate your present knowledge of the word by circling 1, 2, or 3, depending on how familiar you are with the word.

1. And finally, decision and commitment, which **encompass** (in the short run) the decision that one loves another and (in the long run) the commitment to maintain the love.
   Encompass means
   a. includes.
   b. prevents.
   c. excludes.
   d. discusses.

   Level of Understanding   1   2   3

2. According to Sternberg, that is the kind of love that people strive for but find difficult to **sustain.**
   Sustain means to
   a. forgive.
   b. maintain or keep.
   c. describe.
   d. forget.

   Level of Understanding   1   2   3

3. For instance, among the early Greeks, the most **profound** form of love was believed to exist in the friendship of two males, who might also be involved in an erotic love relationship.
Profound means
a. rewarding or fulfilling.
b. religious.
c. common.
d. deep or absolute.

Level of Understanding   1   2   3

4. Evidence that these beliefs may be changing comes from a recent study in which over a quarter of the **respondents** listed a member of the other gender as their best friend.
Respondent means one who
a. shares.
b. organizes.
c. replies.
d. supports a cause.

Level of Understanding   1   2   3

5. The bride's friend said that some of the guests "seemed a little surprised" when he **preceded** her down the aisle.
Preceded means to
a. join.
b. come before in order or rank.
c. follow.
d. stop or halt.

Level of Understanding   1   2   3

6. It is essentially the same type of love that Tennov called *limerence*—a love characterized by **preoccupation**, **acute** longing, exaggeration of the other's good qualities, seesawing emotion, and aching in the chest.
Preoccupation means a state of
a. being absorbed or distracted by something.
b. excitement or joy about a new job.
c. being quiet and inactive.
d. fear about losing a loved one.

Level of Understanding   1   2   3

7. **Acute** (see the above sentence) means
   a. brief or quick.
   b. attractive.
   c. sharp or intense.
   d. regular.

   Level of Understanding   1   2   3

8. Everything you do is **calculated** in terms of how the limerent object would respond—whether he or she would like or dislike it.
   Calculated means
   a. judged or estimated.
   b. rewarded.
   c. experienced or associated.
   d. avoided.

   Level of Understanding   1   2   3

9. **Intrusive** or unintentional thinking about the limerent object. . . .
   Intrusive means
   a. brief.
   b. dream-like.
   c. forcing without invitation.
   d. exciting.

   Level of Understanding   1   2   3

10. Desire for **exclusivity** with the limerent object. . . .
    Exclusivity means a condition of
    a. being special and important.
    b. not wanting to share or divide with others.
    c. wanting freedom from a relationship.
    d. being expensive and rare.

    Level of Understanding   1   2   3

11. Once admiration and sexual attraction are present, the next step is to undergo an experience that raises the probability that these feelings might be **reciprocated.**
    Reciprocated means to
    a. ignore the actions of.
    b. refuse.
    c. show in return.
    d. appreciate.

    Level of Understanding   1   2   3

12. Limerence is a **_tantalizing_** state, which promises great things that never can be fully realized.
    Tantalizing means
    a. satisfying.
    b. emotional.
    c. boring but attainable.
    d. exciting but out of reach.
    Level of Understanding   1   2   3

13. In the beginning it can also be **_devastating_,** especially if the limerent object is lost abruptly.
    Devastating means
    a. overpowering in effect or strength.
    b. pleasing.
    c. discouraging.
    d. relaxing and soothing.
    Level of Understanding   1   2   3

14. In addition to spending a great deal of time intentionally **_fantasizing_** about the limerent object, you find that thoughts about your beloved intrude and interfere with other mental activity in an apparently involuntary way.
    Fantasizing means
    a. discussing or talking about.
    b. imagining and dreaming about.
    c. wanting and longing to be with.
    d. avoiding contact with.
    Level of Understanding   1   2   3

15. The third is through the transfer of attention to another limerent object—a **_continuation_** of the limerent state.
    Continuation means
    a. trying to be alone.
    b. beginning a new course of action.
    c. rejecting the usual or routine.
    d. remaining in the same state, capacity, or place.
    Level of Understanding   1   2   3

PRETEST SCORING DIRECTIONS: Check with your instructor for the answers. Give yourself one point for each item that was correct, and tally the number of 1s, 2s, and 3s you marked.

Number Correct _____

Level of Understanding

1 _____

2 _____

3 _____

 Pretest—Content-Specific Words

DIRECTIONS: For each term list as many descriptions or characteristics as possible based on your knowledge of the word. Then rate your present knowledge of the word by circling 1, 2, or 3, depending on how much information you already possess about the word.

1. cognitive components

_____

_____

_____

   1   **2**   **3**

2. component

_____

_____

_____

   1   **2**   **3**

3. consummate love

_____

_____

_____

   1   **2**   **3**

4. crystallization

_____

_____

_____

   1   **2**   **3**

5. emotional component

          _____

          _____

          _____

      1   2   3

6. erotic love

          _____

          _____

          _____

      1   2   3

7. infatuate

          _____

          _____

          _____

      1   2   3

8. intimacy

          _____

          _____

          _____

      1   2   3

9. limerence

          _____

          _____

          _____

      1   2   3

10. motivational component

          _____

          _____

          _____

      1   2   3

11. nonlove

          _____

          _____

          _____

      1   2   3

12. passion

          _____

          _____

          _____

      1   2   3

13. physiological arousal   **14.** platonic love

_____   _____

_____   _____

_____   _____

    1   **2**   **3**   **1**   **2**   **3**

PRETEST SCORING DIRECTIONS: Check with your instructor for the answers. Since there are no right or wrong answers, simply record the number of 1s, 2s, and 3s you have marked and record them below.

Level of Understanding

    1 _____

    2 _____

    3 _____

Now read the chapter excerpt "Forms of Love," paying attention to the targeted words, particularly those for which you could generate no characteristics or those for which your level of understanding was low.

· ·

Forms of Love

by Elizabeth Rice Allgeier and Albert Richard Allgeier

Psychologist Robert J. Sternberg (1986) has developed a theoretical framework to account for the various forms loving can take. Love, he maintains, can be understood in terms of three components: (a) intimacy, which includes feelings of closeness and connectedness one experiences in loving relationships; (b) passion, which refers to the drives that lead to romance, physical attraction, and sexual interaction in a loving relationship; and (c) decision and commitment, which **encompass** (in the short run) the decision that one loves another and (in the long run) the commitment to maintain the love.

Intimacy, according to Sternberg, is the emotional component of love. It grows steadily at first but later tends to level off. It is the major component of most loving relationships that we have with family, friends, and lovers.

Passion is the motivational component of love. Passion develops quickly in relationships but then tends to level off. It involves a high degree of physiological arousal and an intense desire to be united with the loved one. In its most pure form, it may be seen in the "love at first sight" experience.

Decision and commitment are the cognitive components of love. Commitment increases gradually at first and then grows more rapidly as a relationship develops. The love of a parent for a child is often distinguished by a high level of commitment.

Although these three components are all important parts of loving relationships, their strength may differ from one relationship to another and may change over time within the same relationship. The amount of love that one experiences depends on the absolute strengths of these three components, and the kind of love one experiences depends on their relative strengths. Sternberg represents the various possible relationships as triangles [see figure]. The absence of all three components is nonlove [see part *a* of figure], which describes the majority of our relationships—those with casual acquaintances. When all three components of Sternberg's love triangle are present in a relationship, there exists what he calls consummate or complete love [see part *h* of figure]. According to Sternberg, that is the kind of love that people strive for but find difficult to **sustain.** It is possible only in very special relationships.

FRIENDSHIP

The first type of love that most of us experience outside of our families is a close friendship with a person of the same gender. Friendship, or liking, is reserved for very close friends; it is not felt toward passing acquaintances. According to Sternberg, it occurs when one experiences the intimacy component of love without passion and decision/commitment [see part *b* of figure]. It is possible for friendships to develop into passionate arousal and long-term commitment, but when this occurs the friendship goes beyond liking and becomes another form of love. Also known as *philia* and platonic love, friendship is a form of love in which we are as concerned with the well-being of our friend as we are with our own well-being.

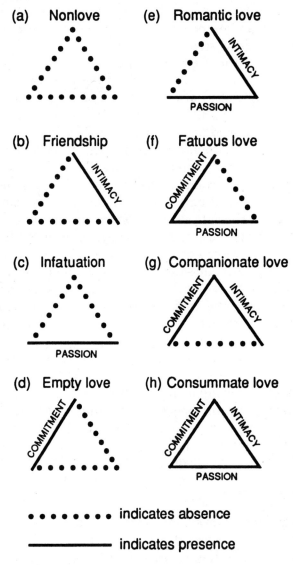

The Forms of Love

philia—a type of love involving concern with the well-being of a friend.
platonic love—nonsexual love for another person, often referred to as spiritual love.

Friendship involves a bond between equals. It is interesting that throughout most of our history, this kind of love between a man and woman was seen as unlikely or impossible. For instance, among the early Greeks, the most **profound** form of love was believed to exist in the friendship of two males, who might also be involved in an erotic love relationship.

With the movement toward equality for men and women in the twentieth century, intense friendship is no longer confined to partners of the same gender. Nonetheless, 75 percent of the **respondents** in a magazine survey (*Psychology Today,* 1979) saw same-gender friendships as different from other-gender friendships. Friendships between men and women were seen as more difficult and complicated because of potential sexual tensions, the lack of social support for male-female friendships, and the belief that men and women have less in common than do friends of the same gender. Evidence that these beliefs may be changing comes from a recent study in which over a quarter of the respondents listed a member of the other gender as their best friend, and about half of the sample claimed at least one person of the other gender as a close friend (Davis, 1985). Although male-female friendships now appear to be more common, most people are not likely to follow the lead of a bride in Washington who selected as her "maid" of honor her best friend, who happened to be male. The bride's friend said that some of the guests "seemed a little surprised" (Krucoff, 1982, p. 2) when he **preceded** her down the aisle.

INFATUATION

The *Merriam-Webster dictionary* (1974) defines to **infatuate** as "a foolish unreasoning, or extravagant passion or attraction." In Sternberg's framework, infatuation involves passionate arousal without the intimacy and decision/commitment components of love [see part *c* of figure]. Infatuated love is "love at first sight." It is essentially the same type of love that Tennov called **limerence**—a love characterized by **preoccupation, acute** longing, exaggeration of the other's good qualities, seesawing emotion, and aching in the chest. These characteristics can be experienced as either intensely pleasurable or painful, depending on the response of the loved one or "limerent object."

infatuation—foolish and irrational love.
limerence (**LIH-mer-ence**)—love that is marked by obsession and preoccupation with the loved one.

Unlike other forms of love, limerence is an all-or-nothing state that is experienced in similar ways by men and women. Based on several hundred descriptions of limerence obtained through personal interviews, Tennov (1979) outlined a number of characteristics a person in this state may exhibit:

1. *Preoccupation with the limerent object.* You are unable to think about anything else but the object of your affection. Everything you do is **calculated** in terms of how the limerent object would respond—whether he or she would like or dislike it. You may feel happy or sad depending on the amount of attention you get from your limerent object.

2. **Intrusive** *or unintentional thinking about the limerent object.* In addition to spending a great deal of time intentionally **fantasizing** about the limerent object, you find that thoughts about your beloved intrude and interfere with other mental activity in an apparently involuntary way. You may be working on a paper or performing some task at work when thoughts and fantasies of the love object come to the fore.

3. *Desire for* **exclusivity** *with the limerent object.* You crave the limerent object and no one else. You want commitment to ensure exclusivity even when it is premature or inappropriate. This can lead you to smother the object of your affection with attention and pressure rather than allowing the relationship to develop gradually.

Tennov proposes that limerence develops in stages, the first being admiration for another person who possesses valued qualities and for whom one feels a basic liking. This stage is followed by an awareness of sexual attraction. Once admiration and sexual attraction are present, the next step is to undergo an experience that raises the probability that these feelings might be **reciprocated**. This experience could be something as simple as observing a look or gesture or being asked to go to dinner or a party.

At this point in the development of limerence, the first "crystallization" occurs: one begins to focus on the good qualities of the limerent object and to disregard his or her bad qualities. After the first crystallization, if the two people develop a mutual attraction, the intensity of the romantic involvement will be relatively mild. Doubt about the limerent object's commitment, however, can lead to extreme or "crazy" limerence. The interaction between hopefulness and uncertainty leads to the second crystallization, which results in one's feeling an intense attraction to the other person. For the individual who is not so infatuated, the developmental process just described stops early, and the intensity of full-fledged limerence is never felt. Nonlimerents are generally more practical about their romantic involvements.

Limerence is a ***tantalizing*** state, which promises great things that never can be fully realized. In the beginning it can also be ***devastating***, especially if the limerent object is lost abruptly. Tennov outlines three ways in which limerent attraction can end. The first is through the development of a deeper relationship, which evolves if one is able to withstand the major disappointments and emptiness of fading limerence. The second is through abandonment due to a lack of reciprocity on the part of the limerent object. The third is through the transfer of attention to another limerent object—a ***continuation*** of the limerent state. Tennov maintains that full-blown limerence cannot develop without an element of uncertainty. □

 Determining Meaning—General Words

PART I DIRECTIONS: Using the generative strategy of the vocabulary card, write a definition, synonym, antonym, and part of speech for each word below. Remember to select the most appropriate definition on the basis of how the word is used in this chapter excerpt. Be sure to pay particular attention to the words that you missed in the pretest. In addition, find a minimum of two more unfamiliar words from "Forms of Love," and make vocabulary cards for those words also.

1. acute
2. calculated
3. continuation
4. devastating
5. encompass
6. exclusivity
7. fantasizing
8. intrusive
9. preceded
10. preoccupation
11. profound
12. reciprocated
13. respondents
14. sustain
15. tantalizing
16.
17.

*As mentioned in Chapter 2, one way to learn the meanings of words that are difficult for you is to use imagery. In addition, in Chapter 3 we stressed that the origin or etymology of a word was another way to make a difficult word more memorable. The word **tantalizing** can be learned using both of these strategies. Look up the word Tantalus in a dictionary.*

Tantalus is the origin of the word **tantalize**. As your dictionary entry reveals, Tantalus was a king who was punished in the lower world for his sins. His specific punishment was that he had to stand in water that always receded when he tried to drink it and under branches of fruit that rose when he tried to reach for them. Can you picture this scene of a frustrated king who could never drink the water or eat the fruit he desired and needed? Could you imagine this scene going on forever and the frustration the king felt? Put a picture of this scene on your vocabulary card and use this image to remember the word.

Now, try to use imagery to learn another difficult targeted word. For example, what image could you develop for the word **acute?**

PART III DIRECTIONS: There are several words from this selection that contain a prefix or suffix. Using the list of prefixes and suffixes provided in Chapter 4, answer the following questions.

1. Which two words contain the prefix meaning *before?* Of the two, which one also contains a Latin root? List that root and its meaning.

   a. _____

   b. _____

2. Which three words end with a noun suffix? List them below and underline the suffix. Then write the root for each of them.

   a. _____

   b. _____

   c. _____

Determining Meaning—Content-Specific Words

DIRECTIONS: Using the vocabulary card format described in Chapter 2, write a definition and examples or characteristics for each content-specific word below. In some cases you will be able to use context (c), and in other cases you will have to rely partially or solely on the dictionary (d). Occasionally you might be able to use your own prior knowledge (pk). Hints are provided in the parentheses following each word. You might wish to go back and skim Chapter 3 before beginning this activity.

1. cognitive components (c/d)
2. component (d)
3. consummate love (c/d)
4. crystallization (c/d)
5. emotional component (c/d)
6. erotic love (d/pk)
7. infatuate (c)
8. intimacy (c/pk)
9. limerence (c)
10. motivational component (c)
11. nonlove (c)
12. passion (c/d/pk)
13. physiological arousal (c/d/pk)
14. platonic love (c/d)

After you have determined the meanings for all content-specific words, discuss these terms with a classmate, a group, or your instructor to gain additional understanding of the terms.

 Organizing Concepts

PART I DIRECTIONS: This activity is a modified version of the generative strategy grouping and labeling outlined in Chapter 2. Find the general and content-specific words that could be grouped under each of the labels. You may not be able to use all of the words, but list as many as you can. One group has been started for you. Be prepared to justify and explain your categorizations in class.

Components of Love

Emotional Component of Love

intimacy

_____

_____

_____

Cognitive Component of Love

_____

_____

_____

Motivational Component of Love

_____

_____

All Components of Love

_____

_____

_____

No Component of Love

_____

_____

_____

PART II DIRECTIONS: *Using the content-specific and general words and the ideas from the text excerpt, complete the following chart. Some categories have been started for you. You probably will not be able to use all of the words, but list as many as you can.*

	Friendship	Infatuation
Components Involved	intimacy	
Synonyms		limerence
Definitions		
Subtypes	platonic love	
Characteristics		preoccupation intrusiveness
Examples		

↰ Beginning Conceptual Understanding

DIRECTIONS: *Answer the following true and false questions about love, paying particular attention to the words that are boldfaced. Then make any of the false statements true by adding, deleting, or in some other way changing the sentence.*

T   F   **1.** According to Robert Sternberg, there are three ***components*** that help define or explain love.

T   F   **2.** ***Consummate love*** is a ***profound*** form of love that is very easy to ***sustain.***

T   F   **3.** One of the ***motivational components*** of love, ***intimacy,*** grows steadily at first and then tends to level off.

T   F   **4.** ***Limerence*** is a form of ***infatuated love.***

T   F   **5.** A friendship with a member of the opposite sex that is not sexual is also called ***erotic love.***

T   F   **6.** The casual acquaintances we have with people at work or in classes are classified as ***nonlove.***

T   F   **7.** ***Passion,*** a ***motivational component*** of love, does not involve any ***physiological arousal.***

T   F   **8.** ***Acute*** longing for the loved one and a desire for ***exclusivity*** with the loved one are the only two characteristics of ***limerence.***

T   F   **9.** The only way limerent attention can end is through the transfer and ***continuation*** of limerence to another individual of desire.

T   F   **10.** The first ***crystallization*** of limerence occurs when the individual begins to become intensely attracted to the limerent object.

T   F   **11.** Friendship is a type of love without the ***intimacy*** and ***passion*** component.

T   F   **12.** Decision and *platonic love* are the *cognitive components* of love.

T   F   **13.** *Infatuation encompasses passion* and *intimacy,* but not decision and commitment.

 Using Concepts

DIRECTIONS: Complete the following sentences, being as specific as possible in order to demonstrate your conceptual understanding of the boldfaced words.

   1. An example of a *cognitive* task you might be assigned might

      be _____

      _____

   2. Some people believe that college should *precede* _____

      _____

   3. People on a diet often *fantasize* about _____

      _____

   4. Once your thoughts begin to *crystallize* about a math

      problem, you _____

      _____

   5. A good example of *consummate* happiness is _____

      _____

   6. An example of a *tantalizing* food would be _____

      _____

7. In the United States we have an *acute* shortage of _____

   _____

8. *Devastating* events include_____

   _____

9. One way to *reciprocate* friendship is to_____

   _____

10. *Respondents* to questionnaires in the mail often _____

    _____

11. When you demand *exclusivity* in a friendship you _____

    _____

12. *Continuations* of movie characters or movie sequels_____

    _____

13. The driver *calculated* that he had _____

    _____

14. After studying for five hours, some people find it difficult to

    sustain _____

    _____

15. When you are trying to study, *intrusive* thoughts include ___

    _____

16. People who exercise two or three hours a day have a

    preoccupation with _____

    _____

17. The movie's ending was so *profound* that the audience_____

_____

18. Success in life *encompasses* the ingredients of _____

_____

19. To build *intimacy* with a friend you should_____

_____

20. She was so *infatuated* with the idea of _____

_____

Reciting and Reviewing

Comprehending Concepts

PART I DIRECTIONS: The questions below are based on your understanding of the content-specific words, some of the general words, and most of the key ideas presented in the chapter excerpt entitled "Forms of Love." At this point you should be able to answer the questions without looking at the textbook excerpt, your vocabulary cards, or your organizing strategies.

1. What are the three components of love? Define each of them.

_____

_____

2. What is the emotional component of love? _____

_____

3. What is the motivational component of love?_____

_____

4. What are the two cognitive components of love? _____

_____

5. If all three components of love are in place, what form of love

would you have?_____

_____

6. Describe one characteristic of the love from Question 5. _____

_____

7. The absence of all three components of love is what form of

love? _____

_____

8. Which of the three components exists in friendships? _____

_____

9. Platonic love is an example of what type of love? _____

_____

10. Which of the three components exists in infatuation? _____

_____

11. What are three characteristics of limerence? _____

_____

PART II WRITING DIRECTIONS: Write an answer to the following essay question that is representative of the kind you might have to answer in a sociology or a human sexuality course.

Love is a common theme in songs, movies, and books. Using Sternberg's theoretical framework, explain the forms of love that are discussed in our popular culture.

_____

_____

_____

_____

_____

_____

 Self-Evaluating

DIRECTIONS: Think about the words that you have studied in this reading. List those for which you have a conceptual understanding in Column A. In Column B, list the words for which you have just a partial understanding. In Column C, list the words for which you have no understanding or just a definitional understanding. You should study and review words listed in Columns B and C before beginning the next chapter.

Column A	Column B	Column C
_____	_____	_____
_____	_____	_____
_____	_____	_____
_____	_____	_____
_____	_____	_____
_____	_____	_____
_____	_____	_____

_____   _____   _____

_____   _____   _____

_____   _____   _____

See your instructor for Posttest II.

6

Readings Concerning Educational Issues

Did You Know?

The word *berserk* originated from Norse mythology. Berserk was a fierce man who used no armor and assumed the form of a wild beast in battle. Supposedly, no enemy could touch him. Today, if you are described as *berserk,* you are wild, dangerous, and crazed.

In this unit you will be reading three different selections that deal with educational issues. In the first selection, "In Praise of the F Word," an adult basic education teacher and mother argues why more students should be failed during their public school education. In the second selection, "The Education of Berenice Belizaire," the author describes how one immigrant from Haiti succeeded in high school and college through pure determination and hard work. In the third selection, "Motivation," the author describes what motivates people to do what they do. This third selection is actually an excerpt from a psychology textbook that would be used in an introductory college course.

There are 52 targeted vocabulary words in this unit. The general words you will learn are varied and will be extremely useful for your reading and writing vocabulary. For example, you will frequently encounter words like ***median, spurn,*** and ***pervasive*** as you complete your textbook assignments for your college courses. In addition, words like ***squelching*** or ***impediments*** will assist you in making your written assignments and papers more precise and vivid. The content-specific words should also be useful to you, even if you never take a

197

psychology course. For example, words like *cardiologist, extrinsic,* and **intrinsic** can be found in many of your assigned textbooks or in your pleasure reading of newspapers or magazines.

In the first selection (Reading A), there are 14 targeted words. As you read the author's ideas about flunking students who have not mastered the necessary skills, decide if she has presented a logical and solid case. In other words, do you agree or disagree with her? The second selection (Reading B) contains 14 targeted words and is informational as well as inspirational. As you read it you may wish to think of students or acquaintances who are similar to Berenice or very different from her. The third selection, the psychology textbook excerpt (Reading C), is the longest. You will be introduced to 17 general words and 7 content-specific words. Before you begin reading, you may wish to define what motivates you to do something such as school work or household chores. Then, as you read, pay careful attention to the various types of motivation and check to see if your ideas about motivation are represented in the text.

Your instructor will probably remind you that you have three options with each unit in this text. After you have finished the activities in Reading A and Reading B, you can choose to:

1. Take **Posttest I** over Readings A and B. Then skip Reading C and turn to Chapter 7.
2. Take **Posttest I** over Readings A and B. Then turn to Reading C and complete those activities. When you have finished, take **Posttest II** over Readings A, B, and C.
3. Turn to Reading C and complete those activities, skipping **Posttest I** altogether. When you have finished, take **Posttest II** over Readings A, B, and C.

In Praise of the F Word

by Mary Sherry

 Targeted Words

abusive	perceive
composure	priority
conspiracy	radical
dooms	reality
equivalency	resentful
flustered	semiliterate
impediments	validity

 Pretest

DIRECTIONS: The words in this pretest will be introduced in the reading selection "In Praise of the F Word." Before reading the selection, however, take the pretest by answering the questions about each boldfaced word. Use the sentence to help you decide the correct answer, and circle that letter. Then rate your present knowledge of the word by circling 1, 2, or 3, depending on how familiar you are with the word. (Check the introduction to Chapters 5–8 to review the scoring procedures.)

1. Their *validity* will be questioned only when their employers discover that these graduates are *semiliterate.*
Validity means a condition of being
   a. practical.
   b. sound or effective.
   c. humorous.
   d. serious.

   Level of Understanding   1   2   3

2. *Semiliterate* (see the above sentence) means
   a. having an elementary level of reading, writing, and math skills.
   b. having some of the capabilities of a college student.
   c. being fluent in two languages.
   d. being late and disorganized half of the time.

   Level of Understanding   1   2   3

3. There, high-school graduates and high-school dropouts pursuing graduate-*equivalency* certificates will learn the skills they should have learned in school.
Equivalency means a condition of being
   a. extremely easy.
   b. significantly different.
   c. equal in force or value.
   d. very common.

   Level of Understanding   1   2   3

4. I am your basic do-gooder, and prior to teaching this class I blamed the poor academic skills our kids have today on drugs, divorce, and other *impediments* to concentration necessary for doing well in school.
Impediments means
   a. people that assist or help.
   b. skills or attitudes that increase.
   c. economic conditions that unite.
   d. something that blocks or prevents.

   Level of Understanding   1   2   3

5. Mrs. Stifter looked at me steely-eyed over her glasses. "I don't move seniors," she said. "I flunk them." I was *flustered.*
Flustered means
a. upset.
b. excited.
c. relieved.
d. confused.

Level of Understanding   1   2   3

6. I regained my *composure* and managed to say that I thought she was right.
Composure means a/an
a. concern.
b. ability to disagree.
c. calmness or peacefulness of mind.
d. speaking voice.

Level of Understanding   1   2   3

7. It was a *radical* approach for these times, but, well, why not?
Radical means
a. out-of-date.
b. extreme.
c. fashionable.
d. violent.

Level of Understanding   1   2   3

8. Suddenly English became a *priority* in his life.
Priority means a/an
a. fear.
b. condition of happiness.
c. burden.
d. item of importance or urgency.

Level of Understanding   1   2   3

9. I know one example doesn't make a case, but at night I see a parade of students who are angry and *resentful* for having been passed along until they could no longer even pretend to keep up.
Resentful means a feeling of
a. quiet happiness because of receiving rewards.
b. rage and violence.
c. anger because of being treated unjustly.
d. relief and acceptance.

Level of Understanding   1   2   3

10. No one seems to stop to think that—no matter what environments they come from—most kids don't put school first on their list unless they *perceive* something is at stake.
Perceive means to
a. understand.
b. demand.
c. ask.
d. cooperate.
Level of Understanding   1   2   3

11. Many students I see at night could give expert testimony on unemployment, chemical dependency, *abusive* relationships.
Abusive means
a. strong, lasting.
b. sexual.
c. hurtful, injurious.
d. meaningful.
Level of Understanding   1   2   3

12. However, making it work again would take a dedicated, caring *conspiracy* between teachers and parents.
Conspiracy means a
a. situation.
b. discussion.
c. strong disagreement over issues.
d. secret plan or plot for a bold purpose.
Level of Understanding   1   2   3

13. It would mean facing the tough *reality* that passing kids who haven't learned the material—while it might save them grief for the short term—*dooms* them to long-term illiteracy.
Reality means a quality of being that is
a. frightening.
b. actual or true.
c. severe or strict.
d. final.
Level of Understanding   1   2   3

14. *Dooms* (see the above sentence) means
a. condemns.
b. criticizes.
c. prevents.
d. insults.
Level of Understanding   1   2   3

PRETEST SCORING DIRECTIONS: Check with your instructor for the answers. Give yourself one point for each item that was correct, and record the number of 1s, 2s, and 3s you marked.

Number Correct _____

Level of Understanding

1 _____

2 _____

3 _____

Now read the selection "In Praise of the F Word," paying attention to the targeted words, particularly those you missed on the pretest and those for which your level of understanding was low.

· ·

In Praise of the F Word

by Mary Sherry

Tens of thousands of 18-year-olds will graduate this year and be handed meaningless diplomas. These diplomas won't look any different from those awarded their luckier classmates. Their **validity** will be questioned only when their employers discover that these graduates are **semiliterate.**

Eventually a fortunate few will find their way into educational-repair shops—adult-literacy programs, such as the one where I teach basic grammar and writing. There, high-school graduates and high-school dropouts pursuing graduate-**equivalency** certificates will learn the skills they should have learned in school. They will also discover they have been cheated by our educational system.

Mary Sherry, "In Praise of the F Word" (My Turn Column), *Newsweek*, May 6, 1991. Reprinted by permission of the author.

As I teach, I learn a lot about our schools. Early in each session I ask my students to write about an unpleasant experience they had in school. No writers' block here! "I wish someone would have had made me stop doing drugs and made me study." "I liked to party and no one seemed to care." "I was a good kid and didn't cause any trouble, so they just passed me along even though I didn't read well and couldn't write." And so on.

I am your basic do-gooder, and prior to teaching this class I blamed the poor academic skills our kids have today on drugs, divorce and other *impediments* to concentration necessary for doing well in school. But, as I rediscover each time I walk into the classroom, before a teacher can expect students to concentrate, he has to get their attention, no matter what distractions may be at hand. There are many ways to do this, and they have much to do with teaching style. However, if style alone won't do it, there is another way to show who holds the winning hand in the classroom. That is to reveal the trump card of failure.

I will never forget a teacher who played that card to get the attention of one of my children. Our youngest, a world-class charmer, did little to develop his intellectual talents but always got by. Until Mrs. Stifter.

Our son was a high-school senior when he had her for English. "He sits in the back of the room talking to his friends," she told me. "Why don't you move him to the front row?" I urged, believing the embarrassment would get him to settle down. Mrs. Stifter looked at me steely-eyed over her glasses. "I don't move seniors," she said. "I flunk them." I was *flustered.* Our son's academic life flashed before my eyes. No teacher had ever threatened him with that before. I regained my *composure* and managed to say that I thought she was right. By the time I got home I was feeling pretty good about this. It was a *radical* approach for these times, but, well, why not? "She's going to flunk you," I told my son. I did not discuss it any further. Suddenly English became a *priority* in his life. He finished out the semester with an A.

I know one example doesn't make a case, but at night I see a parade of students who are angry and *resentful* for having been passed along until they could no longer even pretend to keep up. Of average intelligence or better, they eventually quit school, concluding they were too dumb to finish. "I should have been held back" is a comment I hear frequently. Even sadder are those students who are high-school graduates who say to me after a few weeks of class, "I don't know how I ever got a high-school diploma."

Passing students who have not mastered the work cheats them and the employers who expect graduates to have basic skills. We excuse this dishonest behavior by saying kids can't learn if they come from terrible environments. No one seems to stop to think that—no matter what environments they come from—most kids don't put school first on their list unless they *perceive* something is at stake. They'd rather be sailing.

Many students I see at night could give expert testimony on unemployment, chemical dependency, *abusive* relationships. In spite of these difficulties, they have decided to make education a priority. They are motivated by the desire for a better job or the need to hang on to the one they've got. They have a healthy fear of failure.

People of all ages can rise above their problems, but they need to have a reason to do so. Young people generally don't have the maturity to value education in the same way my adult students value it. But fear of failure, whether economic or academic, can motivate both.

Flunking as a regular policy has just as much merit today as it did two generations ago. We must review the threat of flunking and see it as it really is—a positive teaching tool. It is an expression of confidence by both teachers and parents that the students have the ability to learn the material presented to them. However, making it work again would take a dedicated, caring *conspiracy* between teachers and parents. It would mean facing the tough *reality* that passing kids who haven't learned the material—while it might save them grief for the short term—*dooms* them to long-term illiteracy. It would mean that teachers would have to follow through on their threats, and parents would have to stand behind them, knowing their children's best interests are indeed at stake. This means no more doing Scott's assignments for him because he might fail. No more passing Jodi because she's such a nice kid.

This is a policy that worked in the past and can work today. A wise teacher, with the support of his parents, gave our son the opportunity to succeed—or fail. It's time we return this choice to all students. □

 **Determining Meaning**

PART I DIRECTIONS: Using the generative strategy of the vocabulary card, write a definition, synonym, antonym, and part of speech for each word below. Remember to select the most appropriate definition on the basis of how the word is used in this reading. Be sure to pay particular attention to the words that you missed in the pretest. In addition, find a minimum of two more words from "In Praise of the F Word" with which you are unfamiliar. Make vocabulary cards for those words also.

1. abusive
2. composure
3. conspiracy
4. dooms
5. equivalency
6. flustered
7. impediments
8. perceive

9. priority
10. radical
11. reality
12. resentful
13. semiliterate
14. validity
15.
16.

*PART II DIRECTIONS: As mentioned in Chapter 2, one way to learn the meanings of words that are difficult for you is to use imagery and the keyword strategy. For instance, if you are having difficulty remembering the meaning of **composure,** you might try using this keyword and imagery strategy:*

In the word **composure** you can see the small part **posure.** **Posure** looks very much like the real word **posture** except that the *t* is missing. Picture yourself in a very relaxed posture—perhaps you have just finished an important exam and have nothing to do for the weekend. Maybe you are in a relaxed posture sitting on a beach or on your porch thinking about how well you have done during the week. You are in a relaxed posture because you feel calm and peaceful, the meaning of the word **composure.** You might image something that looks like the following image:

You should draw such an image on the front of your vocabulary card. Then you should try to use a combination of imagery, keywords, or mnemonics to remember the rest of the targeted words. For example, what small part of a word can you see in *conspiracy?*

PART III DIRECTIONS: As mentioned in Chapter 4, word elements can sometimes be useful in determining or recalling the meaning of a word. In the 14 words from this selection, several have interesting prefixes. Using your knowledge of word elements and a dictionary, supply the following words.

1. Which word begins with the prefix meaning half?

   _____

2. What other words do you know that begin with this prefix? Check a dictionary for two examples of words that are new to you. Write each below and then provide a definition for each.

   a. _____

   b. _____

3. Which word begins with the prefix that means to be just or equal in value?

_____

4. What other words do you know that begin with this prefix? Check a dictionary for two examples of words that are new to you. Write each below and then provide a definition for each.

a. _____

b. _____

↰↱ Trying Out Meaning

DIRECTIONS: Select the word from the target list that best answers each of the questions below.

1. Which noun means a state of being sound or effective and thus resistant to attack by another individual?

_____

2. Which noun means a condition of being equal in value or force?

_____

3. Which adjective describes something or someone as being extreme?

_____

4. Which word describes how some people might feel during a difficult math exam—nervous, upset, or in a state of confusion?

_____

5. Which noun means calmness or peacefulness of mind and is the opposite of the word in Question 4?

_____

6. Which word means the same as harmful or injurious?

_____

7. Which noun means the same as an item of importance or urgency in your life, such as your family or school or friends?

_____

8. Which verb means to understand or to see and take notice of?

_____

9. Which word means the same as a secret plan or plot, usually for a bold reason or purpose?

_____

10. Which adjective describes a person who is filled with anger because that person thought he or she was being treated in an unfair manner?

_____

11. Which word describes someone who has a very limited understanding of reading, writing, and math skills?

_____

12. Which word means something or someone that blocks, prevents, or obstructs you from accomplishing what you desire?

_____

13. Which verb with a negative connotation means to condemn or pronounce judgment against?

_____

14. Which noun means a quality or state of being actual or true?

_____

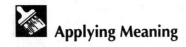 **Applying Meaning**

DIRECTIONS: Complete each of the following sentences, being as specific as possible to demonstrate your thorough understanding of each boldfaced word.

1. After hiring the **semiliterate** adult to do his payroll and

   bookkeeping, the owner _____

   _____

2. **Impediments** to succeeding in college include _____

   _____

3. The beauty pageant contestant quickly lost her **composure**

   when _____

   _____

4. Corporations and businesses place a **priority** upon _____

   _____

5. The English professor's **abusive** comments about the

   freshman's paper _____

   _____

6. She thought it was a **conspiracy** between her parents to _____

   _____

7. The musician's **radical** ideas caused people to _____

   _____

8. During the game, the quarterback became so *flustered* that

_____

_____

9. The younger girl felt *resentful* toward her older sister because

_____

_____

10. Many people feel that a lack of a college education can *doom*

you to _____

_____

11. The bartender questioned the *validity* of _____

_____

12. When talking with people from other cultures, it is sometimes

difficult to *perceive* _____

_____

13. Some college freshmen wonder about the *equivalency*

between _____

_____

14. Everyone has to face the *reality* that _____

_____

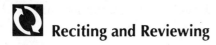 **Reciting and Reviewing**

 Conceptualizing Meaning

PART I DIRECTIONS: Complete the following analogies with one of the targeted vocabulary words listed below. Remember to keep the same part of speech across the analogy. The examples below illustrate how analogies can be organized.

> EXAMPLE ONE   expensive : costly :: attractive : good-looking
>   (Each set contains adjectives that mean the same.)
> EXAMPLE TWO   decrease : increase :: help : hinder
>   (Each set contains verbs that mean the opposite.)

 Targeted Vocabulary Words

> radical   impediment
> conspiracy   perceive
> priority   equivalent

1. extreme: _____ : : harmful: abusive

2. unequal: _____ : : calm: flustered (opposites)

3. to misunderstand: to _____ : : to glorify: to doom (opposites)

4. obstruction: _____ : : peacefulness: composure

PART II DIRECTIONS: When you can provide an example of something, you generally have a good conceptual knowledge of the word. Follow the instructions below, and, if necessary, explain your choices.

1. Give an example of a ***conspiracy*** that you or someone you know has experienced. Explain why it would qualify as a ***conspiracy.*** _____

   _____

2. What items that you possess or own should be ***valid*** (adjective form of the noun ***validity***)? Why is this ***validity*** critical? _____

   _____

3. What daily tasks would a ***semiliterate*** individual find difficult (be specific)? _____

   _____

4. Give two examples of ***priorities*** in your life. Why have you ***prioritized*** (verb form of ***priority***) them? _____

   _____

5. When have you or someone you know been ***resentful?*** What caused this ***resentment*** (noun form of ***resentful***)? _____

   _____

6. When have you lost your ***composure?*** What caused this loss of ***composure?*** _____

   _____

7. As you grow older you learn to face *realities.* List one

unpleasant and one pleasant *reality* that you have faced or

will face. _____

_____

 Self-Evaluating

*DIRECTIONS: Think about the words that you have studied in this
reading. List those for which you have a conceptual understanding
in Column A. In Column B, list the words for which you have just a
partial understanding. In Column C, list the words for which you have
no understanding or just a definitional understanding. You should
study and review words listed in Columns B and C before beginning
the next reading.*

Column A	Column B	Column C
_____	_____	_____
_____	_____	_____
_____	_____	_____
_____	_____	_____
_____	_____	_____
_____	_____	_____
_____	_____	_____
_____	_____	_____
_____	_____	_____

The Education of Berenice Belizaire

by Joe Klein

 Targeted Words

corroded	preconceived
elite	prodding
enduring	propriety
inebriated	reinvigorated
median	spurn
menial	taunts
perverse	valedictory

 Pretest

DIRECTIONS: The words in this pretest will be introduced in the reading selection "The Education of Berenice Belizaire." Before reading the selection, however, take the pretest by answering the questions about each boldfaced vocabulary word. Use the sentence to help you decide the correct answer, and circle that letter. Then rate your present knowledge of the word by circling 1, 2, or 3, depending on how familiar you are with the word. (Check page 128 to review the scoring procedures.)

1. Berenice had always been a good student, but now she was learning a new language while ***enduring*** constant ***taunts*** from the Americans (both black and white).
   Enduring means
   a. exchanging.
   b. suffering through.
   c. arguing.
   d. ignoring.
   Level of Understanding   1   2   3

2. ***Taunts*** (see the above sentence) means a/an
   a. question.
   b. push or shove.
   c. insulting remark.
   d. embarrassment.
   Level of Understanding   1   2   3

3. Within two years Berenice was speaking English, though not well enough to get into one of New York's ***elite*** public high schools.
   Elite means
   a. best.
   b. modern.
   c. exciting.
   d. closest.
   Level of Understanding   1   2   3

4. She gave the speech, after some ***prodding***—a modest address about the importance of hard work and how it's never too late to try hard: an immigrant's ***valedictory***.
   Prodding means to
   a. prevent.
   b. help complete a task.
   c. bribe.
   d. encourage into action.
   Level of Understanding   1   2   3

5. ***Valedictory*** (see the above sentence) means a
   a. farewell speech or address.
   b. point of view.
   c. solution.
   d. situation.
   Level of Understanding   1   2   3

6. The burdens they place on a creaky, *corroded* system are often cited as an argument against liberal immigration policies, but teachers like Judith Khan don't seem to mind.
Corroded means
   a. confused.
   b. dangerous.
   c. dishonest.
   d. worn down.

   Level of Understanding   1   2   3

7. You see Berenice, who had none of the usual, *preconceived* racial barriers in her mind—you see her becoming friendly with the Russian kids, and learning chess from Po Ching [from Taiwan].
Preconceived means
   a. hurtful.
   b. strong.
   c. determined in advance.
   d. in place before birth.

   Level of Understanding   1   2   3

8. Indeed, it is possible that immigrant energy *reinvigorated* not just schools (and more than a few teachers)—but the city itself in the 1980s.
Reinvigorated means to
   a. provide additional technology.
   b. give energy and strength again.
   c. create many confusions.
   d. destroy repeatedly.

   Level of Understanding   1   2   3

9. They restored the retail life of the city, starting a raft of small businesses—and doing the sorts of entry-level, bedpan-emptying jobs that nonimmigrants *spurn.*
Spurn means to
   a. reject.
   b. demand.
   c. appreciate.
   d. learn.

   Level of Understanding   1   2   3

10. Their *median* household income, at $28,853, is about $1,000 less than the citywide *median* (but almost $1,000 higher than Chinese immigrants, often seen as a "model" minority).
Median means the
    a. lower level in a financial statement.
    b. extreme value in a report.
    c. interesting levels in a statement.
    d. middle value in a distribution.

    Level of Understanding   1   2   3

11. Such *perverse propriety* cannot last long.
Perverse means
    a. creative.
    b. stubborn.
    c. immoral or questionable.
    d. destructive.

    Level of Understanding   1   2   3

12. *Propriety* (see the above sentence) means the
    a. condition where land ownership is questioned.
    b. condition where parental standards are rejected.
    c. quality of cooperating on a task.
    d. quality of conforming to existing customs or rules.

    Level of Understanding   1   2   3

13. Some lose hope after years of *menial* labor; others lose discipline, *inebriated* by freedom.
Menial means
    a. servant-like or low in nature.
    b. cruel and destructive.
    c. required or mandatory.
    d. useless and out-of-date.

    Level of Understanding   1   2   3

14. *Inebriated* (see above sentence) means
    a. confused, discouraged.
    b. resentful.
    c. excited.
    d. surprised.

    Level of Understanding   1   2   3

PRETEST SCORING DIRECTIONS: Check with your instructor for the answers. Give yourself one point for each item that was correct, and record the numbers of 1s, 2s, and 3s you marked

Number Correct   _____

Level of Understanding

1   _____

2   _____

3   _____

Now read the article "The Education of Berenice Belizaire," paying attention to the targeted words, particularly those that you missed on the pretest and those for which your level of understanding was low.

· ·

The Education of Berenice Belizaire

by Joe Klein

When Berenice Belizaire arrived in New York from Haiti with her mother and sister in 1987, she was not very happy. She spoke no English. The family had to live in a cramped Brooklyn apartment, a far cry from the comfortable house they'd had in Haiti. Her mother, a nurse, worked long hours. School was torture. Berenice had always been a good student, but now she was learning a new language while *enduring* constant *taunts* from the Americans (both black and white). They cursed her in the cafeteria and threw food at her. Someone hit her sister in the head with a book. "Why can't we go home?" Berenice asked her mother.

Because home was too dangerous. The schools weren't always open anymore, and education—her mother insisted—was the most important thing. Her mother had always pushed her: memorize everything, she ordered. "I have a pretty good memory," Berenice admitted last week. Indeed, the other kids at school began to notice that Berenice always, somehow, knew the answers. "They started coming to me for help," she says. "They never called me a nerd."

Within two years Berenice was speaking English, though not well enough to get into one of New York's *elite* public high schools. She had to settle for the neighborhood school, James Madison—which is one of the magical American places, the alma mater of Ruth Bader Ginsburg among others, a school with a history of unlikely success stories. "I didn't realize what we had in Berenice at first," says math teacher Judith Khan. "She was good at math, but she was quiet. And the things she didn't know! She applied for a summer program in Buffalo and asked me how to get there on the subway. But she always seemed to ask the right questions. She understood the big ideas. She could think on her feet. She could explain difficult problems so the other kids could understand them. Eventually, I realized: she wasn't just pushing for grades, she was hungry for *knowledge* . . . And you know, it never occurred to me that she also was doing it in English and history, all these other subjects that had to be much tougher for her than math."

She moved from third in her class to first during senior year. She was selected as valedictorian, an honor she almost refused (still shy, she wouldn't allow her picture in the school's yearbook). She gave the speech, after some *prodding*—a modest address about the importance of hard work and how it's never too late to try hard: an immigrant's *valedictory.* Last week I caught up with Berenice at the Massachusetts Institute of Technology where she was jump-starting her college career. I asked her what she wanted to be doing in 10 years: "I want to build a famous computer, like IBM," she said. "I want my name to be part of it."

Berenice Belizaire's story is remarkable, but not unusual. The New York City schools are bulging with overachieving immigrants. The burdens they place on a creaky, *corroded* system are often cited as an argument against liberal immigration policies, but teachers like Judith Khan don't seem to mind. "They're why I love teaching in Brooklyn," she says. "They have a drive in them we no longer seem to have. You see these kids, who aren't prepared academically and can barely speak the language, struggling so hard. They just sop it up. They're like little sponges. You see Berenice, who had none of the usual, *precon-*

ceived racial barriers in her mind—you see her becoming friendly with the Russian kids, and learning chess from Po Ching [from Taiwan]. It is *so* exciting."

Dreamy hothouse: Indeed, it is possible that immigrant energy *reinvigorated* not just some schools (and more than a few teachers)—but *the city itself* in the 1980s. "Without them, New York would have been a smaller place, a poorer place, a lot less vital and exciting," says Prof. Emanuel Tobier of New York University. They restored the retail life of the city, starting a raft of small businesses—and doing the sorts of entry-level, bedpan-emptying jobs that nonimmigrants *spurn.* They added far more to the local economy than they removed; more important, they reminded enlightened New Yorkers that the city had always worked best as a vast, noisy, dreamy hothouse for the cultivation of new Americans.

The Haitians have followed the classic pattern. They have a significantly higher work-force participation rate than the average in New York. They have a lower rate of poverty. They have a higher rate of new-business formation and a lower rate of welfare dependency. Their *median* household income, at $28,853, is about $1,000 less than the citywide median (but almost $1,000 higher than Chinese immigrants, often seen as a "model" minority). They've also developed a traditional network of fraternal societies, newspapers and neighborhoods with solid—extended, rather than nuclear—families. "A big issue now is whether women who graduate from school should be allowed to live by themselves before they marry," says Lola Poisson, who counsels Haitian immigrants. "There's a lot of tension over that."

Such *perverse propriety* cannot last long. Immigrants become Americans very quickly. Some lose hope after years of *menial* labor; others lose discipline, *inebriated* by freedom. "There's an interesting phenomenon," says Philip Kasinitz of Williams College. "When immigrant kids criticize each other for getting lazy or loose, they say, 'You're becoming American.'" (Belizaire said she and the Russians would tease each other that way at Madison.) It's ironic, Kasinitz adds. "Those who work hardest to keep American culture at bay have the best chance of becoming American success stories." If so, we may be fixed on the wrong issue. The question shouldn't be whether immigrants are ruining America, but whether America is ruining the immigrants. □

 **Determining Meaning**

PART I DIRECTIONS: Using the generative strategy of the vocabulary card, write a definition, synonym, antonym, and part of speech for each word below. Remember to select the most appropriate definition on the basis of how the word is used in this reading selection. Be sure to pay particular attention to the words that you missed in the pretest. In addition, find a minimum of two more words from "The Education of Berenice Belizaire" with which you are unfamiliar. Make vocabulary cards for those words also.

1. corroded
2. elite
3. enduring
4. inebriated
5. median
6. menial
7. perverse
8. preconceived

9. prodding
10. propriety
11. reinvigorated
12. spurn
13. taunts
14. valedictory
15.
16.

PART II DIRECTIONS: As mentioned in Chapter 4, word elements can be useful in determining or recalling the meaning of a word. In the 14 words from this selection, two have prefixes. Using your knowledge of prefixes, answer the following questions.

1. Which word begins with the prefix meaning **to repeat** or **do over again?**

_____

2. What other words do you know that begin with this prefix? Check a dictionary for two examples of words that are new to you. Write each below and then provide a definition for each.

   a._____

   b._____

3. Which word begins with the prefix meaning **before?**

_____

4. The word you listed in the answer blank above can be altered in form to become a noun. Using your dictionary or your knowledge of suffixes, write that noun form in the answer blank below.

_____

5. Check your dictionary to determine whether the word *propriety* contains the prefix *pro-*. As mentioned in Chapter 3, you will find that information in the etymological entry. Does the word *propriety* contain the prefix *pro-?* Yes or no? __ If not, what are the root and origin of the word *propriety?*

_____

*PART III DIRECTIONS: As mentioned in Chapter 2, one way to learn the meanings of words that are difficult for you is to use imagery and the keyword strategy. For instance, if you are having difficulty remembering the meaning of the word **prodding,** you might try using this keyword strategy:*

The word **prodding** means "encouraging" or "stimulating." In the word **prodding** is the smaller word **rod**. Using the word **rod** as a stimulus for an image, picture yourself holding a fishing **rod** in your hand. You are fishing in a quiet lake for perch, a large northern fish. Use the **p** in **perch** to remember the **p** that precedes **rod.**

*Your keyword sentence could be this: I do not have to prod myself into spending a quiet day with my fishing **rod** at a lake filled with **perch.** Your image might look something like the following:*

Put this image and keyword sentence on your vocabulary card. You could make a similar keyword sentence and image with the words *spurn* (use the little word *urn*) and *taunt* (use the little word *aunt*). Complete one of these below in the space provided.

 Trying Out Meaning

DIRECTIONS: Select the word from the target list that best answers each of the questions below. Write that word in the blank.

1. Which noun means a middle value in a series of numbers?

   _____

2. What plural noun means a remark or statement that insults another person?

   _____

3. What verb means to reject or refuse in a hateful manner?

4. What adjective means lowly in reputation?

5. What adjective means the best or most skilled of a group of people?

6. What word means encouraging into action?

7. What noun means a farewell speech or address?

8. What adjective means to be drunk or overwhelmed with excitement?

9. What adjective means to suffer or last through some event or action for a long period of time?

10. What adjective means opposing in regard to what is typically accepted?

11. What adjective means an opinion that has been established in advance?

12. What adjective means worn away or dissolved gradually over time?

_____

13. What noun means the act of being appropriate or proper by conforming or sticking to existing rules or customs?

_____

14. What verb means to give energy and life again to something or someone?

_____

Applying Meaning

DIRECTIONS: Respond to each of the following questions or statements. Your answer should reflect your understanding of each boldfaced word.

1. Describe some tasks that most college students would consider to be **menial.**

_____

2. What is the **median** for the following numbers: **12, 14, 15, 16, 17?**

_____

3. Would most people **spurn** an inheritance of one million dollars? Why or why not?

_____

4. Would an individual described as **elite** have to endure hunger or homelessness? Why or why not?

_____

5. Describe one technique for *reinvigoration* that you have used after reading and studying for a long period of time.

   _____

6. Give an example of a *taunt* that a young child might say on the playground.

   _____

7. What might a college senior say in her *valedictory* address?

   _____

8. What two factors tend to *corrode* a classroom environment?

   _____

9. Give an example of a *preconceived* opinion that many college students hold. How do you know this?

   _____

10. Would a student who had to be *prodded* in the morning to get out of bed choose to take an eight o'clock class? Why or why not?

    _____

11. Would someone who routinely behaved at work in a *perverse* manner be a candidate for promotion? Why or why not?

    _____

12. On what occasions do individuals become *inebriated* with joy or happiness? Give two examples.

    _____

13. *Propriety* is valued in many situations in our lives. Give two examples of when you have had to act with *propriety.*

    _____

14. Would a student show determination if she **endured** the semester while her mother was very ill? Why or why not?

_____

Reciting and Reviewing

Conceptualizing Meaning

DIRECTIONS: Complete each of the following sentences, being as specific as possible to demonstrate your thorough understanding of the boldfaced word.

1. In her **valedictory** address she encouraged her classmates to

_____

2. The students became **reinvigorated** when they_____

_____

3. After constant **prodding** from his parents, Carlos_____

_____

4. The **median** grade on the first exam _____

_____

5. When people have **preconceived** ideas about _____

_____

6. The college senior **spurned** the job from IBM because _____

_____

7. After receiving **taunts** about her clothes, Marissa _____

_____

8. The new employee was assigned *menial* tasks such as _____

_____

9. The secretary's *perverse* attitude at work caused _____

_____

10. *Elite* colleges and universities can demand students to _____

_____

11. After *enduring* years of sacrifice, the struggling student _____

_____

12. Occasions where *propriety* and respect are expected include

_____

13. Time and pollution *corroded* the building so that _____

_____

14. Senator Hendricks became so *inebriated* with power that he

_____

 **Self-Evaluating**

DIRECTIONS: Think about the words that you have studied in this reading. List those for which you have a conceptual understanding in Column A. In Column B, list the words for which you have just a partial understanding or just a definitional understanding. In Column C, list the words for which you have no understanding. You should study and review words listed in Columns B and C before beginning the next reading.

Column A	Column B	Column C
_____	_____	_____
_____	_____	_____
_____	_____	_____
_____	_____	_____

 Extending and Challenging

PART I DIRECTIONS: Below are twelve words from this chapter and four spaces for the additional words you have chosen to learn. Write your own words in the blanks. Then place each word in either the positive or negative connotation column. If the word has neither a positive nor a negative connotation for you, circle that word. As discussed in Chapter 3, you will react positively to words with pleasant connotations and negatively to words with unpleasant or bad connotations. Be prepared to discuss and defend why you grouped the words as you did. You may wish to compare and contrast your groupings with a classmate or with a small group of classmates.

menial	valedictory	validity	composure
perverse	impediments	spurn	resentful
abusive	conspiracy	radical	corroded
_____	_____	_____	_____

Positive   **Negative**

_____   _____

_____   _____

_____   _____

_____   _____

_____   _____

PART II DIRECTIONS: Below are three words from Reading A and Reading B. Each of them can be changed to a noun with the addition of the suffix -tion. Check the list of suffixes in Chapter 4 or a dictionary for information about this suffix.

As you probably discovered, *-tion* means an action or process. Add *-tion* to each of the three words below. Then, using your knowledge of the words and your background knowledge, write a definition for each new word in the blank provided. You may wish to check a dictionary to confirm your guess as to the meaning and correct spelling. Then finish the exercise by writing a complete sentence that shows your understanding of the word. Add these nouns to the front of your vocabulary cards.

EXAMPLE: *validity* becomes *validation*

A validation is an act of making sound or effective.
I asked the attendant for a *validation* of my parking sticker.

1. *Perceive* becomes _____

   Meaning of the noun _____

   Sentence _____

   _____

2. *Reinvigorated* becomes _____

   Meaning of the noun _____

   Sentence _____

   _____

3. *Inebriated* becomes _____

   Meaning of the noun _____

   Sentence _____

   _____

PART III WRITING ACTIVITIES DIRECTIONS: Writing is an extremely effective way of learning new vocabulary words, especially if you use the words in a personal situation that you have created. The following are short-answer questions and journal-entry questions to which you may wish to respond. Share your responses either with a classmate or with your instructor.

1. What would Mary Sherry, the author of the article "In Praise of the F Word," think about Berenice Belizaire?

_____

_____

_____

_____

_____

2. Have you met a student like Berenice Belizaire or like Mary Sherry's son? Describe him or her.

_____

_____

_____

_____

_____

3. Write an entry in your journal responding to the following questions: Besides the fear of failing a class, what should students do to motivate themselves to learn? What could teachers and schools do to help students become more motivated? How could you be more motivated? Use as many of the new words as possible in your journal entry.

_____

_____

_____

_____

_____

 Posttest I—Readings A and B

DIRECTIONS: Now you are ready for the first posttest for this chapter. Please see your instructor in order to receive a copy of the posttest for Readings A and B.

Reading C

Motivation

by Benjamin Lahey

 Targeted Words

General	Content-Specific
apparatus	achievement motivation
banish	affiliation motivation
detract	cardiologists
diligently	extrinsic motivation
exhibit	intrinsic motivation
explosive	somatic tension
forbidding	Type A personality
inherent	
manifest	
ostracism	

passive
pervasive
presumption
repugnant
squelching
toll
validated

 Pretest—General Words

DIRECTIONS: The following words in this pretest will be introduced in the chapter excerpt "Motivation." Before reading the selection, however, take the pretest by answering the questions about each boldfaced word. Use each sentence to help you decide the correct answer, and circle that letter. Rate your present knowledge of the word by circling 1, 2, or 3, depending on how familiar you are with the word. (Check the Introduction to Chapters 5–8 to review scoring procedures.)

1. Some individuals high in ***n Ach*** experience more than the average amount of ***somatic*** (bodily) tension and stress made ***manifest*** as aches, pains, and illnesses.
   Manifest means to
   a. reveal or make obvious.
   b. cause or contribute.
   c. disagree.
   d. suggest.

   Level of Understanding   1   2   3

2. Other common characteristics of the Type A personality include directing conversation to topics that interest him or her and ***explosive*** speech patterns.
   Explosive means
   a. causing disagreements.
   b. setting out violent arguments.
   c. bursting forth suddenly or sharply.
   d. keeping thoughts inside.

   Level of Understanding   1   2   3

3. In addition, Type A personalities have a *pervasive* sense of time urgency and a belief that people who act quickly succeed. *Pervasive* means a
   a. condition where you convince another person.
   b. tendency that is present throughout.
   c. tendency that becomes weak over time.
   d. condition where you must always win.
   Level of Understanding   1   2   3

4. The reason that two heart specialists are interested in Type A behavior is that it takes a serious *toll* on the body. *Toll* means the
   a. state or condition of labor.
   b. conditions related to health.
   c. fee charged on a special highway.
   d. amount of a loss.
   Level of Understanding   1   2   3

5. If you found yourself in that situation, would you enjoy your success, feel pressured to continue to be first, or fear *ostracism* by jealous classmates? *Ostracism* means a/an
   a. act of excluding or ignoring someone from a group.
   b. situation in which someone is highly respected.
   c. condition of being copied by others.
   d. act of gossiping or talking about a group member.
   Level of Understanding   1   2   3

6. Horner found that fear of success was common in women and felt that it was related to the *passive,* noncompetitive roles that women have been expected to assume in our society. *Passive* means
   a. demanding and intensive.
   b. caring and motherly.
   c. accepting without objection.
   d. rejecting and debating.
   Level of Understanding   1   2   3

7. More strikingly, Ruth Benedict (1934) long ago showed that there are cultures in the world where individual achievement is not only considered undesirable but **repugnant** and embarrassing.
   Repugnant means
   a. silly or ridiculous.
   b. disgusting or offensive.
   c. wasteful or time-consuming.
   d. childlike or immature.
                                    Level of Understanding   1   2   3

8. An individual who found himself in the public spotlight—such as by heroically saving a child from stampeding horses—would be so embarrassed that he would **banish** himself from the tribe and physically punish himself for months before feeling ready to return quietly.
   Banish means to
   a. remove or drive away.
   b. cooperate freely.
   c. work hard.
   d. question politely.
                                    Level of Understanding   1   2   3

9. Some research has looked at factors that influence how much need for affiliation a given person will **exhibit** at a particular point in time.
   Exhibit means to
   a. refuse.
   b. pretend.
   c. show outwardly.
   d. withdraw.
                                    Level of Understanding   1   2   3

10. He told half of the groups of subjects that they would be participating in an experiment involving painful electric shocks—and they were shown the **forbidding** looking shock **apparatus** in the background.
   Forbidding means
   a. commanding or ruling.
   b. large and overwhelming.
   c. sophisticated and advanced.
   d. threatening or unfriendly.
                                    Level of Understanding   1   2   3

11. *Apparatus* (see the above sentence) means
   a. a machine designed for a specified task.
   b. an agreement between two parties.
   c. something extra offered to a company.
   d. a source of revenue or income.
   Level of Understanding   1   2   3

12. Presumably, the first group was made far more anxious than the second group, a *presumption* that was *validated* by the students' own rating of their anxiety.
   Presumption means a/an
   a. belief that certain happenings come first.
   b. general agreement reached from facts.
   c. act of accepting something as true.
   d. belief that something is about to happen.
   Level of Understanding   1   2   3

13. *Validated* (see the above sentence) means
   a. imitated without permission.
   b. provided freely without obligation.
   c. declared or proven true and sound.
   d. increased over time.
   Level of Understanding   1   2   3

14. We speak of intrinsic motivation when the person is motivated by the *inherent* nature of the activity or its natural consequences or both.
   Inherent means
   a. receiving money or property from a close relative.
   b. an essential characteristic existing in something or somebody.
   c. a blocking force which could be dangerous.
   d. an increase or rise to levels considered to be productive.
   Level of Understanding   1   2   3

15. Children who hate to do their math homework often will do it *diligently* if rewarded with additional allowance money.
   Diligently means
   a. working hard with much effort.
   b. showing an increase in profits.
   c. finishing quickly and quietly.
   d. organizing for long-term goals.
   Level of Understanding   1   2   3

16. On the other hand, if the individual is already intrinsically motivated to perform an activity, adding extrinsic motivation will often *detract* from the intrinsic motivation.
Detract means to
a. challenge or frustrate.
b. meet or gather again.
c. support or increase.
d. reduce or decrease.

Level of Understanding   1   2   3

17. We must be careful to avoid *squelching* intrinsic motivation by providing unnecessary extrinsic rewards.
Squelching means
a. encouraging or stimulating.
b. crushing or trampling.
c. measuring or evaluating.
d. defining or explaining.

Level of Understanding   1   2   3

PRETEST SCORING DIRECTIONS: See your instructor for the correct answers. Give yourself one point for each item that was correct, and record the number of 1s, 2s, and 3s you marked.

Number Correct _____

Level of Understanding

1 _____

2 _____

3 _____

 Pretest—Content-Specific Words

DIRECTIONS: Beside each term provide as many descriptions or characteristics as possible based on your knowledge of the word. Then rate your present knowledge of the word by circling 1, 2, or 3, depending on how much information you already possess about the word.

1. achievement motivation   **2.** somatic tension

_____

_____

_____

    1   2   3   1   2   3

3. Type A personality   **4.** cardiologists

_____

_____

_____

    1   2   3   1   2   3

5. affiliation motivation   **6.** intrinsic motivation

_____

_____

_____

    1   2   3   1   2   3

7. extrinsic motivation

_____

_____

_____

    1   2   3

PRETEST SCORING DIRECTIONS: Since there are no right or wrong answers, simply record the number of 1s, 2s, and 3s you have marked and record them below.

Level of Understanding

1 _____

2 _____

3 _____

Now read the chapter excerpt "Motivation," paying attention to the targeted words, particularly those for which you could generate no characteristics or those for which your level of understanding was low.

....

Motivation

by Benjamin Lahey

Achievement motivation

Who was voted "most likely to succeed" in your high school class? Was he or she a "go getter" who was willing to work hard to gain success? Someone who was not afraid to accept responsibility and seemed to perform best in competitive situations? If so, your class probably voted for someone high in achievement motivation, abbreviated as *n Ach* (need to achieve). Achievement motivation is the psychological need for success in school, sports, occupation, and other competitive situations. Chances are very good that this person went into an occupation that provides rewards for *individual* achievement, such as sales, engineering, architecture, or law, rather than one that does not single out successful individuals for rewards, such as a government bureaucratic job. Chances are, too, that your high school's most likely to succeed went into an occupation that was realistically matched to his or her abilities. Persons who are high in *n Ach* generally experience little anxiety or fear of failure, but tend to choose jobs and other challenges (such as college courses) in which they have a realistic chance for success. And when success is achieved, the high *n Ach* individual enjoys the fruits of his or her labors more than the average person (Atkinson, 1964; McClelland, Atkinson, Clark, & Lowell, 1953).

Achievement motivation and the Type A personality

The description of the person high in *n Ach* is a positive one of calm, energetic success, and this is a generally accurate portrait. The price that some high achievers pay, however, is substantial. Some individuals high in *n Ach* experience more than the average amount of somatic (bodily) tension and stress made **manifest** as aches, pains, and illnesses. The key to whether or not a high *n Ach* person will experience serious somatic problems seems to be their amount of *hostility*. Some highly motivated achievers become excessively angry when they are interrupted or, worse still, when they fail. Such individuals compete in an aggressive, hostile manner at all times. They do not play tennis for fun or exercise but to *beat* their opponent, and they become upset if they lose.

Cardiologists Meyer Friedman and Ray Rosenman (1974) have termed this type of hostile, achievement-oriented person the Type A personality. Other common characteristics of the Type A personality include directing conversations to topics that interest him or her and **explosive** speech patterns. In addition, Type A personalities have a **pervasive** sense of time urgency and a belief that people who act quickly succeed; as a result, they often do two things at once to save time. There is a little Type A personality in most of us, and you should be concerned only if it's excessive. The reason that two heart specialists are interested in Type A behavior is that it takes a serious **toll** on the body. In one study of 3,400 men age thirty-nine to forty-nine, the frequency of heart disease was 6.5 times higher than normal in Type A men (Friedman & Rosenman, 1974).

Fear of failure and fear of success

There can be great costs of being high in *n Ach* if the person falls into the hostile Type A pattern. And, even more relaxed high achievers must learn to balance the demands of hard success-oriented work with the need for leisure, family, and friends. However, being low in *n Ach* does not guarantee a happy life either. Many low *n Ach* persons are not interested in achieving status or material success and are happy to spend their time and energy in other ways. Many other individuals low in *n Ach*, however, are very anxious in competitive situations, such as tests and sales competitions, and greatly fear failure. These emotions may lead the individual to avoid competitive occupations for which they are otherwise well suited or to experience considerable discomfort if they do enter such jobs (Atkinson, 1964).

Several researchers have shown that not only is a fear of failure common, but so is a fear of *success*. Individuals are said to fear success if they are overly concerned that success would lead to their rejection by others. Psychologist Matina Horner (1969) studied fear of success by asking women to complete sentences that begin like, "After the first term finals, Anne finds herself at the top of her medical school class. . . ." How would you complete that sentence? If you found yourself in that situation, would you enjoy your success, feel pressured to continue to be first, or fear **ostracism** by jealous classmates? Horner found that fear of success was common in women and felt that it was related to the **passive,** noncompetitive roles that women have been expected to assume in our society. Because many women have been taught that they should be housewives and nurses, they fear rejection from men and other women if they become engineers or physicians, Horner believes.

More recent research using Horner's sentence-completion technique, however, suggests that fear of success is no more common in females than in males (Morgan & Mausner, 1973). However, when males and females were placed in direct competition in laboratory tasks, females were less competitive (House, 1974; Morgan & Mausner, 1973). Although we have come a long way towards eliminating prejudicial stereotypes about women's roles, females in our culture still may be less willing than males to take the risks involved in success. Or alternatively, women may accurately perceive that the risks are still greater for females (Jung, 1978).

Origins of achievement motivation

Achievement motivation is probably a learned motive. Evidence for this proposition comes from several sources. For example, boys with high *n Ach* tend to have fathers who are in occupations that demand individual achievement (Turner, 1970). Probably these fathers encourage, model, and reinforce achievement in their sons. More strikingly, Ruth Benedict (1934) long ago showed that there are cultures in the world where individual achievement is not only considered undesirable but **repugnant** and embarrassing. The Zuñi Indians, who once flourished in the desert southwest of the United States, actively avoid personal achievement or recognition. An individual who found himself in the public spotlight—such as by heroically saving a child from stampeding horses—would be so embarrassed that he would **banish** himself from the tribe and physically punish himself for months before feeling ready to return quietly. Further evidence along these lines has been provided by David McClelland. He was able to show the influence of learning on *n Ach* by *teaching* it to business leaders from countries that were traditionally low in achievement motivation. The teaching not only raised scores on measures of *n Ach* but increased their business productivity as well (McClelland & Winter, 1969).

Affiliation motivation

Do you usually enjoy being with friends? Do you feel lonely during periods when you do not have many friends? Human beings are social creatures: given the opportunity, we generally prefer to be with other people. In this sense, it can be said that people have a motive for affiliation.

The need for affiliation is presumably present in all normal humans, but most research on this topic concerns differences between individuals who have different levels of this motive. Individuals who are high in the need for affiliation, for example, tend to prefer being with others rather than satisfying other motives. When asked to perform a clerical task with a partner, individuals who are high in the need for affiliation, but low in *n Ach*, choose to work with a friend, regardless of how competent the friend is. In contrast, individuals who are low in the need for affiliation, but high in *n Ach*, choose the partner that they believe to be most competent (French, 1956).

Some research has looked at factors that influence how much need for affiliation a given person will **exhibit** at a particular point in time. One important influence on the need for affiliation is anxiety. Stanley Schachter (1959) has conducted a number of experiments on the relationship between anxiety and the need for affiliation. In a typical experiment, female university students were brought to the laboratory in small groups. There they met a man dressed in a white coat who introduced himself as Dr. Gregor Zilstein, a professor of Neurology and Psychiatry. He told half of the groups of subjects that they would be participating in an experiment involving painful electric shocks—and they were shown the **forbidding** looking shock **apparatus** in the background. The other half of the groups were told that they would receive very mild shocks that they would experience as a mere tickle. Presumably, the first group was made far more anxious than the second group, a **presumption** that was **validated** by the students' own ratings of their anxiety. Both groups were given the choice of waiting alone in individual waiting rooms or together in a group waiting room.

As Schachter predicted, almost two-thirds of the subjects who were made to feel anxious chose to wait in groups, indicating a high level of need for affiliation. However, only one-third of the low anxiety group chose to wait together. Apparently, anxiety increases our motive to affiliate—"misery loves company" as the saying goes. Schachter found, however, that the effect of anxiety on the desire to affiliate was strongest for firstborn siblings or only children. Other research has also pointed to the presence of a higher need for affiliation in firstborn males and females (December, 1964). Perhaps there is something about the way that firstborns were raised that makes affiliation more important to them.

Intrinsic and extrinsic motivation

Psychologists have found it useful to distinguish between intrinsic and extrinsic motivation. We speak of intrinsic motivation when the person is motivated by the **inherent** nature of the activity or its natural consequences or both. For example, the monkeys that we mentioned earlier who will take apart mechanical puzzles for no reward other than getting them apart are intrinsically motivated to solve puzzles. Similarly, people who donate anonymously to charity because they wish to contribute without being recognized are intrinsically motivated. Extrinsic motivation, on the other hand, is external to the activity and not an inherent part of it. If a child who hates to do arithmetic homework is encouraged to do so by payment of a nickel for every correct answer, he is extrinsically motivated. That is, he works for the external payment rather than for an intrinsic interest in math.

Perhaps the most interesting and significant issue concerning the distinction between intrinsic and extrinsic motivation is the question of when extrinsic rewards should be supplied by parent, teachers, and employers in an effort to increase motivation. When is it wise to use extrinsic motivation in the form of positive reinforcement to increase the frequency of some behavior (such as completing homework, delivering packages on time, and so on)? There is considerable evidence suggesting that if a behavior occurs infrequently—and its intrinsic motivation can be assumed low for that individual—then extrinsic motivation is successful in increasing the frequency of occurrence of the behavior. Children who hate to do their math homework often will do it **diligently** if rewarded with additional allowance money. And because of the success they experience, they will sometimes come to enjoy math (Rimm & Masters, 1980). On the other hand, if the individual is already intrinsically motivated to perform an activity, adding extrinsic motivation will often **detract** from the intrinsic motivation. For example, when young children who like to draw pictures in school were given certificates for good drawing, they drew pictures less often than children who had not received certificates (Lepper, Greene & Nisbett, 1973). We must be careful to avoid **squelching** intrinsic motivation by providing unnecessary extrinsic rewards. □

 ## Determining Meaning—General Words

PART I DIRECTIONS: Using the generative strategy of the vocabulary card, write a definition, synonym, antonym, and part of speech for each word below. Remember to select the most appropriate definition on the basis of how the word is used in the chapter excerpt. Be sure to pay particular attention to the words that you missed in the pretest. In addition, find a minimum of two more unfamiliar words from "Motivation" and make vocabulary cards for those words.

1. apparatus
2. banish
3. detract
4. diligently
5. exhibit
6. explosive
7. forbidding
8. inherent
9. manifest
10. ostracism
11. passive
12. pervasive
13. presumption
14. repugnant
15. squelching
16. toll
17. validated
18.
19.

*PART II DIRECTIONS: As mentioned in Chapter 2, one way to learn the meanings of words that are difficult for you is to use imagery or the keyword strategy. For example, if you are having difficulty learning the meaning of **manifest**, a word meaning "to reveal or make obvious," you may wish to use this keyword strategy:*

In the word **manifest** is the small word **man** and the word part **fest**, which looks like the word **festival**. Imagine a **man** at an arts festival **displaying** or **revealing** his paintings and sculptures. You like his work a lot and decide to buy it because it **manifests** or makes obvious what it means to be an American.

Your image of this keyword sentence might look something like this:

Now try using the keyword strategy or imagery to remember another word. For example, what strategy could you use with the word *squelching?*

PART III DIRECTIONS: Using the information from Chapter 3 on the dictionary and Chapter 4 on word elements, answer the following questions. You may wish to add this information to your vocabulary cards.

1. Which word begins with the prefix meaning **down** or **from?**

_____

2. Check the etymological entry for that word. You should notice that the word consists of a prefix and a root. What is the root of that word? What is the meaning of that root?

_____

3. List two other words that contain that root.

_____

4. The word **ostracism** has an interesting origin that may help you remember the meaning of the word. Using your dictionary, look up the meaning of **ostracism** or **ostracize.** Explain the origin of the word.

_____

_____

5. One of the words has two meanings, one of which is a verb and one of which is a noun.

Which word is that? _____
Check to make sure you wrote down the correct definition on your vocabulary card.

Determining Meaning—Content-Specific Words

DIRECTIONS: Using the vocabulary card format described in Chapter 2, write a definition and examples or characteristics for each of the content-specific words below. In some cases you will be able to use context (c) and in other cases you will have to rely partially or solely on a dictionary (d). Occasionally, you might be able to use your own prior knowledge (pk). Hints are provided in parentheses following each word. You might wish to go back and skim Chapter 3 before beginning the activity. After you have determined the meaning for all content-specific words, discuss these terms with a classmate, a small group, or your instructor to gain additional understanding of the terms.

1. achievement motivation (c)
2. affiliation motivation (c)
3. cardiologists (pk/d)
4. extrinsic motivation (c/d/pk)
5. intrinsic motivation (c/d/pk)
6. somatic tension (c/d)
7. Type A personality (c)

 Organizing Concepts

DIRECTIONS: Complete the following chart, using as many general and content-specific words as possible. Some categories and explanations have been started for you.

MOTIVATION

Types	Definition	Characteristics Examples	Experiments Research
Achievement		Type A	
			Schacter's shock apparatus
Intrinsic		Inherent	

Beginning Conceptual Understanding

DIRECTIONS: Answer the following true/false questions about motivation, paying particular attention to the boldfaced words. Make any of the false statements true by adding, deleting, or in some other way changing the sentence.

T F **1.** People who **exhibit** high levels of **achievement motivation** generally choose jobs that **squelch** individual efforts to be the best.

T F **2.** Students with **Type A personality** try to **detract** attention away from themselves.

T F **3.** **Somatic tension** occurs commonly in **passive** and easygoing people.

T F **4.** Fear of success is an **inherent** characteristic in females and is more **pervasive** among females than males.

T F **5.** **Cardiologists** believe that excessive **Type A behavior** can take a **toll** on our health.

T F **6.** In some cultures individuals who attempt to glorify themselves because of an individual achievement might be **ostracized** or **banished.**

T F **7.** Schachter's experiment with a **forbidding** looking shock **apparatus** demonstrated that females have more **extrinsic motivation** than males.

T F **8.** Studies have **validated** that most normal human beings have some degree of **affiliation motivation.**

T F **9.** The **presumption** of psychologists is that **extrinsic motivation** is always better than **intrinsic motivation** in terms of shaping human behavior.

T F **10.** People described as being low in **achievement motivation** use **explosive** speech patterns.

T   F   **11.** Students who are ***intrinsically motivated*** to do an assignment will do it ***diligently*** because they like to learn new ideas.

T   F   **12.** ***Somatic tension*** may ***manifest*** itself when you begin to have aches, pains, and illnesses that seem to have no apparent cause.

 Using Concepts

DIRECTIONS: Complete the following sentences, being as specific as possible in order to demonstrate your conceptual understanding of the boldfaced words.

1. An example of ***extrinsic motivation*** for receiving a good

grade point average in your first year of college might be _____

_____

2. An example of a student's ***passive*** behavior in a discussion on

Shakespeare's plays might be _____

3. Someone with a lot of ***somatic tension*** would experience _____

_____

4. People with ***Type A personality*** tend to behave as if _____

_____

5. An example of a ***forbidding*** assignment in a college course

might be _____

_____

6. If you demonstrate ***diligence*** in one of your classes, you

probably would _____

7. A professional athlete might be *banished* from playing if

   he/she _____

8. Examples of *repugnant* cleaning tasks include _____

   _____

9. An example of a course that you might be *intrinsically*

   motivated to study for would be _____

10. You can be *detracted* from your studies if you are worrying

    about _____

11. Examples of *validated* documents that you carry with you or

    have in your possession include _____

12. Diseases that are *pervasive* across the world include _____

    _____

13. *Cardiologists* worry about people who *exhibit* behaviors that

    include _____

14. College students who have a high degree of *affiliation*

    motivation usually _____

15. One way to *squelch* cheating in the classroom is to _____

    _____

16. An example of an *apparatus* essential to a dentist or doctor

    would be a _____

17. Situations that can take a *toll* on a college student's life

    include _____

18. People with *explosive* personalities might *manifest* behavior

such as _____

19. One way to *ostracize* an individual from your group would be

to _____

20. An example of one personality characteristic that is *inherent*

in people with high *achievement motivation* would be _____

_____

21. In our legal system the lawyers, judge, and jury must

presume _____

Reciting and Reviewing

Comprehending Concepts

PART I DIRECTIONS: The questions below are based on your understanding of the content-specific words, some of the general words, and most of the key ideas presented in the chapter excerpt entitled "Motivation." At this point you should be able to answer the questions without looking at the textbook excerpt, your vocabulary cards, or your organizing strategies.

1. What are four types of motivation? _____

_____

2. People with the *Type A personality* might *manifest* what

type of characteristics? _____

_____

3. Is **achievement motivation inherent** in all cultures or

   societies? Explain. _____

   _____

4. What did Stanley Schachter's experiment with a **forbidding**

   apparatus demonstrate about people's desire or motivation

   for **affiliation?** _____

   _____

5. Give an example of both **extrinsic** and **intrinsic motivation**
   for learning. _____

   _____

6. Are the terms **achievement motivation** and **Type A**

   personality equal in meaning? Explain why or why not. _____

   _____

7. How might a parent or teacher **squelch** a child's **intrinsic**

   motivation to learn? _____

   _____

8. Why are **cardiologists** concerned about people with the

   Type A personality? _____

   _____

*PART II WRITING DIRECTIONS: The following essay questions
represent what you might have to answer on an exam in a college
psychology course. For each question, write a clear and specific answer
without using your vocabulary cards or the chapter excerpt.*

1. Discuss the four types of motivation, making sure you define and give examples and characteristics for each.

_____

_____

_____

_____

_____

2. Discuss which type or types of motivation have had the greatest impact on you and your college education.

_____

_____

_____

_____

_____

3. Discuss how males and females might be alike and/or different in terms of motivation.

_____

_____

_____

_____

_____

 **Self-Evaluating**

DIRECTIONS: Think about the words that you have studied in this reading. List those for which you have a conceptual understanding in Column A. In Column B, list the words for which you have just a partial understanding. In column C, list the words for which you have no understanding or just a definitional understanding. You should study and review the words listed in Columns B and C before beginning the next reading.

Column A	Column B	Column C
_____	_____	_____
_____	_____	_____
_____	_____	_____
_____	_____	_____
_____	_____	_____
_____	_____	_____
_____	_____	_____
_____	_____	_____
_____	_____	_____
_____	_____	_____

Posttest II for Readings A, B, and C

DIRECTIONS: Now you are ready for the second posttest for this chapter. Please see your instructor in order to receive a copy of Posttest II for Readings A, B, and C.

_____

_____

_____

C H A P T E R 7

Readings Concerning Health-Related Issues

Did You Know?
The word *sinister* originated from an old superstition that the left side is unlucky and from the Latin word *sinister,* meaning left. Today a *sinister* person is evil.

This thematic chapter focuses on health-related issues and contains three readings. These readings might be similar to those your instructor might ask you to read in either life science courses or a health-related major, such as hospital administration, nursing, or x-ray technician.

Reading A examines the issue of smoking in the workplace. Entitled "If You Light Up on Sunday, Don't Come in on Monday," it is about how some employers are not only prohibiting smoking in the workplace, but also demanding that employees not smoke off the job as well. Nineteen words are introduced in this reading. As you read the article, put yourself in the place of both the employee and employer. Would you be a **proponent** of such a ruling? Does this new hiring rule seem **justifiable?** What has **spurred** such measures?

The selection presented in Reading B, "Health Care: How We Got Into This Mess," focuses on medical care in the United States. More specifically, this article examines the rising costs and efficiency of U.S. medical care and presents some of the reasons for increasingly high health care costs. This article, which is longer than Reading A, contains 23 targeted words. As you read this article, think about how the health care issue affects you and your family. Do you believe in *universal* health care? Can we ever have an ideal system? What is the *grim paradox* about medicine becoming more high-tech? Should there be *restrictions* on health care for certain individuals?

Reading C in the health-related unit is an excerpt from a text, thus it contains content-specific as well as general words. This excerpt, entitled "AIDS," examines this deadly disease of the immune system, for which there is no cure. *AIDS* is one of the most discussed and researched health-related issues today. The general discussion in "AIDS" focuses on the rather brief history of the disease, which emerged in the mid-1970s, only as *isolated* cases. In addition, the authors try to do away with some incorrect perceptions that people often have about *HIV positive* individuals by discussing what *epidemiologists* have discovered concerning how the virus can and cannot be *transmitted.* As you read, think about your own beliefs about the *transmission* of this disease. Were you aware of the ways *AIDS* cannot be transmitted?

When you complete this chapter, you will have been introduced to 66 new general words that cut across a variety of disciplines, as well as 20 content-specific terms that you might encounter in a health-related course.

Your instructor will probably remind you that you have three options with each unit in this text. After you have finished the activities in Readings A and B, you can choose to:

1. Take **Posttest I** over Readings A and B. Then skip Reading C and turn to Chapter 8.
2. Take **Posttest I** over Readings A and B. Then turn to Reading C and complete those activities. When you have finished, take **Posttest II** over Readings A, B, and C.
3. Turn to Reading C and complete those activities, skipping **Posttest I** altogether. When you have finished, take **Posttest II** over Readings A, B, and C.

If You Light Up on Sunday, Don't Come in on Monday

by Zachary Schiller, Walescia Konrad, and Stephanie Anderson Forest

 Targeted Words

banning	levied
communicable	moonlighting
deem	perk
disincentives	proffer
estimates	prohibits
fraternizing	proponents
grim	sentiment
incentives	spurred
incidence	surcharge
justifiable	

 Pretest

DIRECTIONS: The words in the pretest will be introduced in the reading selection entitled "If You Light Up on Sunday, Don't Come in on Monday." Before reading the selection, however, take the pretest by answering the questions about each boldfaced vocabulary word. Use the sentence to help you decide the correct answer, and circle that letter. Then rate your present knowledge of the word by circling 1, 2, or 3,

depending on how familiar you are with the word. (Check the Introduction to Chapters 5–8 to review scoring procedures, if necessary.)

1. The incident helped privacy **proponents** pass an Indiana state law protecting employees who smoke away from work.
   Proponents means those who
   a. are against something.
   b. go on trial for a crime.
   c. are in favor of something.
   d. want to smoke on the job.

   Level of Understanding   1   2   3

2. Johnson & Johnson Health Management Inc. of New Brunswick, N.J., which sells wellness programs to companies, **estimates** that 15% to 20% of corporate health care costs stem from employees' "unhealthy lifestyle conditions."
   Estimates means
   a. comes close to.
   b. wildly guesses.
   c. averages.
   d. believes.

   Level of Understanding   1   2   3

3. With health care costs rising a **grim** 9% each year, employers note, why shouldn't individual employees take responsibility for their behavior—especially since corporate health coverage is a **perk** in the first place?
   Grim means
   a. acceptable.
   b. ugly.
   c. depressing.
   d. average.

   Level of Understanding   1   2   3

4. **Perk** (see above sentence) means
   a. benefit.
   b. requirement.
   c. law.
   d. disadvantage.

   Level of Understanding   1   2   3

5. The employers' concerns are *justifiable.*
Justifiable means
   a. unfounded.
   b. incorrect.
   c. proven.
   d. shown to be valid.
   Level of Understanding   1   2   3

6. So far, only a handful of companies have taken the extreme stance of Ford Meter . . . [b]ut many others are instituting *disincentives* for staffers they *deem* high-risk—charging them more for health insurance, for example.
Disincentives means
   a. advantages.
   b. problems.
   c. penalties.
   d. gifts.
   Level of Understanding   1   2   3

7. *Deem* (see above sentence) means
   a. misinterpret.
   b. suspect.
   c. praise.
   d. judge.
   Level of Understanding   1   2   3

8. But since 1989, 20 states have passed laws *banning* discrimination against smokers, and a few give much broader protection.
Banning means
   a. promoting.
   b. suggesting.
   c. legalizing.
   d. prohibiting.
   Level of Understanding   1   2   3

9. The backers of such laws are tapping a wellspring of
   sentiment that employers have no business telling employees
   how to run their private lives, as long as what they do doesn't
   interfere with how they do their jobs.
   Sentiment means
   a. beliefs.
   b. prejudices.
   c. issues.
   d. comments.
                    Level of Understanding   1   2   3

10. Employers have always had concerns about some off-hours
    activities: *moonlighting,* politicking, *fraternizing* with
    competitors' employees.
    Moonlighting means
    a. working the night shift.
    b. working a second job.
    c. working for a competitor.
    d. being unemployed.
                    Level of Understanding   1   2   3

11. *Fraternizing* (see above sentence) means
    a. associating with others.
    b. making others angry with you.
    c. outdoing others.
    d. spying on others.
                    Level of Understanding   1   2   3

12. The U.S. Supreme Court has upheld a federal law that
    prohibits discrimination by federal contractors against
    persons with *communicable* diseases such as AIDS.
    Prohibits means
    a. allows.
    b. demands.
    c. permits.
    d. forbids.
                    Level of Understanding   1   2   3

13. *Communicable* (see above sentence) means something
    a. that is deadly.
    b. you get from someone.
    c. that is curable.
    d. that is not curable.
                    Level of Understanding   1   2   3

14. Smoking might lead to a higher *incidence* of lung disease among workers who work with mineral fiber used in making tile.
Incidence means
a. ratio.
b. cause.
c. promotion.
d. occurrence.

Level of Understanding   1   2   3

15. Many companies take a positive approach, in the shape of financial *incentives* that give employees who live right the chance to profit by it.
Incentives means
a. benefits.
b. penalties.
c. problems.
d. punishments.

Level of Understanding   1   2   3

16. But while some companies *proffer* a carrot, others favor the stick.
Proffer means
a. donate.
b. take back.
c. give.
d. oppose.

Level of Understanding   1   2   3

17. "Why should we continue to do that when all medical evidence says smoking leads to health problems?" asks Miller of Monsanto, which is toying with a *surcharge.*
Surcharge means
a. incentive.
b. surplus.
c. additional charge.
d. refund.

Level of Understanding   1   2   3

18. **Spurred** by an in-house study showing that smokers' health costs at TI were 50% higher than nonsmokers', the company began charging employees $10 a month for smoking outside work.
Spurred means
a. urged on.
b. held back.
c. discouraged.
d. supplement.

Level of Understanding 1 2 3

19. The sum is **levied** for up to two of the employees' dependents if they smoke too.
Levied means
a. collected.
b. refunded.
c. deposited.
d. enforced.

Level of Understanding 1 2 3

PRETEST SCORING DIRECTIONS: Check with your instructor for the answers before beginning the next activity. Give yourself one point for each item that was correct, and record the number of 1s, 2s, and 3s you marked.

Number Correct _____

Level of Understanding

1 _____

2 _____

3 _____

Now read the article "If You Light Up on Sunday, Don't Come in on Monday," paying attention to the targeted words, particularly those that you missed on the pretest or those for which your level of understanding was low.

If You Light Up on Sunday, Don't Come in on Monday

by Zachary Schiller, Walescia Konrad, and Stephanie Anderson Forest

*Two years ago, Ford Meter Box in Wabash, Ind., decided it would no longer hire any smokers. Janice Bone was a payroll clerk for the small manufacturer. When a urine test uncovered nicotine traces in Bone's sample, Ford fired her. The incident helped privacy **proponents** pass an Indiana state law protecting employees who smoke away from work. But Bone, who has filed suit against Ford, has not gotten her job back. . . .*

Do you smoke? Drink? Eat more than you should? Your employer is getting very interested in your answer. It may cost you more in insurance coverage; there's even an off chance that it could cost you your job. As medical expenses whirl skyward, more companies have begun to see smokers, drinkers, and workers who engage in other "high-risk"—but legal—activities as a burden. Johnson & Johnson Health Management Inc. of New Brunswick, N.J., which sells wellness programs to companies, **estimates** that 15% to 25% of corporate health care costs stem from employees' "unhealthy lifestyle conditions." With health care costs rising a **grim** 9% each year, employers note, why shouldn't individual employees take responsibility for their behavior—especially since corporate health coverage is a **perk** in the first place?

The employers' concerns are **justifiable.** Still, they raise a range of questions about the employee's right to privacy away from the workplace. So far, only a handful of companies have taken the extreme stand of Ford Meter . . . [b]ut many others are instituting **disincentives** for staffers they **deem** high-risk—charging them more for health insurance, for example.

Existing civil rights laws don't generally protect against "lifestyle discrimination," because smokers and skydivers aren't named as protected classes. But since 1989, 20 states have passed laws *banning* discrimination against smokers, and a few give much broader protection. The backers of such laws are tapping a wellspring of *sentiment* that employers have no business telling employees how to run their private lives, as long as what they do doesn't interfere with how they do their jobs. "When they start telling you you can't smoke on your own time, the next thing you know they'll tell you you can't have sex but once a week, and if you have sex twice a week, you're fired," declares Oklahoma State Senator Carl Franklin, a backer of Oklahoma's smoker-protection law.

AFTER HOURS. Employers have always had concerns about some off-hours activities: *moonlighting,* politicking, *fraternizing* with competitors' employees. But the technological advances and social ills of the 1980s brought with them a host of workplace privacy issues. The result was a new generation of laws and court decisions spelling out how far an employer can go in certain areas. Congress has largely banned the use of polygraph testing. The U.S. Supreme Court has upheld a federal law that *prohibits* discrimination by federal contractors against persons with *communicable* diseases such as AIDS. Ten states have restricted drug testing. . . .

SMOKE-BUSTERS. Already, many employers won't hire smokers. Since 1987, USG Corp., a Chicago building-materials maker, has banned smokers from the ranks of 1,200 workers in eight plants. Its concern: Smoking might lead to a higher *incidence* of lung disease among workers who work with mineral fiber used in making tile. Turner Broadcasting System Inc. won't hire smokers at all. "We think we have the right to employ the kind of person we want to have—and that's a nonsmoker," says William M. Shaw, vice-president for administration. . . .

Cracking down on smokers is understandable, because the dangers of tobacco are so well established. The fear, of course, is that once employers start questioning one type of employee behavior, the list of unsuitable habits will grow. "Why would an employer tell you to knock off smoking at home and not tell you to knock off the beer, if the beer is bad for you, too?" asks Lewis L. Maltby, director of the American Civil Liberties Union National Task Force on Civil Liberties in the Work Place. . . .

Many companies take a positive approach, in the shape of financial *incentives* that give employees who live right the chance to profit by it. Half of the 22,000 persons covered by Southern California Edison Co.'s medical plan have reduced their annual premium by $120 under the corporation's good-health rebate program. They qualify if their weight, cholesterol, and other statistics are within certain bounds. . . .

SIN SURCHARGE. But while some companies ***proffer*** a carrot, others favor the stick. In a recent Harris Poll for Metropolitan Life Insurance Co., 86% of 1,175 executives surveyed found it "acceptable" to charge higher premiums for unhealthy habits. Since the presence of smokers in a work force drives the group rate up, there is a growing interest in charging smokers more for their insurance—rather than spreading the cost equally among all employees. "Why should we continue to do that when all the medical evidence says smoking leads to health problems?" asks Miller of Monsanto, which is toying with a ***surcharge.***

No reason at all, or so Texas Instruments Inc. figured. ***Spurred*** by an in-house study showing that smokers' health costs at TI were 50% higher than nonsmokers', the company began charging employees $10 a month for smoking outside work. The same sum is ***levied*** for up to two of the employees' dependents if they smoke, too.

The new charges have prompted no great outcry, perhaps because smokers recognize their puffing is so unpopular. Most of them are bothered, though, that the charge doesn't apply to other habits. "I think they should go and investigate all types of lifestyles that may increase risk to the company," says a TI programmer who pays $20 more each month because he and his wife smoke. "Someone who jumps out of airplanes for jollies or who races cars on weekends, that could cost the company, too.". . . □

 Determining Meaning

PART I DIRECTIONS: Using the generative strategy of the vocabulary card, write a definition, synonym, antonym, and part of speech for each word below. Remember to select the most appropriate definition on the basis of how the word is used in the reading. Be sure to pay particular attention to the words that you missed in the pretest. In addition, find a minimum of two more words from "If You Light Up on Sunday, Don't Come in on Monday" with which you are unfamiliar, and make vocabulary cards for those words also.

1. banning
2. communicable
3. deem
4. disincentives
5. estimates
6. fraternizing
7. grim
8. incentives
9. incidence
10. justifiable
11. levied
12. moonlighting
13. perk
14. proffer
15. prohibits
16. proponents
17. sentiment
18. spurred
19. surcharge
20.
21.

*PART II DIRECTIONS: There are several words in this reading that you might be able to remember more easily by using imagery. For example, **moonlighting**, which means to have a job at night in addition to the job you have during the day, could be easily remembered by creating an image of a person doing work outdoors at night with the moon shining. Your image might look something like this:*

Now you try creating images or keywords for **surcharge** and **prohibits**. What images did you create? How did they help you remember what the words mean? What other words might be imageable? (Hint: You might try the image "Sir Charge" to help you with **surcharge**.)

My images are _____

_____

_____

PART III DIRECTIONS: Several of the words in the reading selection have prefixes or suffixes. Look at each of the word pairs below and think about what happens to the word as a prefix or suffix is added or changed. How do the meaning and part of speech change? Note that in some cases the part of speech may not change, but that the prefix or suffix simply changes the meaning of the word. The first one has been done for you.

1. **communicable**
   part of speech: <u>adjective</u>
   meaning: <u>something that can be transmitted or given to</u>
   <u>someone else, such as a message or a disease</u>

   communicate
   part of speech: <u>verb</u>
   meaning: <u>to pass along or to make known</u>

2. **disincentives**
   part of speech: _____

   meaning: _____

   incentives
   part of speech _____

   meaning: _____

3. fraternizing

part of speech: _____

meaning: _____

fraternity

part of speech: _____

meaning: _____

4. proponents

part of speech: _____

meaning: _____

opponents

part of speech: _____

meaning: _____

5. justifiable

part of speech: _____

meaning: _____

justify

part of speech: _____

meaning: _____

 Trying Out Meaning

DIRECTIONS: Use one of the words from the list in each of the sentences below. Use the vocabulary cards you created in Determining Meaning *to help you select the correct word. Each word is used only once and is in its proper form.*

banning	fraternizing	levied	proponents
communicable	grim	moonlighting	sentiment
deem	incentives	perk	spurred
disincentives	incidence	proffer	surcharge
estimates	justifiable	prohibits	

1. The jury's decision to convict the accused criminal of murder was _____, based on the large amount of evidence presented by the prosecution.

2. The _____ of the bill before Congress to improve health care firmly believed that enough federal money was available to fund the bill.

3. The _____ of smoking on all domestic airplane flights was greeted with praise from flyers who are allergic to cigarette smoke.

4. Once a tax is _____, it is difficult to have it removed.

5. In the 1970s, when oil was in low supply but high demand, many energy companies put a(n) _____ on the fuel people used in their homes, making their bills even higher.

6. At one time the statistics on the number of people who died of smallpox were _____, but with the help of vaccinations, there are hardly any cases anywhere in the word currently.

7–8. In daycare centers, there is a high _____ of _____ diseases because sick children are often not kept at home, and at the centers they are generally in close contact.

9. Samuel was working as a bank teller during the day, but was _____ as a bartender four nights a week to help pay off his college loans.

10. A county or city law often _____ pet owners from letting their dogs roam freely in their neighborhoods.

11. In order to figure out your insurance premiums, a company _____ how likely you are to have an accident, based on your past driving record.

12. Many small business owners believe that providing health insurance to their employees is a(n) _____, not a right.

13. Before her death, it was Lauren's _____ that she be cremated.

14. _____ to doing well in college might include landing a high-paying job or getting into graduate school.

15. Things that you _____ to be important will be things that you give great care and attention to.

16. Because Harley was caught _____ with nonunion workers, he almost lost his job and many friends.

17. When you _____ your opinion, you should be willing to accept the fact that others might disagree with you.

18. A(n) _____ to smoking would be having to pay higher insurance premiums.

19. _____ on by the hoots and hollers of the crowd, the band played another set, which turned out to be their best of the night.

Applying Meaning

DIRECTIONS: Complete each of the following sentences, being as specific as possible, in order to demonstrate your thorough understanding of each boldfaced word.

1. If you have a *communicable* disease _____

_____

2. An *incentive* for making good grades might be _____

_____

3. If you are *prohibited* from smoking in a pubic building, you

would have to _____

4. When one country *levies* a tax against another _____

_____

5. It is *justifiable* to keep something you have found if _____

_____

6. If you are a *proponent* of a piece of legislation, you might _____

_____

7. There is a high *incidence* of disease in poor countries because

_____

8. You might *deem* it unnecessary to attend class when _____

_____

9. Someone who is *banned* from a store for shoplifting would

_____

10. One of the *perks* of having a good job might be_____

_____

11. You might *proffer* a suggestion for improving your workplace if

_____

12. You might have to *moonlight* if _____

_____

13. It might be good to *fraternize* with your competition if _____

_____

14. You might have to pay a *surcharge* on an airline ticket if

_____

15. If your research ideas were often *spurred* by inspiration, you might _____

_____

16. If your *sentiment* about smoking differed from your roommate's, you might _____

_____

17. The *grim* fact about smoking is that _____

_____

18. *Estimates* that the number of AIDS cases will rise _____

_____

19. A *disincentive* to studying might be _____

_____

Reciting and Reviewing

Conceptualizing Meaning

DIRECTIONS: When you can provide an example of something, you generally have a good conceptual knowledge of the word. Follow the instructions below, and if necessary, explain your choice.

1. Give an example of a job you might have if you had to *moonlight.* _____

2–3. Give an example of an *incidence* in which you might have to pay a *surcharge.* _____

4–5. Give an example of something that has been *prohibited* or

banned. _____

6. Give an example of something that you *deem* to be important

to success._____ Why is this important to success?

_____

7. Give an example of a disease that has *grim* consequences. ____

_____

8–9. Give an example of a time when it might be *justifiable* to *levy*

new taxes. _____

10. Give an example of a time when your *sentiments* differed

from everyone else's. _____

_____

11. Give an example of a disease that is *communicable.* _____

_____

12. Give an example of a *perk* you might receive if you worked for

an important movie producer. _____

_____

13. Give an example of when *fraternizing* with your co-workers

may do more harm than good. _____

_____

14–15. Give an example of an *incentive* and *disincentive* for going

to the doctor. _____

_____

16. Give an example of what an animal rights *proponent* might

say at a rally. _____

_____

17. Give an example of something that the federal government

estimates every year. _____

18. Give an example of when a strong belief about something has

spurred you into action. _____

_____

19. Give an example of a situation when you did not want to

proffer your thoughts on something. _____

_____

Reading B

Health Care: How We Got Into This Mess

by Robert J. Samuelson

 **Targeted Words**

ambiguous	impersonal
autonomy	inflation
batteries	massive
beneficiary	paradox
compensation	reimbursement
crank	restrictions
curbs (ed)	scourge
deficits	ultimately
devastating	unbounded
dilemma	universal
enriching	volatile
fosters	

 Pretest

DIRECTIONS: The words in the pretest will be introduced in the reading selection entitled "Health Care: How We Got Into This Mess." Before reading the selection, however, take the pretest by answering the questions about each boldfaced vocabulary word. Use the sentence to help you decide the correct answer, and circle that letter. Then rate

your present knowledge of the word by circling 1, 2, or 3, depending on how familiar you are with the word.

1. Unfortunately, this feeling that people ought to have health care on demand *fosters* the illusion that health care is free.
   Fosters means
   a. detracts from.
   b. promotes.
   c. promises.
   d. defines.
   Level of Understanding   1   2   3

2. Provide ***universal*** insurance coverage—no one should be denied essential care.
   Universal means
   a. narrow.
   b. individual choice.
   c. occasional.
   d. including all.
   Level of Understanding   1   2   3

3. Allow absolute freedom of choice—we should be free to choose our doctors, and they should have ***autonomy*** to select the best treatments for us.
   Autonomy means
   a. independence.
   b. consult.
   c. dependence.
   d. limitations.
   Level of Understanding   1   2   3

4. Every ***crank*** psychotherapy would qualify for insurance coverage.
   Crank means
   a. licensed.
   b. unproven.
   c. strange; odd.
   d. retired.
   Level of Understanding   1   2   3

5. But in a larger sense, the debate represents an awkward attempt to come to terms with the ***ambiguous*** nature of modern medicine.
Ambiguous means
a. well defined.
b. changing.
c. uncertain.
d. cautious.

Level of Understanding   1   2   3

6. We are shuffled between specialists and subjected to ***batteries*** of tests.
Batteries means
a. few.
b. specific.
c. ordered.
d. series.

Level of Understanding   1   2   3

7. When Americans say they want "choice," it means that they don't want health reform to make the system even more ***impersonal.***
Impersonal means
a. user friendly.
b. caring.
c. unemotional.
d. unfair.

Level of Understanding   1   2   3

8. Despite urban violence and the ***scourge*** of AIDS—which have had a ***devastating*** impact on some Americans—most of us are healthier than ever.
Scourge means
a. affliction.
b. beauty.
c. increase.
d. decrease.

Level of Understanding   1   2   3

9. ***Devastating*** (see above sentence) means
a. healthy.
b. destroying.
c. enlightening.
d. personal.

Level of Understanding   1   2   3

10. Nor has there been a *massive* loss of insurance coverage.
Massive means
a. minor.
b. temporary.
c. determined.
d. huge.

Level of Understanding   1   2   3

11. Since 1972, rising insurance costs have eaten up half of workers' increased *compensation.*
Compensation means
a. benefits.
b. penalty.
c. salary.
d. promotions.

Level of Understanding   1   2   3

12. Unless health costs are *curbed,* it may also be impossible to subdue federal budget *deficits.*
Curbed means
a. stopped.
b. increased.
c. monitored.
d. slowed.

Level of Understanding   1   2   3

13. *Deficits* (see above sentence) means
a. windfalls.
b. shortages.
c. profits.
d. increases.

Level of Understanding   1   2   3

14. The basic cause of the spending explosion is the *volatile* mix of generous insurance and high-tech medicine.
Volatile means
a. gentle.
b. odd.
c. recognized.
d. explosive.

Level of Understanding   1   2   3

15. It's wrong to dismiss high-tech medicine merely as the excesses of the health-industrial complex: expensive gadgets and drugs peddled by doctors *enriching* themselves.
Enriching means
a. harming.
b. improving.
c. rewarding.
d. confusing.

Level of Understanding   1   2   3

16. Finally, high-tech medicine creates a grim *paradox:* the more it extends life, the more it raises the cost of living longer.
Paradox means two ideas that
a. mean the same thing.
b. are opposite from one another.
c. are false.
d. seem to contradict each other.

Level of Understanding   1   2   3

17. The *beneficiary* of today's bypass surgery may have a heart attack in five years or develop cancer.
Beneficiary mean one who
a. gains.
b. loses.
c. dies.
d. takes advantage of.

Level of Understanding   1   2   3

18. Open-ended insurance *reimbursement* makes it in doctors' self-interest to provide more treatment.
Reimbursement means a
a. payment.
b. debt.
c. refund.
d. tip.

Level of Understanding   1   2   3

19. A survey done for The Robert Wood Johnson Foundation asked respondents what *restrictions* might be acceptable on insurance to cut costs.
Restrictions means
a. freedoms.
b. additions.
c. limitations.
d. perks.

Level of Understanding   1   2   3

20. Our *dilemma* is that a system that provides *unbounded* benefits for all of us as individuals will hurt us as a society.
Dilemma means
a. suggestion.
b. conclusion.
c. answer.
d. problem.

Level of Understanding   1   2   3

21. *Unbounded* (see above sentence) means
a. without problems.
b. restraints.
c. without rules or restrictions.
d. important.

Level of Understanding   1   2   3

22. The health care debate is *ultimately* a giant guessing game about what kind of system best balances society's need for economic discipline with the individual's need for dignity.
Ultimately means
a. currently.
b. eventually.
c. primarily.
d. logically.

Level of Understanding   1   2   3

PRETEST SCORING DIRECTIONS: Check with your instructor for the answers before beginning the next activity. Give yourself one point for each item that was correct, and record the number of 1s, 2s, and 3s you marked.

Number Correct _____

Level of Understanding

1 _____

2 _____

3 _____

Now read the article "Health Care: How We Got Into This Mess," paying attention to the targeted words, particularly those that you missed on the pretest or those for which your level of understanding was low.

· ·

Health Care: How We Got Into This Mess

by Robert J. Samuelson

The health care debate launched by President Clinton will occur along the ragged border between ethics and economics. Ever since World War II, Americans have come to consider good health care as a right: something that people should receive when they need it. It's not like buying a car or stereo: if you can't afford it, tough luck. Unfortunately, this feeling that people ought to have health care on demand *fosters* the illusion that health care is free. But someone has to pay, the someone is us and, frankly, we don't like that, either. The result is that our ideal health care system is a logical impossibility.

We know exactly what it should do:

Robert J. Samuelson, "Health Care: How We Got Into This Mess," found in *Newsweek,* August 4, 1993, © 1993, Washington Post Writers Group. Reprinted by permission.

- Provide **universal** insurance coverage—no one should be denied essential care;
- Allow absolute freedom of choice—we should be free to choose our doctors, and they should have **autonomy** to select the best treatments for us;
- Control costs—government, businesses and families shouldn't be bankrupted by soaring health spending.

The trouble is that no health care system can fully achieve all these goals. Universal insurance coverage, coupled with absolute freedom of choice, would make costs uncontrollable. Every **crank** psychotherapy would qualify for insurance coverage. Every new lifesaving technology—no matter how huge the expense or brief the benefit—would be used. We can control costs only if some people or some treatments aren't covered by insurance. Some things have to be made unaffordable. We either make these choices directly or tolerate a medical system that makes them for us.

What President Clinton has started is a historic effort to find an acceptable new balance of competing public demands—to reinvent health care in ways that provide somewhat less freedom for patients and doctors and somewhat more cost control. In its mind-numbing complexity, the debate will be about whether his program or any of its rivals can do what they claim. But in a larger sense, the debate represents an awkward attempt to come to terms with the **ambiguous** nature of modern medicine.

We once hailed every medical breakthrough as a triumph of science and a gift to humanity. Now we see the mixed blessings of advanced medicine. Its growing sophistication also makes it more costly and bureaucratic. We can get better care—and feel less cared for. We are shuffled between specialists and subjected to **batteries** of tests. When Americans say they want "choice," it means that they don't want health reform to make the system even more **impersonal.** They still crave a trusting doctor-patient relationship. "When people get sick, they feel they need to reach out to someone," says Dr. Stanley Talpers, a retired family practitioner who now teaches at George Washington University. "If they know the doctor, it's so much easier."

Our health care problem is not that we are less healthy or have become hugely unhappy with our medical care. Just the opposite. Despite urban violence and the **scourge** of AIDS—which have had a **devastating** impact on some Americans—most of us are healthier than ever. In 1950, life expectancy was

68 years; now it is 76 years. Likewise, most Americans (about 80 percent) say they're satisfied with their personal health care. Nor has there been a *massive* loss of insurance coverage. Between 1977 and 1992, the share of Americans without coverage rose only slightly, from 13 to 17 percent. Health costs are the big problem, because today's system essentially provides unlimited care for the insured.

Between 1965 and 1991, health spending rose from 5.9 to 13.2 percent of GDP. If unchecked, it could hit 20 percent in a decade. The increases have squeezed take-home pay and overburdened government. They are draining funds from police and schools. As companies pay more for health insurance, less is left for wages. Since 1972, rising insurance costs have eaten up half of workers' increased *compensation* (pay plus fringe benefits). Unless health costs are *curbed,* it may also be impossible to subdue federal budget *deficits.* Between 1965 and 1992, health costs (mainly for Medicare and Medicaid) rose from 2.5 to 16 percent of federal outlays. By 2000, they could exceed 25 percent.

The final effect of uncontrolled spending is to corrode confidence in the entire medical system. Loss of insurance may not have exploded, but anxiety about it has. Americans correctly sense that a vicious circle is at work. The costlier insurance becomes, the harder it is for individuals and small businesses to afford it. As companies "downsize," more workers worry that they'll become uninsured if laid off. More than a quarter of those with insurance fear losing it, reports a survey done for The Henry J. Kaiser Family Foundation.

The basic cause of the spending explosion is the *volatile* mix of generous insurance and high-tech medicine. The two have fed each other. The more expensive medicine became, the more people wanted protection against its costs. In 1960, patients paid 56 percent of health costs out of their own pockets; by 1991, that was only 22 percent. But the more insurance Americans had, the more doctors and hospitals resorted to expensive technology. Patients wanted the best and doctors could order whatever seemed necessary, because someone else paid.

It's wrong to dismiss high-tech medicine merely as the excesses of the health-industrial complex: expensive gadgets and drugs peddled by doctors *enriching* themselves. Many new drugs really do offer spectacular benefits. In 1977, the first drug (Tagamet) to treat stomach ulcers appeared; more risky and less effective stomach surgery declined sharply. Heart disease is more treatable than ever. Drugs lower blood pressure and dissolve clots. Bypass surgery moves blood around clogged arteries with veins from elsewhere in the body. Since 1963, death rates from heart disease have dropped 56 percent, and some of the decline reflects these advances. (Much of the rest is better diet, less smoking and more exercise).

Even when new treatments don't improve crude health indicators—like life expectancy—they may deliver huge benefits. "A lot of this is quality of life. It's comfort," says economist Henry Aaron of the Brookings Institution. Artificial hips enable grandparents to play with grandchildren. Prozac has relieved depression. Cataract removal allows the elderly to enjoy reading or TV.

But all these medical advances clearly raise total health costs. Indeed, economist Joseph Newhouse of Harvard attributes roughly half of the recent increases in health spending to new medical technologies (much of the rest stems from rising population and *inflation*). The reasons are clear. Some lifesaving procedures are hugely expensive. A liver transplant and follow-up treatment cost $300,000 in the first year, reports the consulting firm Milliman & Robertson. Once a new advance occurs, its use explodes—and there's a tendency to overuse. Between 1970 and 1991, the number of annual bypass operations rose from 14,000 to 407,000. At first, patients were younger. As surgeons' skills improved, older patients (who have less to gain from surgery) became candidates, too.

Finally, high-tech medicine creates a grim *paradox:* the more it extends life, the more it raises the cost of living longer. The *beneficiary* of today's bypass surgery may have a heart attack in five years or develop cancer. Medical advances can be cost-effective in treating individual illnesses, even while raising a person's lifetime health costs. The trouble with our present system is that it imposes no discipline on spending. Open-ended insurance *reimbursement* makes it in doctors' self-interest to provide more treatment. It's often hard to know in advance who will benefit, and patients expect the best.

Any health reform that *curbs* costs must impose some limits. Doctors and/or patients will lose some freedom in determining care. The health care debate is so morally discomforting precisely because it poses questions few of us want to face, either individually or as a society. When do we give up hope for a loved one? Can we embrace medical technology without becoming its victim? In general, we don't believe limits are necessary. A survey done for The Robert Wood Johnson Foundation asked respondents what *restrictions* might be acceptable on insurance to cut costs. Three quarters of the respondents rejected limiting transplants; 70 percent opposed limiting personal choice of doctors or hospitals; 61 percent opposed restricting specialized services to regional medical centers requiring an hour's driving time. . . .

Our **dilemma** is that a system that provides **unbounded** benefits for all of us as individuals will hurt all of us as a society. It will squeeze private incomes and burden government. Yet we all feel uneasy at placing limits on care for family, friends or almost anyone. Ours is a society highly sensitive to individual rights and ever optimistic about the possibilities of improving life. The dilemma will only intensify as America ages and medical technology advances. By 2020, the over-65 population could hit nearly 17 percent, up from 12.5 percent in 1990. Biotechnology makes possible new treatments for everything from cystic fibrosis to cancer.

The health-care debate is **ultimately** a giant guessing game about what kind of system best balances society's need for economic discipline with individuals' need for dignity. No reform can give us everything we want—lower costs, more medicine and total freedom. If we deny choices, we cannot have an honest debate. The debate will have lasting value only if it makes us more accepting of the shortcomings of any health care system. We cannot have an ideal system, but maybe we can have a less imperfect one. □

 Determining Meaning

PART I DIRECTIONS: *Using the generative strategy of the vocabulary card, write a definition, synonym, antonym, and part of speech for each word below. Remember to select the most appropriate definition on the basis of how the word is used in the reading. Be sure to pay particular attention to the words that you missed in the pretest. In addition, find a minimum of two more words from "Health Care: How We Got Into This Mess" with which you are unfamiliar, and make vocabulary cards for those words also.*

1. ambiguous
2. autonomy
3. batteries
4. beneficiary
5. compensation
6. crank
7. curbs (ed)

8. deficits
9. devastating
10. dilemma
11. enriching
12. fosters
13. impersonal
14. inflation

15. massive	21. unbounded
16. paradox	22. universal
17. reimbursement	23. volatile
18. restrictions	24.
19. scourge	25.
20. ultimately	

PART II DIRECTIONS: Select any three words from the list above and create images to help you remember the word. You might want to go back to Chapter 2 and reread the section on imagery. You also might want to look at the example given for Reading A. Put these three images on your vocabulary cards.

PART III DIRECTIONS: There are several targeted words that have multiple meanings, all of which are very different from one another. First, go back and read the context for each of the words below. Then read the definition that you wrote on your vocabulary card from Part I. Now find another meaning as well as the part of speech for the targeted word and write this new information in the space provided below. (Note: The "new" definition may actually be the one with which you are more familiar.)

1. **batteries**

    part of speech: _____

    new definition: _____

    _____

2. **crank**

    part of speech: _____

    new definition: _____

    _____

3. curbs

part of speech: _____

new definition: _____

_____

 Trying Out Meaning

DIRECTIONS: Read each sentence carefully. If the boldfaced word is used correctly, circle C and go on to the next item. If, however, the boldfaced word is used incorrectly, circle I and then make the sentence correct.

C   I   **1.** The *impersonal* nature of large universities *fosters* very small classes and lots of interactions with faculty.

C   I   **2.** The *crank* psychologist's suggestions had *devastating* effects on the decisions Carla made.

C   I   **3.** The *massive* budget *deficit* is one reason why health care costs have climbed.

C   I   **4.** *Universal* health care is reserved only for those who can afford it.

C   I   **5.** The situation was so *volatile* that the police decided it wasn't worth responding to the call.

C   I   **6.** When we are children, we are very *autonomous* individuals.

C   I   **7.** George was the *beneficiary* of many of his father's belongings, which totally *enriched* his life.

C   I   **8.** Tonya's teacher said that her writing was so *ambiguous* that everything in her paper was clear and easy to understand.

C   I   **9.** *Inflation* in the economy usually makes everyone happy since prices tend to fall.

C   I   **10.** Alex tried to ***curb*** his eating by going to an "all you can eat for $5.00" restaurant several times a week.

C   I   **11.** Kendall ***ultimately*** decided to major in biochemistry since she wanted to become a doctor someday.

C   I   **12.** ***Reimbursement*** for a job well done often comes in the form of ***compensation*** other than money.

C   I   **13.** Andrew's parents were faced with the ***dilemma*** of either putting him on ***restrictions*** or not giving him his weekly allowance because he had not even started his assigned chores.

C   I   **14.** The ***scourge*** of deadly diseases such as AIDS has made us realize that our medical resources are ***unbounded.***

C   I   **15.** The ***paradox*** of our health care system is that it is not available to everyone in the same manner.

 Applying Meaning

DIRECTIONS: Select the word from the target word list which best answers each of the questions below. Each word will be used only once. You might have to add or delete an ending in order to put the target word in its proper form.

1. Which word describes the economy when prices of goods and services increase?

_____

2. Which word describes what a tornado does to anything that comes in its path?

_____

3. Which word describes health care that is given to all people regardless of how much money they earn?

_____

4. Which word describes someone's personality that is nice one minute and the next minute throwing things?

_____

5. Which word describes the plot of a play that could have one of several interpretations?

_____

6. Which word describes what you would be if your rich uncle died and left you all his money?

_____

7. Which word describes what you have on your hands if you have two dates on the same night?

_____

8. Which word tells what you are doing if you cut back on the amount of money you spend?

_____

9. Which *two words* describe what your boss might give you if you spent your own money to throw a party for his out-of-town guests?

_____

10. Which word describes a college student who refuses to take any money or support from her parents?

_____

11. Which word describes something very large (such as an iceberg) or very severe (such as a heart attack)?

_____

12. Which word describes universities where you are "just a number" or corporations where you are "just a paycheck"?

_____

13. Which word describes a phone call you might receive in which someone says bizarre and strange things?

_____

14. Which word describes something that might not be necessary but improves the quality of your life?

_____

15. Which word describes land that seems endless, without fences or borders?

_____

16. Which word describes the limitations that some manufacturers put on their warranties or that airlines put on special ticket prices?

_____

17. Which word describes what you have when you spend more money than you can pay back?

_____

18. Which word tells what world leaders try to do during peace negotiations? They try to _____ peace.

19. The following is an example of which word? The longer people live, the higher medical costs become. _____

_____

20. Which word describes things like war, crime, or murder?

_____

21. Which word has to do with your highest goal?

_____

22. Which word describes several series of tests that you may have to take if the doctor cannot figure out what is wrong with you?

_____

Reciting and Reviewing

Conceptualizing Meaning

DIRECTIONS: When you can provide an example of something, you generally have a good conceptual knowledge of the word. Follow the instructions below, and if necessary, explain your choice.

1. Give an example of a *paradox.* _____

_____

2. Give an example of an *impersonal* question. _____

_____

3. Give an example of when you might take a *battery* of tests.

_____

4. Give an example of a health care *dilemma.* _____

_____

5. Give an example of something you do or have just because it is

enriching. _____

_____

6. Give an example of something that *fosters* racism or sexism.

_____

7. Give an example of one thing in life that you would

   ultimately like to accomplish. _____

8. Give an example of something that might *curb* your desire to

   smoke. _____

9. Give an example of an *ambiguous* invitation. _____

   _____

10. Give an example of a situation that might become *volatile.*

    _____

11. Give an example of something a *crank* repairman might do to

    your car. _____

    _____

12. Give an example of something that has happened because of

    inflation in health care. _____

    _____

13. Give an example of something that is *universal* in college

    students' lives. _____

    _____

14. Give an example of something that would happen if there were

    a *deficit* in your bank account. _____

    _____

15. Give an example of a situation in which it might be good to have *restrictions.* _____

_____

16. Give an example of when you might feel *autonomous.* _____

_____

17. Give an example of something you might do in order to receive *compensation.* _____

_____

18. Give an example of when you might become a *beneficiary.* ___

_____

19. Give an example of something that might happen if you were not *reimbursed* for your business expenses. _____

_____

20. Give an example of something that is a *scourge* to society.

_____

21. Give an example of a disease that is *devastating.* _____

_____

22. Give an example of what might happen in a *massive* automobile accident. _____

_____

23. Give an example of why *unbounded* health benefits may be a

bad rather than a good idea. _____

_____

◨ Self-Evaluating

DIRECTIONS: Think about the words that you have studied in this reading. List in Column A those for which you have a conceptual understanding. In Column B, list the words for which you have just a partial understanding. In Column C, list the words for which you have no understanding or just a definitional understanding. You should study and review the words listed in Columns B and C before beginning the next reading.

Column A	Column B	Column C
_____	_____	_____
_____	_____	_____
_____	_____	_____
_____	_____	_____
_____	_____	_____
_____	_____	_____
_____	_____	_____
_____	_____	_____
_____	_____	_____
_____	_____	_____
_____	_____	_____

Extending and Challenging

PART I DIRECTIONS: Complete the analogies below using one of the targeted vocabulary words listed below. Remember to keep the same part of speech across the analogy. Refer to the examples on page 212 in Chapter 6.

 Targeted Vocabulary Words

enrich	foster	paradox
unbounded	devastate	autonomy
surcharge	volatile	

1. crank: legitimate : : _____ : restrictions

2. massive: huge : : _____ : self-supporting

3. clear: ambiguous : : build-up: _____

4. solve: _____ : : enrich: life

5. perk: incentive : : tax: _____

6. encourage: _____ : : forbid: prohibit

PART II DIRECTIONS: Each of the words listed below can be used in a general sense or to specifically talk about health-related fields in some way. Go back over your vocabulary cards and the previous activities (if necessary), and then explain how each of the target words below is specifically related to health-related areas. The first one has been done for you.

1. *crank* Doctors or therapists who are cranks would be able to collect for services that probably are not helping their patient if there was universal health care coverage.

2. *universal* _____

_____

_____

3. *impersonal* _____

_____

_____

4. *deficits* _____

_____

_____

5. *inflation* _____

_____

_____

6. *restrictions* _____

_____

_____

7. *communicable* _____

_____

_____

8. *incentives* _____

_____

_____

PART III WRITING ACTIVITIES DIRECTIONS: Read the following questions and then answer them based on what you have read in Readings A and B. When you write out your answers, try to use as many of the vocabulary words as possible.

1. How does cigarette smoking affect the cost of health care today? _____

   _____

   _____

   _____

   _____

2. Do you believe that health care should be ***universal?*** Should people who engage in habits known to be harmful to health be included in ***universal*** coverage? Why or why not? _____

   _____

   _____

   _____

   _____

   _____

3. The author of "Health Care: How We Got Into This Mess"

states that "high-tech medicine created a grim *paradox.*"

What does he mean? Do you agree? Why or why not? _____

_____

_____

_____

_____

_____

4. Write a journal entry that expresses your viewpoint on what health care should look like in the future. Use as many of the new words you have learned as you can in your writing.

 Posttest I—Readings A and B

DIRECTIONS: Now you are ready for the first posttest for this chapter. Please see your instructor in order to receive a copy of the posttest for Readings A and B.

Reading C

AIDS

by Joseph S. Levine and Kenneth R. Miller

 **Targeted Words**

General	Content-Specific
asymptomatic	AIDS (acquired immune deficiency syndrome)
conduits	antibodies
confirmed	contagious
contaminated	cyclosporin
detect	defense mechanism
ensured	epidemiologists
epidemic	evolution
heterosexually	hemophiliacs
impaired	HIV (human immunodeficiency virus)
insidious	hypodermic
isolated	immune system
latency	intravenous
legions	Kaposi's sarcoma
misconceptions	malaria
predominant	microorganisms
prevalence	opportunistic infections
prudent	pathogen
quarantining	
recipients	
sophisticated	

spawn

stigmatized

suppressed

transmission(tted)

Pneumocystis carinni

protozoan

yellow fever

 Pretest—General Words

DIRECTIONS: The general words in the pretest will be introduced in the reading selection entitled "AIDS." Before reading the selection, however, take the pretest by selecting the word that best completes the sentence. Then rate your present knowledge of the boldfaced word by circling 1, 2, or 3, depending on how familiar you are with the word.

1. To **spawn** a debate about something is to
   a. end it
   b. enjoy it.
   c. believe it.
   d. encourage it.

   Level of Understanding   1   2   3

2. **Sophisticated** techniques would be
   a. immature.
   b. complex.
   c. easily understood.
   d. incomprehensible.

   Level of Understanding   1   2   3

3. When scientists **isolate** a gene they
   a. cut it up.
   b. destroy it.
   c. set it apart from others.
   d. try to alter it.

   Level of Understanding   1   2   3

4. If you **ensure** your findings you
   a. guarantee they are correct.
   b. find the errors.
   c. tell others about them.
   d. destroy them and start over.

   Level of Understanding   1   2   3

5. A person with *legions* of allergies would
   a. love it when spring came.
   b. only be allergic to one thing.
   c. be allergic to many things.
   d. have no allergies.
   Level of Understanding   1   2   3

6. One who is *heterosexual* might
   a. ask someone of the same sex for a date.
   b. ask someone of the opposite sex for a date.
   c. never go out on a date.
   d. be afraid of all sexual interactions.
   Level of Understanding   1   2   3

7. An *epidemic* would
   a. make millions of people ill.
   b. have very little effect.
   c. affect only children.
   d. be confined to a small area.
   Level of Understanding   1   2   3

8. If a disease is *insidious* it would be
   a. easy to stop the spread of.
   b. easy to identify.
   c. cured quickly.
   d. dangerous.
   Level of Understanding   1   2   3

9. If you have a *misconception* about something you
   a. have a good understanding of it.
   b. have the wrong idea about it.
   c. understand nothing about it.
   d. understood it at one time, but now you do not.
   Level of Understanding   1   2   3

10. If your vision is *impaired* you
    a. have perfect vision.
    b. don't need glasses.
    c. can't see very well.
    d. are totally blind.
    Level of Understanding   1   2   3

11. When you *suppress* a sneeze you
    a. try to stop it.
    b. make yourself sneeze.
    c. sneeze really loudly.
    d. sneeze several times in a row.

                                    Level of Understanding 1   2   3

12. To *contaminate* something is to
    a. clean it.
    b. tear it.
    c. contain it.
    d. make it impure.

                                    Level of Understanding 1   2   3

13. When you *confirm* your reservations you
    a. cancel them.
    b. change them.
    c. discuss them.
    d. verify them.

                                    Level of Understanding 1   2   3

14. When you *detect* smoke you
    a. discover it.
    b. ignore it.
    c. fear it.
    d. appreciate it.

                                    Level of Understanding 1   2   3

15. If you are the *recipient* of a gift you
    a. return it.
    b. receive it.
    c. evaluate it.
    d. pay for it.

                                    Level of Understanding 1   2   3

16. People who are *asymptomatic*
    a. are in the final stages of a disease.
    b. have a disease but show no symptoms.
    c. have early symptoms of a disease.
    d. were exposed to a disease but will never get it.

                                    Level of Understanding 1   2   3

17. When animals are *quarantined* they are
    a. isolated.
    b. destroyed.
    c. starved.
    d. separated by gender.
    Level of Understanding 1   2   3

18. A *prevalence* of bacteria in the water supply would mean that
    a. no bacteria were present.
    b. a small number of bacteria were present.
    c. only harmful bacteria were present.
    d. an abundance of bacteria were present.
    Level of Understanding 1   2   3

19. When you are *stigmatized* you are
    a. congratulated.
    b. noticed.
    c. ignored.
    d. labeled.
    Level of Understanding 1   2   3

20. During a *latency* period an animal might
    a. be very active.
    b. eat more than usual.
    c. rest.
    d. mate.
    Level of Understanding 1   2   3

21. People who are *prudent* with their money
    a. spend most of it.
    b. give it to their heirs.
    c. live in large homes and drive expensive cars.
    d. spend and save wisely.
    Level of Understanding 1   2   3

22. A *conduit* for a disease would be
    a. how it spreads.
    b. how it is described.
    c. how contagious it is.
    d. where it was found.
    Level of Understanding 1   2   3

Number Correct _____

Level of Understanding

1 _____

2 _____

3 _____

 Pretest—Content-Specific Words

DIRECTIONS: For each term list as many descriptions and characteristics as possible based on your knowledge of the word. Then rate your present knowledge of the word by circling either 1, 2, or 3, depending on how much information you already possess about the word.

1. pathogen   **2.** evolution

_____   _____

_____   _____

_____   _____

1   2   3   1   2   3

AIDS

by Joseph S. Levine and Kenneth R. Miller

And I looked and beheld a pale horse: and his name that sat on him was Death. —Revelations 6:8

That a new disease should appear is not in itself surprising; the jungles of equatorial Africa *spawn* diseases new to science with alarming regularity. But this disease was caused by a virus close to perfection in terms of pathogen evolution. Not only had this pathogen developed ways to avoid every single defense mechanism of the immune system, but is also attacked that system directly, lived inside it, and destroyed it. This was the virus that came to be called HIV—the human immunodeficiency virus.

HIV spread through central Africa, where it went unrecognized for years, both because its victims died of other, already recognized diseases and because *sophisticated* medical care was usually wanting. It spread slowly to Europe and to Haiti, and then to the United States, Latin America, and Asia. There the first *isolated* cases—a few in Europe and one or two in the United States in the mid-1970s—were puzzles that left physicians wringing their hands helplessly and scratching their heads in amazement. Their patients were dying of infections from microorganisms they should have fought off easily, and no one could imagine why.

Finally, the virus found its way into two Western populations whose behaviors *ensured* its explosive spread: the gay community, where sexual freedom was a way of life, and the *legions* of intravenous drug users whose ritual sharing of needles spread infected blood with deadly speed and efficiency. At about the same time, the disease began to spread among *heterosexually* active individuals throughout central Africa.

These recognized modes of HIV *transmission*—through sexual activity and via infected blood—seriously interfered with world society's ability to react to and ultimately to control this new disease. Many medical researchers and science journalists note that AIDS has brought out both the best and the worst in everyone connected with the *epidemic.* On the one hand, we have learned more about this *insidious* virus in a shorter period of time than we have about nearly any other disease in history. On the other hand, fear, prejudice, and denial created major obstacles to effective action to protect the health of those at risk of infection. Because AIDS remains incurable, and because it presents a threat to the health of many Americans, we will try to correct some of the *misconceptions* about AIDS by reviewing what is now known about its history and mode of action.

The History of AIDS in the United States

In the early 1980s, physicians in California and New York noticed an increasing number of patients with unusual infections and a form of skin cancer so rare that most cancer specialists had never even seen a case before. The infections, including a type of pneumonia attributed to *Pneumocystis carinni* (a proto-zoan), were caused by organisms that are common in the environment and cause serious disease only in extremely rare cases. The purple skin tumors were identified as *Kaposi's sarcoma,* a cancer normally seen only in elderly patients with impaired immune systems or in patients whose immune systems had been *suppressed* with drugs such as cyclosporin.

Thoughtful physicians soon recognized that these were opportunistic infections—infections that were successful only because the immune system of the patient was impaired for some other reason. The first six recognized cases of the disease were described in Los Angeles in 1981, and the name AIDS (for acquired immune deficiency syndrome) was suggested for the disorder.

Because the disease was first reported among gay men, physicians—rather than looking immediately for an infectious agent—assumed that something about these men's lifestyles led to the breakdown of the immune response. But a few epidemiologists conducted studies among the growing number of gay and IV-drug-using AIDS patients. They suggested by the fall of 1981 that AIDS was a contagious disease that might be spread through blood (by the sharing of *contaminated* needles) and sexual intercourse. By 1982, the first cases of AIDS were reported among infants born to infected mothers and among hemophiliacs and surgical patients who had received transfusions of blood or blood products.

Then, in 1983, Luc Montagnier and his associates at the Institut Louis Pasteur in France announced that a virus had been identified as the cause of AIDS. The discovery was quickly **confirmed** by a team led by Robert Gallo at the National Institutes of Health in the United States. Federal funds were released to support development of a test to **detect** AIDS in donated blood, and all blood donated in the United States has been screened for antibodies to the virus since 1986. Research on the disease is now progressing in laboratories all over the world, and we have learned a great deal about the biology of AIDS in a relatively brief period of time.

The Spread of HIV Infection

Although a cure for AIDS has not yet been developed, we are certain how the disease is spread: through blood, through sexual intercourse, and from infected mother to unborn child. It is important to realize that AIDS is not exclusively a "gay and bisexual" disease. An unknown number of heterosexual transfusion **recipients,** hemophiliacs, intravenous drug users, and the sexual partners of all these individuals are currently carrying the virus though they show no signs of infection. These **asymptomatic** carriers are probably concentrated in major metropolitan areas, but the mobility of American society makes it likely that significant numbers of them have traveled widely across the nation. Because there is so much confusion and inaccurate information about the transmission of AIDS, we will examine the biologically relevant facts in detail.

How AIDS Is *Not* Transmitted

Although AIDS is one of the deadliest diseases known, it is *not* easy to catch. Numerous studies conducted over several years have shown that AIDS is *not* **transmitted** through casual contact. There is *no* evidence that HIV can spread via food or water or through coughing, sneezing, dry kissing, hugging, or sharing clothing, bedding, or eating utensils. Everyday contact with AIDS victims, including shaking hands and engaging in close conversation, poses no risk of infection. There is, therefore, neither purpose in nor need of **quarantining** or isolating either HIV-positive individuals or AIDS patients.

There is no evidence that AIDS can be transmitted by mosquitoes. The mosquito that transmits (malaria) cannot carry (yellow fever) and vice versa. Furthermore, the bite of the mosquito transmits malaria only because the disease-causing organism enters the insect's salivary glands. There is no evidence that HIV either lives in the mosquito's system or enters its salivary secretions. Because the insect does not actually inject blood from a previous meal into new victims, there is no way for a mosquito bite to transmit this particular disease. Authorities and the media often referred to "high-risk groups," by which they meant gay and bisexual men and intravenous drug users. It is now clear that the disease is not restricted to any specific group of people. Rather, the disease can be contracted by anyone who engages in specific high-risk *behaviors*. Those behaviors are clearly identifiable: sexual intercourse of any kind and the sharing of (hypodermic) syringes.

Sexual transmission   The initial **prevalence** of AIDS in the United States among non-drug-using gay men, many of whom practice anal intercourse, misled many people into thinking that AIDS is not transmitted through vaginal intercourse. Across most of Africa, however, heterosexual intercourse is the **predominant** mode of transmission and the ratio of infected females to infected males is close to 1:1. Some individuals insist that differences in sexual practices between Africa and the United States make it unlikely that heterosexual transmission has occurred or will occur here. Most responsible physicians and researchers, however, now agree that this is not the case. Estimates of the number of Americans already infected with HIV range from 500,000 to nearly 2 million. Estimates of the global HIV-infected population also vary widely, in part because many countries have not reported the disease to the World Health Organization until recently for fear of being **stigmatized.**

Luckily, it does not appear that the virus is spreading explosively through the population at large, as some researchers feared it would; the number of infected individuals outside of those participating in high-risk behaviors is still small. But because of the virus's long **latency** period, because of uncertainty about the rate of transmission through heterosexual intercourse, and because of an almost total lack of knowledge about the sexual activities of the American public, **prudent** epidemiologists advise caution.

Sharing of syringes   The AIDS virus is clearly transmitted in the infected blood spread from person to person through the use of shared needles among intravenous drug users. In 1988, estimates of the percentage of intravenous drug users who are infected with the AIDS virus ranged from 50 to 75 percent in various parts of the country. Because AIDS is spread through sexual activity, the sexual partners of intravenous drug users are directly at risk and—if sexually active themselves—may serve as *conduits* for the virus into non-drug-using populations.

Transmission from mother to fetus   The AIDS virus easily crosses the placenta from the mother's blood supply to that of the fetus. The percentage of babies born to infected mothers, many of whom are non-drug-using sexual partners of intravenous drug users, is rising annually. By early 1988, nearly 2 percent of the babies born in New York State tested positive for HIV.

Transfusion-borne AIDS   Before 1985, there were numerous cases in which the HIV infection was transmitted to hemophiliacs and surgical patients through transfusions of infected blood. Such cases have been nearly eliminated by two concurrent strategies:

1. The nation's blood supply is now screened for antibodies to HIV, and public health officials assure us that the nation's blood supply is safe. Because not all infected persons produce antibodies to the virus at all times, however, and because of the *latency* period between infection and first antibody production, it is possible for the blood that tests antibody-negative to carry the AIDS virus. Intensive research and development are currently in progress to develop a commercially usable test for minute quantities of viral RNA. This technique will further minimize the risk of transmission through transfusion.

2. The blood industry is doing everything it can to discourage potentially infected individuals from donating blood in the first place.
   Note that because all licensed health care providers use sterile equipment when handling blood and blood products, it is virtually impossible to contract AIDS when giving blood at a recognized and licensed blood-donating facility. □

Determining Meaning—General Words

PART I DIRECTIONS: Using the generative strategy of the vocabulary card, write a definition, synonym, antonym, and part of speech for each word below. Remember to select the most appropriate definition on the basis of how the word is used in the reading. Be sure to pay particular attention to the words that you missed in the pretest. In addition, find a minimum of two more words from "AIDS" with which you are unfamiliar, and make vocabulary cards for those words also.

1. asymptomatic	14. misconceptions
2. conduits	15. predominant
3. confirmed	16. prevalence
4. contaminated	17. prudent
5. detect	18. quarantining
6. ensured	19. recipients
7. epidemic	20. sophisticated
8. heterosexually	21. spawn
9. impaired	22. stigmatized
10. insidious	23. suppressed
11. isolated	24. transmission (transmitted)
12. latency	25.
13. legions	26.

*PART II DIRECTIONS: Create mnemonics to help you remember the words **prudent** and **insidious**. You can use imagery or another kind of mnemonic. Put these on your vocabulary cards and use them when you recite and review your words.*

To help you remember **prudent,** you might use a combination of imagery and the keyword strategy. **Prudent,** which means a wise and practical handling of something or using good judgment, contains the smaller word **dent.** You might image a woman named **Prudence** who refused to put a **dent** in the money she had saved. **Prudence** was being **prudent** in saving her money rather than spending all of it.

Now see if you can create a mnemonic for **insidious.**

PART III DIRECTIONS: As you read in Chapter 4, knowing and understanding word parts can help you figure out word meanings. There are several words in this list that use prefixes. First, write the meaning of the prefixes given. Second, write down the meaning of the targeted word. Third, list another word that uses the same prefix, and finally, tell what your word means.

1. *hetero-* means _____

   heterosexual means _____

   my word: _____

   meaning: _____

2. *mis-* means _____

   misconceptions means_____

   my word: _____

   meaning: _____

3. *epi-* means _____

   epidemic means _____

   my word: _____

   meaning: _____

4. *a-* means _____

   asymptomatic means _____

   my word: _____

   meaning: _____

5. *pre-* means_____

   predominant means _____

   my word: _____

   meaning: _____

Determining Meaning—Content-Specific Words

PART I DIRECTIONS: Using the vocabulary card format described in Chapter 2, write a definition and examples or characteristics for each of the content-specific words below. In some cases, you will be able to use context (c), and in other cases, you will have to rely either partially or solely on a dictionary definition (d). Occasionally you might be able to use your own prior knowledge (pk). (You might wish to skim Chapter 3 before beginning this activity.) Occasionally you will have to rely solely on a dictionary definition. Hints are provided in parentheses following each word.

1. pathogen (c/d)
2. evolution (d)
3. defense mechanism (pk/d)
4. immune system (d)
5. HIV (human immunodeficiency virus) (c/pk)
6. microorganisms (d)
7. intravenous (c/d)
8. *Pneumocystis carinni* (c)
9. protozoan (d)
10. Kaposi's sarcoma (c)
11. AIDS (acquired immune deficiency syndrome) (c/d/pk)
12. cyclosporin (c/d)
13. opportunistic infections (c)
14. epidemiologists (d)
15. contagious (c/d)
16. hemophiliacs (c/d)
17. malaria (d/pk)
18. yellow fever (d/pk)
19. hypodermic (c/d)
20. antibodies (d)

PART II DIRECTIONS: After you have determined the meaning for all content-specific words, discuss them with a partner or your instructor as a way of gaining additional understanding of the terms.

Organizing Concepts

DIRECTIONS: Look at the headings in "AIDS." Then, using both general and content-specific terms, use the generative group and label strategy to organize the words around the following headings. Some terms may be included in two or more headings if appropriate. Be prepared to explain and justify your ideas in class.

AIDS

History of

1980 – CA & NY _____

_____

_____

_____

_____

1981 – LA   <u>AIDS named</u>

1982   _____

1983 – France   <u>virus identified and_____</u>

How NOT _____

(_____)

1. casual contact

_____ not necessary

2. mosquitos

Spread of

How _____

1. Sex

2. Drugs

_____

_____

Beginning Conceptual Understanding

*PART I DIRECTIONS: From your readings of "AIDS," finish each of the following sentences by explaining how each of the following is related to the disease **AIDS**. The first one has been completed for you.*

1. ***Pathogen evolution*** is related to ***AIDS*** because AIDS is <u>caused by an agent (pathogen). This pathogen changes or evolves so that the body cannot fight it.</u>

2. ***HIV*** is related to ***AIDS*** _____

_____

_____

3. *Pneumocystis carinni* is related to **AIDS** _____

_____

_____

4. *Kaposi's sarcoma* is related to **AIDS** _____

_____

_____

5. *Epidemiologists* are related to **AIDS** _____

_____

_____

6. *Hemophiliacs* are related to **AIDS** _____

_____

_____

7. *Hypodermic* is related to **AIDS** _____

_____

_____

8. The *immune system* is related to **AIDS** _____

_____

_____

9. *Intravenous* is related to **AIDS** _____

_____

_____

PART II DIRECTIONS: Respond to each of the following statements or questions. Some of the answers are stated in the article, but others are related to applications of the words and will require you to think about and generate your own answers. Your answers should reflect understanding of the boldfaced words.

1. What would happen if your **immune system** were

    suppressed? _____

    _____

2. Why are individuals who are **HIV** positive often **stigmatized?**

    _____

    _____

3. List two **misconceptions** about **AIDS.** _____

    _____

4. Where were the first **isolated** cases of **AIDS?** _____

    _____

5. Name two **predominant** ways that **AIDS** can be

    transmitted. _____

    _____

    _____

6. Do you think that the number of **AIDS** cases is of **epidemic**

    proportion? Why or why not? _____

    _____

7. What is an **opportunistic** infection? _____

    _____

8. Name two diseases for which individuals may be

quarantined. _____

_____

9. Why are people who are *HIV* positive often *asymptomatic?*

_____

_____

10. What is the relation between *contaminated hypodermic*

needles and *HIV?* _____

_____

11. What do the words *microorganisms* and *protozoa* have in

common?_____

_____

12. What might happen if your *immune system* is *impaired?*

_____

_____

13. Why is *AIDS* referred to as an *insidious* disease? _____

_____

_____

14. How was the *HIV* virus first *detected?* _____

_____

15. In what part of the world is there a *prevalence* of people who are *HIV* positive?_____

16. At this point, what is *ensured* to happen to an *HIV* recipient? _____

_____

17. What is meant when we say that *HIV* is a *latent* virus? _____

_____

18. Why should everyone be *prudent* in his or her sexual practices?_____

_____

Using Concepts

DIRECTIONS: Use one of the words from the general list in each of the blanks below. Use vocabulary cards you created in Determining Meaning *to help you select the best word. Each word is used only once, but you may need to change its form.*

1. Which word describes incorrect ideas that people have about something? _____

2. Which words describes an idea that is advanced or complex?

_____

3. Which word describes those who receive something?

_____

4. Which word is an antonym for clean or pure?

_____

5. Which two words describe what HIV does to one's immune system? _____

6. Which word is the antonym for homosexual?

_____

7. Which word describes something that is dangerous or harmful?_____

8. Which word describes what researchers try to do with viruses in order to study them? _____

9. Which word tells what you should do if you want to be sure that a restaurant has your dinner reservations correct?

_____

10. Which word tells what you should be with your money now if you want to be rich in the future? _____

11. Which word describes someone who is HIV positive but has no outward signs of the virus?_____

12. Which word tells what health officials used to do to people who had diseases that were contagious? _____

13. Which word describes what we might call a sudden outbreak of measles in which thousands of people come down with the disease? _____

14. Which word tells what you would try to do if you thought your office was bugged? _____

_____

15. Which two words have to do with an abundance or what is most important? _____

16. Which word describes what happens to you if you are disgraced? _____

17. Which word describes many or groups of people?

_____

18. Which word tells what you have done when you have given someone a cold or other illness? _____

_____

19. Which word describes something, like talent, that has the potential to develop but has not yet developed?

_____

20. Which word means to cause or to give rise to?

_____

21. Which word describes the person who would pass HIV to another person? _____

Reciting and Reviewing

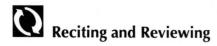 **Comprehending Concepts**

DIRECTIONS: The questions below are based on your understanding of the content-specific words, some of the general words, and many of the key concepts presented in the reading "AIDS." At this point, you should be able to answer the questions without looking at the text excerpt, your vocabulary cards, or your organizing strategies.

1. How does the *intravenous* use of shared *hypodermic*

   needles *spawn* the *transmission* of HIV?_____

   _____

   _____

2. Why are *Kaposi's sarcoma* and *Pneumocystis carinni* both

   considered *opportunistic infections?* _____

   _____

   _____

3. What happens when *pathogens* are able to avoid the *defense*

   mechanisms of the *immune system?* _____

   _____

   _____

4. What happens to *hemophiliacs* if they are the *conduits* for

   contaminated blood? _____

   _____

5. How do we know that **AIDS** is not *transmitted* in the same way that *malaria* and *yellow fever* are?_____

_____

_____

6. What role do *antibodies* play in *detecting AIDS* in the nation's blood supply?_____

_____

7. Explain some of the research that *epidemiologists* are conducting that examines the *contagiousness* of **AIDS.**_____

_____

_____

8. Describe the *evolution* of **HIV.** _____

_____

_____

9. What role does *cyclosporin* play in the *immune system?* What might *cyclosporin* be used for? _____

_____

_____

10. Why is **HIV** considered a *microorganism?*_____

_____

PART II WRITING ACTIVITY DIRECTIONS: The following essay questions represent what you might have to answer on an exam in a college course related to the health care professions. For each question, write a clear and specific answer without referring to your vocabulary cards or to your chapter excerpt.

1. There are many misconceptions about how HIV is transmitted. Discuss these misconceptions as well as why you think that the misconceptions came about.

   _____

   _____

   _____

   _____

   _____

   _____

2. Trace the history of AIDS in the United States. Include in your answer why epidemiologists think that the disease is "new."

   _____

   _____

   _____

   _____

   _____

 **Self-Evaluating**

DIRECTIONS: Think about the words that you have studied in this reading. List those for which you have a conceptual understanding in Column A. In Column B, list the words for which you have just a partial understanding. In Column C, list the words for which you have no understanding or just a definitional understanding. You should study and review the words listed in Columns B and C before beginning the next reading.

Column A	Column B	Column C
_____	_____	_____
_____	_____	_____
_____	_____	_____
_____	_____	_____
_____	_____	_____
_____	_____	_____
_____	_____	_____
_____	_____	_____
_____	_____	_____
_____	_____	_____

 Posttest II for Readings A, B, and C

DIRECTIONS: Now you are ready for the second posttest for this chapter. Please see your instructor in order to receive a copy of Posttest II for Readings A, B, and C.

8

Readings Concerning the Environment

Did You Know?
The word *stigma* originated from a Greek custom. They would place an identifying brand or *stigma* on slaves, criminals, and soldiers. Today a *stigma* is a mark of shame.

In this thematic chapter you will be reading three very different articles concerning aspects of pollution in our environment. Because the environment is such a critical and important issue, you will probably be exposed to environmental issues in several college courses. You might read about environmental concepts in physical science, chemistry, biology, geography, and perhaps even in sociology courses. Some campuses also offer courses that focus totally on environmental issues. In addition, colleges that offer degrees in forestry and agriculture build entire degrees around environmental studies. This is probably why college graduates tend to be considerably more knowledgeable of and sensitive to the effects and problems of pollution.

The purpose of this chapter is to expose you to numerous words, all drawn from readings that concern the environment. Some of the words are very general and, therefore, could be used across a variety of disciplines or topics. Other words are considerably more content-specific in that you would expect to see them more frequently in articles dealing with the environment than you would in another content area such as history or psychology.

The first reading, "A Fable for Tomorrow," may sound familiar to you since it is an excerpt from the well-known book *Silent Spring* by

327

Rachel Carson. The excerpt, which was written about 30 years ago, describes a town that was at one time streaming with life until plagued by the ugly blight called pollution. As you read this article, think about what Carson says in relation to the city or town from which you come. What kinds of pollutants are evident in your hometown? What are some of the more obvious results of this pollution? Is your city or town doing anything to curb pollution so that what is described in "A Fable for Tomorrow" doesn't happen in every city and town nationwide? This reading has 12 words targeted for learning.

Reading B, "Reusing and Recycling Materials," has 18 targeted words. It also makes some predictions about the future, but it is more specific since the content focuses on what might occur in the future if we fail to recycle materials. This reading also offers reasons why recycling will become imperative in the future. During your reading, think about what you personally do to reuse and recycle materials. What kind of an effort does your family make? What is being done on your campus? What kinds of efforts could you help organize?

The final reading, containing 19 general and 18 content-specific words, is an excerpt taken from a biology textbook chapter. Many of the words can also be found in writings on ecology, geography, or physical science. Words such as *biosphere, ecosystems, pesticides,* and *carbonates* are much more science-related than more general words such as *surmise, lauded,* and *tangible.* Whereas Reading B focused primarily on the recycling problem, this excerpt examines the relation between ecology and economics as well as what is known as the *greenhouse effect,* which has to do with *global warming.* As you are reading this excerpt, look for other articles in newspapers and magazines that discuss global warming. Numerous television shows also discuss this issue, particularly when there seem to be dramatic shifts in weather. Pay attention to those problems that occur in your own area. What has caused the *greenhouse effect?* Is there anything that can be done about it?

Your instructor will probably remind you that you have three options with each unit in this text. After you have finished the activities in Reading A and Reading B, you can choose to:

1. Take **Posttest I** over Readings A and B and skip Reading C.
2. Take **Posttest I** over Readings A and B. Then turn to Reading C and complete those activities. When you have finished, take **Posttest II** over Readings A, B, and C.
3. Turn to Reading C and complete those activities, skipping **Posttest I** altogether. When you have finished, take **Posttest II** over Readings A, B, and C.

Reading these articles, learning the 67 new words contained in them, and thinking and talking about what you have read and learned will help you to understand pollution problems better. It will also give you a vocabulary of concepts on which you can build further knowledge about environmental issues.

Reading A

A Fable for Tomorrow

by Rachel Carson

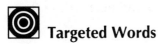 **Targeted Words**

anglers	maladies
blight	moribund
brooded	prosperous
counterparts	specter
droned	stark
harmony	withered

 Pretest

DIRECTIONS: The words in the pretest will be introduced in the reading selection entitled "A Fable for Tomorrow." Before reading the selection, however, take the pretest by answering the questions about each boldfaced vocabulary word. Use the sentence to help you decide the correct answer, and circle that letter. Then rate your present knowledge of the word by circling 1, 2, or 3, depending on how familiar you are with the word. (Check the Introduction to Chapters 5–8 to review scoring procedures.)

1. There was once a town in the heart of America where all life seemed to live in **harmony** with its surroundings.
   Harmony means
   a. conflict.
   b. relation.
   c. agreement.
   d. hardship.

   Level of Understanding   1   2   3

2. The town lay in the midst of a checkerboard of **prosperous** farms, with fields of grain and hillsides of orchards where, in spring, white clouds of bloom drifted above the green fields.
   Prosperous means
   a. well-to-do.
   b. small.
   c. hidden.
   d. useless.

   Level of Understanding   1   2   3

3. Then a strange **blight** crept over the area and everything began to change.
   Blight means
   a. fungus.
   b. disease.
   c. evil.
   d. odor.

   Level of Understanding   1   2   3

4. Some evil spell had settled on the community: mysterious **maladies** swept the flocks of chickens; the cattle and sheep sickened and died.
   Maladies means
   a. sicknesses.
   b. deaths.
   c. weather.
   d. quietness.

   Level of Understanding   1   2   3

5. The few birds seen anywhere were ***moribund;*** they trembled violently and could not fly.
Moribund means
a. slightly ill.
b. crippled.
c. near death.
d. without song.

Level of Understanding   1   2   3

6. On the farms, the hens ***brooded,*** but no chicks hatched.
Brooded means
a. pondered.
b. cackled.
c. mated.
d. sat on eggs.

Level of Understanding   1   2   3

7. The apple trees were coming into bloom but no bees ***droned*** among the blossoms, so there was no pollination and there would be no fruit.
Droned means
a. made a continuous sound.
b. flew from flower to flower.
c. made honey.
d. produced offspring.

Level of Understanding   1   2   3

8. The roadsides, once so attractive, were now lined with browned and ***withered*** vegetation as though swept by fire.
Withered means
a. only a small amount.
b. dried up.
c. extremely hot.
d. attractive.

Level of Understanding   1   2   3

9. ***Anglers*** no longer visited them, for all the fish had died.
Anglers
a. fight.
b. trade.
c. argue.
d. fish.

Level of Understanding   1   2   3

10. This town does not actually exist, but it might easily have a thousand ***counterparts*** in America or elsewhere in the world. ***Counterparts*** means
  a. something with similar characteristics.
  b. opposite in characteristics.
  c. something that does not really exist.
  d. small portions of a whole.

  Level of Understanding   1   2   3

11. A grim ***specter*** has crept upon us almost unnoticed, and this imagined tragedy may easily become a ***stark*** reality we all shall know.
  Specter means
  a. picture.
  b. plague.
  c. reality.
  d. threatening possibility.

  Level of Understanding   1   2   3

12. ***Stark*** (see above sentence) means
  a. naked.
  b. obvious.
  c. harsh.
  d. unrealistic.

  Level of Understanding   1   2   3

PRETEST SCORING DIRECTIONS: Check with your instructor for the answers before beginning the next activity. Give yourself one point for each item that was correct and tally the number of 1s, 2s, and 3s you marked.

Number Correct _____

Level of Understanding

1 _____

2 _____

3 _____

Now read the article "A Fable for Tomorrow," paying attention to the targeted words, particularly those that you missed on the pretest or those for which your level of understanding was low.

A Fable for Tomorrow

by Rachel Carson

There was once a town in the heart of America where all life seemed to live in **harmony** with its surroundings. The town lay in the midst of a checkerboard of **prosperous** farms, with fields of grain and hillsides of orchards where, in spring, white clouds of bloom drifted above the green fields. In autumn, oak and maple and birch set up a blaze of color that flamed and flickered across a backdrop of pines. Then foxes barked in the hills and deer silently crossed the fields, half hidden in the mists of the fall mornings.

Along the roads, laurel, viburnum and alder, great ferns and wildflowers delighted the traveler's eye through much of the year. Even in winter the roadsides were places of beauty, where countless birds came to feed on the berries and on the seed heads of the dried weeds rising above the snow. The countryside was, in fact, famous for the abundance and variety of its bird life, and when the flood of migrants was pouring through in spring and fall people traveled from great distances to observe them. Others came to fish the streams, which flowed clear and cold out of the hills and contained shady pools where trout lay. So it had been from the days many years ago when the first settlers raised their houses, sank their wells, and built their barns.

Then a strange **blight** crept over the area and everything began to change. Some evil spell had settled on the community: mysterious **maladies** swept the flocks of chickens; the cattle and sheep sickened and died. Everywhere was a shadow of death. The farmers spoke of much illness among their families. In the town the doctors had become more and more puzzled by new kinds of sickness appearing among their patients. There had been several sudden and unexplained deaths, not only among adults but even among children, who would be stricken suddenly while at play and die within a few hours.

There was a strange stillness. The birds, for example—where had they gone? Many people spoke of them, puzzled and disturbed. The feeding stations in the backyards were deserted. The few birds seen anywhere were **moribund;** they trembled violently and could not fly. It was a spring without voices. On the mornings that had once throbbed with the dawn chorus of robins, catbirds, doves, jays, wrens, and scores of other bird voices there was now no sound; only silence lay over the fields and woods and marsh.

On the farms the hens **brooded,** but no chicks hatched. The farmers complained that they were unable to raise any pigs—the litters were small and the young survived only a few days. The apple trees were coming into bloom but no bees **droned** among the blossoms, so there was no pollination and there would be no fruit.

The roadsides, once so attractive, were now lined with browned and **withered** vegetation as though swept by fire. These, too, were silent, deserted by all living things. Even the streams were now lifeless. **Anglers** no longer visited them, for all the fish had died.

In the gutters under the eaves and between the shingles of the roofs, a white granular powder still showed a few patches; some weeks before it had fallen like snow upon the roofs and the lawns, the fields and streams.

No witchcraft, no enemy action had silenced the rebirth of new life in this stricken world. The people had done it themselves.

This town does not actually exist, but it might easily have a thousand **counterparts** in America or elsewhere in the world. I know of no community that has experienced all the misfortunes I describe. Yet every one of these disasters has actually happened somewhere, and many real communities have already suffered a substantial number of them. A grim **specter** has crept upon us almost unnoticed, and this imagined tragedy may easily become a **stark** reality we all shall know.

What has already silenced the voices of spring in countless towns in America? This book is an attempt to explain. ☐

Determining Meaning

PART I DIRECTIONS: Using the generative strategy of the vocabulary card, write a definition, synonym, antonym, and part of speech for each of the words below. Remember to select the most appropriate definition on the basis of how the word is used in the reading. Be sure to pay particular attention to the words that you missed in the pretest. In addition, find a minimum of two more words from "A Fable for Tomorrow" with which you are unfamiliar, and make vocabulary cards for those also.

1. anglers
2. blight
3. brooded
4. counterparts
5. droned
6. harmony
7. maladies
8. moribund
9. prosperous
10. specter
11. stark
12. withered
13.
14.

*PART II DIRECTIONS: You might want to try to use imagery to help you remember some of the words. For example, the word **drone** means to go on and on without stopping. **Drone** is also usually associated with the bumblebee, an insect. Therefore, to remember **drone,** you might image the face of someone whom you consider long-winded on the body of a bumblebee. Your image might look something like this:*

*PART III DIRECTIONS: Several of the words in this reading contain roots that are fairly common. Because these roots are common, they can help you unlock the meanings to other words with which you might be unfamiliar. In the following activity, we will examine two roots—**mal** and **mori**.*

1. The word ***maladies*** contains the root ***mal.*** Use your dictionary to find out what this root means.

   mal means _____

   _____

2. Find two other words in your dictionary that also contain ***mal.*** Write these words and their meanings on the lines below. _____

   _____

3. The word ***moribund*** contains the root ***mori.*** Use your dictionary to find out what this root means.

   mori means _____

   _____

4. Find two other words in your dictionary that also contain ***mori.*** Write these words and their meanings on the lines below. _____

   _____

➥ Trying Out Meaning

DIRECTIONS: Read each of the following sentences carefully. If the boldfaced word is used correctly, circle C and go on to the next item. If, however, the boldfaced word is used incorrectly, circle I and then make the sentence correct.

C   I   **1.** The **blight** that swept across Africa provided an abundance of food for the winter.

C   I   **2.** We could tell by looking at the **withered** leaves that the plant was in good shape and required very little attention.

C   I   **3.** Individuals who are **prosperous** live in small houses and drive inexpensive cars.

C   I   **4.** Young children are often plagued with a variety of **maladies** that they pick up from their playmates.

C   I   **5.** The **anglers** went on a weekend camping trip to hunt deer.

C   I   **6.** Because Sarah had little furniture and no pictures on the walls, her new apartment looked **stark** to everyone who visited.

C   I   **7.** Every time you entered Sam's home and heard the constant yelling, you could sense the **harmony** there.

C   I   **8.** In an attempt to keep cool on the hot, humid day, the air-conditioner **droned** on in Bev's small apartment.

C   I   **9.** The puppy appeared **moribund** as he frolicked with his new owner in the yard.

C   I   **10.** A small, rural town might be considered a **counterpart** to a big city.

C   I   **11.** Before the eggs hatched, the hens **brooded** in the henhouse.

C   I   **12.** The ***specter*** of a destroyed environment is a major problem in the future.

 Applying Meaning

DIRECTIONS: Complete each of the following sentences, being as specific as possible, in order to demonstrate your thorough understanding of the boldfaced words.

1. A ***moribund*** animal might _____

_____

2. If the leaves on your plants began to ***wither*** you would _____

_____

3. When we say that people and nature need to live in ***harmony,***

we mean _____

_____

4. ***Anglers*** would enjoy a vacation where _____

_____

5. The woods might appear ***stark*** when _____

_____

6. Mammals do not ***brood*** because _____

_____

7. If you had a ***malady,*** you might _____

_____

8. If there were a ***blight*** upon the land in the Midwest, _____

_____

9. When your professor *drones,* you might _____

_____

10. The *specter* of failure might haunt you if _____

_____

11. Your *counterparts* are _____

_____

12. One who is *prosperous* might own _____

_____

Reciting and Reviewing

Conceptualizing Meaning

PART I DIRECTIONS: Choose the word or phrase that does not relate to the other three. Write this in the blank after "Exclude." In the blank labeled "General concept" write the concept that describes the remaining words.

1. moribund
lively
deathlike
specter

   a. **Exclude** _____

   b. **General concept** _____

_____

2. malady
blight
withered
harmony

   a. **Exclude** _____

   b. **General concept** _____

_____

3. rifle
angler
reel
sinker

   a. **Exclude** _____

   b. **General concept** _____

_____

4. harmony
   peace
   prosperous
   moribund

   a. Exclude _____

   b. General concept_____

   _____

5. stark
   plain
   specter
   undecorated

   a. Exclude _____

   b. General concept_____

   _____

PART II DIRECTIONS: When you can provide an example of something, you generally have a good conceptual knowledge of the word. Follow the instructions below, and if necessary, explain your choice.

1. Give an example of a ***blight*** that might hit college

   campuses. _____

2. Give two examples of something that an ***angler*** would need.

   _____

3. Give an example of something, other than a bee, that ***drones.***

   _____

4. Give an example of two countries that live in ***harmony.***

   _____

5. Give an example of a situation in which your home or dorm

   room might look ***stark.*** _____

 Self-Evaluating

DIRECTIONS: Think about the words that you have studied in this reading. List in Column A those for which you have a conceptual understanding. In Column B, list the words for which you have just a partial understanding. In Column C, list the words for which you have no understanding or just a definitional understanding. You should

study and review the words listed in Columns B and C before beginning the next reading.

Column A	Column B	Column C
————	————	————
————	————	————
————	————	————
————	————	————
————	————	————
————	————	————
————	————	————
————	————	————
————	————	————
————	————	————

Extending and Challenging

PART I DIRECTIONS: Use each word in a sentence. As you do this activity, first recall all the connotative and denotative information you can about the word. Then construct a sentence that lets the reader know you have a conceptual understanding of the word. You may change the form of the word if you wish; for example, it is all right to change **harmony** *to* **harmonious.** *Put your sentences on the vocabulary cards you made for* Determining Meaning *earlier in the chapter. A sentence such as "He is my* **counterpart***" would show little conceptual knowledge. After you have written your sentence, rate it on a scale from 1 to 3. Give yourself a "1" if you think you have written a poor sentence and really do not have a very good conceptual understanding of the word. Rate yourself a "3" if you think you wrote an outstanding sentence and have an excellent understanding of the word. Rate yourself a "2" if you fall somewhere in the middle.*

1. angler(s)   1   2   3

2. blight   1   2   3

3. brooded   1   2   3

4. droned   1   2   3

5. harmony   1   2   3

6. counterpart(s)   1   2   3

7. malady(ies)   1   2   3

8. moribund   1   2   3

9. prosperous   1   2   3

10. specter   1   2   3

11. stark   1   2   3

12. withered   1   2   3

13.   1   2   3

14.   1   2   3

Any words that you or your instructor marked as a "1" are words that you need to go back and work on further. Use your vocabulary cards, your personal dictionary, context, and other activities that you completed to improve your conceptual understanding.

1. Why do you think Rachel Carson titled this chapter of *Silent Spring* "A Fable for Tomorrow"? How much of this fable has come true today? _____

   _____

   _____

   _____

2. If you were to read all of Carson's book *Silent Spring,* you would find that much of what she wrote about focused on the effects of pesticides. What are pesticides? Find a newspaper or magazine article that discusses how the use of pesticides currently influences our environment. Would Carson have been pleased with what you find? Why or why not? _____

   _____

   _____

   _____

   _____

   _____

Reading **B**

. . . .

Reusing and Recycling Materials

by the World Watch Institute

 **Targeted Words**

aberration	modestly
composting	obsolescence
comprehensive	revenue
dispersed	scarcity
embodied	simplification
emits	slash
ethic	sustainable (-ability)
facilitate	systematic (-ally)
hierarchy	transition

 Pretest

DIRECTIONS: The words in the pretest will be introduced in the reading selection entitled "Reusing and Recycling Materials." Before reading the selection, however, take the pretest by answering the questions about each boldfaced vocabulary word. Use the sentence to help you decide the correct answer, and circle that letter. Then rate your present knowledge of the word by circling 1, 2, or 3, depending on how familiar you are with the word.

1. The throwaway society that has emerged during the late twentieth century uses so much energy, *emits* so much carbon, and
   generates so much air pollution, acid rain, water pollution,
   toxic waste, and rubbish that it is strangling itself.
   Emits means
   a. processes.
   b. gives off.
   c. reuses.
   d. destroys.
                                Level of Understanding   1   2   3

2. Rooted in the concept of planned *obsolescence* and appeals to
   convenience, it will be seen by historians as an *aberration.*
   Obsolescence means the process of
   a. becoming worn out.
   b. becoming depended upon.
   c. needing to recycle.
   d. something unnecessary becoming necessary.
                                Level of Understanding   1   2   3

3. *Aberration* (see above sentence) means
   a. something ordinary.
   b. a passing fad.
   c. something not typical.
   d. a situation needing restructuring.
                                Level of Understanding   1   2   3

4. Society will become dramatically less energy-intensive and
   less polluting only if the throwaway mentality is replaced by
   a recycling *ethic.*
   Ethic means
   a. plan.
   b. moral code.
   c. convenience.
   d. increase.
                                Level of Understanding   1   2   3

5. And recycling glass saves up to a third of the energy ***embodied*** in the original product.
   Embodied means
   a. incorporated.
   b. released.
   c. discarded.
   d. collected.

   Level of Understanding   1   2   3

6. A ***hierarchy*** of options can guide materials policy.
   Hierarchy means
   a. list.
   b. supply.
   c. variety.
   d. ranking.

   Level of Understanding   1   2   3

7. In the early stages, countries will move toward ***comprehensive, systematic*** recycling of metal, glass, paper, and other materials, beginning with source separation at the consumer level.
   Comprehensive means
   a. extensive.
   b. minimal.
   c. understanding.
   d. narrowly defined.

   Level of Understanding   1   2   3

8. ***Systematic*** (see above sentence) means
   a. uncontrolled.
   b. careless.
   c. step-by-step.
   d. discarded.

   Level of Understanding   1   2   3

9. Steady advances in technologies are speeding the ***transition.***
   Transition means
   a. idea.
   b. change.
   c. priority.
   d. reduction.

   Level of Understanding   1   2   3

10. By 2030, the industry will be widely *dispersed.*
Dispersed means
a. owned.
b. expensive.
c. banned.
d. distributed.

Level of Understanding   1   2   3

11. Further, they will provide jobs and *revenue,* while eliminating a source of waste.
Revenue means
a. salaries to individuals.
b. high-paying administrative jobs.
c. money paid to the government.
d. corporations.

Level of Understanding   1   2   3

12. In the *sustainable* economy of 2030, the principal source of materials for industry will be recycled goods.
Sustainable means
a. profitable.
b. substantial.
c. conscientious.
d. maintainable.

Level of Understanding   1   2   3

13. One of the most obvious places to reduce the volume of waste generated is in industry, where a restructuring of manufacturing processes can easily *slash* wastes by a third or more.
Slash means
a. reduce.
b. increase.
c. destroy.
d. create.

Level of Understanding   1   2   3

14. Another major potential source of waste reduction lies in the *simplification* of food packaging.
Simplification means the process of making something
a. more difficult.
b. less complex.
c. easier to handle.
d. more difficult to understand.

Level of Understanding   1   2   3

15. Perhaps the best model is Shanghai: after *modestly* expanding its urban political boundaries to *facilitate* sewage recycling, the city now produces an exportable surplus of vegetables.
Modestly means
a. drastically.
b. embarrassingly.
c. moderately.
d. totally.

Level of Understanding   1   2   3

16. *Facilitate* (see above sentence) means to make
a. more complex.
b. more efficient.
c. larger.
d. easier.

Level of Understanding   1   2   3

17. In a society with a *scarcity* of protein, such an approach, modeled after nature's nutrient recycling, can both eliminate a troublesome waste problem and generate a valuable food resource.
Scarcity means
a. insufficient amount.
b. abundance.
c. withered.
d. poisoned.

Level of Understanding   1   2   3

18. A lost art in many communities, ***composting*** not only reduces garbage flows, it provides a rich source of humus for gardening, lessening the need to buy chemical fertilizers to maintain lawn and garden fertility.

Composting means

a. mixing leaves and decaying food so that it can be used as a fertilizer.

b. recycling cardboard, newspaper, and plastic so as not to pollute the environment.

c. taking trash to the landfill and then selling the decomposed trash as fertilizer.

d. communities getting together and establishing a recycling center.

Level of Understanding   1   2   3

PRETEST SCORING DIRECTIONS: Check with your instructor for the answers before beginning the next activity. Give yourself one point for each item that was correct, and tally the number of 1s, 2s, and 3s you marked.

Number Correct   _____

Level of Understanding

1   _____

2   _____

3   _____

Now read the article "Reusing and Recycling Materials," paying attention to the targeted words, particularly those that you missed on the pretest or those for which your level of understanding was low.

Reusing and Recycling Materials

by the World Watch Institute

In the sustainable, efficient economy of 2030, waste reduction and recycling industries will have largely replaced the garbage collection and disposal companies of today. The throwaway society that has emerged during the late twentieth century uses so much energy, *emits* so much carbon, and generates so much air pollution, acid rain, water pollution, toxic waste and rubbish that it is strangling itself. Rooted in the concept of planned *obsolescence* and appeals to convenience, it will be seen by historians as an *aberration.*

Most materials used today are discarded after one use—roughly two-thirds of all aluminum, three-fourths of all steel and paper, and an even higher share of plastic. Society will become dramatically less energy-intensive and less polluting only if the throwaway mentality is replaced by a recycling *ethic.* Just 5 percent as much energy is needed to recycle aluminum as to produce it from bauxite, the original raw material. For steel produced entirely from scrap, the saving amounts to roughly two-thirds. Newsprint from recycled paper takes 25–60 percent less energy to make than that from wood pulp. And recycling glass saves up to a third of the energy *embodied* in the original product.

Recycling is also a key to getting land, air, and water pollution down to acceptable levels. For example, steel produced from scrap reduces air pollution by 85 percent, cuts water pollution by 76 percent, and eliminates mining wastes altogether. Paper from recycled material reduces pollutants entering the air by 74 percent and the water by 35 percent, as well as reducing pressures on forests in direct proportion to the amount recycled.

A *hierarchy* of options can guide materials policy: The first priority, of course, is to avoid using any nonessential item. Second is to directly reuse a product—for example, refilling a glass beverage container. The third is to recycle the material to form a new product. Fourth, the material can be burned to extract whatever energy it contains, as long as this can be done safely. And finally, the option of last resort is disposal in a landfill.

The first check on the worldwide movement toward a throw-away society came during the seventies as oil prices and environmental consciousness climbed. Rising energy costs made recycling more attractive, reversing the trend toward tossing out more metal, glass, and paper. The second boost came during the eighties as many urban landfill sites filled, forcing municipal governments to ship their garbage to faraway places for disposal. For many U.S. cities, garbage disposal costs during the last decade increased severalfold, making it cost-effective for them to help establish recycling industries.

During the nineties, this trend will be reinforced by the need to reduce carbon emissions, air pollution, acid rain, and toxic waste. In the early stages, countries will move toward *comprehensive, systematic* recycling of metal, glass, paper, and other materials, beginning with source separation at the consumer level. Many communities in Europe, Japan, and, more recently, the United States have already taken steps in this direction.

Steady advances in technologies are speeding the *transition.* The electric arc furnace produces high-quality steel from scrap metal using far less energy than a traditional open hearth furnace does. In the United States, a leader in this technology, roughly a third of all steel is already produced from scrap in such furnaces.

Historically, the steel industry has been concentrated near areas with coal and iron ore, such as Wales in the United Kingdom or western Pennsylvania in the United States. By 2030, the industry will be widely *dispersed.* Electric arc furnaces can operate wherever there is electricity and a supply of scrap metal, and they can be built on a scale adapted to the volume of locally available scrap.

The steel mills of the future will feed heavily on worn-out automobiles, household appliances, and industrial equipment. Further, they will provide local jobs and *revenue,* while eliminating a source of waste.

In the *sustainable* economy of 2030, the principal source of materials for industry will be recycled goods. Most of the raw material for the aluminum mill will come from the local scrap collection center, not from the bauxite mine. Paper and paper products will be produced at recycling mills, with recycled paper moving through a hierarchy of uses, from high-quality bond to newsprint and, eventually, into cardboard boxes. When, after several rounds of recycling, the fibers are no longer reusable, they can be burned as fuel in a cogenerating plant. In a paper products industry that continually uses recycled materials, wood pulp will play a minor role. Industries will feed largely on what is already within the system, turning to virgin raw materials only to replace any losses in use and recycling.

Although early moves away from the throwaway society are concentrating on recycling, *sustainability* over the long term depends more on eliminating waste flows. One of the most obvious places to reduce the volume of waste generated is in industry, where a restructuring of manufacturing processes can easily *slash* wastes by a third or more. The 3M Company halved its hazardous waste flows within a decade of launching a corporation-wide program. A pioneer in waste reduction, 3M also boosted its profits in the process.

Another major potential source of waste reduction lies in the *simplification* of food packaging. In the United States, consumers spent more on food packaging in 1986 than American farmers earned selling their crops. In the interest of attracting customers, items are sometimes buried in three or four layers of packaging. For the final trip from supermarket to home, yet another set of materials is used in the form of paper or plastic bags, also typically discarded after one use. Forty years from now, government regulation is likely to have eliminated excessive packaging. Throwaway grocery bags will have been replaced by durable, reusable bags of canvas or other material.

Societies in 2030 may also have decided to replace multi-sized and shaped beverage containers with a set of standardized ones made of durable glass that can be reused many times. These could be used for most, if not all, beverages, such as fruit juices, beer, milk, and soda pop. Bottlers will simply clean the container, steam off the old label, and add a new one. Containers returned to the supermarket or other outlet might become part of an urban or regional computerized inventory, which would permit their efficient movement from supermarkets or other collection centers to local dairies, breweries, and soda bottling plants as needed. Such a system will save an enormous amount of energy and materials.

In addition to recycling and reusing metal, glass, and paper, a sustainable society also recycles nutrients. In nature, one organism's waste is another's sustenance; in urban societies however, human sewage has become a troublesome source of pollutants in rivers, lakes, and coastal waters. The nutrients in human wastes can be reused safely as long as the process includes measures to prevent the spread of disease.

Fortunately, cities in Japan, South Korea, and China already provide some examples of this kind of nutrient recycling. In these countries, human waste is systematically returned to the land in vegetable-growing greenbelts around cities. Intensively farmed cropland surrounding some cities there produces vegetables year-round using greenhouses or plastic covering during the winter to extend the growing season. Perhaps the best model is Shanghai: after *modestly* expanding its urban political boundaries to *facilitate* sewage recycling, the city now produces an exportable surplus of vegetables.

Some cities will probably find it more efficient to use treated human sewage to fertilize aquacultural operations. A steady flow of nutrients from human waste into ponds can supply food for a vigorously growing population of algae that in turn are consumed by fish. In Calcutta, a sewage-fed aquaculture system now provides 20,000 kilograms of fresh fish each day for sale in the city. In a society with a *scarcity* of protein, such an approach, modeled after nature's nutrient recycling, can both eliminate a troublesome waste problem and generate a valuable food resource.

As recycling reaches full potential over the next 40 years, households will begin to compost yard wastes rather than put them out for curbside garbage pickup. A lost art in many communities, *composting* not only reduces garbage flows, it provides a rich source of humus for gardening, lessening the need to buy chemical fertilizers to maintain lawn and garden fertility.

By *systematically* reducing the flow of waste and reusing or recycling most remaining materials, the basic needs of the planet's growing number of human residents can be satisfied without destroying our very life-support systems. Moving in this direction will not only create a far more livable environment with less air and water pollution, it will also reduce the unsightly litter that blights the landscape in many industrial societies today. □

 **Determining** Meaning

PART I DIRECTIONS: Using the generative strategy of the vocabulary card, write a definition, synonym, antonym, and part of speech for each word below. Remember to select the most appropriate definition on the basis of how the word is used in the reading. Be sure to pay particular attention to the words that you missed in the pretest. In addition, find a minimum of two more words from "Reusing and Recycling Materials" with which you are unfamiliar, and make vocabulary cards for those words also.

1. aberration
2. composting
3. comprehensive
4. dispersed
5. embodied
6. emits
7. ethic
8. facilitate
9. hierarchy
10. modestly

11. obsolescence
12. revenue
13. scarcity
14. simplification
15. slash
16. sustainable
17. systematically
18. transition
19.
20.

*PART II DIRECTIONS: As previously discussed, keyword strategies can be helpful because they help you associate the meaning of an unknown word with another word that is difficult to remember. Often students will also use imagery along with keywords to make remembering easier still. For three words from the list above, use a combination of both keywords and images. The word **scarcity** could use both of these mnemonics. **Scarcity,** which means not having enough or a shortage of something, sounds very much like the word scary. Think of something that it would be scary to have a **scarcity** of—money, perhaps, or food. Get an image in your head of a family with several small children frightened because of a **scarcity** of food. Now think of three more images for other words. Put these mnemonics on your vocabulary cards.*

*PART III DIRECTIONS: Several words from this reading contain word elements. **Sustainable** consists of a prefix, a root, and a suffix. Using what you already know about this word, context, and your dictionary, answer the following questions about **sustainable**.*

1. What do you already know about the word **sustainable?** If your knowledge is at Stage 1, write nothing. Otherwise, predict what you think it means. _____

_____

2. What information do you gain from context? _____

_____

3. What is the prefix? What does it mean? _____

_____

4. What is the root word? What does it mean? _____

_____

5. What is the dictionary definition of **sustainable,** based on the way it is used in context?_____

_____

6. Did using word elements help, hinder, or add nothing to figuring out the meaning of this word? Why?_____

_____

Trying Out Meaning

DIRECTIONS: Select the word from the target list that best answers each of the questions below. You might have to add or delete a word ending.

1. Which word describes a recycling program that takes every aspect of pollution into consideration?

   _____

2. Which word tells what a storekeeper might do to the price of day-old bread in order to get rid of it?

   _____

3. Which word describes what a world with no pollution might currently be called?

   _____

4. Which is another word for the taxes you must pay to the state and federal governments?

   _____

5. Which word describes what you might do with your leftover food scraps, leaves, and so on, in order to fertilize your garden?

   _____

6. Which word tells what you form when you put information in some sort of rank order?

   _____

7. Which word describes the state of old, out-of-date encyclopedias, phonograph record players, and typewriters?

   _____

8. Which word describes making the recycling process easier so that more individuals would participate?

_____

9. Which word describes the level of effort made by someone who recycles, but recycles only old newspapers?

_____

10. Which word describes an individual who organizes his or her life in order to do the same thing at the same time every day?

_____

11. Which word tells what an automobile does when it releases carbon monoxide into the air?

_____

12. Which word describes something that you have only a little of?

_____

13. Which word describes the action of a crowd after a baseball game ended and everyone went their separate ways?

_____

14. Which word tells what I might try to do if my roommates are arguing about something, and I would help them work out their problems but not take sides?

_____

15. Which word tells what I have if I have strong morals?

_____

16. Which word tells what something contained inside another thing would be?

_____

17. Which word refers to the process that takes place as I move from childhood to adolescence to adulthood?

_____

18. Which word describes what you must try to do when you want to keep or maintain your enthusiasm?

_____

Applying Meaning

DIRECTIONS: _Answer yes or no to each of the following statements and then explain your answer in the space provided._

_____ **1.** Would a computer be considered **obsolete?** Why or

why not? _____

_____

_____ **2.** Would **withered** fruit and leaves be good for

composting? Why or why not? _____

_____

_____ **3.** Would a **blight** upon the land cause a **scarcity** of

food? Why or why not? _____

_____

_____ **4.** Would a human who lived to be 115 years old be

considered an **aberration?** Why or why not?_____

_____

5. Would a human who lived to be 115 years old have many *counterparts?* Why or why not? _____

_____

6. Would a company that *dispersed* raw sewage into a city's water supply have *ethics?* Why or why not?

_____

_____

7. If the land was *prosperous,* would it be important for everyone to eat *modestly?* Why or why not?

_____

_____

8. Would the United States be *sustainable* without *revenue?* Why or why not? _____

_____

9. Would you get good grades if you studied *comprehensively* and *systematically?* Why or why not? _____

_____

10. Would talks between two unfriendly nations *facilitate harmony?* Why or why not? _____

_____

_____ **11.** Is Georgia *embodied* in the United States? Why or

why not? _____

_____

_____ **12.** Would an automobile that *emitted* too much carbon

monoxide be dangerous? Why or why not? _____

_____

_____ **13.** Would 30, 31, 35, 46, and 51 be considered a

hierarchy of numbers? Why or why not? _____

_____

_____ **14.** Would a *simplification* of directions make it more

difficult to connect a VCR or a stereo system? Why or

why not? _____

_____

_____ **15.** Would getting a raise result in a *slash* in your

salary? Why or why not? _____

_____

_____ **16.** Would *anglers* be happy if there were a *scarcity* of

fish? Why or why not? _____

_____

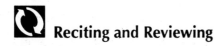 **Reciting and Reviewing**

 Conceptualizing Meaning

DIRECTIONS: Write a meaningful sentence for each of the following words. Your sentence should illustrate that you have a conceptual knowledge of the word. You can change the form of the word; for example, **obsolescence** *can be changed to* **obsolete.** *The example should help you see the difference between what is acceptable and what is not. When you have finished, place these sentences on the backs of your vocabulary cards.*

Example using *comprehensive:*

Weak: Our family engages in a *comprehensive* recycling program.

Good: Recycling cans, glass, newspapers, cardboard, and plastic, as well as composting foodstuffs, is all part of our family's *comprehensive* recycling program.

1. aberration _____

2. composting _____

3. comprehensive _____

4. dispersed _____

5. embodied _____

6. emits _____

7. ethic _____

8. facilitate _____

9. hierarchy _____

10. modestly _____

11. obsolescence _____

12. revenue _____

13. scarcity_____

14. simplification _____

15. slash _____

16. sustainable (-ability)_____

17. systematic (-ally) _____

18. transition _____

 Self-Evaluating

DIRECTIONS: Think about the words that you have studied in this reading. List in Column A those for which you have a conceptual understanding. In Column B, list the words for which you have just a partial understanding. In Column C, list the words for which you have no understanding or just a definitional understanding. You should study and review the words listed in Columns B and C before beginning the next reading.

Column A	Column B	Column C
_____	_____	_____
_____	_____	_____
_____	_____	_____
_____	_____	_____
_____	_____	_____
_____	_____	_____
_____	_____	_____

	Column A	Column B	Column C
	_____	_____	_____
	_____	_____	_____

◤ Extending and Challenging

PART I DIRECTIONS: Several words found in "Reusing and Recycling Materials" can take different forms. Such words generally change part of speech as the endings change. Look at each of the changes below and the sentences that follow. Then change each ending so that the word changes to the part of speech indicated. Write a sentence using each word form following the examples below.

1. dispersed — verb   dispersion — noun
   Because the oil spill ***dispersed*** over several miles, it was extremely difficult to clean up.

   The ***dispersion*** of the oil over several miles made it extremely difficult to clean up.

2. emits — verb   emission — noun
   If a car ***emits*** too much carbon monoxide, you should check the catalytic converter.

   When carbon monoxide ***emission*** is high, you should have your catalytic converter checked.

3. simplification — noun   _____ — verb

   _____

   _____

4. transition — noun   _____ — adjective

   _____

   _____

5. sustainable — adjective   _____ — noun

_____

_____

Note from the above exercise that *-tion, -sion,* and *-ion* endings are generally noun forms and *-able* and *-ability* are generally adjective forms.

PART II WRITING ACTIVITIES DIRECTIONS: Respond to each of the following questions.

1. What do you think Rachel Carson, author of *Silent Spring,*

would think about recycling as described in "Using and

Recycling Materials"? What else might she suggest? _____

_____

_____

_____

_____

_____

_____

2. Discuss at least three ways that the general public and industry can cut down on the amount of waste material that we generate. Then list three specific things that you can do in your home._____

_____

_____

_____

_____

_____

_____

3. Examine your local newspaper for articles dealing with pollution and ecological concerns. What are the issues in your city? What is being done? Write a one-page journal entry that addresses these issues, using as many of the words from Readings A and B as possible.

 Posttest I for Readings A and B

DIRECTIONS: Now you are ready for the first posttest for this chapter. Please see your instructor in order to receive a copy of the posttest for Readings A and B.

Reading C

Ecology and Economics: Tending Our Houses

by Joseph S. Levine and Kenneth R. Miller

 Targeted Words

General	Content-Specific
avid	biogeochemical view
befouled	biosphere
cartel	botanist
decimated	carbonates
depletion	ecology
diverged	ecologist
hospitable	economics
inhabitants	ecosystems
lauded	environmentalist
lethal	geochemical view
myriads	global warming
obliged	greenhouse effect
pivotal	greenhouse gases
precipitate	incubator
predecessors	organic processes
successors	ozone layer
surmise	pesticides
sweltered	sedimentary rocks
tangible	toxic

Pretest—General Words

DIRECTIONS: The words in the pretest will be introduced in the reading selection entitled "Ecology and Economics: Tending Our Houses." Before reading the selection, however, take the pretest by selecting one of the words from the general vocabulary list to complete each of the sentences. Each word will be used only once and each is in its proper form. Then rate your present knowledge of the word by circling 1, 2, or 3, depending on how familiar you are with the word.

1. People who live in New York City are called _____ of that city.

   Level of Understanding   1   2   3

2. So many of our waters have been _____ to the point that it is not even safe to swim in them.

   Level of Understanding   1   2   3

3. All members of society are _____ to do their fair share to help save the environment.

   Level of Understanding   1   2   3

4. Individuals who are _____ environmentalists might be members of Greenpeace.

   Level of Understanding   1   2   3

5. The _____ of our natural resources will occur unless there are measures taken that will help conserve them.

   Level of Understanding   1   2   3

6. _____ amounts of toxic chemicals have been dumped into some rivers and lakes before newer standards were set.

   Level of Understanding   1   2   3

7. Much of the data gathered in the 1970s about the effects of pollution on the environment had little _____ effect.

   Level of Understanding   1   2   3

8. Environmental agencies were _____ by budget cuts and unable to take any action to prevent chemical dumping.

   Level of Understanding   1   2   3

9. Our planet's _____ temperature is due to the gases that allow sunlight through but keep all of the heat from escaping.
                              Level of Understanding   1   2   3

10. _____ of pollution problems face our planet that must be addressed if we expect to survive.
                              Level of Understanding   1   2   3

11. Rubber tappers of the Amazon correctly _____ that if rain forests are kept intact, animal and plant resources will be renewed.
                              Level of Understanding   1   2   3

12. Chico Mendez, an environmentalist, was _____ by the United Nations for his efforts to save the rain forest.
                              Level of Understanding   1   2   3

13. The disciplines of ecology and economics ran parallel until the eighteenth century when they _____.
                              Level of Understanding   1   2   3

14. Rachel Carson's book, *Silent Spring,* _____ much interest in the use of pesticides.
                              Level of Understanding   1   2   3

15. The economic recession of the late 1970s and early 1980s was caused, in part, by an oil shortage created by a _____ of oil-producing nations.
                              Level of Understanding   1   2   3

16. Thoreau, and his _____ who followed him, encouraged society to live within environmental limitations.
                              Level of Understanding   1   2   3

17. During the 1960s and early 1970s, scientists strengthened the beliefs of the _____ such as Carson and Thoreau.
                              Level of Understanding   1   2   3

18. During the summer of 1995, many people _____ when temperatures reached into temperatures over 100° for several days in a row.
                              Level of Understanding   1   2   3

19. Rachel Carson's book played a _____ role in bringing attention to the problems of chemical pesticide use.

Level of Understanding   1   2   3

PRETEST SCORING DIRECTIONS: Check with your instructor for the answers before completing the pretest for content-specific words. Give yourself one point for each item that was correct and tally the number of 1s, 2s, and 3s you marked.

Number Correct   _____

Level of Understanding

1   _____

2   _____

3   _____

Pretest—Content-Specific Words

DIRECTIONS: For each term list as many descriptions or characteristics as possible based on your knowledge of the word. Then rate your present knowledge of the word by circling 1, 2, or 3, depending on how much information you already possess about the word.

Example:

1. biogeochemical view   **2.** biosphere

relationships _____   _____

_____   _____

_____   _____

1   2   3   1   2   3

3. botanist

_____

_____

_____

    1   **2**   **3**

4. carbonates

_____

_____

_____

    1   **2**   **3**

5. ecology

_____

_____

_____

    1   **2**   **3**

6. economics

_____

_____

_____

    1   **2**   **3**

7. ecosystems

_____

_____

_____

    1   **2**   **3**

8. environmentalist

_____

_____

_____

    1   **2**   **3**

9. geochemical view

_____

_____

_____

    1   **2**   **3**

10. global warming

_____

_____

_____

    1   **2**   **3**

11. greenhouse effect

     1   **2**   **3**

12. greenhouse gases

     1   **2**   **3**

13. incubator

     1   **2**   **3**

14. organic processes

     1   **2**   **3**

15. ozone layer

     1   **2**   **3**

16. pesticides

     1   **2**   **3**

17. sedimentary rocks

     1   **2**   **3**

18. species

     1   **2**   **3**

19. toxic

_____

_____

_____

    1   **2**   **3**

PRETEST SCORING DIRECTIONS: Compare your descriptors and characteristics with those in your instructor's answer key. Since there are no right or wrong answers, simply tally the number of 1s, 2s, and 3s you have marked and record them below.

Level of Understanding

    1   _____

    2   _____

    3   _____

Now read the article "Ecology and Economics: Tending Our Houses," paying attention to the targeted words, particularly those for which you could generate no characteristics or those for which your level of understanding was low.

Ecology and Economics: Tending Our Houses

by Joseph S. Levine and Kenneth R. Miller

Francisco (Chico) Mendez wasn't born into circumstances that you'd expect to propel him onto the front pages of international newspapers. He spent most of his life in a jungle town called Xapuri, deep in the Amazon, where he earned a living by tapping rubber trees for their sap. But as the leader of a rubber tappers union, Mendez found himself smack in the middle of a national dispute that made global headlines.

Rubber tappers, you see, are people who harvest products of the rain forest for a living. By virtue of both their temperament and their profession, they prefer to see most of the jungle left standing. They correctly *surmise* that their region will produce more valuable goods for a longer period of time if the rain forest remains intact, allowing them to harvest its rich and valuable store of plants and animals as renewable resources. That philosophy puts rubber tappers squarely at odds with wealthy and powerful ranchers, who prefer to destroy the rain forest to plant forage grasses for cattle.

Campaigning to save the rain forest, Mendez found himself first labeled an environmentalist, then *lauded* as a self-styled ecologist. His precious rain forests received more and more national attention. Mendez received an award from the United Nations for his efforts. Things seemed to be going well. But in December 1988, at the age of 44, he was shot and killed outside his jungle home by the son of a cattle rancher.

Like Joanne O'Donnell, Chico Mendez was caught up in a firestorm that, although heavily involved with ecological science, was driven by economics and politics. To those who study the history of human interactions with the environment, these complex stories of environment, intrigue, money, and power are not surprising. That's because the disciplines of ecology and economics have affected one another since ancient times. We will not trace the details of human interactions with the global environment. . . . Here we will concentrate on certain **pivotal** points in the relationship between human society and its environment, illustrating our current difficulties with a single major issue of global significance.

A Historical Perspective on Ecology and Economics

The words ecology and economics are both derived from the Greek word *oikos,* which means "house." Over time, economics has become concerned primarily with the art of human household management, whereas ecology deals with the study of nature's "houses" and their **inhabitants.** For some time the disciplines ran in parallel, but by the eighteenth century their philosophies had diverged.

The split began in 1749, when Swedish botanist Carl von Linné (Linnaeus) wrote an essay entitled "The Oeconomy of Nature," in which he argued that God created "nature's economy" exclusively to serve the human economy. Adam Smith, the founder of modern economics and an avid disciple of Linnaeus, adopted a similar view of the biosphere as a global warehouse of raw materials for human use. Smith also believed that it was humanity's birthright to dominate nature through hard work and technological advancement. Thus the writings of a biologist spawned a very human-centered view of people's interactions with nature.

As Smith's successors, most economists adopted a human-centered view of human interactions with nature and developed economic models that analyzed some aspects of human activity quite accurately. But until recently, economic theory failed to consider the long-term ecological effects of human activities: **depletion** of nonrenewable resources such as coal and oil, loss or pollution of renewable resources such as air and water, and the disappearance of species and ecosystems.

In contrast, biologists and natural philosophers, as far back as Linnaeus's time, realized that unrestricted growth and development could have serious environmental consequences. The proponents of this view who were best known to the public were not ecological researchers but gentleman–naturalist–authors such as Henry David Thoreau. Thoreau, an early champion of a less human-centered perspective, embraced the natural world as home to *all* life. He and his **successors** counseled society to recognize, and learn to live within, environmental limitations.

During the mid-twentieth century, it became apparent that human activities were, in fact, disturbing many local ecosystems. Then, in 1962, biologist Rachel Carson published *Silent Spring*, a disturbing documentary of the destructive power of chemical pesticides then widely used in agriculture. *Silent Spring* inaugurated the environmental movement by warning of ecological apocalypse—a spring without the sounds of birds and insects.

The scientific environmental movement, often at odds with local and national governments and economists, grew during the 1960s and early 1970s. Throughout this period, ecological researchers strengthened the scientific underpinnings of their **predecessors'** philosophical and emotional appeals. The concern over environmental matters shown by the general public was reflected in several important pieces of legislation designed to protect the environment.

Unfortunately, the public image of "ecology" fell on hard times in the mid-1970s and early 1980s. The country suffered an economic recession, triggered in part by the sudden shortage of imported oil created by a **cartel** of oil-producing nations. It became popular during those years to attribute financial hardships to convenient local scapegoats, including environmental activists. One bumper sticker that was popular in New England during those years read "Hungry? Cold? Eat an environmentalist!"

Ecologists kept working, of course, and they continued to amass important data about the local and global effects of human activities on the environment. But that increasing body of data did not—for an unfortunately long time—have any **tangible** effect on either public perceptions or national environmental policy. All politicians paid lip service to the environment, but given the public mood, few wanted to confront their constituents with the cost of paying for a cleaner environment. Although the environmental agencies set up earlier remained in place, several were **decimated** by budget cuts and executive-branch decisions not to spend money that Congress had earmarked for environmental action. Offered a choice between investing large sums of money in waste treatment and quietly dumping toxic material where they could, many corporations similarly chose the easy route to short-term profits.

Then, sometime between the beginning of 1988 and the middle of 1989, the world at large suddenly woke up. During the summer of 1988, much of the country *sweltered* under a heat wave with temperatures regularly above 100°F. At the same time, agricultural areas from California to Georgia were scorched by a drought that cut grain harvests by 31 percent. Scientists detected dangerous holes in the earth's protective ozone layer. Raw sewage, garbage, and discarded syringes washed up, not only onto public beaches around New York and Boston, but onto exclusive resorts on the islands of Nantucket and Martha's Vineyard. During one weekend, coastal waters in Alaska, Rhode Island, California, and Delaware were all being fouled by oil from separate, major tanker accidents. One of those spills, caused by navigational errors aboard the tanker Exxon *Valdez*, *befouled* more than 1355 miles of formerly pristine Alaska coastline.

None of these events was either new or unexpected from a scientific point of view. Scientists even rushed to point out that the American heat wave and drought could not definitely be cited as evidence that a global warming trend had begun. But somehow, this time, the total of these human-caused disturbances in the planetary environment finally shifted the balance and changed the attitudes of both the mass media and the public.

Finally, world political leaders felt obligated to get into the act. During a global economic meeting among leaders of the world's seven largest industrial nations in the summer of 1989, environmental issues took center stage. Their meeting, in fact, came to be called "The Green Summit." "What defense has been to world leaders for the past 40 years," an editorial in Britain's *The Economist* predicted at that time, "the environment will be for the next 40."

To give you a taste of what all the excitement is about and a sample of the ongoing debates among scientists over uncertainties in models of the way the world works, we will take a brief look at one of the most talked-about phenomena in ecology today: global warming and the greenhouse effect.

The Greenhouse Effect: Atmosphere as <u>Incubator</u>

Temperatures in our part of the solar system vary enormously, and virtually everywhere except on Earth, conditions are *lethal* to life as we know it.

We owe our planet's *hospitable* temperature in large part to levels of atmospheric carbon dioxide, water vapor, and certain other gases that readily admit sunlight to the planet's surface but retard the escape of heat. Because these gases act in much the same way as the glass in a greenhouse, this phenomenon is called the greenhouse effect, and the gases involved are often called greenhouse gases.

Greenhouse gases are critically important in balancing incoming solar radiation and escaping heat. If their concentration were to increase beyond a certain point, more heat would be retained and the planet would get warmer. And if Earth's average temperature were to rise by only a few degrees, global weather patterns could change, heat waves and droughts would plague important agriculture areas, and polar ice caps could melt, flooding coastal cities. If, on the other hand, greenhouse gas concentrations were to fall, Earth's temperature would drop. And a fall of only a few degrees in average temperature could trigger an ice age.

If this much is clear to most scientists, why does so much controversy exist among scientists and politicians regarding "the greenhouse effect?" The answer—as is usually the case in science—is complex.

Carbon Dioxide and Its Effect on Global Temperature

The key to Earth's constant temperature lies in the changes our atmosphere's carbon dioxide concentration has undergone through time. During Earth's early years, our atmosphere had close to 1000 times as much carbon dioxide as it does today. The greenhouse effect of all that carbon dioxide kept Earth warm, even though the sun at the time was much dimmer. But over millions of years, as the sun grew warmer, much of the planet's early surplus of carbon dioxide dissolved in the oceans, formed carbonate rocks, and thus left the atmosphere. Later, after life evolved, many living organisms took up carbon dioxide and incorporated it either into their bodies or into protective body coverings.

Since that time, atmospheric carbon dioxide concentrations have dropped to a present level of about 0.03 percent, allowing more and more heat to escape from Earth's surface. Somehow—and scientists still do not agree on just how—the decrease in the greenhouse effect paralleled the rise in the sun's output so closely that planetary temperatures stayed nearly constant.

Was this blind luck, or does the Earth have some sort of "thermostat" that regulates its temperature? There are two different sets of explanations. Some researchers suggest that the control mechanisms are the result of geological and chemical processes alone. The other explanation involves living organisms as well.

The geochemical view Those who credit geochemistry alone as a temperature regulator argue that Earth's carbon dioxide revolves in a giant cycle the most important pathways of which involve strictly physical processes. Atmospheric carbon dioxide dissolves in rainwater, forming a weak acid that erodes rocks composed of calcium, silicon, and oxygen. The resulting mixture of elements travels through rivers and streams to the oceans, where the carbon dioxide may combine with calcium and magnesium to form insoluble compounds called carbonates. These carbonates *precipitate* out of solution and accumulate on the ocean bottom, where they harden into the sedimentary rocks called limestone and dolomite. In certain places, geological activity forces those rocks underneath the continents, sometimes so deeply that intense heat drives the carbon dioxide out in gaseous form. When volcanoes erupt, this underground carbon dioxide is reinjected into the atmosphere.

According to the strictly geochemical view, changes in atmospheric carbon dioxide content result exclusively from changes in this cycle that are caused by variations in planetary temperature. Although those who hold this view do not deny the effect of living organisms on atmospheric carbon dioxide, they believe that geologic processes are far more important.

The biogeochemical view Other scientists believe that living organisms play a major role in regulating carbon dioxide levels. They point out that most carbonate rocks created today are formed not geochemically, but biologically; *myriads* of single-celled marine organisms incorporate dissolved carbon dioxide into their shells. When these organisms die, their shells fall to the ocean bottom and accumulate into vast deposits such as, for example, the famous white cliffs of Dover. As this process removes carbon dioxide from the sea, more of the gas in the atmosphere goes into solution to replace it. At the same time, terrestrial plants incorporate carbon dioxide from the air into living tissue. Much of this organic carbon is continually recycled, but a great deal was buried in the form of vast organic deposits that, over time, became coal and oil.

The biogeochemical view argues that changes in the growth rates of plants and other organisms significantly affect the amount of carbon dioxide left in the atmosphere. Such organic processes, which could easily be affected by any change in global temperature, may have acted as a sort of "living thermostat," adjusting the atmosphere's carbon dioxide concentration ever since life became established.

Which theory is correct? We don't know yet. At the present time, insufficient data are available for us to determine whether strictly geochemical or biogeochemical processes are dominant today. Even fewer data are available about what happened 3 billion years ago.□

 Determining Meaning—General Words

PART I DIRECTIONS: Using the generative strategy of the vocabulary card, write a definition, synonym, antonym, and the part of speech for each word below. Remember to select the most appropriate definition on the basis of how the word is used in the reading. Be sure to pay particular attention to the words that you missed in the pretest. In addition, find a minimum of two more words from "Ecology and Economics: Tending Our Houses" with which you are unfamiliar and make vocabulary cards for those words also.

1. avid
2. befouled
3. cartel
4. decimated
5. depletion
6. diverged
7. hospitable
8. inhabitants
9. lauded
10. lethal
11. myriads
12. obliged
13. pivotal
14. precipitate
15. predecessors
16. successors
17. surmise
18. sweltered
19. tangible
20.
21.

*PART II DIRECTIONS: As in past chapters, you can use images and mnemonics to help you remember the meanings of some general words. For example, you might be able to remember the meaning of the word **befouled** by imaging dead "foul" (chickens, ducks, or geese) along a polluted riverbank. Here the "foul" may have been **befouled** by drinking the polluted water, but they are also **befouling** the riverbank.*

*Now you try this technique with at least two other words. **Sweltered, lethal,** and **decimated** would all lend themselves well to using imagery or mnemonics.*

Determining Meaning—Content-Specific Words

DIRECTIONS: Using the vocabulary card format described in Chapter 2, write a definition and examples or characteristics for each of the content-specific words below. In some cases you will be able to use context (c), and in other cases you will have to rely either partially or solely on a dictionary (d). Occasionally you might be able to use your own prior knowledge (pk). Hints are provided in parentheses following each word. You might wish to go back and skim Chapter 3 before beginning the activity. After you have determined the meaning for all of the content-specific words, discuss them with a partner or your instructor as a way of gaining additional understanding of the terms.

1. biogeochemical view (c)
2. biosphere (c/d)
3. botanist (d/pk)
4. carbonates (c/d)
5. ecology (c/d/pk)
6. economics (c/d/pk)
7. ecosystems (d)
8. environmentalist (c/d/pk)
9. geochemical view (c)
10. global warming (c/d)
11. greenhouse effect (c/d)
12. greenhouse gases (c)
13. incubator (d)
14. organic processes (c)
15. ozone layer (c/d)
16. pesticides (c/d)
17. sedimentary rocks (c/d)
18. toxic (d)

Organizing Concepts

PART I DIRECTIONS: This activity is a modified version of the generative group and label strategy outlined in Chapter 2. From the lists, find the general and content-specific words that could be grouped under each of the labels. You probably will not be able to use all of the words, but list as many as you can. Both groups have been started for you. Be prepared to explain and justify your ideas in class.

Historical Perspective

Economics

Ecology

↓
_____

_____

_____

_____

_____

_____

_____

↓
Greenhouse Effect

_____

_____

_____

↓
Role of Carbon Dioxide

Geochemical View

_____

_____

_____

Biogeochemical View

_____

_____

_____

PART II DIRECTIONS: As you learned in Chapter 4, the suffix -tion *creates nouns. One example is found in this reading—**decimated**. The verb **decimated** becomes the noun **decimation** when -tion is added. Read the following sentences and note the differences.*

Verb—   The rain forest was **decimated** by ranchers who wanted the land for cattle grazing.

Noun—   The **decimation** of the rain forest by the ranchers gave them a place to graze their cattle.

Change each of the following words to noun forms by adding -tion. Then change the sentence so that the word is used in its noun form.

Verb—   Because Shawna had agreed to help her friend move, she felt **obliged** to do it, even though she didn't feel well.

Noun—   _____

_____

Verb—   Exercising outdoors during the hottest part of the day **depletes** the body of fluids quickly.

Noun—   _____

_____

 Beginning Conceptual Understanding

DIRECTIONS: Read each sentence carefully, paying particular attention to the boldfaced words. Mark T if the statement is true, and go on to the next item. If, however, the statement is false, mark F and then make it correct by adding, deleting, or in some other way changing the sentence.

T   F   **1.** A **botanist** believes that the **decimation** of plants would help protect our **ozone layer**.

T   F   **2.** Some **pesticides** have been shown to **befoul** our **ecosystem.**

T   F   **3.** The *geochemical view* states that earth's temperature is regulated by biological processes only.

T   F   **4.** Silicon and calcium are examples of *sedimentary rocks.*

T   F   **5.** *Greenhouse gases* are *lethal* to our *ecosystems.*

T   F   **6.** According to the *greenhouse effect,* changes in weather patterns would not be *precipitated* if the earth's temperature increased by only a few degrees.

T   F   **7.** According to the *biogeochemical view, myriads* of living things play a role in regulating carbon dioxide levels in the environment.

T   F   **8.** The words *ecology* and *economy* both come from the Greek word *oikos,* which means "house."

T   F   **9.** An *environmentalist* might believe that the government is *obliged* to clean up *toxic* waste.

T   F   **10.** All living things live in earth's *biosphere.*

T   F   **11.** *Organic processes* include the growth rate of plants and other organisms in the *biosphere.*

T   F   **12.** When carbon dioxide combines with calcium and magnesium, *carbonates* are formed.

T   F   **13.** *Global warming* is thought to have resulted from the sun slowly moving closer to the earth.

T   F   **14.** *Incubators* are used to keep things from *sweltering.*

 **Using Concepts**

DIRECTIONS: Complete each of the following sentences, being as specific as possible, in order to demonstrate your conceptual understanding of the boldfaced words.

1. If a company were **lauded** for its environmental efforts _____

   _____

2. If you are **sweltering** you might _____

   _____

3. If our natural resources were **depleted**_____

   _____

4. An example of **divergent** opinions on the environment would

   be _____

   _____

5. If a town is **hospitable** to its **inhabitants,**_____

   _____

6. If an area has been **befouled** with **lethal** chemical pollutants,

   _____

7. When you have a **myriad** of choices, you _____

   _____

8. A forest that has been **decimated** would _____

   _____

9. If you see *tangible* results of your efforts, you _____

_____

10. If you *surmise* that you did well on an exam, _____

_____

11. You might feel *obliged* to invite someone to your home for

dinner if _____

_____

12. A *predecessor* of President Reagan would be _____

_____

13. A *successor* of President Reagan would be _____

_____

14. If you are an *avid environmentalist,* you _____

_____

15. The oil *cartel* is responsible for _____

_____

16. Something that might *precipitate* an oil spill would be _____

_____

17. An example of a *pivotal* event in American history would be

_____

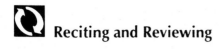 **Reciting and Reviewing**

 Comprehending Concepts

DIRECTIONS: The questions below are based on your understanding of the content-specific words, some of the general words, and many of the key concepts presented in the reading entitled "Ecology and Economics: Tending Our Houses." At this point, you should be able to answer the questions without looking at the text excerpt, your vocabulary cards, or your organizing strategies.

1. What is the difference between the ***geochemical view*** and the ***biogeochemical view*** of the earth's "thermostat"? _____

    _____

    _____

    _____

    _____

2. How were ***environmentalists*** viewed in the 1970s? Why were they viewed this way?_____

    _____

3. What is the ***greenhouse effect?*** _____

    _____

    _____

4. How do ***greenhouse gases*** influence our ***biosphere?***_____

    _____

    _____

5. Why is the earth's atmosphere considered to be an *incubator?*

   _____

   _____

6. What influence did Rachel Carson's book, which examined the use of *pesticides,* have on the environmental movement?_____

   _____

   _____

7. What caused the areas of *ecology* and *economics* to *diverge?*

   _____

   _____

8. Linnaeus could be called an *avid* human-centered *botanist.* Why?_____

   _____

9. How is carbon dioxide *pivotal* in the formation of carbonates?_____

   _____

   _____

10. What role does the *ozone layer* play? What might occur if the earth's *ozone layer* were damaged?_____

   _____

   _____

11. How does the *biogeochemical view* incorporate *organic processes?* _____

_____

_____

12. Give two examples of *sedimentary rocks.* _____

_____

13. What happens to our *ecosystems* when *toxic* chemicals are released into rivers and streams? _____

_____

14. What might happen to weather patterns as a result of *global warming?* _____

_____

Self-Evaluating

DIRECTIONS: *Think about the words that you have studied in this reading. List those for which you have a conceptual understanding in Column A. In Column B, list the words for which you have just a partial understanding. In Column C, list the words for which you have no understanding or just a definitional understanding. You should study and review the words listed in Columns B and C before taking the chapter posttest.*

Column A	Column B	Column C
_____	_____	_____
_____	_____	_____
_____	_____	_____

_____   _____   _____

_____   _____   _____

_____   _____   _____

_____   _____   _____

_____   _____   _____

_____   _____   _____

_____   _____   _____

 Posttest II for Readings A, B, and C

DIRECTIONS: See your instructor for a copy of Posttest II for Readings A, B, and C.

Word Lists

Word List—General

(Annotations refer to chapter [5–8] and reading [A–C] in which each word appears.)

aberration 8B

abolition 5B

abusive 6A

acute 5C

ambiguous 7B

androgyny 5B

anglers 8A

apparatus 6C

applicable 6C

asymptomatic 7C

autonomy 7B

averted 5A

avid 8C

baffled 5B

banish 6C

banning 7A

batteries 7B

befouled 8C

beneficiary 7B

blight 8A

brooded 8A

calculated 5C

cartel 8C

chauvinism 5B

communicable 7A

compensation 7B

composting 8B

composure 6A

comprehensive 8B

condescension 5A

conduits 7C

confirmed 7C

consolation 5A

conspiracy 6A

contaminated 7C

continuation 5C

corroded 6B

counterparts 8A

crank 7B

curbs(ed) 7B

decimated 8C

decipher 5A

deem 7A

deficits 7B

déjà vu 5B

depletion 8C

detect 7C

detract 6C

devastating 5C, 7B

deviousness 5B

diligently 6C

dilemma 5B

disincentives 7A

disparate 5A

dispersed 8B

distinction 5A

diverged 8C

domestic 5B

dominance 5A

dooms 6A

droned 8A

egalitarian 5B

elite 6B

embodied 8B

emits 8B

encompass 5C

endowed 5A

enduring 6B

enhance 5A

enriching 7B

ensured 7C

entrepreneur 5B

epidemic 7C

equivalency 6A

estimates 7A

ethic 8B

exclusivity 5C

exhibit 6C

explosive 6C

facilitate 8B

fantasizing 5C

flustered 6A

forbidding 6C

fosters 7B

fraternizing 7A

grim 7A

harmony 8A

heterosexually 7C

hierarchy 8B

hospitable 8C

impaired 7C

impediments 6A

impersonal 7B

incentives 7A

incidence 7A

inclined 5A

indicted 5B

inebriated 6B

inferiority 5A

inflation 7B

inhabitants 8C

inherent 6C

insidious 7C

instinctively 5A

intriguing 5B

intrusive 5C

isolated 7C

jargon 5B

justifiable 7A

latency 7C

lauded 8C

legions 7C

lethal 8C

levied 7A

liberation 5B

maladies 8A

manifest 6C

massive 7B

median 6B

menial 6B

misconceptions 7C

modestly 8B

moonlighting 7A

moribund 8A

myriads 8C

nostalgic 5B

obliged 8C

obsolescence 8B

oppressed 5B

ostracism 6C

paradox 7B

passive 5B, 6C

perceive 6A

perk 7A

pervasive 6C

perverse 6B

phenomenon 5A

pivotal 8C

preceded 5C

precipitate 8C

preconceived 6B

predecessors 8C

predominant 7C

preoccupation 5C

presumption 6C

prevalence 7C

priority 6A

prodding 6B

proffer 7A

profound 5C

prohibits 7A

proponents 7A

proposition 5B

propriety 6B

prosperous 8A

provisional 5B

prudent 7C

quarantining 7C

radical 6A

reality 6A

recipients 7C

reciprocated 5C

reimbursement 7B

reinvigorated 6B

repugnant 6C

resentful 6A

respondents 5C

restrictions 7B

revenue 8B

scarcity 8B

scourge 7B

semiliterate 6A

sentiment 7A

simplification 8B

slash 8B

sophisticated 7C

spasms 8C

spawn 7C

specter 8A

spurn 6B

spurred 7A

squelching 6C

stark 8A

stigmatized 7C

successors 8C

suppressed 7C

surcharge 7A

surmise 8C

sustain 5C

sustainable (-ability) 8B

sweltered 8C

systematic (-ally) 8B

tangible 8C

tantalizing 5C

taunts 6B

tedious 5B

toll 6C

transition 8B

transmission 7C

transmitted 7C

ultimately 7B

unbounded 7B

universal 7B

valedictory 6B

validated 6C

validity 6A

volatile 7B

withered 8A

Word List—Content-Specific

(Annotations refer to chapter [5–8] and reading [A-C] in which each word appears.)

achievement motivation 6C

affiliation motivation 6C

AIDS 7C

antibodies 7C

biogeochemical view 8C

biosphere 8C

botanist 8C

carbonates 8C

cardiologists 6C

cognitive components 5C

components 5C

consummate love 5C

contagious 7C

crystallization 5C

cyclosporin 7C

defense mechanism 7C

ecologist 8C

ecology 8C

economics 8C

ecosystems 8C

emotional component 5C

environmentalist 8C

epidemiologists 7C

erotic love 5C

evolution 7C

extrinsic motivation 6C

flora 8C

geochemical view 8C

global warming 8C

greenhouse effect 8C

greenhouse gases 8C

hemophiliacs 7C

HIV 7C

hypodermic 7C

immune system 7C

incubator 8C

infatuate 5C

intimacy 5C

intravenous 7C

intrinsic motivation 6C

Kaposi's sarcoma 7C

limerence 5C

malaria 7C

microorganisms 7C

motivational component 5C

nonlove 5C

opportunistic infections 7C

organic processes 8C

ozone layer 8C

passion 5C

pathogen 7C

pesticides 8C

physiological arousal 5C

platonic love 5C

Pneumocystis carinni 7C

protozoan 7C

relative humidity 8C

sedimentary rocks 8C

somatic tension 6C

toxic 8C

Type A personality 6C

yellow fever 7C

Word List—All

(Annotations refer to chapter [5–8] and reading [A-C] in which each word appears.)

aberration 8B

abolition 5B

abusive 6A

achievement motivation 6C

acute 5C

affiliation motivation 6C

AIDS 7C

ambiguous 7B

androgyny 5B

anglers 8A

antibiotics 7C

apparatus 6C

applicable 6C

asymptomatic 7C

autonomy 7B

averted 5A

avid 8C

baffled 5B

banish 6C

banning 7A

batteries 7B

befouled 8C

beneficiary 7B

biogeochemical view 8C

biosphere 8C

blight 8A

botanist 8C

brooded 8A

calculated 5C

carbonates 8C

cardiologists 6C

cartel 8C

chauvinism 5B

cognitive component 5C

communicable 7A

compensation 7B

components 5C

composting 8B

composure 6A

comprehensive 8B

condescension 5A

conduits 7C

confirmed 7C
consolation 5A
conspiracy 6A
consummate love 5C
contagious 7C
contaminated 7C
continuation 5C
corroded 6B
counterparts 8A
crank 7B
crystallization 5C
curbs(ed) 7B
cyclosporin 7C
decimated 8C
decipher 5A
deem 7A
defense mechanism 7C
deficits 7B
déjà vu 5B
depletion 8C
detect 6C
detract 6C
devastating 5C
deviousness 5B
diligently 6C
dilemma 5B
disincentives 7A
disparate 5A
dispersed 8B
distinction 5A
diverged 8C
domestic 5B
dominance 5A
dooms 6A
droned 8A
ecologist 8C
ecology 8C
economics 8C

ecosystems 8C
egalitarian 5B
elite 6B
embodied 8B
emits 8B
emotional component 5C
encompass 5C
endowed 5A
enduring 6B
enhance 5A
enriching 7B
ensured 7C
entrepreneur 5B
environmentalist 8C
epidemic 7C
epidemiologists 7C
equivalency 6A
erotic love 5C
estimates 7A
ethic 8B
evolution 7C
exclusivity 5C
exhibit 6C
explosive 6C
extrinsic motivation 6C
facilitate 8B
fantasizing 5C
flora 8C
flustered 6A
forbidding 6C
fosters 7B
fraternizing 7A
geochemical view 8C
global warming 8C
greenhouse effect 8C
greenhouse gases 8C
grim 7A
harmony 8A

hemophiliacs 7C
heterosexually 7C
hierarchy 8B
HIV 7C
hospitable 8C
hypodermic 7C
immune system 7C
impaired 7C
impediments 6A
impersonal 7B
incentives 7A
incidence 7A
inclined 5A
incubator 8C
indicted 5B
inebriated 6B
infatuate 5C
inferiority 5A
inflation 7B
inhabitants 8C
inherent 6C
insidious 7C
instinctively 5A
intimacy 5C
intravenous 7C
intriguing 5B
intrinsic motivation 6C
intrusive 5C
isolated 7C
jargon 5B
justifiable 7A
Kaposi's sarcoma 7C
latency 7C
lauded 8C
legions 7C
lethal 8C
levied 7A
liberation 5B

limerence 5C
maladies 8A
malaria 7C
manifest 6C
massive 7B
median 6B
menial 6B
microorganisms 7C
misconceptions 7C
modestly 8B
moonlighting 7A
moribund 8A
motivational component 5C
myriads 8C
nonlove 5C
nostalgic 5B
obliged 8C
obsolescence 8B
oppressed 5B
opportunistic infections 7C
organic processes 8C
ostracism 6C
ozone layer 8C
paradox 7B
passion 5C
passive 5B, 6C
pathogen 7C
perceive 6A
perk 7A
pervasive 6C
perverse 6B
pesticides 8C
phenomenon 5A
physiological arousal 5C
pivotal 8C
platonic love 5C
Pneumocystis carinni 7C
preceded 5C

precipitate 8C
preconceived 6B
predecessors 8C
predominant 7C
preoccupation 5C
presumption 6C
prevalence 7C
priority 6A
prodding 6B
proffer 7A
profound 5C
prohibits 7A
proponents 7A
proposition 5B
propriety 6B
prosperous 8A
protozoan 7C
provisional 5B
prudent 7C
quarantining 7C
radical 6A
reality 6A
recipients 7C
reciprocated 5C
reimbursement 7B
reinvigorated 6B
relative humidity 8C
repugnant 6C
resentful 6A
respondents 5C
restrictions 7B
revenue 8B
scarcity 8B
scourge 7B
sedimentary rocks 8C
semiliterate 6A
sentiment 7A
simplification 8B

slash 8B
somatic tension 6C
sophisticated 7C
spasms 8C
spawn 7C
specter 8A
spurn 6B
spurred 7A
squelching 6C
stark 8A
stigmatized 7C
successors 8C
suppressed 7C
surcharge 7A
surmise 8C
sustain 5C
sustainable (-ability) 8B
sweltered 8C
systematic (-ally) 8B
tangible 8C
tantalizing 5C
taunts 6B
tedious 5B
toll 6C
toxic 8C
transition 8B
transmission 7C
transmitted 7C
Type A personality 6C
ultimately 7B
unbounded 7B
universal 7B
valedictory 6B
validated 6C
validity 6A, 6C
volatile
withered 8A
yellow fever 7C

Part I—Word List—Chapters 1–4

abundance
adaptation
admonish
ample
anchors
assertive
asymmetrical
atheism
benign
binge
bland
celebratory
chlorofluorocarbons
circadian rhythms
compel
concept
conception
confirmation
conservative
considerably
consistent
convenience
conveys
cripple
demonstrated
developmental period
dimensions
disgruntled
diurnal
dominance
dormant
egalitarian
elaboration
emulate
endangered
engrossing

enhance
environmental influence
estivation
expounded
fatality
feigned
fervent
forecast
genetic
glucagon
graver
hibernation
hormone
impose
incidence
inevitable
injects
innate
instinct
instinctual
intensify
interactions
leptin
martyr
migration
mimics
moderation
neutral
nocturnal
nondenominational
nonreciprocal
nonverbal
obese
orated
peptide
plaintiff

portentously

prerogative

presumptuous

psychologist

quota

receptors

reciprocate

recital

regulators

rehabilitation

replication

reverence

riffling

riveted

socioeconomic

solidarity

solvents

stratosphere

stringent

subordinate

tumult

verify

vistas

voraciously

Instructor's Resource Manual
Developing Vocabulary Concepts
for College Thinking
Second Edition

Sherrie L. Nist
University of Georgia

Michele L. Simpson
University of Georgia

HOUGHTON MIFFLIN COMPANY   BOSTON   NEW YORK

Both authors contributed equally to this textbook. Hence, the determination was made to list their names in alphabetical order.

Sponsoring Editor: Renée Deljon
Senior Associate Editor: Linda Bieze
Associate Project Editor: Gabrielle Stone
Associate Production Coordinator: Deborah Frydman
Senior Manufacturing Coordinator: Michael O'Dea
Marketing Manager: Nancy Lyman

Printed in the U.S.A.

ISBN: 0-669-41851-X

123456789–QM–00 99 98 97 96

Contents

Answer Keys   31

Preface

The purpose of the Instructor's Resource Manual is to provide individuals using *Developing Vocabulary Concepts for College Thinking*, Second Edition, with some additional information, not only about how to use the book, but also about vocabulary instruction in general. We have divided the guide into four major sections. The first one, Philosophical Questions and Research About Teaching Vocabulary, provides information on levels of word knowledge beyond what is given in the student text, and how these levels relate to assessing vocabulary understanding. It discusses the role of active learning as well as characteristics of effective vocabulary instruction. Basically, it addresses the philosophical and research underpinnings that guided the writing of *Developing Vocabulary Concepts for College Thinking*. Instructors will notice that the textbook is inextricably tied to the philosophy and research outlined in the first section.

The second section, Using *Developing Vocabulary Concepts for College Thinking* in the Classroom, assists instructors in adapting the text to their unique situations. Suggestions are given that can assist you in using *Developing Vocabulary Concepts for College Thinking* flexibly, depending on your particular situation. The pedagogy behind the textbook is also drawn from the philosophical and research bases discussed in the first section and further delineated in section two.

Section three, Sample Lesson Plans, presents a generic lesson plan that can be used as a guide for all of the readings presented in *Developing Vocabulary Concepts for College Thinking*. We have divided each lesson into five stages: Preparing, Focusing, Practicing, Monitoring/ Assessing, and Evaluating. Not only have we discussed each of these five stages generally, but we have also presented two very specific lesson plans. One plan is for a narrative reading, whereas the other is for a selection with more difficult content. These examples should be helpful as instructors work on pacing their own specific courses and course demands. At the end of this section, there is also a suggested reading list for those who would like additional information on vocabulary research and instruction.

Finally, the last section provides the answer keys for all of the activities presented in the textbook. We have tried to be as complete as possible in writing these keys, but instructors should keep in mind that many activities do not have pat answers. In keeping with our philosophy as well as current research on vocabulary, these activities were purposefully planned to allow for student analysis and varying opinions.

We have used reviewers' comments as well as unsolicited ideas from students and colleagues as we have revised both the student text and the Instructor's Resource Manual. We welcome any additional input, particularly on how you adapted the text to your own teaching situation. Let us know what you think.

Sherrie L. Nist
Michele L. Simpson

....

Philosophical Questions and Research About Teaching Vocabulary

PHILOSOPHICAL BACKGROUND

What Does It Mean to "Know" a Word?

What factor determines whether students have learned a new word? This question is difficult to answer, but we do know that word knowledge becomes more intricate as students increase their associations with the word and their own experiences in the world.

We also know that students' understanding of a word could probably be placed on a continuum much like the one by Dale (1958) that we discuss in Chapter 1. For example, students who have never seen or heard the word *exacerbate* would be at Dale's first stage of word knowledge. Many college students, especially those who are taking developmental or remedial college reading courses, are at Dale's first or second stage.

Dale's fourth stage comes the closest to capturing what is meant by knowing a word. That is, students understand a word when they recognize it and can provide an appropriate and precise definition that fits the context. Dixon and Jenkins (1984) have described this fourth stage of word knowledge as full conceptual knowledge. Full conceptual knowledge of a word is in contrast to partial conceptual knowledge and verbal associational knowledge, where students have only memorized the word in meaningful sentences that are syntactically correct. Moreover, they rarely understand the nuances or subtleties of the word. For example, a student lacking the fourth stage of knowledge about the word *exacerbate* would probably write a sentence similar to this: John always *exacerbated* his sister, which made his mother angry. Dale (1958) and Dixon and Jenkins (1984) imply that it is best for students to know a new word as a full concept, especially if knowing a word is to have a long-term impact on their reading and listening comprehension.

But what does it mean to know a word conceptually? What processes are involved? After reviewing the literature, we believe that students should be able to perform the following key processes:

1. Recognize and generate critical attributes, examples, and non-examples of a concept (Beck, McCaslin, & McKeown, 1980; Graves, 1985; Tennyson & Park, 1980).
2. Sense and infer relationships between concepts and their own backgrounds (Ausubel, 1968; Beck, McCaslin, & McKeown, 1980; O'Rourke, 1974).
3. Recognize and apply the concept to a variety of contexts (Carnine, Kameenui, & Coyle, 1984; Mezynski, 1983; Stahl, 1983).
4. Generate novel contexts for the targeted concept (Beck, McCaslin, & McKeown, 1980; Gipe, 1979; Stahl, 1983, 1986).

Hence, "knowing" a word is more than reciting a memorized definition, which might be a surprise to many students who have religiously memorized definitions for quizzes and then forgotten the words once they left the classroom environment. In order to help students understand this conceptual approach to learning new words, we have created some steps for learning general and content-specific words. These steps can be found in the Introduction to Part II, Thematic Chapters.

How Can Vocabulary Knowledge Be Measured?

The type of format used for student practice and also to measure students' understanding of a word should be closely related to the philosophical definition of what it means to "know" a word (Kameenui, Carnine, & Freschi, 1982). If there is not a match between philosophy, instruction, and test format, then there is a strong possibility that a test will mask students' understanding and provide inaccurate data about achievement. For example, if a matching test is used to determine whether students conceptually understand the targeted words, students with only partial conceptual or verbal associational understanding might be able to do well because the format asked them only to recognize the definitions they had memorized.

Relying solely on recognition formats such as matching and multiple choice as measures of students' understanding has been criticized for many reasons. Anderson and Freebody (1981) stress that choices in a multiple-choice question affect performance and that test-taking strategies can camouflage students' real understanding. Kaneenui, Dixon, and Carnine (1987) have argued that multiple-choice vocabulary tasks are "useless at best and dangerous at worst" because they cannot reveal the dimensions of a student's conceptual understanding (p.15). Consequently, in *Developing Vocabulary Concepts for College Thinking* we have used multiple-choice and other recognition formats sparingly.

Rather than depending upon recognition formats, we have included a variety of practice and test formats to enable students to practice the processes characterizing conceptual thinking. Listed below are those four processes and specific formats that are used for both practice and measurement formats in this text.

Recognizing and Generating Characteristics, Examples, and Nonexamples

1. Request for an example or characteristic
2. Exclusion activities

Sensing and Inferring Relationships

1. Paired-word questions
2. Classifying and categorizing via list, group, and label; charting; semantic feature analysis; mapping; subsuming
3. Analogies

Applying Concepts to a Variety of Contexts

1. Sentence judgment
2. Cloze or sentence completion

Generating Novel Contexts

1. Paired-word sentence generation
2. Sentence writing

What Should Be the Student's Role in Learning New Words?

Many students are passive rather than active learners. Research suggests, however, that students who actively try to make sense of what they see and hear are those who will learn more (Craik & Tulving, 1975; Johnson-Laird, Gibbs, & de Mowbrey, 1978). Tyler, McCallum, and Ellis (1979) have proposed that the amount of cognitive effort required by a task is an important determinant of later recall performance, with greater student cognitive effort leading to greater recall.

These research findings probably come as little surprise. That is, the more students try to actively engage themselves in learning, the more they will remember and understand. But how does that translate into practice with respect to learning vocabulary? Stahl (1985) describes active involvement of the learner as "generative processing." Generative processing engages students in activities such as restating formal definitions in their own words, creating semantic maps, studying definitional characteristics, creating sentences using targeted words, and participating in discussions. In contrast, Stahl describes the passive involvement of the learner as "associational tasks." Passive associational tasks related to vocabulary instruction are characterized by worksheet-type activities asking students to match words with definitions or by instructional methods such as asking students to repeat words and definitions aloud several times.

In this text we have used a variety of activities and tests that actively involve and engage students. Many of these activities involve solving problems that demand higher-level thinking and processing. Students will also be monitoring their conceptual word understanding. In addition, we have encouraged students to interact with their classmates and instructor as they work their way through the steps. In short, we stress that students can learn new words and improve their comprehension only if they are actively involved.

CHARACTERISTICS OF EFFECTIVE VOCABULARY INSTRUCTION

Although the present research cannot conclusively recommend one vocabulary approach over another, there is enough evidence to describe some characteristics of effective vocabulary instruction. We will examine five of these characteristics, all of which guided the development of *Developing Vocabulary Concepts for College Thinking*.

Generative Approach

There are two divergent vocabulary instructional approaches that guide classroom instruction and commercial materials (Stahl, Brozo, &

Simpson, 1987). The first is the additive approach, an instructional orientation that focuses on improving vocabulary by learning a predetermined set of words. In contrast, the generative approach emphasizes the teaching of strategies which facilitate students' growth in vocabulary beyond the specific instructional materials. Even though the former dominates commercial materials, research suggests that generative vocabulary approaches, when appropriately taught, are superior to additive approaches in promoting word knowledge and improving students' understanding of text (Stahl & Fairbanks, 1986).

Generative vocabulary instruction teaches students strategies for independently learning new words. Those strategies might include such approaches as analyzing context, mapping, charting, using a dictionary, or applying knowledge of word elements. The generative approach assumes that no one strategy in isolation is superior to another. Rather, students learn to use the strategies collectively to understand a word conceptually. For example, a student might use the context from a textbook, a dictionary, and a map or graphic organizer to develop the concept of **demographic transformation** for a geography class.

Although both additive and generative strategies may appear in most vocabulary commercial materials, how the activities are organized determines the approach. That is, there is a difference between asking students to use their knowledge of word elements to determine the meaning of difficult or unknown words and asking students to use word elements to complete matching or multiple-choice exercises using words like **transportation** and **photography**. Hence, the teacher should examine an activity and ask whether it is teaching students strategies that they can apply independently to new contexts using words they will encounter in their academic careers. If not, then the approach is not generative but additive.

Developing Vocabulary Concepts for College Thinking uses the generative approach. In the first four chapters students learn vocabulary strategies that they can employ independently in their own reading and learning. They learn these strategies with general words and content-specific words taken from college-level narrative and expository material. Not only does the text encourage students to apply these strategies to these preselected words, but it also encourages them to practice these strategies on words they self-select from the readings.

Mixed Methods

From the reviews of research on vocabulary acquisition, Stahl (1983, 1985) suggested that a student who really knows a word has both definitional and contextual knowledge about that word. Definitional knowledge is the knowledge of the relationships between a word and other known words, such as those that appear in a dictionary definition. Contextual knowledge is the knowledge of a core concept, first acquired in a specific context, that becomes generalized or decontextualized through a number of exposures in different situations.

When a method of vocabulary instruction involves students in both definitional and contextual knowledge of the word, it can be termed a "mixed method." Several studies with college students (Anderson & Kulhavey, 1972; Carr, 1985; Crist, 1981) support the mixed-method approach.

What does the research on the mixed method specifically suggest for teachers who want to teach vocabulary? Most importantly, instruction that emphasizes memorization (i.e., verbal understanding) and pairing of labels to synonyms (e.g., *arduous* means *difficult* or *hard*) imparts only definitional knowledge. Such knowledge is likely to have a negligible impact on students' subsequent reading comprehension and learning (Kameenui, Dixon, & Carnine, 1987). Thus, the best vocabulary instruction should emphasize both definitional and contextual information about a word, but with emphasis on the latter (Stahl, 1985).

We developed *Developing Vocabulary Concepts for College Thinking* so students would be challenged to understand words beyond the definitional level. In fact, the second step of learning general vocabulary words is "Determining Meaning," but this step is followed by five other steps (Trying Out Meaning, Applying Concepts, Reciting and Reviewing, Conceptualizing Meaning, and Self-Evaluating) that emphasize contextual information about words. Hence, this text, following research findings, uses mixed methods to help students improve their vocabulary.

Active Role of the Learner

Researchers who required their subjects to be actively involved in their own vocabulary development (Carr, 1985; Diekhoff, Brown, & Dansereau, 1982; Pressley, Levin, & Miller, 1982) found that such learners performed significantly better than other subjects on measures designed to evaluate vocabulary knowledge. From their reviews, Stahl and Fairbanks (1986) and Mezynski (1983) likewise concluded that active processing is critical for vocabulary acquisition.

The implications of these findings are clear. Students will not improve their vocabulary on a long-term basis if they merely fill in blanks and match definitions to words in an individualized setting. We need to use instructional materials and strategies that stimulate students to engage in elaborative processing. In addition, instruction needs to provide more opportunities for discussions and interactions between student and teacher or between students.

As we mentioned earlier, the practice activities, steps, and pre/posttest formats in *Developing Vocabulary Concepts for College Thinking* emphasize students interacting with words in creative ways. Furthermore, students are encouraged to select and study words not from lists in the textbook. This feature is especially crucial since students must develop the drive, curiosity, and strategies to learn words on their own if they are to become successful independent learners. Finally, throughout the text there are suggestions for writing activities, small group discussions, and paired work with other students that will assist students in becoming active learners and provide them with immediate feedback about their thinking.

Vocabulary in Context

The findings from numerous research studies suggest that vocabulary should be taught from a unifying context (Jenkins & Dixon, 1983; Mezynski, 1983). Words taught in a context of a subject area will be learned more effectively than words in isolation or from unrelated lists, because context allows students to integrate words with previously acquired knowledge.

The implication, of course, is that students will not improve long-term vocabulary acquisition by memorizing definitions to words from a list provided in the textbook. In the ideal world students would spontaneously select words to study from their own textbooks or reading materials such as newspapers and novels. However, this is slightly unworkable since many students lack the strategies, curiosity, and motivation to begin or sustain an independent program of vocabulary development on their own. The next-best solution would be to provide students college-level material organized around relevant themes and then preselect the vocabulary words to study. In this scenario students encounter targeted words in some meaningful context.

In order to teach words in a meaningful context, we incorporated several features in *Developing Vocabulary Concepts for College Thinking*. The reading selections are arranged so that there are four overall themes in the book. This arrangement facilitates students' comprehension, since the ideas from the first reading will assist students in building background for the second and third readings. Words are introduced in lists, but students first interact with them in their original context when they take the pretest. Finally, the practice activities require students to place the words back in a context, whether it be the original context or another meaningful but slightly different context.

Intensity of Instruction

Research reviews by Jenkins and Dixon (1983), Mezynski (1983), and Stahl and Fairbanks (1986) have concluded that for vocabulary instruction to be effective it should be intense. Intense instruction is characterized by the use of multiple examples, repetitions, and review in differing contexts over a long period of time. These researchers have suggested that students will remember words learned via intense instructional methods because the multiple repetitions and review lead to a decontextualized word understanding. However, intense instruction, by itself, will not guarantee conceptual understanding of new words. As we mentioned earlier, instruction must emphasize contextual word knowledge and actively involve students in the processes involved in understanding a word conceptually.

The implications of this research have also been incorporated into this text. The book teaches fewer words than traditional texts and provides more instructional time for meaningful reinforcement activities and cumulative reviews. These activities and reviews will, in turn, promote the breadth of word knowledge necessary for students' long-term retention and use.

We have provided intense instruction within *Developing Vocabulary Concepts for College Thinking* in two ways. Most importantly, each of the four thematic chapters introduces students to the words via a multi-step procedure (seven steps for general words and eight steps for content-specific words) that incorporates multiple repetition and review. In turn, the repetition and review occurs within differing activity formats that gradually require more sophisticated levels of conceptual processing. Second, each thematic chapter contains a comprehensive posttest over Readings A and B and a comprehensive posttest over Readings A, B, and C. Students doing all three readings and the subsequent activities will definitely receive intensive instruction.

REFERENCES

Anderson, R. C., & Freebody, P. (1981). Vocabulary knowledge. In J. T. Guthrie (Ed.), *Comprehension and teaching: Research reviews* (pp. 77–117). Newark, DE: International Reading Association.

Anderson, R. C., & Kulhavy, R. W. (1972). Imagery and prose learning. *Journal of Educational Psychology, 63,* 242–243.

Ausubel, D. P. (1963). *The psychology of meaningful verbal learning.* New York: Grune & Stratton.

Beck, J., McCaslin, E., & McKeown, M. G. (1982). The effects of long-term vocabulary instruction on lexical access and reading comprehension. *Journal of Educational Psychology, 74,* 506–521.

Carnine, D., Kameenui, E. J., & Coyle, G. (1984). Utilization of contextual information in determining the meaning of unfamiliar words. *Reading Research Quarterly, 19,* 188–204.

Carr, E. (1985). The vocabulary overview guide: A metacognitive strategy to improve vocabulary comprehension and retention. *Journal of Reading, 21,* 684–689.

Craik, F. I. M., & Tulving, E. (1975). Depth of processing and the retention of words in episodic memory. *Journal of Experimental Psychology: General, 104,* 268–294.

Crist, R. L. (1981). Learning concepts from contexts and definitions: A single subject replication. *Journal of Reading Behavior, 13,* 271–277.

Dale, E. (1958). Vocabulary measurement: Techniques and major findings. *Elementary English, 42,* 895-901.

Diekhoff, G. M., Brown, P. J., & Dansereau, D. F. (1982). A prose learning strategy training program based on network and depth of processing models. *Journal of Experimental Education, 50,* 180–184.

Dixon, R. C., & Jenkins, J. R. (1984). *An outcome analysis of receptive vocabulary knowledge.* Unpublished manuscript, University of Illinois, Champaign.

Gipe, J. (1979). Investigating techniques for teaching word meanings. *Reading Research Quarterly, 14,* 624–645.

Graves, M. F., & Hammond, H. K. (1979). A validated procedure for teaching prefixes and its effect on students' ability to assign meaning to novel words. In M. L. Kamil and A. J. Moe (Eds.), *Perspectives on reading research and instruction* (pp. 184–188). Washington, D.C.: National Reading Conference.

Kameenui, E. J., Carnine, D. W., & Freschi, R. (1982). Effects of text construction and instruction procedures for teaching word meanings on comprehension and recall. *Reading Research Quarterly, 17,* 367–388.

Kameenui, E. J., Dixon, R. C., & Carnine, D. W. (1987). Issues in the design of vocabulary instruction. In M. G. McKeown & M. G. Curtis (Eds.), *The nature of vocabulary acquisition* (pp. 129–145). Hilsman, N.J.: Erlbaum.

Mezynski, K. (1983). Issues concerning the acquisition of knowledge: Effects of vocabulary training on reading comprehension. *Review of Educational Research, 53,* 253–279.

Nagy, W. E., Diakidaj, I. A., & Anderson, R. C. (1993). The acquisition of morphology. Learning the contribution of suffixes to the meanings of derivatives. *Journal of Reading Behavior, 25 (2),* 155–170.

O'Rourke, J. P. (1974). *Toward a science of vocabulary development.* The Hague: Mouton.

Pressley, M., Levin, J. R., & Miller, G. E. (1981). How does the keyword method affect vocabulary, comprehension, and usage. *Reading Research Quarterly, 16,* 213–225.

Stahl, N. A., Brozo, W. G., & Simpson, M. L. (1987). A content analysis of college vocabulary textbooks. *Reading Research and Instruction, 26,* 203–221.

Stahl, S. A. (1983). Differential word knowledge and reading comprehension. *Journal of Reading Behavior, 15,* 33–50.

Stahl, S. A. (1985). To teach a word well: A framework for vocabulary instruction. *Reading World, 24,* 16–27.

Stahl, S. A., & Fairbanks, M. M. (1986). The effects of vocabulary instruction: A model-based meta-analysis. *Journal of Educational Research, 56,* 72–110.

Tennyson, R. D., & Park, O. (1980). The teaching of concepts: A review of instructional design literature. *Review of Educational Research, 50,* 55–70.

Tyler, S. W., Hertel, P. T., McCallum, M. C., & Ellis, H. C. (1979). Cognitive effort and memory. *Journal of Experimental Psychology: Human Learning and Memory, 5,* 607–617.

Using *Developing Vocabulary Concepts for College Thinking* in the Classroom

PEDAGOGY

Those of you who have used other vocabulary texts with students will immediately notice that *Developing Vocabulary Concepts for College Thinking* is different both in format and approach. Most other texts on the market today purposefully design vocabulary books that can be used by students on an individual basis. Books using this approach generally give students a list of words, instruct them to look the words up in a dictionary, and then have them do a series of tasks, usually in a multiple-choice format. Students then check their own work and, if their performance is adequate, they go on to the next set of words and activities. Rarely do such texts have students discuss words with each other; rarely is there any direct instruction and modeling of strategic processes by the teacher. *Developing Vocabulary Concepts for College Thinking,* however, is a text and vocabulary program that is rooted in the belief that direct instruction, instructor modeling, discussion, writing, and student interaction are imperative if students are to learn generative vocabulary strategies that will lead to conceptual word knowledge. The purpose of this section, then, is to focus on how to use *Developing Vocabulary Concepts for College Thinking* in the classroom.

Before discussing the actual pacing of the text, we will first present the overriding pedagogy which encompasses the text. There are four key pedagogical features that instructors should incorporate regardless of the specific pacing of the course. Some of these features were mentioned earlier as we discussed the philosophy and research encompassing this text. These features are highlighted below.

Words are always presented in context. Although the words for each reading are isolated for convenience in a list at the beginning of each reading, all words are presented within the context of a longer reading. Instructors should always have students read the passage so that they can get a feeling for real uses of the words. As students work through the activities, they should refer to the reading selection to see how their interactions with the words in the activities compare and contrast to the way they initially saw the word in the reading.

Direct instruction is important if conceptual understanding is to occur. Straightforwardly, this text was not primarily designed for individualized use, although some of the reviewers stated they had great success with students using the text on their own. Students would probably learn words using it in that manner, but *maximum* learning will occur when the instructor is willing to guide students through the strategies and words. When we use the term "direct instruction," we are not referring to the instruction of discrete skills. Rather, we mean that direct instruction involves instructor modeling of the processes and thinking that students should be employing as they learn the generative strategies. For Chapters 1 through 4, instructors should teach the strategies using instructor modeling, discussion, and the reading and activities included in each of these chapters. It is important that students have a basic understanding of the generative strategies introduced in the first four chapters before interacting with the four thematic units.

When teaching the words in the four thematic units, instructors might want to follow the example lessons presented later in this Instructor's Guide. We encourage you to make modifications based on students' ability levels and on the course in which you are using the text. For example, students with very weak vocabularies will probably need more direct instruction than those with somewhat better vocabularies. We assume that those using this text know their students' needs, and as they become more familiar with the context of the text, they can adjust instruction accordingly.

Discussion and writing help students learn words conceptually. Discussion and writing are integral parts of vocabulary instruction. Encourage students to discuss the readings and the words. From the time students' prior knowledge is activated until the time they are preparing for the posttest, we encourage you to use teacher-guided discussion, as well as paired discussion between students. The classroom environment should be such that students do not feel threatened about making mistakes or about asking for further clarification and explanation about word meaning. During discussion, instructors and students can work together to determine which generative strategies would be most appropriate for specific words. For example, you might encourage students to generate images or keywords to help them learn and remember more concrete words. Students working in pairs might first discuss and create these images and then bring them back to the entire class for discussion. Discussion might also include *why* certain strategies are appropriate or inappropriate for a given word or group of words. If, for example, students have a very difficult time evoking an image or a keyword for a word or group of words, another strategy would be a better choice. You should always encourage students to use a variety of strategies since, as we stated in the previous section, mixed methods appear to be the most effective way of learning new words.

Writing activities are also important ways to help students understand new words at a conceptual level. The more students write sentences and paragraphs using the targeted words, the more secure they will feel about using the words outside the classroom. Writing activities also demand students to interact and think about the words and ideas in an elaborative fashion. Because of this elaborative interaction, students will remember the words more and store them in their long-term memory. The activities in this textbook provide students with many opportunities for writing. The thematic arrangement in Part II of the text (e.g., Gender Issues, Educational Issues, Health-Related Issues, and Environmental Issues) provides students with the background and stimulus for responding to probes and questions about important ideas and the targeted words. In addition to sentence writing, each chapter contains short answer and essay questions pertinent to the themes.

Repetition is important. The amount of repetition needed to learn and remember a word depends on several factors. First, it depends on the students' level of understanding at the time they are introduced to the word. For example, if students are at Stage 1 and state that they have never seen the word before and that they have no idea of the word's meaning, they will certainly require more exposure to the word than if they are at Stage 3 and have at least a fuzzy notion of what the word means.

Second, the number of repetitions depends on the concreteness of the word. Imagery, mnemonic, and keyword research shows that concrete words are more easily learned and remembered than are abstract words. For example, words such as **anglers** and **egomaniac** should require fewer repetitions than more abstract words such as **distinction** and **asymptomatic.**

Third, the level of students' interest in the topic being studied and the selection being read is also a factor. Words that are in some way related to students' interests or major fields of study will not only require fewer repetitions but also will be learned at a deeper conceptual level than those for which a lack of interest exists.

Because of the importance of repetition within the thematic units, students interact with the words numerous times. We have attempted to provide a minimum of five exposures to the word in the activities alone. These exposures do not include any of the discussions in which you may engage students during direct instruction and modeling, nor does it include repetitions of the words in pairs and in self-evaluating. Our experience with this text is that students conceptually know the words presented by the time they complete the activities.

USING THE TEXT FLEXIBLY

After using the text with our own students, and considering the comments from many of the instructors who also used the text, we realized how important it was to make the text more flexible. Hence, the second edition of *Developing Vocabulary Concepts for College Thinking* has been revised so that you can use the textbook with your students in a variety of ways. We highly recommend that all instructors begin with Part I of the text, which teaches students the basic generative strategies for expanding their vocabulary. In addition to practicing the use of strategies such as context clues, the dictionary, and word elements, students will also read selections in Part I that are tied to one of the themes of the book, and then study targeted words taken from the selections. In Part I there are approximately 95 words for students to study and learn.

After completing the activities and mastering the words in Part I, instructors and students have a variety of options in using Part II of *Developing Vocabulary Concepts for College Thinking*. It is important to remember that Part II of the textbook has been written so it contains a multitude of assessment, teaching, reinforcement, and evaluation material. These include:

1. Pretests for each reading selection in each chapter.
2. Writing activities to promote elaborative thinking.
3. Word elements, word origin, dictionary, context, and keyword/imagery activities.
4. Posttests for Readings A and B in each chapter.
5. Posttests for Readings A, B, and C in each chapter.
6. Self-monitoring activities to promote students' self-evaluation of their mastery of the words.

Instructors and students can choose to approach Part II in the three following ways:

1. Select only the first two readings for each chapter in Part II of the text. Readings A and B are shorter in length, contain fewer vocabulary words, and are typically narrative in format. There is a comprehensive posttest for Readings A and B for each chapter in the Instructor's Guide.

   The third reading, Reading C, is a lengthy excerpt from a college content area textbook. Reading C is not only longer, but it also contains a lot more words. In addition, students study and learn both content-specific and general words.
2. Select only one or two chapters in Part II and focus on them intensively. The criteria for selecting these chapters should probably be the themes which fit in best with your other course goals and text materials. Hence, with this option students will complete Readings A, B, and C, and all the activities for each. In addition, students can take two posttests for each chapter (i.e., posttest over Readings A and B; posttest over Readings A, B, and C).
3. Assign all four chapters in Part II of the textbook and select additional readings from other texts or magazines which support these themes. Then use the additional readings to practice basic comprehension and study skills, or any of the goals of your course. We should mention that we have written a college reading text, *Developing Textbook Fluency*, which has been written and organized thematically. This book would make an excellent companion for *Developing Vocabulary Concepts for College Thinking*.

The options you choose will, of course, depend on the characteristics of your program, your students, and your institution. In the next section, we offer some suggestions for helping you decide how you will use this textbook.

PACING

The pace at which you use *Developing Vocabulary Concepts for College Thinking* can best be estimated by answering the following questions:

1. What is the length of the term? Will the text be used in a 10-week quarter or in a 14- to 16-week semester or trimester?
2. How many hours weekly does the course meet? Is it a two-, three-, or five-credit course?
3. Is this the sole text used in the course or is it used in conjunction with another text?
4. What ratio of guided practice, paired practice, and independent practice will work best with the students who are using this text? In other words, will the students using this text be at Stage 1 understanding for most of the words, or will they be closer to Stages 2 and 3?

Rather than attempting to give an example of a generic syllabus that could not address all of the above factors, we have chosen to provide some general guidelines for each of the four questions. Using these guidelines, you should then be able to construct a syllabus appropriate to the circumstances under which you will teach.

Length of term. Regardless of the length of the term, it is of primary importance that students study the first four chapters. Instructors teaching on a semester or trimester system should be able to cover everything in *Developing Vocabulary Concepts for College Thinking* in one term. Instructors using the text on a quarter system that is approximately 10 weeks long will probably not be able to include all the readings.

Number of credit hours awarded. Pacing will vary based on the number of weekly meetings for the course. In situations in which students attend daily, certainly you will be able to cover more readings than those in which students attend only two or three times weekly. Of course, you will also need to consider the other factors discussed here. For example, instructors teaching a three-credit semester course will be able to cover considerably more material than would those teaching a three-credit quarter course.

Amount of emphasis placed on teaching vocabulary. This consideration actually focuses on the goal of the course. Although the primary purpose of *Developing Vocabulary Concepts for College Thinking* is to improve students' vocabularies, the text also stresses the importance of comprehension. Our philosophy that comprehension and vocabulary are inseparable enables you to use this text for both purposes. Hence, if you use this text and exclude another reading or studying text, pacing will differ considerably than if you use this as a supplementary text. As we note in the specific lesson plans presented at the end of this section, we believe that some daily attention to vocabulary is important. This does not mean that every minute of every period need be vocabulary related, but that at least 10 to 15 minutes be devoted to one of the five steps outlined in the generic lesson plan: Preparing, Focusing, Practicing, Monitoring/Assessing, Evaluating. As with learning any kind of material, distributed practice, in which students interact with information to be learned a little at a time rather than in one large mass, leads to more efficient and effective learning. Therefore, what you should think about is how much emphasis the particular course places on vocabulary. In those courses with a strong vocabulary emphasis, you will be able to devote more time to direct vocabulary instruction and will probably be able to cover more of the text in a comprehensive manner. For those courses in which vocabulary instruction is more ancillary, either you will cover less of the text or you will cover it in less detail. You should always keep in mind, however, that (a) it is much better for students to learn fewer words but learn them conceptually, and (b) a little knowledge of a vocabulary word is perhaps worse than no knowledge of that word at all.

Ratio of guided, paired, and independent practice necessary. As we mentioned earlier, the success that students have with this text is related to the level of modeling, discussion, and interaction that they have with you and with each other. However, the stage of vocabulary understanding at which students begin will determine the ratios of guided to paired to independent practices students need. Students who start at Stage 1 will need more guided and paired practice. If they don't receive it, they will have more difficulty completing the independent practice activities which focus more on conceptual understanding. On the other hand, students who are at Stage 2 or 3 will need less guided and paired practice prior to engaging in independent practice. Again, instructors who have a good idea about the entry-level characteristics of their students will be able to provide a balance among the three types of practice so that students can effectively and conceptually learn the words. In addition, you may alter the ratio as the term progresses. As students become better versed in applying generative strategies to unknown words, even Stage 1 words, they will require less guided and paired practice.

Pacing, then, involves many factors, all of which should be considered as you plan a vocabulary program suitable for your students. As such, there is no one best way to pace the use of *Developing Vocabulary Concepts for College Thinking*. Part of what makes the text so attractive is the flexibility available to instructors to custom-design vocabulary-building programs based on generative strategies that suit their particular groups of students.

Sample Lesson Plans

Because *Developing Vocabulary Concepts for College Thinking* differs in philosophy, content, and format from most vocabulary texts, we want to assist you by providing a generic lesson plan, as well as plans for two of the readings. The generic plan not only gives the steps that you might want to follow, but also ties these steps to the progression of activities within the text. The generic plan is followed by a specific plan for the easier reading "If You Light Up on Sunday, Don't Come in on Monday" found in Chapter 7, Readings Concerning Health-Related Issues, and the more difficult content reading "Motivation" found in Chapter 6, Readings Concerning Educational Issues.

GENERIC LESSON PLAN

You might want to use the following five steps for each of the readings. Remember that these steps can be either streamlined or expanded, depending on students' ability levels, interest in the topics, and familiarity with the words. We do suggest, however, that you pay some attention to each step so that students can work toward conceptual understanding.

    1. Preparing. Before students actually read the article containing the targeted words, it is important that you prepare them. First, students should take the **pretest.** Answers to the pretest are now included in the Instructor's Guide rather than in the student's text, as was the case in the first edition. If your class is pressed for time, students can take the pretest at home and check it against the key when they come to class. Once students have taken the pretest, you should then **activate prior knowledge and create interest** in the overall theme and, more specifically, in the particular article on which students will be working. You can create interest through discussion, showing films, short paper and pencil activities, listening to recordings, or other types of "fun" activities that can get students thinking about what they already know about the topic. Finally, students **skim** the reading to find the targeted words. At this time, students and instructor should also discuss how students performed on the pretest, and you might point out any words that were particularly troublesome. Then assign students to read the article and do the **Determining Meaning/Organizing Meaning** activity for homework. Students should bring their completed vocabulary cards to class and also should be ready to discuss the words and the article. For information on how students should complete their vocabulary cards, please see Chapter 2 in *Developing Vocabulary Concepts for College Thinking.*

Goal statement: After **preparing,** students should have an idea of which words might be difficult for them. They should have read the selection and be prepared to discuss it.

2. **Focusing.** During this step, students begin to gain understanding of the targeted words, although most will not have reached the conceptualization stage. Here, you should formally introduce students to the words through discussing the article and the way the targeted words are used in context. At this point, encourage students to make any changes on their vocabulary cards.

Goal statement: After **focusing,** students should have an understanding of the reading selection. They should also have a good set of vocabulary cards for referral as they engage in practice activities.

3. **Practicing.** Three different types of practice take place during this step: **guided practice, paired practice,** and **independent practice.** During **guided practice,** you should review definitions and then, together with the students, go over the first two or three items in the **Trying Out Meaning/Beginning Conceptual Understanding** and **Applying Meaning/Using Concepts** activities. When discussing the examples, you should be sure to **model** for students how to think through the correct answers as well as how to use vocabulary cards and

context clues from the reading selection to help determine the correct answers. **Modeling** is particularly important early in the term and may be used less intensively as students are able to use the strategies in a more generative manner.

During **paired practice,** students work in pairs with their vocabulary cards as they **Recite and Review.** They can work in either dyads or triads and each member of each small group should provide clear definitions, synonyms, antonyms, parts of speech, and sentences for words. You should also encourage students to practice their cards front-to-back and back-to-front and to mix them up so as not to learn the words in one specific order. In pairs, students can compare answers to **Trying Out Meaning/Beginning Conceptual Understanding, Writing Activities,** and **Applying Meaning/Using Conceptual Understanding** exercises, rather than simply turning these activities in to you. Activities such as these broaden conceptual understanding and help get words into long-term memory.

Independent practice is simply that. At this point students should be familiar enough with the words and have a deep enough understanding so that they can do the **Conceptualizing Meaning/Comprehending Concepts** activity **independently** and, when present, the **Extending and Challenging** activity. These activities can be assigned for homework and turned in so that you can provide feedback to students. At this point, you might lead a final discussion of the words to ensure that students have conceptualized meaning.

Goal statement: After **practicing,** students should be approaching conceptual word understanding.

4. Monitoring/Assessing. At this step, students should engage in the **Self-Evaluating** activity as they list the words they know at a conceptual level in Column A, words they have a partial understanding of in Column B, and words they have little or no understanding of in Column C. For words listed in Columns B and C, students need to get additional assistance and engage in additional **Reciting and Reviewing** prior to taking the posttests. This step is important for students to undertake before they are assessed with each of the posttests.

Goal statement: After **monitoring/assessing,** students should be able to identify words that are still problematic and get additional assistance before taking the posttest.

5. Evaluating. The final step, **Evaluating,** takes place after students have taken the posttest and after you have graded the tests. Return the tests to students and discuss each of the items. Encourage students to make any final additions or modifications to their vocabulary cards and to correct the wrong answers on their tests.

LESSON PLAN OUTLINE

1. Preparing
   Pretest
   Activate prior knowledge and stimulate interest
   Skim reading
   Assignment: Read the article
         Determining Meaning/Organizing Meaning
             Make vocabulary cards
2. Focusing
   Discuss reading and words
3. Practicing
   Guided practice
         First 2 or 3 items in Trying Out Meaning/Beginning
             Conceptual Understanding and Applying
               Meaning/Using
             Concepts
   Modeling and discussing
   Paired practice
         Reciting and Reviewing
   Independent practice
         Conceptualizing Meaning/Comprehending Concepts
             and, when appropriate, Extending and Challenging
4. Monitoring/Assessing
   Self-Evaluating
   Posttest (A and B, A, B, and C)
5. Evaluating (at the end of each Thematic Unit)
   Go over Posttest (A and B, A, B, and C)
   Additional discussion and vocabulary card modification

LESSON PLAN FOR "IF YOU LIGHT UP ON SUNDAY, DON'T COME IN ON MONDAY" TAKEN FROM CHAPTER 7

1. **Preparing:** Day 1 in vocabulary instruction cycle.
   Time: Approximately 20–30 minutes

In order to gain an idea of their understanding about the words, students should first take the pretest. When they have finished, you should score their tests using the keys provided in the Instructor's Guide for *Developing Vocabulary Concepts for College Thinking*.

After students have taken and received a score on the pretest, activate their prior knowledge and stimulate their interest for the topic. You might use the following questions as a starting point: Do you think that smokers should have the right to smoke where and when they want? Why or why not? Should businesses be permitted not to hire individuals who smoke? Do you believe it is fair for insurance companies to make smokers pay more for health insurance? Why or why not? If you owned a business, would you want to make it a smoke-free environment? Use your own judgment about additional questions and activities.

With your guidance, students should then skim the article, noting the underlined target words and that the main focus of the reading is on how some businesses try to discourage their employees from smoking. If time permits, you could have different students read aloud each sentence in which each of the targeted words is found and begin to make some predictions about what each word means.

Assignment: Students read "If You Light Up . . . " for homework and do the **Determining Meaning** activity. They should put the words, definitions, synonyms, antonyms, part of speech, and, if possible, a sentence on each of their vocabulary cards using the format presented in Chapter 2 of the text.

2. **Focusing:** Day 2 in vocabulary instruction cycle.
   Time: Approximately 30–40 minutes

On the second day in the cycle, you and the students should discuss the article and the words. The following questions are representative of those that you might pose and discuss with students: What percentage of corporate health care costs comes from "unhealthy lifestyle conditions"? How may states have **banned** discrimination against smokers? What kinds of **disincentives** are companies like Ford Motor instituting? Why do some companies **levy** a **surcharge** against their employees who smoke? Questions such as the above serve two purposes. First, they provide a check that students have read and understood the article, and second, they incorporate the targeted vocabulary words into the discussion. You might choose to ask questions such as the above and then discuss the words and the article at the same time. You should encourage students to change or add to the definitions and other information included on their cards as they discuss the words. You should also encourage them at this point to add any mnemonics to their cards that might better enable them to remember what each word means.

3. *Practicing:* Also carried out on Day 2 in vocabulary instruction cycle.

Guided Practice: You should then introduce the next two activities, **Trying Out Meaning** and **Applying Meaning,** modeling the thinking processes that take place using the first two or three items as examples. We will "talk through" the first item in **Trying Out Meaning** here as an example. The item reads as follows: "The jury's decision to convict the accused criminal of murder was (_____) based on the large amount of evidence presented by the prosecution." First, you should read the sentence out loud, saying "blank" in the part of the sentence where the word should be inserted. Then you might say something such as the following: "Let's take a closer look at this sentence." If you read the sentence without the missing word, it would still make sense. It would read, "The jury's decision to convict the accused criminal of murder was based on the large amount of evidence presented by the prosecution." So the word that we want to put in this sentence should be one that tells us something about the jury's decision to convict. What king of a decision was it? We know that there was a lot of evidence, which means that they probably had sufficient grounds to bring back a guilty verdict. What word means "a decision where one has sufficient grounds or information"? (justifiable). Then either model a second example or perhaps ask a student to talk through the next item. Follow the same process for the first two or three items on **Applying Meaning.**

Assignment: Complete **Trying Out Meaning** and **Applying Meaning.** These activities should be turned in to you during the next class period. (Day 3 in vocabulary instruction cycle. No additional activity would take place on the third day because you need to score the two activities and provide feedback to students.)

4. *Practicing:* Day 4 in vocabulary instruction cycle.
Time: Approximately 15 minutes

You should return **Trying Out Meaning** and **Applying Meaning** activities. Give the group feedback about common errors that students made as they engaged in the activities. Allow students time to ask any specific questions they might have. Try to clear up any confusion that exists about the words.

Paired Practice: Students should work in pairs to **Recite and Review** with their vocabulary cards and the **Trying Out Meaning** and **Applying Meaning** activities, which you have returned to them. Encourage students not only to provide definitions, antonyms, synonyms, and parts of speech, but also, at this point, to generate sentences, or to provide new examples modeled after those in **Trying Out Meaning** and **Applying Meaning.**

Assignment: Provide independent practice by assigning for homework **Conceptualizing Meaning.** After they complete this activity on their own, students should then engage in monitoring by doing the **Self-Evaluating** activity found in the chapter.

5. *Monitoring:* Day 5 in vocabulary instruction cycle.
Time: Approximately 10 minutes

You should collect the homework assignments and then ask students which words are still giving them problems. These words should appear in Column C of the **Self-Evaluating** activity. Some additional clarification still might be in order for words that students have included in Column B.

6. *Monitoring/Assessing:* Day 6 in vocabulary instruction cycle.
Time: Approximately 10–15 minutes

Return the **Conceptualizing Meaning** activity to students. Discuss the words one last time by going over these two activities. Encourage students to do continued **Reciting and Reviewing** on the words from "If You Light Up . . ." so that they will be ready to take Posttest I following the next reading, "Health Care: How We Got Into This Mess."

Note: Although students are not given a formal assessment after this selection, you could choose from several alternatives if you think that some sort of formal assessment is necessary. First, you could use the **Conceptualizing Meaning** activity as a final assessment. Second, you could have students turn in their vocabulary cards. Third, you could construct your own short quiz which practiced formats that would appear on Posttest I.

LESSON PLAN FOR "MOTIVATION" TAKEN FROM CHAPTER 6

1. *Preparing:* Day 1 in vocabulary instruction cycle.
   Time: Approximately 15 minutes (if pretest is given as a homework assignment)

Begin with the **pretest** which can be an assignment out-of-class or an activity during class. After grading the pretest in class or allowing students to grade their own work, stimulate interest and activate prior knowledge of the chapter excerpt. You can do this in several ways. One method would be to ask the students to write their own definition of what it means to be motivated. Then ask the students to share their definitions, writing them on the overhead or board. After students have finished sharing, stimulate the discussion by asking questions such as: Are there differences in the definitions? What? If possible, combine the individual student definitions into a single class definition and ask students to copy this definition. The stage should now be set for skimming the reading excerpt.

Ask students to turn to the chapter excerpt "Motivation." Skim the chapter excerpt with the students, modeling the steps they should use when beginning a reading assignment. Stress the following ideas during the skimming activity: (a) the three main subheadings—Achievement Motivation, Affiliation Motivation, and Intrinsic and Extrinsic Motivation; (b) the use of boldface type that highlights important words; and (c) the 24 general and content-specific words to be studied.

Assignment: Students should read the chapter excerpt and be prepared for discussion during the next class session. Either establish a purpose for reading or ask students to suggest some possible purposes from their skimming. For example, students could read to determine how their definition of motivation differs from those in the text. Also assign students to complete vocabulary cards for the 7 content-specific words listed before the pretest.

2. *Focusing:* Days 2 and 3 in vocabulary instruction cycle.
   Time: Two class periods

During Day 2 give students an opportunity to discuss the chapter excerpt and the 7 content-specific words. Some of the students will be able to determine appropriate definitions for the words, as well as to write sensible sentences. Some, however, will have difficulty, so class discussion will be important. You can discuss the chapter excerpt first and then the 7 content-specific words, or the discussion can weave together the ideas from the excerpt with the content-specific words. The following are possible discussion questions: According to the chapter, what are four types of motivation? Which ones most resemble your definition? Which type of motivation have you ever experienced in school or in another setting? What do you think is the most powerful and productive type of motivation? Explain why. Do you think that there are any other types of motivation that the authors of this chapter have overlooked?

An effective way to summarize the discussion is to assign students the completion of the first Organizing Activity. Students can do this chart in small groups or pairs, or the entire class can complete it in a large group discussion.

Assignment: Students complete vocabulary cards for the 17 general words and the second Organizing Activity for the next class session.

During Day 3, discuss the general words, paying particular attention to sentence construction, synonyms, and antonyms. Encourage students to share mnemonics and add them to their cards in order to improve their recognition and recall.

3. *Practicing:* Days 4, 5, and 6 in vocabulary instruction cycle.
Time: Approximately 15 minutes each day

Guided Practice could begin on Day 4 by discussing some of the problems or questions students have about synonyms, antonyms, or sentences for their vocabulary cards. Then model and discuss some of the questions from **Beginning Conceptual Understanding** and **Using Concepts.** For example, after you model aloud how to answer the first two questions in **Beginning Conceptual Understanding,** the students could complete the next three items by themselves or in pairs. If students seem unsure of either activity or unsure of the words, then it might be appropriate for them to work in pairs on their vocabulary cards. They then could compare synonyms, antonyms, and sentences with each other.

Assignment: Students should complete **Beginning Conceptual Understanding** and **Using Concepts** in the text.

During Day 5 discuss the answers to **Beginning Conceptual Understanding** and **Using Concepts.** This can be done as a class or small groups or pairs of students. Students may still need to revise and complete some of their vocabulary cards during this discussion. Collect the work and provide students feedback in time for the next class session.

If **Paired Practice** has not yet occurred during class, then some time should be reserved for pairs to **Recite and Review.** Students might need to see the reciting and reviewing process modeled, especially the idea of reviewing the vocabulary cards front to back and back to front.

Assignment: Students should complete **Comprehending Concepts.** Remind students that they are to complete this activity without looking at the chapter excerpt, the charts, or their vocabulary cards. However, you should not assign students this final activity unless they have comprehensive vocabulary cards and have successfully completed previous activities. You can determine this only through class discussion, observation of students working in paired practice, and checking their work. Some students may need individual help at this point.

Independent Practice will occur when students have completed **Comprehending Concepts.** Collect this activity and check it in order to determine what content-specific or general words need to be reviewed with the students. Then on Day 6 discuss the activity and any troublesome words. In addition, you might also reserve class time for students to work in pairs on all the words in this thematic chapter.

Assignment: In preparation for **Monitoring and Assessing,** assign students to **Recite and Review** all the general and content-specific words for this thematic chapter.

4. *Monitoring/Assessing:* Days 7 and 8 in instruction cycle.
Time: Day 7, approximately 15 minutes;
Day 8, approximately 45 minutes

On Day 7 students will be **Monitoring** their readiness for the posttest. This should be facilitated by their previous independent reciting and reviewing. After discussing any problem words/concepts, ask students to complete the **Self-Evaluating** activity in the text. This should stimulate some more discussion of the targeted words.

Then inform the students of the format for the Posttest for Readings A, B, and C. End this session by brainstorming with the students about how they could prepare/study for the test. Students should mention reciting and reviewing their vocabulary cards and studying their charts and other previous activities in the text.

Assignment: Students should study for the posttest.

On Day 8 or when appropriate, **assess** the students' conceptual understanding of the targeted words with the Posttest for Readings A, B, and C. Collect and correct these.

5. *Evaluating:* Day 9 in vocabulary instruction cycle.
            Time: 20 minutes

Day 9 allows you and the students time to **evaluate** what was learned and what is still to be learned. To evaluate, return the posttest and discuss the answers with the students. As you discuss each question, encourage students to make additions/deletions/modifications to their vocabulary cards. Encourage students who have not done well on the exam to come in for individual assistance.

SUGGESTED READINGS

Theory, Research, Research Reviews

McKeown, M. G., & Curtis, M. G. (1987). *The nature of vocabulary acquisition.* Hilsman, NJ: Erlbaum.

Mezynski, K. (1983). Issues concerning the acquisition of knowledge: Effects of vocabulary training on reading comprehension. *Review of Educational Research, 53,* 253–279.

Simpson, M. L., & Dwyer, E. J. (1991). Vocabulary acquisition and the college student. In Flippo, R. F., & Caverly, D. C. (Eds.), *Teaching reading and study strategies at the college level* (pp. 1–41). Newark, DE: International Reading Association.

Stahl, N. A., Brozo, W. G., & Simpson, M. L. (1987). A content analysis of college vocabulary textbooks. *Reading Research and Instruction, 26*(3), 203–221.

Stahl, S. A. (1983). Differential word knowledge and reading comprehension. *Journal of Reading Behavior, 15,* 33–50.

Stahl, S. A. (1985). To teach a word well: A framework for vocabulary instruction. *Reading World, 24,* 16–27.

Stahl, S. A., & Fairbanks, M. M. (1986). The effects of vocabulary instruction: A model-based meta-analysis. *Journal of Educational Research, 56,* 72–110.

General Articles or Monographs

Haggard, M. R. (1982). The vocabulary self-collection strategy: An active approach to word learning. *Journal of Reading, 26,* 203–207.

Haggard-Ruddell, M. R. (1992). Integrated content and long-term vocabulary learning with the vocabulary self-collection strategy. In E. K. Dishner, T. W. Bean, J. E. Readence, & D. W. Moore (Eds.), *Reading in the content areas* (pp. 190–196). Dubuque, IA: Kendall Hunt Publishing.

Konopak, B. C., & Mealey, D. L. (1992). Vocabulary learning in the content areas. In E. K. Dishner, T. W. Bean, J. E. Readence, & D. W. Moore (Eds.), *Reading in the content areas* (pp. 174–182). Dubuque, IA: Kendall Hunt Publishing.

Nagy, W. E. (1988). *Teaching vocabulary to improve reading comprehension.* Newark, NJ: International Reading Association.

Nist, S. L. and Olejnik, S. (1995). The role of context and dictionary definitions on varying levels of word knowledge. *Reading Research Quarterly, 30,* 172–193.

Simpson, M. L. (1987). Alternative formats for evaluating content area vocabulary understanding. *Journal of Reading, 31,* 20–27. [Also in E. K. Dishner, T. W. Bean, J. E. Readence, & D. W. Moore (Eds.), *Reading in the content areas* (pp. 413–422). Dubuque, IA: Kendall Hunt Publishing.]

Simpson, M. L., Nist, S. L., & Kirby, K. (1987). Ideas in practice: Vocabulary strategies designed for college students. *Journal of Developmental Education, 11*(2), 20–24.

Stahl, S. A. (1986). Three principles of effective vocabulary instruction. *Journal of Reading, 29*(7), 662–668.

Answer Keys

CHAPTER 1   KNOWING A WORD

Activity 1.1

(Answers will vary since they represent students' opinions.)

Activity 1.2

Student responses may vary, but they should have answers such as the following:

1. **riveted**
   Synonym: engrossed; held the attention of
   Antonym: bored; uninterested
2. **expounded**
   Synonym: explained in detail
   Antonym: ignored; explained shallowly or superficially
3. **inevitable**
   Synonym: unpreventable; impossible to avoid
   Antonym: preventable
4. **feigned**
   Synonym: pretended; faked; gave a false appearance of
   Antonym: real; actuality

Activity 1.3

Answers will vary, but responses may be similar to the following:

2. God existed or that there was such a thing as a supreme being.
3. you were in a car accident and you received only minor injuries.
4. domestic animals such as cats or dogs; most birds (they migrate).
5. when your boss was explaining something to you; when you are driving a car.

Activity 1.4

1. **impression**
   Verb: impress
   Definition: to strongly influence, often favorably.

2. **options**
   Adjective: optional
   Definition: left to choice; not mandatory or compulsory.

3. **correspondence**
   Verb: correspond
   Definition: several definitions; they include: to be in agreement; to be similar; to communicate, often by letter.

4. **contained**
   Noun: options include: container, containment
   Definition: container—something in which material is held or carried.
   containment—the act of holding something back; the policy of checking the influence or expansion of a hostile power or ideology.

5. **dormant**
   Noun: dormancy
   Definition: a state of biological rest or inactivity.

Activity 1.5

Answers will vary since students will select different words from the article.

Activity 1.6

1. Correct
2. Incorrect (Sam's *atheistic* beliefs were obvious when he refused to say grace at the Thanksgiving dinner. . .)
3. Correct

4. Incorrect (The movie was so *engrossing* that I was able to stay awake past my usual bedtime.)
5. Incorrect (The secretary who constantly *feigned* sickness was put on probation for three months.)
6. Incorrect (Professor Miller's lectures were always so *riveting* that most of the class chose to attend even at eight o'clock in the morning.)
7. Correct
8. Incorrect (If you avoid reading, it is *inevitable* that you will have a weak vocabulary and slow reading rate.)
9. Correct
10. Correct
11. Correct
12. Correct

Activity 1.7

(Answers will vary, but the following are meant to be representative.)

1. The little girl who *feigned* illness was caught in a lie by her teacher when she was seen at the grocery store after school.
2. After the gymnast received extensive *rehabilitation,* she was able to compete for a spot on the Olympic team.
3. The book was so *engrossing* that I read it even though I was invited to go out with my friends for dinner.
4. The *vistas* gained from attending college include new friends from many different cultures and new viewpoints on important issues.
5. The student's *dormant* hunger was awakened when he smelled his mother's homemade bread in the oven.
6. After *riffling* through the books on the shelf, I decided to check out Stephen King's latest novel.
7. People who are *atheists* believe that there is no superior being or God.
8. After the insurance salesman reached his *quota* for the week, he took off to go fishing in the mountains.
9. Parents often *expound* about the virtues of a college education.
10. If you study hard and attend class, it is *inevitable* that you will do well on exams.
11. The class became *riveted* to the former Green Beret's description of his experiences in Vietnam.
12. Many serious college students attempt to *emulate* their professors because of their expertise.

CHAPTER 2   GENERATIVE VOCABULARY STRATEGIES

Activity 2.1

1. No. Answers to stage will vary depending on students' knowledge.
2. No. Answers to stage will vary depending on students' knowledge.
3. Yes, a little. Answers to stage will vary depending on students' knowledge.
4. Yes, a little. Answers to stage will vary depending on students' knowledge.
5. No. Answers to stage will vary depending on students' knowledge.
6. No. Answers to stage will vary depending on students' knowledge.

Activity 2.2

(Answers will vary, especially for the cues.)

1. **Abhors** means hates or detests.
   Cues: Because he tried to avoid classes that require him to take essay exams, he probably doesn't like to write very much.
2. **Zealously** means enthusiastically and diligently pursuing a cause, ideal, or goal.
   Cues: No one outside the organization can see its records, thus indicating that its members are a bit fanatical about it.
3. **Mundane** means ordinary or commonplace.
   Cues: Examples are used to indicate *mundane* jobs. These examples include an envelope stuffer, a busboy, and a traffic counter.
4. **Chicanery** means trickery or deception.
   Cues: The context tells you only that *chicanery* means something bad, not necessarily the nature of the badness. We can pick up that *chicanery* has a negative connotation.
5. **Quixotic** means idealistic without being practical.
   Cues: For most people, running away to a desert island and never having to work would just be impractical and impossible.
6. **Lethargic** means sluggish or inactive.
   Cues: The context tells you only that heat may cause you to react in a certain way. It does not give you very much information about the precise meaning of *lethargic*.

7. **Taciturn** means quiet or untalkative.
   Loquacious means very talkative.
   Cues: Because the words are opposite in nature and *loquacious* is defined through example (i.e., "carry on a conversation with anyone at the drop of a hat"), *taciturn* would have to mean someone who did not carry on conversations very much.

8. **Exacerbated** means made worse or aggravated.
   Cues: Getting dirt in a wound can only make it worse, so we get an idea that *exacerbation* of a wound cannot be good for it.

9. **Inane** means dumb or stupid; lacking sense.
   Cues: The word is defined in the sentence as "just plain stupid."

10. **Incessant** means continuous or nonstop.
    Cues: We know that *incessant* means something negative, since the residents were angered by the dog's barking. But we cannot tell the precise meaning just by context. (It could mean loud, for instance.)

Activity 2.3

(Answers will vary, but the following can serve as examples.)

Dictionary Definitions

fervent—having or showing great emotion or zeal.

stringent—imposing rigorous standards of performance; severe.

conception—something conceived in the mind, such as an idea or a plan.

portentously—with unspecifiable significance.

1. The author uses the word **fervent** to describe the observers because this would refer to those who were very emotionally involved in this issue, not just a little involved.
2. Someone's beliefs about other controversial issues such as women's choice or the death penalty.
3. Juanita's **fervent** beliefs in favor of a women's right to choose were shown when she organized demonstrations and donated large sums of money to women's rights organizations.
4. Because they were **fervent**, or very strong in their beliefs.
5. A teenager being grounded for two months after missing a curfew by five minutes; a 45-mile-an-hour speed limit on major interstate highways.

6. My professor, who has a **stringent** attendance policy, dropped our course grade by a whole letter if we missed more than two classes.
7. **Conception**—idea.
8. One's **conception** might change if he or she read new information or had a personal experience that caused him or her to rethink something.
9. The witness's **conception** of what happened at the crime scene was quite different from that of the person in custody for committing the crime.
10. Because he thought that the ruling was as important as tampering with the flag.
11. Answers will vary.
12. Answers will vary.

Activity 2.4

(Answers will vary.)

Activity 2.5

Vocabulary cards should include the following information, and be in the same format as the example on page 51 of the student text.

recital

Part of speech: noun
Sentence: A thunderclap of outrage and shock cracked across the land last week following a U.S. Supreme Court decision forbidding the **recital,** in New York public schools, of this 22-word prayer to a **nondenominational** God.
Definition: the act of reading or saying something in front of others.
Sentence: Martin was nervous about taking a foreign language class because he had heard that students had to do a lot of classroom **recital.**
Synonym: saying out loud
Antonym: reading to yourself

nondenominational

Part of speech: adjective
Sentence: See sentence above.

Definition: not restricted to, or associated with, any one particular religion.

Sentence: Some churches claim to be **nondenominational,** where people of any religion may attend.

Synonym: without affiliation

Antonym: one religious affiliation

tumult

Part of speech: noun

Sentence: For pure **tumult,** the reaction was unequaled since the Court's 1954 ruling on school desegregation.

Definition: disorderly commotion or disturbance; agitation.

Sentence: The speaker's comment caused so much **tumult** in the audience that people were shouting at each other at the top of their lungs.

Synonym: commotion

Antonym: calmness; orderliness

orated

Part of speech: verb

Sentence: "Somebody," **orated** West Virginia's Senator Robert Byrd, "is tampering with America's soul."

Definition: spoken in a formal, pompous manner.

Sentence: The politician **orated** about the importance of getting the bill (that he put before the Senate) passed on the first vote.

Synonym: spoken formally; professed

Antonym: chatted

reverence

Part of speech: noun

Sentence: The prayer which caused the clash dates back to 1951, when the New York State Board of Regents, the highest educational authority in the state, recommended that the schools, at their option, adopt an act of **reverence.**

Definition: act of showing profound respect or love for someone or something.

Sentence: Joel was taught always to remove his cap, as an act of ***reverence,*** whenever entering a place of worship.
Synonym: respect
Antonym: disrespect

impose

Part of speech: verb
Sentence: Lawrence Roth, father of two sons, one in the community's elementary school and one in high school, was disturbed by the idea that the state could ***impose*** any prayer on his children.
Definition: to establish or comply as compulsory.
Sentence: Often people try to ***impose*** their beliefs on you when you already have strong, differing beliefs of your own.
Synonym: force
Antonym: remove

prerogative

Part of speech: noun
Sentence: "We believe religious training is the ***prerogative*** of the parent," he said, "and not the duty of the government."
Definition: the right of a person or group.
Sentence: It is every person's ***prerogative*** to decide for whom they will vote in the next election.
Synonym: choice
Antonym: imposition

disgruntled

Part of speech: adjective
Sentence: When a group of ***disgruntled*** taxpayers confronted the president of the school board, however, the official reportedly told them, "The board has voted on this."
Definition: discontented.
Sentence: When they received a poor grade on the exam, many students were ***disgruntled*** and complained that the test was simply unfair.
Synonym: discontented; angry; mad
Antonym: happy; contented

martyr

Part of speech: noun
Sentence: Roth, although not a ***martyr*** by nature, was willing to go to court.
Definition: one who makes a great sacrifice or suffers because of a cause, belief, or principle.
Sentence: Children often believe that their parents act like ***martyrs*** because they are always telling them how much they have given up in order that their children might have things.
Synonym: sacrificer
Antonym: coward

compel

Part of speech: verb
Sentence: Lower state courts maintained that the prayer was constitutional, so long as schools did not ***compel*** any pupil to join in over his parents' objection.
Definition: to force, drive, or constrain.
Sentence: Since Bart did not receive a grade, or any credit, for doing the assigned homework, he did not feel ***compelled*** to do it.
Synonym: forced; obliged
Antonym: elected; chose

Activity 2.6

(Cards will vary depending on what course and terms students select.)

Activity 2.7

(Responses to this writing activity will vary. The activity will help students identify which strategy works best for them.)

Figure 2.7 Charting for Innate and Learned Behavior

	Innate Behavior	**Learned Behavior**
Role of genetics	genetically programmed	not genetically programmed
Types of organisms	less complex organisms (less advanced brains)	complex organisms (those with complex nervous systems)
Role of environment	patterns repeated in response to environment (e.g., hibernation, migration)	Behaviors can change dramatically as a result of environmental change.
Role of experience	life span short	The longer the life span, the more that can be learned.
Example	digger wasp	humans

Activity 2.8

(Answers will vary, but the following answers serve as examples.)

1. try to make them believe as you do.
2. someone steals her backpack; she fails the first three exams in a college course.
3. you have to say your speech in front of an audience.
4. turn off the TV; offer them small rewards.
5. are probably suing someone.
6. people of all religions would attend.
7. might die for a cause they really believe in.
8. it is proper to respect religious places.
9. there is much agitation and disorganization.
10. that is a right given in the Constitution.
11. are always talking about something.

Activity 2.9

1. Answers will vary, but most students will probably find "Vats, Fats, and Rats" easier to image because of the topic and because many of the words are more highly imageable.

2. Answers will vary, but words such as *obese, tumult, ample, fervent,* and *plaintiff* should be more easily imaged than *admonish, prerogative,* and *consistent.*
3. Answers will vary.

Activity 2.10

Answers will vary.

Figure 2.6   Answer for Activity 2.11

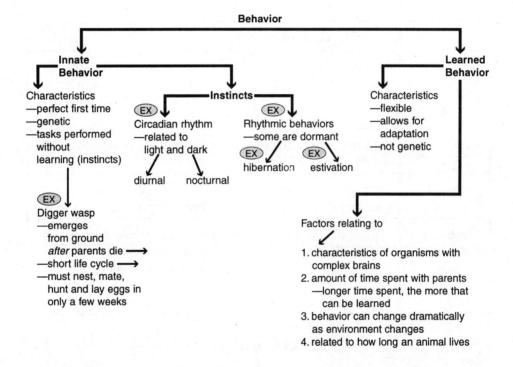

Activity 2.12

Innate	**Learned**
genetic	adaptation
instinctual	developmental period
circadian rhythm	parental attachment
migration	environmental influence
estivation	
hibernation	
diurnal	
digger wasp	

Activity 2.13

Before Bimbi
hustler
uneducated
atheistic
foul mouth

After Bimbi
persistent
educated
different attitude
mentally alive
enlightened
politically active

Activity 2.14

	Old Guidelines	**New Guidelines**
Meat	said nothing about fatty meats	Do not eat meat heavy in fat, such as sausage or salami; meatless diets are okay.
Fat	said nothing about fatty meats	Do not eat fat-laden meats.
Vegetables	vegetarianism never mentioned	Meatless diets can provide enough protein.
Alcohol	Do not drink; alcohol has no benefits.	Alcohol in moderation can reduce risk of heart problems (moderation means 2 drinks for men, 1 for women).

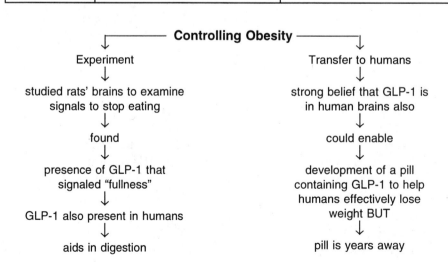

```
───── Controlling Obesity ─────
      ↓                              ↓
  Experiment                  Transfer to humans
      ↓                              ↓
studied rats' brains to examine    strong belief that GLP-1 is
signals to stop eating             in human brains also
      ↓                              ↓
   found                        could enable
      ↓                              ↓
presence of GLP-1 that         development of a pill
signaled "fullness"            containing GLP-1 to help
      ↓                        humans effectively lose
GLP-1 also present in humans   weight BUT
      ↓                              ↓
  aids in digestion            pill is years away
```

Activity 2.15

Answers will vary, but the following answers serve as examples.

1. When you had a very strong opinion, especially about something that might happen in the future.
2. You might gain weight or even become *obese.*
3. Waiting in long lines in the bookstore at the beginning of the term.
4. If your stomach is bothering you or if it is suspected that you have an ulcer.
5. A very strong belief in a cause, such as abortion or the death penalty.
6. Because he chewed up one of your best pairs of shoes.
7. If you don't eat breakfast or lunch, you would be very hungry at dinner time.
8. When they were your role model.

Activity 2.16

Answers will vary, but the following answers serve as examples.

1. Innate behavior is behavior that is done perfectly the first time it happens. It's genetic in that the organism knows how to do it when it is born.
2. Because digger wasps are born knowing how to do everything they need to do. No one teaches them anything.
3. An example of a diurnal animal would be most birds.
4. An example of a nocturnal animal would be bats or owls.
5. Hibernation and estivation are two rhythmic behaviors that are dormant.
6. Learning occurs when experience results in a change of behavior.
7. The three factors are a complex nervous system, the amount of time developing animals spend with their parents, and changing behaviors as the environment changes.

CHAPTER 3   DICTIONARY USE

Activity 3.1

1. 4
2. 2
3. 4
4. 5

Activity 3.2

(Answers will vary.)

1. 1, 2, 3, 4, 5	4
2. none of the characteristics	1
3. 1, 2	2
4. 1, 2, 3, 4, 5	5

Activity 3.3

(Answers will vary.)

1. The subscripts signal different ways in which the word *grave* can be used.
2. Definition and subscript number 2.
3. Four.
4. *Grave* is a mark used on some words to indicate pronunciation.
5. As a transitive and intransitive verb.
6. The transitive definition, definition 1.
7. Look up the word *intense.*
8. *Intensify* means to make stronger or more powerful.
9. As a noun and a verb.
10. As a verb.
11. To damage.
12. As a verb or a noun.
13. Transitive means that you must have a direct object to complete meaning. Intransitive means that you do not need a direct object to complete meaning. Look in the abbreviation section of the dictionary and then look up the word in the dictionary.
14. The second definition.

Activity 3.4

1. The word *grave* has many origins. As a verb and noun the word originated from the Middle English, Old English, Old High

German, and Old Slavic languages. As an adjective the word originated from the Middle French or Italian languages.

2. The word *cripple* originated from Middle and Old English. The Old English word was *creopan*, which meant to creep. If you were crippled, you would probably creep instead of walk.

3. The word *fatality* originated from Middle English, Middle French, and Latin.

4. The word *anchor* originated from Middle English, Old English, Latin, and Greek.

5. The word *stratosphere* originated from French and New Latin.

Activity 3.5

(Answers will vary.)

1. From Greek mythology—*Mentor* was Odysseus' trusted counselor. Teachers have been my mentors.

2. From Greek mythology—*Narcissus* was a youth who pined away in love for his own image in a pool of water; he was later transformed into a flower that bears his name. Some athletes and rock stars can be narcissistic.

3. The word comes from two French words—**faux,** meaning false and **pas,** meaning step. My most embarrassing faux pas was to incorrectly introduce my mother to the principal of my school.

4. From Greek—there is a river in Turkey called **Maeander** that is noted for its winding course. I usually meander through shopping centers.

5. The word comes from a character named Mrs. Malaprop in a play by Richard Sheridan. Using the word **humility** in place of **humiliation.**

6. Chortle is a blend of the words chuckle and snort. Yes, usually.

7. Curio is a shortened version of the word curiosity. Yes, I received a small crystal cat from my sister.

8. The word **quixotic** refers to the hero of a romance which was written by Cervantes.

9. *Nemesis* is the name of the Greek goddess of retributive justice, or vengeance.

10. *Snafu* is a slang acronym meaning all confused or chaotic.

Activity 3.6

1. Answers will vary. A solvent must be some type of chemical that does something to dissolve other substances. Some solvents must

have chlorine in them to do this. These solvents must be dangerous to the ozone layer.
 2. Noun.
 3. A liquid capable of dissolving another substance. This definition
    is best because the adjective does not fit nor does the other noun
    definition (something that solves a problem).

Activity 3.7

(Answers may vary according to the dictionaries students use.)

 1. four
 2. specialized or technical language of a group
 3. jargonize, jargoning
 4. three
 5. The word *androgynous* is from the Latin and Greek languages.
 6. being neither distinguishably masculine nor feminine, as in dress,
    appearance, or behavior; unisex
 7. two
 8. The word *impediment* is from Latin.
 9. Yes, there is a legal definition. The legal definition does not
    exactly fit because it means something that obstructs the making
    of a legal contract.
 10. a hindrance or obstruction.
 11. Answers will vary. The clause following the semicolon contains
     an explanation of how birds would act if they were moribund.
 12. adjective
 13. The word *moribund* originates from Latin.
 14. Answers will vary. Morbid
 15. Moribund means about to die or at the point of death.

Activity 3.8

(Students' cards will vary.)

Activity 3.9

 1. Ban CFCs entirely by 2000.
 2. The ozone layer loss is more than expected and more skin cancer
    deaths have occurred than expected.
 3. 200,000; the fatality estimate is 21 times more than was forecast.
 4. They cause cataracts, weaken our immune system, damage
    crops, and interfere with the reproduction of plankton.

5. They have tried to find substitutes for ozone-eating substances.
6. No, they are pessimistic since the damage has already occurred in our stratosphere.

Activity 3.10

1. Correct
2. Incorrect (After failing the accounting midterm, the business major decided to *intensify* his efforts by hiring a tutor and studying more.)
3. Correct
4. Incorrect (After learning that the damage to her car was *graver* than she expected, Louise felt extremely depressed.)
5. Incorrect (Chris was extremely happy when the doctor told her that her tumor was not cancerous, but *benign.*)
6. Correct
7. Incorrect (In the United States the *incidence* of measles and smallpox has significantly increased.)
8. Incorrect (The bus driver who had caused several passenger *fatalities* was released from his job.)
9. Incorrect (When estimating how much pizza and beverages are needed for a party of hungry college students, it is never wise to be *conservative.*)
10. Correct
11. Correct
12. Incorrect (It was impossible for Anthony to fly his kite through the *stratosphere.*)
13. Incorrect (The United States and Britain are encouraging under-developed nations not to use any more *chlorofluorocarbons.*)
14. Correct

CHAPTER 4   WORD ELEMENTS

Activity 4.1

1. *Pseudo-* means false or fake, *intellectual* means smart, so *pseudo-intellectual* means that Brian wasn't very smart.
2. Someone or something who professes to be intellectual or appeals to the tasks of intellectuals, but actually is or does not.
3. *Pseudo-* means false or fake, *-nym* means name, so pseudonym would mean a name that does not belong to the person using it.
4. A fictitious name assumed by an author; a pen name.
5. Something to do with low and high ratings.
6. A group organized according to rankings from high to low in authority or importance. Answers will vary.

Activity 4.2

1. *Acro-* means top; summit; height.
2. *Aqua-* means water.
3. *Dementi-* means insane.
4. *Herpeto-* means reptile.
5. *Phono-* means sound; voice; speech.
6. *Pyro-* means fire.
7. *Xeno-* means stranger; foreigner.

Activity 4.3

(Answers will vary based on the words students select. Below are representative answers.)

1. Acrobat—One skilled in feats of agility or balance.
2. Aquatic—Of or in water; living or growing in or on the water; taking place in the water.
3. Dementia—Irreversible deterioration of intellectual faculties with accompanying emotional disturbance resulting from organic brain disorder.
4. Herpetologist—One who is engaged in the scientific study of reptiles and amphibians.
5. Phonology—The science of speech sounds, including phonetics and phonemics.
6. Pyromania—The uncontrollable impulse to start fires.
7. Xenocurrency—A currency that is in circulation outside its own country.

Activity 4.4

1. Phonophobia.
2. Xenophobia.
3. Acrophobia.
4. Pyrophobia.
5. Aquaphobia.
6. Herpetophobia.
7. Dementophobia.

Activity 4.5

(Answers may vary.)

1. Where you stand when you are talking to someone.
2. Touch indicating dominance.
3. Touch indicating friendship.

Activity 4.6

1. *a*symmetrical   from, away
2. *inter*actions   between
3. *psych*ologist   mind, mental
4. *socio*economic   social, society
5. *non*reciprocal   not
6. *sub*ordinate   below, under
7. asymmetrical
8. same, together
9. -al
10. presumptuous

Activity 4.7

1. subordinate
2. psychologist
3. interactions
4. nonreciprocal
5. asymmetrical
6. socioeconomic

Activity 4.8

1. anthropology
2. archaeology
3. biology
4. geology
5. gynecology
6. neurology
7. pathology
8. theology

Activity 4.9

(Finally, write in the last blank the original form of the word.)

2.	*tion*	noun	confirm
3.	*ably*	adverb	consider
4.	*ance*	noun	dominate
5.	*tion*	noun	elaborate
6.	*ity*	noun	solid
7.	*tion*	noun	replicate

Activity 4.10

1. replication
2. elaboration
3. confirmation
4. solidarity
5. assertive
6. dominance
7. considerably

Activity 4.11

(Answers will vary.)

1. verify
2. subordinate
3. generative

Activity 4.12

(Answers will vary.)

1. she's not sure of the results she got the first time.
2. everyone liked me.
3. you will not lose your hotel room to someone else as long as you can give your confirmation number.
4. when someone was pressuring you to change your mind about something you believed in strongly.
5. go into detail about your thoughts.
6. not take any side.
7. make some phone calls to your friends to see if they had heard anything.
8. often lets others dominate him.

Activity 4.13

1. Through touch; how close they stand.
2. Because they are not equal. The superior has the right to be more familiar than does the subordinate.
3. Touch that is reciprocal is returned, as between friends, husbands and wives, or boyfriends and girlfriends.
4. Any kind of message that is sent in a way that is not verbal.
5. When men and women are in approximately the same socioeconomic status, men touch women much more than women touch men. Touch therefore appears to be gender rather than socioeconomically related.
6. Through a handshake or hug that is mutually given and received.
7. By studying the conditions under which individuals touch each other.
8. Both would be on equal ground; one would not dominate the other.

Activity 4.14

(Answers will vary—see index.)

Activity 4.15

(Answers will vary.)

CHAPTER 5   READINGS CONCERNING GENDER ISSUES

Reading A—"When Harry Called Sally . . ."

Pretest

1. c	**6.** a	**11.** c
2. d	**7.** b	**12.** b
3. b	**8.** b	**13.** d
4. c	**9.** b	
5. d	**10.** a	

Determining Meaning

Part I—Parts of Speech

1. verb	**8.** verb
2. noun	**9.** verb
3. noun	**10.** verb
4. verb	**11.** noun
5. adjective	**12.** adverb
6. noun	**13.** noun
7. noun	

Part I—Definitions

(Answers will vary depending on the dictionary used.)

1. *averted*—prevented.
2. *condescension*—act of dealing with people in a superior manner.
3. *consolation*—act of comforting someone who is troubled or grieving.
4. *decipher*—to decode, read, or interpret something confusing.
5. *disparate*—completely distinct; dissimilar.
6. *distinctions*—differences, distinguishing features or characteristics.
7. *dominance*—condition or fact of being influential or in control; in governance.
8. *endowed*—equipped or provided with a talent or supply.
9. *enhance*—to make greater or to increase.
10. *inclined*—to have a certain tendency or preference.
11. *inferiority*—state or condition of feeling low in quality or value.
12. *instinctively*—naturally, without thinking; unlearned.
13. *phenomenon*—occurrence or fact that one can sense or perceive.

Part II

phenomenon—no and men (Answers will vary.)

Part III

1. vert; turn
2. a; from or down
3. to turn from or away; yes, because the definition of *prevent* is similar to the definition of *turning from or away*. However, the *prevent* definition is closer to how the word is used in the selection.
4. *Re* is a prefix meaning back or again; *vert* is a root meaning to *turn;* the word *revert* must mean to turn back or turn again.
5. to return to a former condition, practice, or belief.
6. convert, invert, subvert (Answers will vary.)

Trying Out Meaning

(Answers will vary for the corrected sentences. The responses here reflect the ideas that students should be thinking about.)

1. C
2. I (The elderly woman did not *avert* financial disaster when she invested her life savings with the con artists.)
3. C
4. I (The dropout who had not learned how to read quickly could not *decipher* the letter from his lawyer.)
5. I (The proud and hard-working couple found it difficult to accept the *condescension* of their wealthy landlord who inherited his fortune from his grandfather.)
6. C
7. I (Her feelings of *inferiority* caused her to feel uncomfortable seeking out new friends and unfamiliar situations.)
8. I (The English professor criticized the student on his term paper because he had overlooked the *distinction* between paraphrasing and copying someone's ideas as if they were his own.)
9. C
10. C
11. C
12. I (When the school year began, none of the American students in Beginning Russian knew how to speak and write the language *instinctively*.)
13. C

Applying Meaning

(Answers will vary. The responses here reflect the ideas that students should be thinking about.)

1. Probably not, since the penmanship skills of two-year-olds are not very well developed.
2. No, since they probably think they are better than everyone else and thus treat others badly.
3. Speed, quickness, excellent eye-hand coordination.
4. That individual would probably stand in a corner and avoid talking with other people.
5. Obtain good grades, get useful work experiences and internships, work hard in these jobs in order to obtain excellent references, attend college or specialized training.
6. Study two hours for every hour in class; attend class regularly; do assigned readings; ask questions when he or she does not understand.
7. Social worker, minister, a member of a church.
8. Yes, because the lawyer would probably wear a three-piece suit while the rock star would probably wear something to attract attention, more like a costume for a performance.
9. Yes, because we are born with this reflex and we do not think about it.
10. Hockey has a goalie; football players throw a football while hockey players use sticks to pass a puck.
11. Probably, if he/she wanted the class to listen to the lectures or discussions.
12. Walk the stairs, because they enjoy physical activities and see the elevator as not providing any physical benefits.
10. Computers, fertility research, gene research.

Conceptualizing Meaning

(Answers will vary.)

Reading B—"Confessions of a Former Chauvinist Pig"

Pretest

1. b	8. a	15. c
2. c	9. b	16. b
3. a	10. d	17. c
4. b	11. b	18. a
5. d	12. a	19. d
6. b	13. a	
7. a	14. d	

Determining Meaning

Part I—Parts of Speech

1. noun
2. noun
3. adjective
4. noun
5. noun
6. noun
7. adjective
8. adjective
9. noun
10. verb
11. adjective
12. noun
13. noun
14. adjective
15. adjective
16. adjective
17. noun
18. adjective
19. adjective

Part I—Definitions

(Answers will vary depending on the dictionary used.)

1. *abolition*—an act of destroying or getting rid of completely.
2. *androgyny*—unisex, being neither male or female in appearance or behavior.
3. *baffled*—frustrated, confused.
4. *chauvinism*—prejudiced or biased belief in the superiority of one's own group.
5. *déjà vu*—the illusion of having already experienced something before.
6. *deviousness*—not straightforward; shifty; not honest or direct; tricky.
7. *domestic*—pertaining to the household.
8. *egalitarian*—adhering to the belief or doctrine of equal rights for all individuals.
9. *entrepreneur*—one who organizes, operates, and assumes the risks for a business venture.
10. *indicted*—accused or charged.
11. *intriguing*—arousing the interest or curiosity of.
12. *jargon*—specialized language or talk of a trade, business, specialty.
13. *liberation*—act of releasing or freeing from.
14. *nostalgic*—bittersweet longing for things, persons, or situations in the past.
15. *oppressed*—persecuted; bothered unjustly through the use of force or action.
16. *passive*—not participating; inactive; acting without objection.
17. *proposition*—a plan, scheme, statement.

18. *provisional*—providing for the time being; pending a permanent arrangement.
19. *tedious*—uninteresting, tiresome.

Part II
(Answers will vary.)

Part III
1. chauvinism
2. déjà vu
3. egalitarian
4. entrepreneur

Trying Out Meaning

1. chauvinism
2. domestic
3. androgyny
4. tedious
5. passive
6. déjà vu
7. entrepreneur
8. baffled
9. abolition
10. deviousness
11. provisional
12. egalitarian
13. proposition
14. jargon
15. intriguing
16. liberation
17. nostalgic
18. indicted
19. oppressed

Applying Meaning

(Answers will vary. The responses here reflect the ideas that students should be thinking about.)

1. be confused or get easily discouraged doing math homework.
2. their high school or college days.
3. spend more time with that person so you can get to know him/her.
4. became upset because it took him/her away from watching television.
5. tried to turn in her best friend's homework as her own.
6. think you had been in that room before.
7. called the female judge a "gal" or "broad."
8. cannot tell whether the person with long hair and jeans is a boy or girl.
9. worked hard to prove himself so he could gain permanent status.

10. wanted the law removed from the books because it seemed so unfair.
11. washing windows or cleaning bathrooms.
12. that he offered a statement describing a business deal.
13. feel as if people around you did not like you and were trying to upset you with their actions and words.
14. probably not cheer or get excited during the game.
15. participated in marches that protested the treatment of minorities who were employed as migrant laborers.
16. tried to escape from prison in order to avoid the trial.
17. raise your hand and ask questions about the difficult words you do not understand.
18. taking risks and starting new businesses.
19. women and gays.

Conceptualizing Meaning

(Answers will vary. The responses here reflect the ideas that students should be thinking about.)

Part I

1. chauvinism; the other two words have something to do with equal rights for all.
2. tedious; the other two describe something or someone in a positive manner, suggesting that they are interesting.
3. honest; the other two describe something or someone in a negative manner, suggesting that trickery or unfairness is being practiced.

Part II

1. jeans, hats, jacket.
2. capital punishment. Capital punishment should be abolished since it is wrong to take another human's life.
3. I was baffled in a geometry course because the teacher never discussed the homework.
4. When I went to a play that I thought I had seen before.
5. Ironing and washing clothes. They seem acceptable because they benefit me by giving me more clothes to wear.
6. murder, robbery, blackmail.
7. slider, pick-off, shutout. Baseball.
8 sleeping, putting your head down on the desk, staring out the window.

9. at my parent's twenty-fifth wedding anniversary.
10. The proposition was this: if I worked hard and earned good grades, I might receive a scholarship.
11. Provisional approval for a credit might be satisfactory, but provisional approval for a driver's license or job might make you nervous or angry.
12. Ted Turner; Donald Trump; Dick Clark.

Extending and Challenging

Part I

1. Positive words: enhance, distinction, egalitarian, entrepreneur, liberation
2. Negative words: inferiority, deviousness, passive, oppressed, tedious, chauvinism, indicted, condescension, consolation, domestic

Part II

1. ous; androgynous. Some people like the androgynous look in clothing, but I do not.
2. ness, ity; passiveness, passivity. The passiveness of the class annoyed the professor, who enjoyed student discussion and debate.
3. sion, or; oppression, oppressor. The oppressor tortured his victims one minute and lavished attention on them the next.

Posttest I—Readings A and B

PART I DIRECTIONS: Complete the following sentences, being as specific as possible in order to demonstrate your conceptual understanding of the boldfaced words.

1. After feeling a sense of **déjà vu,** I _____

   _____

2. After the **liberation** of the rare tigers, _____

   _____

3. My mother always gets **nostalgic** when _____

   _____

4. Our co-workers offered us **consolation** because _____

_____

5. The new corporate leader established his **dominance** by _____

_____

6. Cats and dogs have **instinctive** behaviors that _____

_____

7. The businessman turned down the **proposition** because _____

_____

PART II DIRECTIONS: Using the word below, complete the following analogies. Remember to keep the part of speech the same for all four words.

abolition	distinctions	provisional
disparate	endowed	decipher

1. inactive: passive :: equipped or supplied: _____

2. similar: _____ :: honest: devious

3. enhanced: increased :: _____: interpret or read

4. temporary: _____ :: longing for the past: nostalgic

PART III DIRECTIONS: Use each of the following pairs in one meaningful sentence in order to demonstrate your full understanding of the words.

1. jargon, inclined

_____

2. inferiority, avert

_____

3. entrepreneur, indicted

_____

4. phenomenon, intriguing

_____

PART IV DIRECTIONS: Answer the following questions that use one or more of the vocabulary words. Make sure your answer demonstrates your understanding of the boldfaced words.

1. Would someone involved in an **egalitarian** relationship feel **oppressed?** Why or why not?

   _____

2. Are **domestic** tasks or jobs generally considered **tedious?** Why or why not?

   _____

3. Is there a **distinction** between experiencing **condescension** or **chauvinism?** Why or why not?

   _____

4. Are most older individuals **baffled** by **androgyny?** Why or why not?

   _____

Answers to Posttest—Readings A and B

Part I
(Answers will vary. Samples follow.)

1. decided that I had been in the room before and had seen that mysterious man before.
2. the people who had supported the effort cheered wildly.
3. she thinks about the picnics and reunions that she used to go to with her family.
4. we had lost our parents in a car crash.
5. firing all the secretaries and the office manager.
6. surprise many of us as we watch them.
7. it would mean that he would be away from home almost all of the time.

Part II

1. endowed
2. distinction
3. decipher
4. provisional

Part III
(Answers will vary. Samples follow.)

1. Lawyers and doctors are inclined to use a lot of jargon when they explain themselves to us.
2. In order to avert his sense of inferiority in playing tennis, he decided to take lessons.
3. The entrepreneur was indicted for cheating elderly people out of their money.
4. The phenomenon was so intriguing that writers from *Newsweek* were sent to cover the event for their next issue.

Part IV
(Answers will vary. Samples follow.)

1. No, because they are treated as if they are important and equal to other individuals.
2. Yes, because they require no special skills or thinking, merely time and effort.
3. There is a slight difference between the two words, but the feelings you would experience as a result of **condescension** or **chauvinism** would be similar.
4. Yes, in most cases. This is because the older generation is used to clearly defined male and female roles and appearances.

Reading C—"Forms of Love"

Pretest—General Words

1. a	**6.** a	**11.** c
2. b	**7.** c	**12.** d
3. d	**8.** a	**13.** a
4. c	**9.** c	**14.** b
5. b	**10.** b	**15.** d

Pretest—Content-Specific Words
(Answers will vary.)

1. a part of something
2. some type of component or part; something to do with cognition
3. something to do with love
4. to crystallize or form
5. some type of component or part; a component having to do with emotions
6. a kind of love; a love emphasizing sex and passion

7. a feeling or emotion that you think you are in love
8. knowing someone well; a situation you have with someone you like or love very much
9. some type of verse; to be limerent
10. having to do with being motivated; a component having to do with motivation
11. not being in love
12. feelings of sexual arousal and physical attraction
13. a type of arousal; arousal emphasizing the body
14. Greek love; a kind of love; Plato's love

Determining Meaning

General Words

Part I—Parts of Speech

1. adjective
2. verb
3. noun
4. adjective
5. verb
6. noun
7. verb
8. adjective
9. verb
10. noun
11. adjective
12. verb
13. noun
14. verb
15. adjective

Part I—Definitions

(Answers will vary depending on the dictionary used.)

1. *acute*—sharp, intense, extremely severe.
2. *calculated*—estimated.
3. *continuation*—state of remaining in the same condition, capacity, or place.
4. *devastating*—overwhelming, confounding, overpowering in effect or strength.
5. *encompass*—includes, surrounds.
6. *exclusivity*—condition of not sharing or dividing with others; undivided attention.
7. *fantasizing*—imagining in the mind.
8. *intrusive*—forcing on oneself or others without being asked or welcomed.
9. *preceded*—to come before in order or rank.
10. *preoccupation*—state of being disturbed or concerned about something so that it takes a lot of your time and effort.

11. *profound*—far-reaching, deep beyond what is obvious; absolute.
12. *reciprocated*—to show or feel in response or in return.
13. *respondents*—persons who respond or reply.
14. *sustain*—to maintain, to keep, to keep in existence.
15. *tantalizing*—exciting, but out of reach.

Part II
(Answers will vary.)

Part III

1. a. precede; *cede* is a root meaning *to go*
   b. preoccupation
2. a. continua*tion;* continue
   b. exclusiv*ity;* exclusive
   c. preoccupa*tion;* preoccupy

Determining Meaning

Content-Specific Words

1. *component*—a part; love has three parts or components.
2. *cognitive component*—having to do with thinking; a thinking part to something; a part of love that deals with decision and commitment.
3. *consummate love*—complete love; a form of love involving commitment, intimacy, and passion.
4. *crystallization*—the act of giving a definite and permanent form to something.
5. *emotional component*—one of the parts of love dealing with feelings and involving intimacy.
6. *erotic love*—involving sexual love and desire.
7. *infatuate*—loving at first sight; foolishly or extravagantly loving or admiring; loving without intimacy, decision, or commitment.
8. *intimacy*—feelings of closeness and connectedness experienced in a loving relationship; one of the three components of love; the emotional component of love.
9. *limerence*—a love characterized by preoccupation, acute longing, exaggeration of the other's good qualities, seesawing emotions, and aching in the chest; these characteristics can be intensely pleasurable or painful; Tennov says there are three characteristics: preoccupation, intrusive thinking or unintentional thinking about the person, and a desire for exclusivity with the person.

10. ***motivational component***—one of the three parts of love; passion is the motivational component which develops quickly and then levels off as quickly; passion is similar to "love at first sight."
11. ***nonlove***—the absence of intimacy, passion, and decision/commitment; a form of Sternberg's love.
12. ***passion***—one of the three components of love; the drives that lead to romance, physical attractions, and sexual interaction in a loving relationship.
13. ***physiological arousal***—a characteristic of passion; arousal involving all the vital processes of an individual.
14. ***platonic love***—a form of spiritual love in which we are concerned about the well-being of a friend; a form of love that goes beyond and does not include physical desire.

Organizing Concepts

Part I

Components of Love

Emotional Component of Love

intimacy

Cognitive Components of Love

decision

commitment

Motivational Component of Love

passion

All Components of Love

consummate love

hard to sustain

No Components of Love

nonlove

Part II

Types of Love

	Friendship	Infatuation
Components Involved	intimacy	passion
Synonyms		limerence
Definitions	liking reserved for close friends	love at first sight; foolish love
Subtypes	platonic love	
Characteristics	bond between equals; gender does not matter; male-female friendship is difficult, but possible	preoccupation; all-or-nothing state; intrusiveness; need for exclusivity; acute longing; seesawing emotions; tantalizing state
Examples	bride's maid of honor; the Greeks	

Beginning Conceptual Understanding

(Answers will vary. The responses here reflect the ideas that students should be thinking about.)

1. T
2. F (*Consummate love* is a *profound* form of love that is very difficult to *sustain.*)
3. F (One of the *emotional components* of love, *intimacy,* grows steadily at first and then tends to level off.)
4. T
5. F (A friendship with a member of the opposite sex that is sexual is also called *erotic love.*)
6. T
7. F (*Passion,* a *motivational component* of love, does involve *physiological arousal.*)

8. F (*Acute* longing for the loved one and a desire for *exclusivity* with the loved one are two of the many characteristics of *limerence.*)

9. F (One of the ways limerent attention can end is through the transfer and *continuation* of limerence to another individual of desire.)

10. F (The first *crystallization* of limerence occurs when one begins to focus on the good qualities of the limerent object and to disregard his or her bad qualities.)

11. F (Friendship is a type of love without the *passion* and decision/commitment components.)

12. F (Decision and commitment are the *cognitive components* of love.)

13. F (*Infatuation* encompasses *passion,* but not *intimacy,* decision, or commitment.)

Using Concepts

(Answers will vary. The responses here reflect the ideas that students should be thinking about.)

1. to solve ten word problems or to write an essay on pollution.
2. your chosen profession or job.
3. food.
4. solve it.
5. having good health and sufficient money.
6. homemade pasta or fresh chocolate chip cookies.
7. nurses, special education, and math teachers.
8. floods, hurricanes, tornadoes, earthquakes.
9. be kind, remember special occasions for the other person.
10. send in their answers in order to receive free coupons.
11. do not want your friend to see anyone else.
12. often are not as good as the originals.
13. enough time to cross the tracks before the train would come.
14. their concentration, interest.
15. your hunger, your desire for some decent sleep.
16. being fit or slender; being the best; winning.
17. remained seated for quite a while after; cried; clapped.
18. hard work, luck, and knowing someone important.
19. be honest, caring, and giving.
20. becoming an actress that she left school and traveled to New York.

Comprehending Concepts—Part I

1. intimacy—feelings of closeness and connectedness one experiences in loving relationships

   passion—drives that lead to romance, physical attraction, and sexual interaction in a loving relationship

   decision and commitment—the decision that one loves another and the commitment to keep the love
2. intimacy
3. passion
4. decision and commitment
5. consummate love
6. It is the kind of love we all strive for; it is possible only in a few special relationships; it is difficult to sustain.
7. nonlove
8. intimacy
9. friendship
10. passion
11. preoccupation with the limerent object; intrusive thinking about the limerent object; desire for exclusivity (see insert on back) with the limerent object.

Posttest II—Readings A, B, and C

PART I DIRECTIONS: Read each sentence carefully. If the italicized word is used correctly, circle C and go on to the next item. If, however, the italicized word is used incorrectly, circle I and then correct the sentence.

C I 1. Most ***entrepreneurs*** are known to be followers who avoid taking risks.

C I 2. The ***condescending*** waiter received many generous tips for his friendly and courteous behavior.

C I 3. Many people believe that the drives to sleep and eat are ***instinctive***.

C I 4. The ***disparate*** roommates had so many hobbies and interests in common that they became close friends.

C I 5. Some women try to ***enhance*** their beauty by exercise, surgery, and cosmetics.

C I 6. ***Chauvinistic*** politicians receive significant contributions and support from women concerned about their quality of life.

C I   **7.** *Domestic* tasks are usually the ones that we dislike the most.

C I   **8.** Because the lawyer had a reputation for *deviousness,* he was an immediate choice for the judgeship.

C I   **9.** The college student was so *baffled* by the statistics problem that he decided to offer help to other students who were having problems.

C I **10.** Some homeowners try to *avert* possible thefts of their possessions with alarms and security systems.

C I **11.** The professor was thrilled to see that a large group of his students reacted in a *passive* manner to his lecture.

C I **12.** There are many *oppressed* minorities in our society who still need *liberation* from unfair practices and laws.

C I **13.** The student was so *devastated* by his low grades that he decided to seek help.

C I **14.** Death is sometimes *preceded* by illness.

C I **15.** The quiet and shy student was avoided by classmates because of his *intrusive* behavior.

C I **16.** The student with the short attention span found it easy to *sustain* his concentration while studying.

PART II DIRECTIONS: Select a word from the list below in order to complete each sentence. Each word is used only once and is in its proper form.

abolition	distinctions
proposition	encompassed
continuation	inferiority
déjà vu	indicted
dominance	nostalgically

17. The young girl felt a sense of _____ when she became surrounded by her older sisters who were attractive, intelligent, and extremely successful in their careers.

18. The directors, writers, and actors hoped that they could persuade their sponsors for _____ of the new and experimental television series.

19. There are several _____ between soccer and football.

20. The young man who crashed his car into another car while he was under the influence of alcohol was _____ for manslaughter.

21. The holidays are often a time for friends and relatives to gather and _____ remember past events together.

22. In the United States football has been able to maintain its _____ as the favored fall sport for many years.

23. The overworked students who had just finished their fourth research paper for the history professor begged for the _____ of all remaining papers and exams.

24. When the college freshman entered the room for the first time, she immediately had a feeling of _____ because the surroundings and people seemed so familiar to her.

25. Wise students always ask their professor what readings and lectures will be _____ in their exams.

26. The college graduate decided to decline IBM's generous business _____ and return to college for more education.

PART III DIRECTIONS: Choose the word or phrase that does not relate to the other two, and write it in the blank after "Exclude." In the blank labeled "General concept" write the concept that describes the remaining words.

27. tantalizing
    intriguing
    tedious

   a. **Exclude** _____

   b. **General concept** _____

   _____

28. calculate
    acute
    decipher

   a. **Exclude** _____

   b. **General concept** _____

   _____

29. platonic love
    limerence
    infatuation

   a. **Exclude** _____

   b. **General concept** _____

   _____

30. exclusivity
condescension
egalitarian

    a.   **Exclude** _____

    b.   **General concept** _____

    _____

31. intimacy
crystallization
passion

    a.   **Exclude** _____

    b.   **General concept** _____

    _____

PART IV DIRECTIONS: Answer each of the following questions so that it is clear that you understand the meaning of the italicized word.

32. When might you offer someone *consolation?*

_____

_____

33. For what items might a dieter be inclined to *fantasize?*

_____

_____

34. Why might a student be accepted at a college with a *provisional* status?

_____

_____

35. What are some examples of *androgynous* looks in clothing and hair styles?

_____

_____

36. Give two examples of *jargon* and identify the profession that would use the jargon.

_____

_____

37. During the winter what sports seem to **preoccupy** the couch potatoes who watch television?

_____

_____

38. What book, play, poem, song, or movie has had a **profound** influence on you? Why?

_____

_____

Total Correct _____

Part I
(Answers will vary.)

1. I (Most **entrepreneurs** are known to be leaders who enjoy taking risks.)
2. I (The **condescending** waiter received hardly any tips for his snotty and conceited behavior.)
3. C
4. I (The **disparate** roommates had so few hobbies and interests in common that they went their separate ways.)
5. C
6. I (**Chauvinistic** politicians receive no significant contributions and support from women concerned about their quality of life.)
7. C
8. I (Because the lawyer did not have a reputation for **deviousness,** he was an immediate choice for the judgeship.)
9. I (The college students was so **baffled** by the statistics problems that he decided to seek help from other students.)
10. C
11. I (The professor was not thrilled to see that a large group of his students reacted in a **passive** manner to his lecture.)
12. C
13. C
14. C
15. I (The nosy and pushy student was avoided by his classmates because of his intrusive behavior.)
16. I (The student with the short attention span found it difficult to **sustain** his concentration while studying.)

Part II

(Answers will vary.)

17. inferiority
18. continuation
19. distinctions
20. indicted
21. nostalgically
22. dominance
23. abolition
24. déjà vu
25. encompassed
26. proposition

Part III

(Answers will vary.)

27. tedious; something or someone who is extremely interesting and arousing.
28. acute; to figure or interpret.
29. platonic love; foolish or extravagant love.
30. egalitarian; treating others badly because of a belief of superiority or a need to monopolize.
31. crystallization; components of love.

Part IV

(Answers will vary.)

32. for a death, a loss of some kind.
33. pizza, desserts.
34. because that student had low standardized test scores, low entrance exam scores, or a low high school grade point average.
35. jeans, long hair, t-shirts.
36. slider and curve ball for a baseball pitcher.
37. basketball, hockey, football, wrestling.
38. *The Color Purple* because it had marvelous characters who made me feel the emotions that they were experiencing.

CHAPTER 6 READINGS CONCERNING EDUCATIONAL ISSUES

Reading A—"In Praise of the F Word"

1. b	**6.** c	**11.** c
2. a	**7.** b	**12.** d
3. c	**8.** d	**13.** b
4. d	**9.** c	**14.** a
5. a	**10.** a	

Determining Meaning

Part I—Parts of Speech

1. adjective	**8.** verb
2. noun	**9.** noun
3. noun	**10.** adjective
4. verb	**11.** noun
5. noun	**12.** adjective
6. adjective	**13.** adjective
7. noun	**14.** noun

Part I—Definitions
(Answers will vary depending on the dictionary used.)

1. *abusive*—hurtful, injurious, treating harmfully.
2. *composure*—calmness or peacefulness of mind.
3. *conspiracy*—secret plan or plot, usually to do evil for a bold purpose.
4. *dooms*—to condemn, to pronounce judgment against.
5. *equivalency*—a state or condition of being equal in value or force.
6. *flustered*—confused, nervous, or upset.
7. *impediments*—things that block, prevent, or obstruct.
8. *perceive*—to understand, to see and take notice of, to become aware of.
9. *priority*—an item of importance or urgency.
10. *radical*—extreme.
11. *reality*—quality or state of being true or actual.
12. *resentful*—feeling angry because of unjust treatment; feeling offended.
13. *semiliterate*—having limited understanding; having an elementary level of reading, writing, and mathematics.

14. *validity*—state of being effectively sound, resistant to attack, or well-grounded.

Part II

con; spir for the word *spirit*

Part III

1. semiliterate
2. answers will vary
3. equivalency
4. answers will vary

Trying Out Meaning

1. validity
2. equivalency
3. radical
4. flustered
5. composure
6. abusive
7. priority
8. perceive
9. conspiracy
10. resentful
11. semiliterate
12. impediment
13. doom
14. reality

Applying Meaning

(Answers will vary. The responses here reflect the ideas that students should be thinking about.)

1. found many errors in the checks that were made out to people.
2. a lack of money, a lack of necessary study strategies, and a lack of motivation and goals.
3. the judge asked her opinion on abortion.
4. being a hard-working and dedicated individual.
5. caused the student to cry.
6. force her to attend the local college.
7. applaud and ask for an encore.
8. he had five passes intercepted.
9. she received all the attention from her parents and relatives.
10. working in a fast-food chain.
11. the student's identification.
12. how they react and feel about what we say.
13. different English professors and the way they evaluate essays.
14. life is not fair and never will be.

Conceptualizing Meaning

Part I

1. radical
2. equivalent
3. perceive
4. impediment

Part II

(Answers will vary. The responses here reflect the ideas that students should be thinking about.)

1. when my parents and all my relatives decided that they wanted me to attend the local university instead of Harvard.
2. birth certificate, driver's license.
3. income-tax forms, insurance documents.
4. Priorities in my life include my family and my job because they are important to me and give my life some meaning.
5. Some people can have resentment because they come from families that were not wealthy. They feel resentful because they have to work their way through school.
6. I lost my composure when I forgot the words to a speech and thus felt very foolish standing up there alone without anything to say.
7. unpleasant—death of parents; pleasant—success in your profession.

Reading B—"The Education of Berenice Belizaire"

Pretest

1. b	6. d	11. b
2. c	7. c	12. d
3. a	8. b	13. a
4. d	9. a	14. c
5. a	10. d	

Determining Meaning

Part I—Parts of Speech

1. verb		8. adjective
2. adjective		9. verb
3. verb		10. noun
4. verb		11. verb
5. adjective		12. verb
6. adjective		13. noun
7. adjective		14. adjective

Part I—Definitions

(Answers will vary depending on the dictionary used.)

1. *corroded*—worn down or eaten away over time.
2. *elite*—the best or most skilled members of a given social group.
3. *enduring*—suffering or lasting through something.
4. *inebriated*—excited or exhilarated as if with alcohol.
5. *median*—the middle value in a distribution or set of numbers.
6. *menial*—of or relating to work or jobs that are regarded as servant-like or low in nature or status.
7. *perverse*—stubbornly persisting in an error or fault; strong-willed.
8. *preconceived*—determined in advance.
9. *prodding*—encouraging into action.
10. *propriety*—conformity to existing customs and usages of a society or group.
11. *reinvigorated*—made vigorous again or given new energy and strength.
12. *spurn*—to reject, refuse, or scorn disdainfully.
13. *taunts*—insulting or scornful remarks.
14. *valedictory*—farewell speech or address, especially one delivered by a valedictorian.

Part II

1. reinvigorated
2. Answers will vary.
3. preconceived
4. preconception
5. no; the word is from Middle English and Old French. The original word, *propriete,* meant a particular character.

Part III
(Answers will vary.)

Trying Out Meaning

1. median
2. taunts
3. spurn
4. menial
5. elite
6. prodding
7. valedictory
8. inebriated
9. enduring
10. perverse
11. preconceived
12. corroded
13. propriety
14. reinvigorated

Applying Meaning

(Answers will vary. The responses here reflect the ideas that students should be thinking about.)

1. Cleaning their rooms, washing their clothes.
2. 15
3. No, most people would want to have more money, especially 1 million dollars.
4. No, most elite people have enough money to prevent them from being hungry or homeless.
5. Exercising, drinking some coffee, talking to friends.
6. A child might tell another child that he/she is ugly, fat, or short.
7. A college senior might say that success can be gained only through hard work, or that success can be measured only by what you give back to society.
8. Lack of discipline, a teacher's lack of content knowledge and teaching methods.
9. Examples of preconceived opinions: (a) If you work hard you should pass all your classes, (b) A college degree guarantees financial success.
10. No. If a student hates to get up in the morning, early classes would be bad for him/her.
11. No. Professionals who are stubborn or strong-willed are viewed as ones who cannot compromise or get along with other people.
12. Graduation, marriage, birth of a child.
13. Church weddings or funerals, ceremonies at a school, job interviews.
14. Yes. If a student can go to classes and study while her mother is sick, that shows that she is determined to last or stick it out.

Conceptualizing Meaning

(Answers will vary. The following are samples.)

1. value family and friends and not let their professions dictate their belief systems.
2. saw the piles of pizzas and Cokes awaiting them.
3. decided to do his homework every night on a volunteer basis.
4. was a D so the professor decided to give extra-credit work to the students.
5. race or gender it is difficult to change their minds.
6. the company was too far away from his family and friends.
7. went home and changed into a plain skirt and sweater.
8. making coffee, filing memos, and cleaning up the workroom.
9. her to be disliked by everyone in the department.
10. purchase computers for taking lecture notes, and to study at least five hours each day.
11. graduated from college with honors and received several job offers.
12. funerals, weddings, and graduation ceremonies.
13. it was falling apart and had no specific color or design on the outside.
14. decided to vote on bills the way he wanted to instead of talking to the people he represented.

Extending and Challenging

Part I
(Answers will vary.)

Positive	Negative
valedictory	menial
validity	perverse
composure	abusive
	impediments
	conspiracy
	spurn
	radical
	resentful
	corroded

Part II

1. perception
Perception means a process of understanding something, or seeing and taking notice of something.
(Answers will vary. Sample follows.)
His visual perception at night was not good, so he let his wife drive the car.

2. reinvigoration
Reinvigoration means a state of becoming energized or gaining strength.
(Answers will vary. Sample follows.)
Because of the long hours he worked and the stress he absorbed, his doctor ordered a month of reinvigoration in the mountains.

3. inebriation
inebriation means a state of being intoxicated; exhilaration.
(Answers will vary. Sample follows.)
Her feelings of inebriation after graduation wore off quickly when she had to begin work the next day.

Part III

(Answers will vary, but some sample answers follow.)

1. Mary Sherry would be impressed and proud of Berenice Belizaire because she overcame a lot of handicaps to graduate from school as the valedictorian, and to be accepted into MIT. Mary Sherry would probably say that more American students should work as hard as Berenice did.
2. Answers will vary.
3. Answers will vary.

Posttest I—Readings A and B

PART I DIRECTIONS: Read each sentence carefully. If the boldfaced word is used correctly, circle C and go on to the next item. If, however, the word is used incorrectly, circle I and then make the sentence correct.

C I **1.** The **semiliterate** clerk at the checkout register was able to make change quickly and correctly even though the register was broken.

C I **2.** The **elite** party in New York City included politicians, famous athletes and celebrities, and wealthy and respected families.

C   I   **3.** The **flustered** lawyer was able to present a smooth and convincing closing argument for his client.

C   I   **4.** It was difficult for many people to **perceive** the differences between the identical twins.

C   I   **5.** A lack of math skills can **doom** any college student hoping to be an accountant.

C   I   **6.** The student remembered fondly the **taunts** he had received from his classmates in elementary school.

C   I   **7.** A lack of education is usually an **impediment** to a high-paying career.

C   I   **8.** The college student who wanted to keep his scholarship decided to make studying a **priority.**

C   I   **9.** An average salary is the same as a **median** salary.

C   I   **10.** The tense and argumentative pitcher seldom lost his **composure** during the game.

PART II DIRECTIONS: Using the words below, complete the following analogies. Remember to keep the part of speech the same for all words. An example is shown following the list of words.

radical	abusive	menial
propriety	elite	spurn

EXAMPLE: tense: calm :: evil: good

        (Notice that the relationships on both sides of the equation are adjectives which are opposite in meaning.)

11. reject: _____ :: corrode: wear away

12. skilled: _____ :: easy going: perverse

13. kindly: _____ :: equivalent: unequal

14. appropriateness: _____ :: farewell address: valedictory

Part III DIRECTIONS: Select a word from the list below in order to make the sentences complete. Each word is used only once and is in its proper form.

resentful	inebriated	prodding	enduring	radical
perceive	conspiracy	reinvigorate	valid	median

15. The child felt there was a _____ between his parents and friends to make sure he would practice his piano every night.

16. Your driver's license must be _____ if you hope to avoid receiving a ticket from a policeman.

17. Many people believe that the legalization of drugs would be a _____ and unwise idea.

18. A trip to the mountains or to a quiet beach can _____ most people who feel burned out from work.

19. After _____ the wait in line for four hours, the students were able to get tickets for the concert.

20. Because of his _____ views on women and feminist theory, he found the guest speaker a total waste of time.

21. The awkward and insecure freshman felt _____ toward her roommate, who was popular and extremely attractive.

22. After receiving a gentle _____ from his mother, the young boy wrote his grandmother a thank-you note for the birthday present.

23. Politicians can become _____ with the power they receive while they are in elective office.

Total Correct _____

Posttest I—Readings A and B

Part I
(Changes to the incorrect items will vary. The responses here reflect the kind of changes students should be thinking about.)

1. I (The semiliterate clerk at the checkout register was not able to make change quickly and correctly when the register broke.)
2. C

3. I (The flustered lawyer was not able to present a smooth and convincing closing argument for his client.)
4. C
5. C
6. I (The student remembered with anger the taunts he had received from his classmates in elementary school.)
7. C
8. C
9. I (An average salary is slightly different from the median salary.)
10. I (The tense and argumentative pitcher frequently lost his composure during the game.)

Part II

11. spurn
12. menial
13. abusive
14. propriety

Part III

15. conspiracy
16. valid
17. radical
18. reinvigorate
19. enduring
20. preconceived
21. resentful
22. prodding
23. inebriated

Reading C—"Motivation"
Pretest—General Words

1. a	7. b	13. c
2. c	8. a	14. b
3. b	9. c	15. a
4. d	10. d	16. d
5. a	11. a	17. b
6. c	12. c	

Pretest—Content-Specific Words

(Answers will vary.)

1. a psychological need for achieving or obtaining a certain goal.
2. some kind of tension or tightening.
3. hostile, angry, very driven people; people who get mad if they are hindered with their goals.
4. concerning the heart and the diseases of the heart.
5. wanting to belong.
6. motivated by goals within yourself.
7. motivated by goals outside yourself.

Determining Meaning—General Words

Part I—Parts of Speech

1. noun
2. verb
3. verb
4. adverb
5. verb
6. adjective
7. adjective
8. adjective
9. verb
10. noun
11. adjective
12. adjective
13. noun
14. verb
15. adjective
16. noun
17. verb

Part I—Definitions

(Answers will vary depending on the dictionary used.)

1. *apparatus*—a machine or group of machines used to perform a specific task.
2. *banish*—to drive away, expel; to force to leave a country or area.
3. *detract*—to take away a desirable part; diminish.
4. *diligently*—characterized by painstaking effort; by working hard.
5. *exhibit*—to show; display outwardly.
6. *explosive*—tending to burst forth suddenly, violently, or sharply.
7. *forbidding*—unfriendly, disagreeable, threatening.
8. *inherent*—existing as an essential characteristic in something or somebody.
9. *manifest*—to make obvious, reveal, demonstrate painfully.
10. *ostracism*—banishment or exclusion from a group.
11. *passive*—accepting without objection or resistance; not acting or operating.

12. *pervasive*—tending to be present throughout; spreading or flowing everywhere.
13. *presumption*—an act of accepting to be true or reasonable.
14. *squelching*—putting down or silencing; crushing or trampling.
15. *repugnant*—arousing disgust; repulsive; offensive.
16. *toll*—the amount or extent of loss or destruction, as of life, health, or property.
17. *validated*—declared or proven true, sound, or effective.

Part II
(Answers will vary.)

Part III

1. detract
2. **trahere**—to pull
3. Answers will vary, but could include: traction, tractable, intractable, subtract.
4. In Greece, potsherds were used as ballots in voting for ostracism; the Greek word for *potsherd* is **ostrakon.**
5. toll

Determining Meaning—Content-Specific Words

1. *achievement motivation*—psychological need for success in school, sports, occupation, and other competitive situations; persons with achievement motivation generally experience little anxiety or fear of failure; when success is achieved, they enjoy the fruits of their labor more than the average individual.
2. *affiliation motivation*—present in all humans; tendency to prefer being with others rather than satisfying other motives.
3. *cardiologist*—one who studies the heart or the diseases of the heart.
4. *extrinsic motivation*—situation in which an individual is motivated or driven by external conditions, such as being paid for correct answers.
5. *intrinsic motivation*—situation in which an individual is motivated or driven by the inherent nature of an activity or its natural consequences or both; for example, doing puzzles because you like to do so.
6. *somatic tension*—tension existing in your body.
7. *Type A personality*—hostile, achievement-oriented persons; persons with Type A personality have explosive speech patterns and tend to rush around to finish tasks.

Organizing Concepts

DIRECTIONS: Complete the following chart, using as many general and content-specific words as possible. Some categories and explanations have been started for you.

MOTIVATION

Types	Definition	Characteristics Examples	Experiments Research
Achievement	psychological need for success	Type A: little anxiety or fear	Men (39–49 years) had more heart disease if Type A.
Affiliation	high need to be with others	prefer to work with others even if the friend is incompetent	Schacter's shock apparatus
Extrinsic	reward external to the activity	giving money to do math problems	
Intrinsic	reward internal in doing or completing a task	inherent; donating to charity because you like to do so	Extrinsic motivation can squelch those who are intrinsically motivated.

Beginning Conceptual Understanding

(Changes to the false items will vary. The responses here reflect the kind of changes students should be thinking about.)

1. F (People who exhibit high levels of achievement motivation generally do not choose jobs that squelch individual efforts to be the best.)
2. F (Students with a Type A personality do not try to detract attention away from themselves.)
3. F (Somatic tension occurs rarely in passive and easy going people.)

4. T
5. T
6. T
7. F (Schachter's experiment with a forbidding-looking shock apparatus demonstrated that anxiety increases our need to affiliate.)
8. T
9. F (The presumption of psychologists is that intrinsic motivation is usually better than extrinsic motivation in terms of shaping human behavior.)
10. F (People described as being high in achievement motivation use explosive speech patterns.)
11. T
12. T

Using Concepts

(Answers will vary. Samples follow.)

1. a check for fifty dollars, a new stereo, a computer.
2. putting his head down on his desk, sleeping.
3. body aches, tight muscles.
4. they are always in a hurry; each is the most important person in the room.
5. a research paper 100 pages long.
6. go to every class, take notes, read all the assignments.
7. took illegal drugs, bet on the game he/she was playing in.
8. cleaning toilet bowls or showers, cleaning out the garbage can.
9. a class on how to write a job resume or conduct a successful job interview.
10. money, your health or the health of your family, your love life.
11. driver's license, passport.
12. AIDS, malaria, cholera.
13. being overweight, stressed, eating poorly.
14. like to study in groups.
15. move students so they are not so close together; make alternative forms of the test.
16. x-ray machine.
17. a lack of money, being sick all the time, having a disagreeable roommate.
18. screaming, hitting the wall when angry, physically abusing another individual.
19. ignore them or send them away.

20. that they experience little anxiety or fear of failure; they enjoy the fruits of their labor more than others do.
21. innocence.

Comprehending Concepts

Part I

1. achievement, affiliation, intrinsic, extrinsic.
2. explosive speech patterns, directing all conversations to themselves, a pervasive sense of time urgency.
3. No. Because achievement motivation is a learned motive, there are some cultures that consider it repugnant or inappropriate.
4. When we experience a lot of anxiety, we have more of a need to affiliate.
5. Example of extrinsic motivation: money for grades. Example of intrinsic motivation: finishing a task because it makes you feel good to do it correctly.
6. People who have the Type A personality are high in achievement motivation, but not all individuals with achievement motivation suffer from the Type A personality. The person with a Type A personality is far more destructive and hostile than the individual who wishes to achieve.
7. If children are give a reward for doing a task they already enjoy doing, the reward may detract from their intrinsic motivation.
8. People with the Type A personality tend to put themselves under a lot of stress and, as a result, have heart problems.

Part II
(Answers will vary. Samples follow.)

1. According to the psychologists, there are four types of motivation. The first type of motivation is achievement motivation. Achievement motivation, or **n ACH**, is the psychological need for success in whatever we do, whether it be in school, sports, or work. People with high amounts of achievement motivation generally choose jobs that challenge them, yet provide them with reasonable promises of success. People high in **n ACH** generally experience little or no anxiety or fear of failure, and enjoy the fruits of hard work more than most people do. Most psychologists believe that achievement motivation is a learned motive and not common to all cultures.

   The second type of motivation is the need for affiliation. People who are motivated by affiliation prefer being with others rather than satisfying their other motives. The need for affiliation can exhibit itself during times of stress. Research has also demonstrated that first-born or only children have more need for affiliation.

Intrinsic motivation is the third type. Individuals with intrinsic motivation complete tasks because they inherently like doing them, or the consequences of finishing a task, or both. For example, if you like figuring out problems, you would probably be intrinsically motivated to finish a puzzle.

The final type is extrinsic motivation. Individuals who need a reward that is external to an activity or task are the ones who need extrinsic motivation. That reward could be money, awards, certificates, or special privileges. Research has suggested that students who resist doing a specific task will do the task more frequently if rewarded. However, students who already enjoy a task and are intrinsically motivated should not receive external rewards because these rewards could detract from their internal motivation.

2. Answers will vary.
3. In terms of motivation, some males and females differ in terms of how they view competition and achievement. According to Horner's research in laboratory settings, females are less competitive in direct laboratory situations. Some researchers believe that females are less competitive and achievement-oriented because of their environment and learning. It may be that females in our culture are less willing than males to take the risks necessary to be a success because of what it means to be a female. In contrast, males are directly and indirectly taught that competition and achievement are good and masculine. They learn these lessons from their fathers and the media, and from participating in and watching sporting events.

Posttest II—Readings A, B, and C

PART I DIRECTIONS: Read each sentence carefully. If the boldfaced word is used correctly, circle C and go on to the next item. If, however, the boldfaced word is used incorrectly, circle I and then correct the sentence.

C I 1. The pitcher lost his **composure** when the coach decided to take him out of the game in the second inning.

C I 2. People who need **extrinsic motivation** want to learn because it is **inherently** exciting and stimulating.

C I 3. **Cardiologists** do not consider healthy eating habits or a routine of exercise to be a **priority** for their patients.

C I 4. As a result of the accountant's **diligent** work, he was praised by his supervisor.

C I 5. Professional athletes earn salaries **equivalent** to those of most other individuals, such as teachers and nurses.

C I 6. The **passive** girl was known by her friends as one who would constantly pick arguments and challenge rules.

C I 7. Going to sleep for four or five days can take a **toll** on most people's lives.

C I 8. The million-dollar winner of the lottery was **inebriated** with joy and excitement.

C I 9. The potential juror was excused because the lawyers felt she had **preconceived** notions about the defendant.

C I 10. The timid child was thrilled to learn that he would have to receive a treatment from a **forbidding apparatus**.

PART II DIRECTIONS: Circle the word that does not belong with the other two. Then, in the space provided, explain how the two remaining words are similar.

11. banish
ostracize
validate

_____

12. repugnant
menial
intrinsic

_____

13. perceive
impede
fluster

_____

14. manifest
spurn
exhibit

_____

PART IV DIRECTIONS: Answer the following questions, making sure to demonstrate your knowledge of the boldfaced words.

15. Would you want to **squelch** a **conspiracy** concerning you and your family? Why or why not? _____

16. Would a **semiliterate** adult have difficulty **enduring** college? Why or why not? _____

17. Would someone with **somatic tension** need to **reinvigorate** herself? Why or why not? _____

18. Would a **Type A personality** be pleased to receive the **median** income from his employer? Why or why not? _____

PART V DIRECTIONS: Select a word from the list below in order to complete each sentence. Each word is used only once and is in its proper form.

composure	perverse	exhibit	forbidding
elite	reality	corroded	toll

19. abusive: hurtful :: worn down: _____

20. radical: extreme :: best: _____

21. rare: pervasive :: easy going, flexible: _____

22. prod: discourage :: hide, withdraw: _____

PART VI DIRECTIONS: Select a word from the list below in order to make the sentences complete. Each word is used only once and is in its proper form.

resentful	propriety	valedictory	presumption
doomed	explosive	reality	detract

23. The insurance salesperson's _____ speech patterns offended many of his clients.

24. After missing twenty days of lab and the midterm, the college student felt he was _____ to failure in chemistry.

25. The older child was _____ of his baby brother because his parents spent all their time caring for the new infant.

26. Sometimes the _____ of college forces students to adopt new study habits.

27. The high school senior's _____ address urges everyone to give more time and money to those less fortunate in our society.

28. Unlike many European countries, in our legal system there is a _____ of innocence for the defendant in a court case.

29. The chewing of gum and the constant use of slang can _____ from a candidate's desirability during a job interview.

30. The dinner guest violated _____ when he chewed his food with his mouth open and used his fingers, rather than the fork and spoon, to eat.

Total Correct _____

Posttest II—Readings A, B, and C

Part I
(Changes to the incorrect items will vary. The responses here reflect the kind of changes students should be thinking about.)

1. C
2. I (People who need intrinsic motivation want to learn because it is inherently exciting and stimulating.)
3. I (Cardiologists consider healthy eating habits and a routine of exercise to be a priority for their patients.)
4. C
5. I (Professional athletes earn salaries that are not equivalent to those of most other individuals, such as teachers and nurses.)
6. I (The passive girl was known by her friends as one who was quiet and rarely challenged rules or ideas.)
7. C
8. C
9. C
10. I (The timid child was upset to learn that he would have to receive a treatment from a forbidding apparatus.)

Part II

11. validate. The other two words mean to send away or to ignore someone.

12. intrinsic. The other two words are negative in connotation and mean something that is lowly or disgusting.
13. perceive. The other two words mean something or someone that is having difficulty completing a task.
14. spurn. The other two words mean to show or to reveal.

Part III

15. Yes, because the conspiracy would be an act that could endanger you and your family. Hence, you would want to stop it immediately.
16. Yes, because the ability to read, write, and compute is necessary for passing almost all college courses.
17. Yes. When you have tensions in your body, you need to relax and remove the stress. This can be done by reinvigorating yourself through rest and exercise.
18. No. The median income is in the middle of a distribution; the Type A personality would want to make the top income in a distribution.

Part IV

19. corroded
20. elite
21. perverse
22. exhibit

Part V

23. explosive
24. doomed
25. resentful
26. reality
27. valedictory
28. presumption
29. detract
30. propriety

CHAPTER 7 READINGS CONCERNING HEALTH-RELATED ISSUES

Reading A—`If You Light Up on Sunday, Don't Come in on Monday"

Pretest

1. c	8. d	15. a
2. a	9. a	16. c
3. c	10. b	17. c
4. a	11. a	18. a
5. d	12. d	19. a
6. c	13. b	
7. d	14. d	

Determining Meaning

Part I—Parts of Speech

1. verb	11. verb
2. adjective	12. noun
3. verb	13. noun
4. noun	14. verb
5. verb	15. verb
6. verb	16. noun
7. adjective	17. noun
8. noun	18. verb
9. noun	19. noun
10. adjective	

Part I—Definitions
(Answers will vary depending on dictionary used.)

1. *banning*—prohibiting, especially by official decree.
2. *communicable*—something transmittable between humans or species; contagious.
3. *deem*—to have as an opinion; to judge.
4. *disincentives*—things that do not motivate effort or cause one to take action; punishments.
5. *estimates*—calculates approximately.
6. *fraternizing*—associating with others in a friendly way.
7. *grim*—dismal; gloomy.
8. *incentives*—things that cause one to take action or motivate effort.
9. *incidence*—extent or frequency of an occurrence.

10. *justifiable*—having sufficient grounds to declare or demonstrate that something is right or valid.
11. *levied*—imposed or collected, as a tax, for example.
12. *moonlighting*—the act of working at another job, usually at night, in addition to one's full-time job.
13. *perk*—reward; something extra received.
14. *proffer*—to offer for acceptance; to tender.
15. *prohibits*—forbids by authority.
16. *proponents*—those who are in favor of something.
17. *sentiment*—an opinion about a specific matter; a view.
18. *spurred*—urged on; stimulated.
19. *surcharge*—a sum added to the usual amount.

Part II
(Answers will vary.)

Part III

2. *disincentives*—noun; something that is not an incentive; punishments.
   incentives—noun; things that cause one to take action; rewards.
3. *fraternizing*—verb; associating with others in a friendly way.
   fraternity—noun; a body of people associated for a common purpose or interest.
4. *proponents*—noun; those who are in favor of something.
   opponents—noun; those who are against something.
5. *justifiable*—adjective; having sufficient grounds to demonstrate that something is right or valid.
   justify—verb; demonstrate that something is right or valid.

Trying Out Meaning

1. justifiable
2. proponents
3. banning
4. levied
5. surcharge
6. grim
7–8. incidence; communicable
9. moonlighting
10. prohibits
11. estimates
12. perk
13. sentiment
14. incentives
15. deem
16. fraternizing
17. proffer
18. disincentive
19. spurred

Applying Meaning

(Answers will vary, but the following serve as examples.)

1. you would not want to be out in public very much since you could give your disease to someone else.
2. rewarding yourself with a trip to the beach!
3. go outside the building if you wanted to smoke.
4. they make them pay some money, perhaps when they import goods.
5. you have tried everything possible to find the owner.
6. support the legislation by lobbying your state representative.
7. there is generally a lack of food and poor sanitation.
8. you totally understood the topic being covered that day.
9. not be allowed in that store anymore.
10. getting a company car, profit sharing, and a high commission.
11. you thought your boss might like it.
12. your day job didn't pay very much and you had a lot of bills to pay.
13. you thought you could find out some of their ideas.
14. you suddenly had to change your flight.
15. you might be making a great contribution to your field.
16. have to get a new roommate or come to an understanding.
17. it has been linked to lung cancer in numerous studies.
18. are coming true.
19. studying hard and then failing the test anyway.

Conceptualized Meaning

(Answers will vary.)

1. a waiter or waitress; working at the 7-11.
2–3. if you draw out your retirement too early.
4–5. having more than one spouse at any given time; smoking in all federal buildings.
6. making a contribution to your field. Because then you leave something behind.
7. AIDS; some forms of cancer.
8–9. when money is needed locally to build a new school.
10. on controversial issues such as abortion or smokers' rights.
11. the common cold; AIDS; measles.
12. a chance to break into acting!
13. when one or several of them are trying to get your job.
14–15. incentive—feeling better; disincentive—the cost.
16. "It should be against the law to use animal fur to make coats."

17. the amount of money it will need for the military, education, welfare, etc.
18. equal pay and rights for all races and sexes.
19. when you are the only one in the group with differing thoughts and opinions.

Reading B—"Health Care: How We Got Into This Mess"
Pretest

1. b	9. b	17. a
2. d	10. d	18. c
3. a	11. a	19. c
4. c	12. a	20. d
5. c	13. b	21. c
6. d	14. d	22. b
7. c	15. c	
8. a	16. d	

Determining Meaning

Part I—Parts of Speech

1. adjective	13. adjective
2. noun	14. noun
3. noun	15. adjective
4. noun	16. noun
5. noun	17. noun
6. adjective	18. noun
7. verb	19. adjective
8. noun	20. adjective
9. adjective	21. adjective
10. noun	22. adjective
11. adjective	23. adverb
12. verb	

Part I—Definitions
(Answers will vary depending on dictionary used.)

1. *ambiguous*—open to more than one interpretation.
2. *autonomy*—the condition or quality of being independent.
3. *batteries*—an array of similar things intended to be used together.
4. *beneficiary*—one who receives a benefit, aid, or help.

5. *compensation*—the act or state of receiving payment for something.
6. *crank*—of, being, or produced by an eccentric or strange person.
7. *curb(s, ed)*—to check, restrain, or control.
8. *deficits*—inadequacies or insufficiencies.
9. *devastating*—laying waste; destroying.
10. *dilemma*—a situation that requires a choice between equally unfavorable or mutually exclusive options.
11. *enriching*—making more meaningful or rewarding.
12. *fosters*—brings up; nurtures; promotes.
13. *impersonal*—showing no emotion or personality.
14. *inflation*—a persistent increase in the level of consumer prices.
15. *massive*—very large; huge.
16. *paradox*—a seemingly contradictory statement that may be nonetheless true.
17. *reimbursement*—the act of paying back or compensating another for money spent.
18. *restrictions*—acts of limiting or confining.
19. *scourge*—a source of widespread affliction and devastation.
20. *unbounded*—having no boundaries or restrictions.
21. *universal*—including, relating to, or affecting all members of a class or group under consideration.
22. *ultimately*—at last; in the end.
23. *volatile*—tending to vary widely; inconsistent.

Part II
(Answers will vary.)

Part III
(In some cases, there is more than one correct answer for these words.)

1. **batteries (battery)**
   Part of speech—noun
   New Definition—the unlawful beating or striking of another person; OR a set of guns or other military equipment.
2. **crank**
   Part of speech—verb OR noun
   New Definition—(verb) to start or operate something by turning a handle; OR (noun) one who is in a bad mood.
3. **curb(s)**
   Part of speech—noun
   New Definition—a concrete border along the edge of a street.

Trying Out Meaning

1. I The impersonal nature of large universities fosters very large classes and few interactions with faculty.
2. C
3. C
4. I Universal health care would be received by everyone.
5. I The situation was so volatile that there were several police cars called to the scene.
6. I When we are adults, we should be autonomous individuals.
7. C
8. I Tonya's teacher said that her writing was so ambiguous that nothing in her paper was understandable or easy to read.
9. I Inflation in the economy usually makes everyone unhappy since prices tend to rise.
10. I Alex tried to curb his appetite by chewing gum and eating filling, low-calorie foods.
11. C
12. C
13. C
14. I The scourge of deadly diseases such as AIDS has made us realize that our medical resources are limited.
15. I The paradox of our health system is that everyone needs it and few can afford to have it.

Applying Meaning

1. inflation
2. devastates
3. universal
4. volatile
5. ambiguous
6. beneficiary
7. dilemma
8. curbing
9. reimbursement; compensation
10. autonomous
11. massive
12. impersonal
13. crank
14. enriching
15. unbounded
16. restrictions
17. deficit
18. foster
19. paradox
20. scourges
21. ultimate
22. batteries

Conceptualizing Meaning

(Answers will vary. The following serve as examples.)

1. The faster I go, the more behind I get.
2. "Nice day today, isn't it?"
3. If you were sick and the doctor couldn't figure out what was wrong with you.
4. The cost keeps rising and it is unaffordable to most people unless they have medical insurance.
5. Plants in the house; classical music; a pet.
6. Teachers treating male and female students differently.
7. Students might put a career goal here.
8. Chewing gum; hard candy.
9. "Maybe we could get together sometime."
10. A hostage situation.
11. Forget to put the plug in after he has changed your oil.
12. Hospitals turning people away who do not have insurance.
13. Studying; late nights.
14. Your checks would bounce.
15. If there were a drought it would be necessary to have restrictions on watering your lawn.
16. When you live in your own apartment for the first time.
17. Work at a part-time job.
18. If someone in your family dies and leaves you something in his will.
19. If you had a lot of business expenses that were not reimbursed, you might talk to your boss or even look for another job.
20. AIDS; war; famine.
21. Some forms of cancer; AIDS.
22. Many cars would be wrecked and people might be seriously injured.
23. Doctors might order unnecessary tests or surgery just because it's covered.

Extending and Challenging

Part I

1. unbounded
2. autonomy
3. devastate
4. scourge
5. dilemma
6. surcharge
7. foster

Part II

(Answers will vary somewhat.)

2. Universal health care would be available to everyone in society, not just those who have jobs that provide medical insurance.
3. Not being able to choose your own physician makes health care more impersonal.
4. Federal budget deficits will continue to rise unless medical costs come down because many people receive Medicare or Medicaid.
5. New technical advances, as well as inflation, lead to high medical costs.
6. Some restrictions on the kind of services provided, as well as who is eligible for these services, may help the costs of health care, come down.
7. Those who have communicable diseases, such as AIDS, are not allowed to be discriminated against in the workplace.
8. Some companies give employees incentives in the form of money if they keep things such as their weight and cholesterol down, thus making them less of a health risk.

Part III

(Answers will vary.)

1. Cigarette smoking affects the cost of health care in several ways. First, employers often have to pay more medical insurance for those employees who smoke. Thus some companies are **banning** the hiring of smokers. Second, smokers' illnesses tend to be **grim**, often costing thousands of dollars. These costs are passed along to everyone in terms of higher-priced medical care.
2. Answers will vary since this question requires a personal response.
3. That we have the technology to keep people alive for a longer period of time. The **grim paradox** is that older people often cannot afford this care.
4. Journal entries will vary. Students should be encouraged to use some of the words in their entries.

Posttest I—Readings A and B

PART I DIRECTIONS: Fill in each of the blanks with the correct word taken from the list below:

batteries
beneficiary
communicable
curbs
deem
devastating
disincentive
grim
justifiable

moonlight
proffered
prohibited
reimbursement
spurred
surcharge
universal
volatile

1. Smoking is _____ in many public and in all federal buildings currently.

2. If _____ health coverage was available, everyone would have at least a minimum of coverage.

3. Because smoking can cause _____ health problems, the criticism against it may be _____.

4. Some companies force their employees to pay a(n) _____ on their health insurance as a(n) _____ to smoking.

5. Some doctors order _____ of tests so that they can receive large _____ for services rendered.

6. The rights of smokers is a _____ topic, _____ by accusations of First Amendment rights violations.

7. Many who have tried to quite smoking have _____ this suggestion: Chewing gum _____ your desire to have a cigarette.

8. Diseases that are _____ are passed from person to person.

9. Because they have no health care plan and make low wages, many individuals _____ it necessary to _____ at night and work a full-time job during the day.

10. Those who are the _____ of a good health care plan often do not understand the _____ facts that many Americans are one illness away from financial disaster.

PART II DIRECTIONS: Use each of the word pairs below in one sentence so that it is clear you conceptually understand each one. You can change the form of the word if you like.

1. enrich/proponents

_____

2. levied/restrictions

_____

3. fosters/dilemma

_____

4. ban/compensation

_____

5. perk/unbounded

_____

PART III DIRECTIONS: Circle the word that is closest to the antonym of the boldfaced target word.

1. **fraternize** (verb)
   a. socialize
   b. organize
   c. reflect
   d. isolate

2. **ambiguous**
   a. hazy
   b. inaccurate
   c. precise
   d. clear

3. **scourge**
   a. punishment
   b. reward
   c. gift
   d. suffering

4. **perk**
   a. punishment
   b. salary
   c. benefit
   d. reimbursement

5. massive
   a. small
   b. severe
   c. huge
   d. unknown

PART IV DIRECTIONS: Read each sentence, paying particular attention to the target word in bold print. If the word is used correctly in the sentence, mark C and go on to the next item. If the word is used incorrectly, mark I and then make the sentence correct.

C   I   **1.** It is good to have a **deficit** in your checking account so that you can go on an occasional shopping spree.

C   I   **2.** Cal was given the **incentive** to work harder when his boss told him he would get a **massive** reduction in his salary.

C   I   **3.** It was everyone's **sentiment** that **inflation** had caused grocery store prices to drop.

C   I   **4.** Martin was tired of getting **crank** phone calls in the middle of the night, so he had his number changed.

C   I   **5. Unbounded** benefits in health care systems would **ultimately** lead to their destruction.

C   I   **6.** The **paradox** of the field of medicine today is that people live longer but have to pay more for health care.

C   I   **7.** The **impersonal** conversation focused on things that Margaret had felt ashamed to talk about for years.

Posttest I—Readings A and B

Part I

1. prohibited
2. universal
3. devastating (or *grim* would also work); justifiable
4. surcharge; disincentive
5. batteries; reimbursement
6. volatile; spurred
7. proffered; curbs
8. communicable
9. deem; moonlight
10. beneficiary; grim (or *devastating* would also work)

Part II
(Answers will vary. The following serve as examples.)

1. **Proponents** of environmental concerns believe that clean air **enriches** the life of everyone on earth.
2. Environmentalists believe that the **restrictions levied** against polluters are necessary and justifiable.
3. Controversial issues, such as just how "clean" the environment should be, not only **foster** debate, but also create **dilemmas**.
4. When the use of pesticides such as DDT was **banned**, people who had been injured by it received **compensation** from large companies that produced it.
5. The **perks** that the CEO received were **unbounded**: a big expense account, private planes at his disposal, and six weeks of vacation every year.

Part III

1. isolate
2. clear
3. reward
4. punishment
5. small

Part IV

1. I It is harmful to have a **deficit** because you will never be able to go on a shopping spree.
2. I Cal was given the incentive to work harder when his boss told him he would get a huge salary increase.
3. I It was everyone's sentiment that inflation had caused grocery store prices to go up.
4. C
5. C
6. C
7. I The impersonal conversation focused on the weather, our dogs, and what we liked to eat.

Reading C—"AIDS"

Pretest

1. d	9. b	17. a
2. b	10. c	18. d
3. c	11. a	19. d
4. a	12. d	20. c
5. c	13. d	21. d
6. d	14. a	22. a
7. a	15. b	23. b
8. d	16. b	24. b

Determining Meaning

Part I—Parts of Speech

1. adjective	13. noun
2. noun	14. noun
3. verb	15. adjective
4. adjective	16. noun
5. verb	17. adjective
6. verb	18. verb
7. noun	19. noun
8. adverb	20. adjective
9. adjective	21. verb
10. adjective	22. verb
11. adjective	23. verb
12. adjective	24. noun, verb

Part I—Definitions
(Answers will vary depending on dictionary used.)

1. *asymptomatic*—having no symptoms.
2. *conduits*—channels for the transmission of something.
3. *confirmed*—made valid; verified.
4. *contaminated*—made unclean or impure by contact with something.
5. *detect*—to discover or ascertain the presence of.
6. *ensured*—made sure or certain.
7. *epidemic*—a rapid spread, growth, or development, often of a disease.
8. *heterosexuality*—being sexually oriented to persons of the opposite sex.
9. *impaired*—diminished, as in strength or quality.

10. *insidious*—working or spreading harmfully in a subtle or stealthy manner.
11. *isolated*—separated from others; solitary.
12. *latency*—the state or quality of something that is present or potential but not evident or active.
13. *legions*—large numbers; multitudes.
14. *misconceptions*—mistaken thoughts, ideas, or notions; misunderstandings.
15. *predominant*—having the greatest importance, influence, authority, or force.
16. *prevalence*—the condition of being widely occurring, existing, accepted, or practiced.
17. *prudent*—wise in handling practical matters; using good judgment.
18. *quarantining*—isolating.
19. *recipients*—those who receive or are receptive.
20. *sophisticated*—complex and refined.
21. *spawn*—to give rise to.
22. *stigmatized*—characterized or branded as disgraceful.
23. *suppressed*—put an end to; subdued.
24. *transmission*—the act or process of sending from one person, place, or thing to another.

Part II
(Answers will vary.)

Part III
(Answers will vary to the last two portions of each of the following activities. The following serve as examples.)

1. hetero- means *other or different.*
   heterosexual means *being sexually oriented to persons of the opposite sex.*
   My word: *heterogeneous.*
   Heterogeneous means *consisting of dissimilar elements or parts.*
2. mis- means *bad; badly, wrong; wrongly.*
   misconceptions means *mistaken or wrong ideas or notions.*
   My word: *misfortune.*
   Misfortune means *bad fortune or ill luck.*
3. epi- means *over or above.*
   epidemic means *rapid growth or above normal growth of something.*
   My word: *epicure.*

Epicure means *one who has refined taste in food and wine (above-average taste).*

4. a- means *without or not.*
   asymptomatic means *without symptoms.*
   My word: *atheist.*
   Atheist means *having no belief in God or any supreme being.*

Determining Meaning—Content-Specific Words

(Answers will vary. The responses below indicate the kinds of information about which students should be thinking.)

1. *AIDS*—acquired immune deficiency syndrome; an opportunistic infection that attacks the immune system.
2. *antibodies*—protein substances produced in the blood or tissues in response to a specific antigen.
3. *contagious*—transmissible by direct or indirect contact; communicable.
4. *cyclosporin*—a drug that suppresses the immune system; this drug is used primarily in patients who have organ transplants, to keep the body from rejecting the organ.
5. *defense mechanism*—a physiological reaction of an organism used in self-protection or against infection.
6. *epidemiologists*—those who deal with the causes, distribution, and control of disease in populations.
7. *evolution*—the idea that organisms change gradually over time.
8. *hemophiliacs*—persons (mostly male) whose blood fails to clot normally because of a defective clotting factor.
9. *HIV*—a retrovirus that causes AIDS; stands for human immunodeficiency virus; a virus that attacks and destroys the immune system.
10. *hypodermic*—injected in or beneath the skin; hypodermic syringes are used for giving injections.
11. *immune system*—the integrated body of organs, tissues, cells, or cell products that identifies and neutralizes potentially pathogenic organisms or substances.
12. *intravenous*—within or administered into a vein.
13. *Kaposi's sarcoma*—a purple skin tumor normally seen in elderly patients with impaired immune systems but found in individuals who are HIV positive, regardless of age.
14. *malaria*—an infectious disease characterized by cycles of chills, fever, and sweating, caused by the infection of blood cells by a protozoan.

15. *microorganisms*—an organism, such as a bacterium or a protozoan, that you can see only under a microscope.
16. *opportunistic infections*—infections that are successful only because the immune system of the individual is impaired for some other reason.
17. *pathogen*—an agent that causes disease.
18. *Pneumocystis carinni*—a type of pneumonia caused by a parasitic protozoan; most common in individuals with an immunodeficiency disease such as AIDS.
19. *protozoan*—any of a large group of single-celled, usually microscopic, organisms.
20. *yellow fever*—an infectious tropical disease caused by mosquitoes.

Part II
(Students should discuss the words with a partner.)

Organizing Concepts

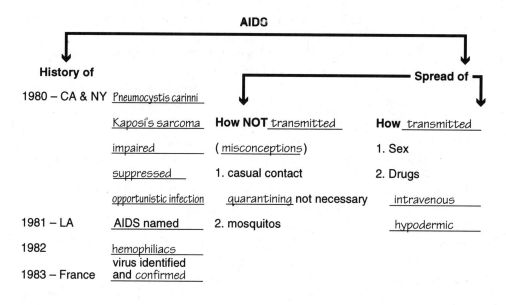

Beginning Conceptual Understanding

Part I

(Answers will vary. The answers here reflect the ideas that students should be thinking about.)

2. **HIV** is related to **AIDS** in that HIV is the virus that causes AIDS. Someone can be HIV positive and be **asymptomatic** of the AIDS disease.
3. **Pneumocystis carinni** is related to **AIDS** in that it is one of the infections that can result in someone who has a suppressed immune system, as AIDS patients have.
4. **Kaposi's sarcoma** is related to **AIDS** in a way similar to the way **Pneumocystis carinni** is. That is, it occurs in AIDS patients who have **suppressed immune systems**. It is a form of skin cancer generally found only in elderly patients with suppressed immune systems.
5. **Epidemiologists** are related to **AIDS** since they are the individuals who deal with the cause, development, and spread of the disease.
6. **Hemophiliacs** are related to **AIDS** in that some hemophiliacs received blood transfusions from blood tainted with **HIV**, the virus that causes AIDS.
7. **Hypodermic** is related to **AIDS** in that the sharing of hypodermic needles is one key way that HIV is spread.
8. The **immune system** is related to **AIDS** in that it is the immune system that is attacked and destroyed in AIDS patients.
9. **Intravenous** is related to **AIDS** in that intravenous drug users who share needles cause the spread of AIDS.

Part II

(Answers will vary. The answers here reflect the ideas that students should be thinking about.)

1. You would become ill and be unable to fight off diseases that your body normally has no problem fighting.
2. Because people are afraid that they can catch the disease from just being around someone who is HIV positive. Although this perception is incorrect, many people label HIV positive individuals as disgraceful.
3. You can catch it from casual contact, such as from eating utensils or hugging; it is transmitted by mosquitoes.
4. In Los Angeles in 1981.
5. Through sexual contact and through the sharing of hypodermic needles.

6. (Personal opinion called for here. While numbers have stabilized somewhat, many who carry HIV have yet to be diagnosed, so it may be hard to tell. We do know that the number of cases has risen dramatically since it was first isolated in 1981.)

7. An **opportunistic infection** is one that is successful only because the immune system was impaired for some other reason.

8. Measles (in a sense), since you are not allowed to go to school if you have measles; something such as coming in contact with the Ebola virus, typhoid, or cholera.

9. Because the HIV can remain dormant in the body for long periods of time without causing any symptoms of AIDS.

10. This is one major way in which HIV is spread—from one drug user to another.

11. Both are organisms that are so small that they can be seen only under a microscope.

12. If your **immune system** were **impaired**, you would have trouble fighting off infections since the job of the immune system is to destroy "invading" organisms.

13. Because it is a very harmful and damaging disease.

14. It was detected during the early 1980s when doctors in California and New York noticed that increasing numbers of patients were dying of rare and unusual infections that they had never seen before.

15. Africa.

16. HIV will attack his/her immune system and the individual will eventually get AIDS.

17. That HIV can be present in the body for a long time without the individual showing any symptoms of AIDS.

18. Because the major way that HIV is communicated is through sex.

Using Concepts

1. misconceptions
2. sophisticated
3. recipients
4. contaminated
5. suppresses; impairs
6. heterosexual
7. insidious
8. isolate
9. confirm
10. be prudent
11. asymptomatic
12. quarantine
13. epidemic
14. detect
15. predominant; prevalence
16. stigmatized
17. legions
18. transmitted
19. latency
20. spawn
21. conduit

Comprehending Concepts

Part I

1. One of the ways that HIV can be passed along to another person is through the sharing of contaminated needles by drug users.
2. Because they are both successful only in the bodies of individuals whose immune systems have been impaired.
3. Pathogens can destroy the immune system, making it open to any and all infections.
4. Hemophiliacs can become HIV positive if they are given transfusions of blood that contain HIV. They in turn will come down with AIDS.
5. Because there is no evidence that HIV lives in a mosquito's system, and because the insect does not inject blood from a previous meal, there is no way that a mosquito bite can transmit HIV.
6. Public health officials screen all blood to see if HIV antibodies are present. If such antibodies are present, the blood is not used for transfusions.
7. They are further examining the way that AIDS is transmitted by examining sexual practices and habits of intravenous drug users. In addition, they are studying ways to make our blood supply safer.
8. Probably began in Africa; the pathogen developed in such a way that it avoided all defenses of the immune system and attacked and destroyed it as well; went unrecognized for years; spread slowly to Europe, Haiti, and then to the U.S.; a few cases identified in the early 1970s, but it wasn't until the early 1980s that AIDS was attached as a name for the disease.
9. It suppresses the immune system. This drug is used most widely by organ transplant patients to avoid rejection of the transplanted organ.
10. Because you need a microscope to see it.

Part II—Writing Activities

1. Many people still believe that AIDS is spread through casual contact, through the food and water supply, and through mosquito bites. There is absolutely no evidence that AIDS can be spread through any of these conduits. These misconceptions may have come about because AIDS was spreading rapidly, and people did not want to accept the fact that a disease could spread so rapidly only through behaviors that were high-risk, such as unprotected sex or the sharing of hypodermic needles.

2. Researchers believe that the disease probably began in Africa. They know that the pathogen developed in such a way that it avoided all defenses of the immune system and that it attacked and destroyed it as well. The disease went unrecognized for years. Then it spread slowly to Europe and Haiti, and then to the U.S., where a few cases were identified in the early 1970s, but it wasn't until the early 1980s that AIDS was attached as a name for the disease. Epidemiologists believe that the disease is "new" because it has been around for a relatively brief period of time. In addition, it was spawned in the jungles of Africa, where "new" diseases arise all the time.

Posttest II—Readings A, B, and C

DIRECTIONS: The items in this posttest are based on all three readings in this chapter: "If You Light Up on Sunday, Don't Come in on Monday," "Health Care: How We Got Into This Mess," and "AIDS."

Part I
(Answer each of these questions in such a way that it is clear that you have a conceptual understanding of the words in bold print.)

1. How does **quarantining** curb the **contagiousness** of **communicable** diseases? _____

   _____

2. When might **moonlighting** be a **prudent** thing to do? _____

   _____

   _____

3. What might happen if the **restrictions**, health care were **unbounded?** _____

   _____

4. When might it be to your advantage to act **sophisticated?**

   _____

   _____

5. What about the health care system is a **paradox?** Why is it considered a **paradox?** _____

   _____

6. Why is smoking **deemed insidious** by many people? _____

_____

_____

7. What would you have to do if your doctor **detected** that your sight was **impaired?** _____

_____

8. Why are many people who are **HIV** positive **asymptomatic**?

_____

_____

9. What might happen if a number of questions on your test were **ambiguous?** _____

_____

PART II DIRECTIONS: Use the directions on page 317.

10. Give an example of a **volatile incident**.

_____

11. Give an example of a **contagious** and **universal** illness.

_____

12. Give an example of a situation for which you might receive **massive compensation.**

_____

13. Give an example of what you might discuss in an **impersonal** conversation.

_____

PART III DIRECTIONS: Use the directions on page 325.

14. batteries
legions
disincentives

15. devastating
levied
insidious

16. fosters
spawned
estimates

17. proffers
    incentives
    reimbursements

18. suppressor
    conduit
    transmitter

19. intravenous
    antibodies
    hypodermic

PART VI DIRECTIONS: *Use directions on page 297.*

predominant   crank   sentiment
epidemiologists   surcharge   recipient
epidemic

20. **dilemma**: problem :: _____ : widespread

21. **prevalence**: _____ :: **grim**: **scourge**

22. **deficit**: **inflation** :: _____ : tax

23. _____ : **AIDS** :: **proponents**: causes

24. **fraternize**: loner :: _____ : taker

25. _____ : serious :: **stigmatize**: praise

PART V DIRECTIONS: *Use directions on page 322.*

26. Is it **justifiable** to **ban** something that **contaminates** the air
    we breath? Why or why not? _____

    _____

27. Why is it sometimes appropriate to receive **perks** for something
    you have done? _____

    _____

28. Is it always a good idea to **confirm** your airplane reservations?
    Why or why not? _____

    _____

29. Why are there so many **misconceptions** about how **AIDS** is transmitted? _____

_____

30. Are you an **autonomous** learner? How do you know? _____

_____

Posttest II—Readings A, B, and C

Part I
(Answers will vary.)

1. People who are quarantined are isolated so that they cannot infect anyone else. Therefore, the disease cannot be spread.
2. When you are just starting out and don't make very much money. You might want to work a second job in order to save some money or to buy some things you need.
3. Health care providers would have to charge excessive amounts of money, or they may even have to go out of business.
4. If you were in a social situation with your new boss, you would want her to think that you could handle yourself.
5. The fact that people are living longer, but they don't have the money to pay for the health care they need.
6. Because smoking is harmful not only to those who smoke, but also to nonsmoking people who happen to be around those who are smoking.
7. You would have to get glasses or contact lenses.
8. Because the HIV virus can be present in the body for many years without showing any visible signs or symptoms.
9. You might have a hard time answering them, because what the instructor wanted would not be very clear.

Part II
(Answers will vary. The following are meant to serve as examples.)

10. Right to life and prochoice groups demonstrating outside an abortion clinic.
11. The common cold.
12. A malpractice suit against a hospital.
13. You might discuss the weather, sports, or your garden.

Part III

(Answers to *b* will vary somewhat. Answers should reflect the over-all concept of the two like words.)

14. a. disincentives
    b. a number or quantity of something
15. a. levied
    b. harmful; damaging
16. a. estimates
    b. caused to happen
17. a. proffers
    b. something you get back; rewards
18. a. suppressor
    b. something that serves to transport
19. a. antibodies
    b. inside something

Part IV

20. epidemic
21. predominant
22. surcharge
23. epidemiologists
24. recipient
25. crank

Part V

(Answers may vary.)

26. Yes; because it can cause health damage to everyone.
27. Because if you have worked really hard, it is appropriate to receive a little something extra for your efforts.
28. Yes; because planes are more often late than they are on time, and sometimes flights are canceled altogether.
29. Because people seem not to know the facts about AIDS; they rely on what people have told them.
30. Yes; because I like to study alone and I know what to do in order to make good grades.

CHAPTER 8   READINGS CONCERNING THE ENVIRONMENT

Reading A—"A Fable for Tomorrow"

Pretest

1. c	5. c	9. d
2. a	6. d	10. a
3. c	7. a	11. d
4. a	8. b	12. b

Determining Meaning

Part I—Parts of Speech

1. noun
2. noun
3. verb
4. noun
5. verb
6. adjective
7. noun
8. adjective
9. adjective
10. noun
11. adjective
12. verb

Part I—Definitions
(Answers will vary depending on the dictionary used.)

1. *anglers*—fishermen who use hooks.
2. *blight*—an adverse environmental condition, such as air pollution.
3. *brooded*—sat on or hatched eggs.
4. *counterparts*—things which are similar to each other.
5. *droned*—made a continuous low, dull humming sound.
6. *harmony*—agreement in feeling, opinion, accord.
7. *maladies*—diseases, disorders, or ailments.
8. *moribund*—approaching the point of death; about to die.
9. *prosperous*—having success; flourishing.
10. *specter*—a threatening or haunting possibility.
11. *stark*—extreme or harsh.
12. *withered*—dried up or shriveled from lack of moisture.

Part II
(Answers will vary.)

Part III

1. *mal* means bad, badly, or abnormal.
2. Answers will vary depending on words chosen.
3. *mori* means to die.
4. Answers will vary depending on words chosen.

Trying Out Meaning

(Answers will vary. The responses here reflect the ideas that students should be thinking about.)

1. I (The *blight* that swept across Africa destroyed what little food was left in the fields.)
2. I (We could tell by looking at the *withered* leaves that the plant was in terrible shape and required some tender, loving care.)
3. I (Individuals who are *prosperous* live in big houses and drive expensive cars.)
4. C
5. I (The *anglers* went on a weekend camping trip to fish.)
6. C
7. I (Every time you entered Sam's home and saw him playing with his children, you could sense the *harmony* there.)
8. C
9. I (The puppy appeared *moribund* as he lay in a corner, hardly moving a muscle.)
10. I (A small, rural town would not be considered a *counterpart* to a big city.)
11. C
12. C

Applying Meaning

(Answers will vary. The responses here reflect the ideas that students should be thinking about.)

1. lie very still and whine because it is in pain.
2. water them or ask someone at a nursery what the problem might be.
3. that people would not pollute and destroy the environment.
4. they stayed in a cabin by a lake or stream and there were plenty of fish to catch.
5. a forest fire had destroyed many acres.
6. their young grow inside their bodies and therefore their young are not hatched.

7. go see a doctor.
8. grains might be very highly priced.
9. fall asleep in class.
10. you kept making the same mistakes over and over.
11. people with whom you have much in common.
12. a big house, a condo on the beach, and an expensive sports car.

Conceptualizing Meaning

Part I
(Answers to *b* will vary somewhat. Answers should reflect the overall concept of the three like words, however.)

1. a. lively
   b. death or death-like
2. a. harmony
   b. disease or sickness
3. a. rifle
   b. all associated with fishing
4. a. moribund
   b. positive terms that have to do with peace
5. a. specter
   b. plain or not fancy

Part II
(Answers will vary. The responses here reflect the ideas that students should be thinking about.)

1. An epidemic of some illness such as mononucleosis or measles.
2. A rod and reel.
3. A boring professor or a minister.
4. The United States and Canada.
5. If you were getting ready to paint the walls and had just removed everything from the walls.

Extending and Challenging, Part II: Writing Activity

(Answers will vary.)

1. A fable is defined as a short narrative that often has a cautionary message, which is what "A Fable for Tomorrow" is. Using an imaginary town, Carson cautions readers about what might happen if people don't take care of the environment. She says that this has not occurred yet, but without changing our actions, it may.

2. Pesticides are chemicals that are used on plants to kill pests, generally insects that harm plants. In newspaper articles, students might find information about the unknown risks of pesticides, how pesticides have been made safer, natural pesticides, and what might happen to crops and food production if all pesticides were banned. For the most part, very dangerous pesticides (such as DDT) have been taken off the market. But because the long-term effects of pesticides are really not known, Carson would probably not be pleased with what we read in the paper today about them.

Reading B—"Reusing and Recycling Materials"

Pretest

1. b	7. a	13. a
2. a	8. c	14. b
3. c	9. b	15. c
4. b	10. d	16. d
5. a	11. c	17. a
6. d	12. d	18. a

Determining Meaning

Part I—Parts of Speech

1. noun	10. adverb
2. noun	11. noun
3. adjective	12. noun
4. verb	13. noun
5. verb	14. noun
6. verb	15. verb
7. noun	16. adjective
8. verb	17. adjective/adverb
9. noun	18. noun

Part I—Definitions
(Answers will vary depending on the dictionary used.)

1. *aberration*—a deviation from the proper or expected course.
2. *composting*—converting decaying, organic matter such as leaves or vegetables into fertilizer.
3. *comprehensive*—large in scope or content.
4. *dispersed*—broken up or scattered in various directions.
5. *embodied*—represented in concrete form.
6. *emits*—releases; sends out.

7. *ethic*—a principle of right and good conduct.
8. *facilitate*—to make easier.
9. *hierarchy*—a body of entities arranged in a graded or ranked series.
10. *modestly*—moderately.
11. *obsolescence*—the process of becoming outdated or outmoded in style or design.
12. *revenue*—a source of income.
13. *scarcity*—insufficient amount or supply; shortage.
14. *simplification*—made simpler or less complex.
15. *slash*—to reduce or curtail dramatically.
16. *sustainable*—keeping in existence; maintainable.
17. *systematic*—carried out in a step-by-step procedure.
18. *transition*—the process or an instance of changing from one form, state, activity, or place to another.

Part II
(Answers will vary depending on words chosen.)

Part III
1. Answers will vary.
2. You get little from context. If you don't know something about this word, context probably will not help much.
3. There is no prefix.
4. Latin, *sustinere*, meaning "to hold up."
5. Enduring or withstanding.
6. They really didn't add much because it would be hard to recognize the root word. It has changed somewhat from the original Latin root.

Trying Out Meaning
1. comprehensive
2. slash
3. aberration
4. revenue
5. composting
6. hierarchy
7. obsolescence
8. simplification
9. modest
10. systematic
11. emits
12. scarcity
13. disperse
14. facilitate
15. ethics
16. embodied
17. transition
18. sustain

Applying Meaning

(Explanations of *why* may vary. The responses here reflect the kinds of ideas that students should be thinking about.)

1. No. Computers are still widely used and their uses continue to grow.
2. Yes. Fruit and leaves would be organically rich and could make good fertilizer.
3. Yes. Diseases could kill both plants and animals, causing food supplies to become less and less.
4. Yes. Living that long is a rare occurrence and would be considered strange.
5. No. There are few people who live that long that he or she could be compared to.
6. No. Releasing sewage into the water supply would not be a very moral thing to do.
7. No. Everyone could eat as much as they wanted if the land was doing very well.
8. No. The government must generate money through taxes or the entire country would come to a stop.
9. Yes. If you studied everything in a step-by-step manner you would probably do well in all of your courses.
10. Yes. They might be able to work something out through discussion.
11. Yes. Georgia is a state within the continental United States.
12. Yes. It would cause too much pollution and should receive attention from an automobile mechanic.
13. Yes. The series goes from the lowest to the highest number.
14. Yes. The directions are often so complex that they are impossible to understand. Making them easier might also make it easier to connect the VCR.
15. No. If your salary were raised, you would expect to see more in your take-home pay, not a drastic reduction in it.
16. No. The more fish the merrier for anglers!

Conceptualizing Meaning

(Sentences that students write will vary.)

Extending and Challenging

3. *simplification*—noun   *simplify*—verb

   The *simplification* of the tax form made it easier for people to complete it without the assistance of an accountant.

When the government decided to *simplify* the tax form, many people were able to complete it without the assistance of an accountant.

4. *transition*—noun   *transitional*—adjective

When our college made the *transition* from the quarter to the semester system, it was difficult for both students and faculty at first.

After switching from the quarter to the semester system, both faculty and students went through a difficult *transitional* period.

5. *sustainable*—noun   *sustenance*—verb

Although the food we ate during our week at the spa was *sustainable*, just about everyone was hungry all the time.

Although the food we ate during our week at the spa provided us *sustenance* to stay alive, just about everyone was hungry all the time.

Part II Writing Activities Directions:

(Answers will vary.)

1. She would most likely approve since Carson was for any and all measures that would improve the environment. She might suggest that laws become harsher on polluters and that people be fined if they don't recycle.

2. Manufacturers can make more containers that are biodegradable; more research can be conducted to discover pesticides that are environmentally friendly; use some garbage to compost. In your home you should recycle, bring your groceries home in reusable cloth bags; reuse plastic bags.

3. Answers will vary.

Posttest I—Readings A and B

PART I DIRECTIONS: Answer each of the following questions so that it is clear that you understand the meaning of the word in bold print.

1. **Anglers** might worry about a **scarcity** of what?

_____

2. What would you do if your dog appeared **moribund?**

_____

3. Why might a gardener try **composting?**

_____

4. When might you have to make a **transition** of some kind?

_____

5. In what occupation might you make a **modest** salary?

_____

6. What kind of **malady** might put you in the hospital?

_____

PART II DIRECTIONS: Complete the analogies using one of the targeted vocabulary words listed below. Remember to keep the same part of speech across the analogy. Refer to the examples on page 212 in Chapter 6.

withered	stark
specter	dispersed

7. obsolete: new :: _____: cluttered

8. _____: scattered :: emitted: leaked

9. droned: bees :: _____: flowers

PART III DIRECTIONS: When you can provide an example of a word, you generally have a good conceptual knowledge of that word. Follow the instructions below, and if necessary, explain your choices.

10. Give an example of when a department store might **slash** prices.

_____

11. Give an example of when you might **brood** about something.

_____

12. Give an example of something that might cause a **blight** in the nation's farmland.

_____

13. Give an example of something you might try to do to **facilitate** learning.

_____

14. Give an example of how someone would behave if he or she had a strong work **ethic.**

_____

15. Give an example of someone who would be your **counterpart.**

_____

*PART IV DIRECTIONS: Read each sentence carefully, paying particular attention to the boldfaced words. Mark **T** if the statement is true, and go on to the next item. If, however, the statement is false, mark **F** and then make it correct by adding, deleting, or in some other way changing the sentence.*

T   F   **16.** Snow in July would be considered an **aberration** in most states.

T   F   **17.** People who are **prosperous** are eligible for welfare.

T   F   **18.** A **comprehensive** exam would cover just the basics of a course.

T   F   **19.** Students who study in a **systematic** way rarely make good grades.

T   F   **20.** Couples often break up when their relationship is **harmonious.**

Posttest I—Readings A and B

Part I
(Answers may vary.)

1. Fish.
2. Take him to the veterinarian.
3. So she would have rich soil to put on her garden.
4. When you go back to school; when you move; when you get married.
5. A secretary; a teacher; a police officer.
6. Appendicitis; heart problems; a broken leg.

Part II

7. stark
8. dispersed
9. withered

Part III
(Answers may vary.)

10. After inventory, when they want to get rid of merchandise.
11. If someone said something to you that hurt your feelings.

12. An abundance of insects, such as grasshoppers; a drought.
13. Being an active reader; getting help when you don't understand something.
14. They would go to work every day and do a good job.
15. Your peers or someone who has the same job that you have.

Part IV

16. T
17. F People who are prosperous do not need welfare.
18. F A comprehensive exam would cover everything presented in a course.
19. F Students who study in a systematic way usually make good grades.
20. F Couples generally stay together when their relationship is harmonious.

Reading C—"Ecology and Economics: Tending Our Houses"

Determining Meaning

Part I—Parts of Speech

1. adjective
2. verb
3. noun
4. verb
5. noun
6. verb
7. adjective
8. noun
9. verb
10. adjective
11. noun
12. verb
13. adjective
14. verb
15. noun
16. noun
17. verb
18. verb
19. adjective

Part II—Definitions
(Answers will vary depending on the dictionary used.)

1. *avid*—marked by keen interest and enthusiasm.
2. *befouled*—made dirty or soiled.
3. *cartel*—a combination of independent business organizations formed to regulate production, pricing, and marketing of goods.
4. *decimated*—inflicted great destruction or damage on.
5. *depletion*—the act or process of using something up or emptying out.
6. *diverged*—went in different directions from a common point.

7. *hospitable*—favorable; agreeable.
8. *inhabitants*—those who live or reside in a certain place.
9. *lauded*—praised; glorified.
10. *lethal*—capable of causing death; extremely harmful.
11. *myriads*—many; vast numbers of something.
12. *obliged*—made indebted or grateful.
13. *pivotal*—being of vital importance; critical.
14. *precipitate*—to cause to happen, often suddenly or prematurely.
15. *predecessors*—those who come before others in time.
16. *successors*—those who come after others in time.
17. *surmise*—to make a conjecture or guess, often without sufficient evidence.
18. *sweltered*—suffered from oppressive heat.
19. *tangible*—real or concrete; touchable.

General Words

1. inhabitants
2. befouled
3. obliged
4. avid
5. depletion
6. lethal
7. tangible
8. decimated
9. hospitable
10. Myriads
11. surmise
12. lauded
13. diverged
14. precipitated
15. cartel
16. successors
17. predecessors
18. sweltered
19. pivotal

Content-Specific Words

(Answers will vary. The following are examples of what students might say. NOTE: Students may be totally unfamiliar with many of these content-specific terms.)

1. *biogeochemical view*—biological, chemical, geological
2. *biosphere*—earth, life, environment
3. *botanist*—plants, scientist, research
4. *carbonates*—carbon, rocks, chemistry
5. *ecology*—environment, conservation, recycling
6. *economics*—money, business, spending
7. *ecosystems*—ecology, balance, plants, animals
8. *environmentalist*—ecology, protection, pollution
9. *geochemical view*—geological, chemical, belief

10. *global warming*—hotter temperatures, little rain, warmer winters
11. *greenhouse gases*—oxygen, carbon dioxide, air
12. *greenhouse effect*—warmth, oxygen, carbon monoxide
13. *incubator*—greenhouse effect, warmth, protection
14. *organic processes*—living things, plants, fertilizer
15. *ozone layer*—protection, "holes," radiation
16. *pesticides*—bugs, chemicals, spraying
17. *sedimentary rocks*—hard, carbonates, bottom
18. *species*—plants, animals, types
19. *toxic*—pesticides, poisonous harmful

Part II
(Answers will vary.)

1. *sweltered*—students could make an association with the word *sweat*, with an image of the sun beating down, and think "When it swelters, you sweat!"
2. *lethal*—those who saw the movie "Lethal Weapon" should have no problems with this word.
3. *decimated*—students could make an association with the word *desert*, with an image of a desert, which often looks *decimated*.

Determining Meaning—Content-Specific Words

(Answers will vary. The responses below indicate the ideas students should be thinking about.)

1. *biogeochemical view*—the belief that living organisms play a major role in regulating carbon dioxide levels in the environment.
2. *biosphere*—the part of the earth and its atmosphere capable of supporting life.
3. *botanist*—one who specializes in the study of plants.
4. *carbonates*—when carbon dioxide combines with elements such as calcium and magnesium to form insoluble compounds.
5. *ecology*—the science of the relationships between organisms and their environment.
6. *economics*—the social science that deals with the production, distribution, and consumption of goods and services.
7. *ecosystems*—an ecological community together with its environment, functioning as a unit.
8. *environmentalist*—one who works toward protecting the natural environment.

9. *geochemical view*—the belief that Earth's carbon dioxide cycle is strictly physical (rather than also biological) in nature.
10. *global warming*—the belief that Earth's average temperature is increasing and causing strange weather patterns.
11. *greenhouse gases*—carbon dioxide, water vapor, and certain other gases that are involved in the greenhouse effect.
12. *greenhouse effect*—the phenomenon in which the earth's atmosphere traps solar radiation, caused by the presence of gases such as carbon dioxide that allow incoming sunlight to pass through, but absorb heat radiated back from the earth's surface.
13. *incubator*—a device for controlling temperature, humidity, and oxygen level.
14. *organic processes*—processes related to living things.
15. *ozone layer*—a protective layer in the upper atmosphere that protects against ultraviolet radiation.
16. *pesticides*—a chemical used to kill pests, especially insects.
17. *sedimentary rocks*—rocks formed by the deposit of fragments of inorganic material, such as limestone.
18. *toxic*—poisonous.

Organizing Concepts

Part I

(Answers may vary.)

HISTORICAL PERSPECTIVE

inhabitants

Economics → **def.** *economics = human*

household management

Ecology → **def.** *ecology = study of*

↓   *nature's "houses"*

ecosystems

environmentalist

biosphere

↓

Greenhouse Effect

greenhouse gases

hospitable

_____

↓

Role of Carbon Dioxide

Geochemical View   **Biogeochemical View**

carbonates   *organic process*

sedimentary rocks   *myriads*

precipitate

Part II
(Answers will vary.)

Beginning Conceptual Understanding

(Answers for false statements will vary. The responses here reflect the kind of changes that students should be thinking about.)

1. F A botanist believes that the decimation of plants would help destroy the ozone layer.
2. T
3. F The geochemical view states that the earth's temperature is regulated by physical processes only.
4. F Limestone and dolomite are examples of sedimentary rocks.
5. F Greenhouse gases are not lethal to our ecosystems.
6. F According to the greenhouse effect, changes in weather patterns would be precipitated if the earth's temperature increased by only a few degrees.
7. T
8. T
9. T
10. T
11. T
12. T
13. F Global warming has resulted from the earth slowly moving closer to the sun.
14. F Incubators are used to keep things warm.

Using Concepts

(Answers will vary. The responses here reflect the ideas that students should be thinking about.)

1. if it helped clean up toxic waste in the community and upgraded its antipollution devices.
2. go inside where it is air-conditioned.
3. we would have to import fuels such as oil.
4. the group Greenpeace, who are very pro-environment, to those who believe that any environmental regulations should be done away with.
5. it treats everyone who lives there nicely.
6. it would take considerable time and money to clean up the mess.
7. can choose the one that is best for you.
8. not be of any use to anyone, animals or persons.

can actually notice that something has been done.
] . you believe that you did well, but you haven't seen your grade to confirm your beliefs.
1. they have invited you to their home on several occasions.
12. Jimmy Carter.
13. President Bush or Clinton.
14. might recycle everything, compost your trash, and join environmental organizations.
15. regulating the price of oil.
16. a tanker crashing into some rocks.
17. World War II.

Comprehending Concepts

(Answers will vary. The responses here reflect the ideas that students should be thinking about.)

1. Those who believe in the **geochemical view** of temperature regulation think that the carbon dioxide cycle involves strictly physical processes rather than biological and physical processes that are part of the **biogeochemical view**.
2. Generally not in a positive light. They were often at odds with government and economists. However, researchers strengthened some of their predecessors' findings, and some important ecological bills were passed.
3. Gases in the earth's atmosphere let in sunlight but keep heat from escaping, working much like a greenhouse, thus the name, **greenhouse effect**.
4. **Greenhouse gases** enable us to regulate the earth's temperature so that it is a hospitable place to live.
5. Because the makeup of the atmosphere helps to keep the earth warm.
6. The book began the environmental movement by warning of the dangers that **pesticides** had on the environment.
7. The split occurred over botanist Linnaeus's essay which argued that nature was there to serve man. Others such as Thoreau argued that man must learn to live in harmony with nature, not abuse it.
8. Because he believed that God created nature exclusively for the use of man.
9. Because the carbon dioxide in the atmosphere dissolves in rain and forms a weak acid that erodes rocks made of calcium, silicon, and oxygen. This mixture travels in streams to oceans, where it combines with calcium and magnesium to form carbonates.

10. The **ozone layer** protects us from harmful radiation. Holes in the ozone layer can cause increased cases of skin cancer.
11. Because the biogeochemical view believes that living things also play a role in regulating the earth's temperature. Organic processes also involve living things rather than just nonliving things, such as rocks.
12. Limestone and dolomite are two **sedimentary rocks**.
13. **Ecosystems** can become damaged or even destroyed.
14. Weather patterns could change, resulting in things such as droughts and heat waves.

Posttest II—Readings A, B, and C

PART I DIRECTIONS: When you can provide an example of a word, you generally have a good conceptual knowledge of that word. Follow the instructions below, and if necessary, explain your choices.

1. Give an example of something that is ***obsolete.***

_____

2. Give an example of something that could be ***slashed.***

_____

3. Give an example of when you might ***swelter.***

_____

4. Give an example of something that can be ***composted.***

_____

5. Give an example of something that is ***toxic.***

_____

6. Give an example of a ***malady.***

_____

7. Give an example of something that parents are ***obliged*** to do for their children.

_____

8. Give an example of a substance that would ***befoul*** water.

_____

9. Give an example of something that most people would *laud.*

_____

10. Give an example of something that you might have to learn *hierarchically.*

_____

11. Give an example of a course in which you might be required to learn a *myriad* of theories.

_____

PART II DIRECTIONS: Answer each of the following questions so that it is clear that you understand the meaning of the italicized word.

12. How might you *deplete* your bank account? _____

_____

13. How do *anglers* like to spend their free time? _____

_____

14. When might it be very important to do something in a *systematic* fashion? _____

_____

15. What might be considered a *blight* upon the land? _____

_____

16. What might *precipitate* a concern about *global warming?*

_____

17. When might it be important to be *hospitable?* _____

_____

18. In what country is there a *scarcity* of food? _____

_____

19. What might an *avid* gardener do? _____

_____

20. When can *pesticides* be *lethal* to humans? _____

_____

21. When might you appear *moribund?* _____

_____

*PART III DIRECTIONS: Read each sentence carefully. If the
italicized word is used correctly, circle C and go on to the next item.
If, however, the italicized word is used incorrectly, circle I and then
make the sentence correct.*

C   I   **22.** The *withered* fruit was plump, juicy, and picked only
this morning.

C   I   **23.** Someone who drives a Mercedes would be considered by
most to be a *prosperous* individual.

C   I   **24.** Jimmy Carter was a *predecessor* of Ronald Reagan.

C   I   **25.** Oil is easily *dispersed* in water.

C   I   **26.** A *comprehensive* test in a course would cover only a
portion of the information.

C   I   **27.** Those who are *modest* need to be the center of attention
whenever they are with a crowd of people.

C   I   **28.** We must pay our share of *revenue* in order for this
country to operate properly.

C   I   **29.** Forest fires are a major reason why some timberlands
are very *stark.*

C   I   **30.** *Pivotal* decisions rarely make a difference.

C   I   **31.** *Environmentalists embody* the idea that we must save
our *ecosystems*.

C   I   **32.** The *decimation* of the *ozone layer* presents little
problem for our environment.

C   I   **33.** Pollution is an *aberration* that has *diverged* to include
most areas of the United States.

C   I   **34.** The *ecologists* study pollutants that are *emitted* into
the air.

C   I   **35.** When plants *wither* we can *surmise* that they need to
be watered.

PART IV DIRECTIONS: Circle the word that does not belong, and then, in the space provided, explain what is similar about the two remaining words.

36. toxic   harmonious   lethal

_____

37. harmonious   tangible   hospitable

_____

38. carbonates   sedimentary rocks   pesticides

_____

39. cartel   composting   organic processes

_____

40. scarcity   depletion   diverged

_____

41. facilitate   oblige   brood

_____

Total Correct _____

Posttest

Part I
(Answers will vary.)

1. Typewriter.
2. The top of a convertible.
3. When the temperature reaches 100°.
4. Leaves, pine needles.
5. Mercury; many pesticides.
6. The common cold.
7. Feed and care for them; provide guidance.
8. Oil.
9. Giving money to charity.
10. Mathematics.
11. Psychology.

Part II
(Answers will vary.)

12. By going on an expensive vacation.
13. Fishing.
14. When you have to put something together and you have to follow the directions step-by-step in order for the object to be usable.
15. A severe drought.
16. When there is an extended heat wave or drought.
17. When you are entertaining your boss.
18. Some countries in Africa; other Third World countries.
19. Work in her garden all the time.
20. If they are exposed to too much of a pesticide.
21. During a bad illness.

Part III
(Changes to the incorrect items will vary. The responses here reflect the kind of changes that students should be thinking about.)

22. I (The *withered* fruit was rotten and dried out and looked like it had been picked a week ago.)
23. C
24. C
25. I (Oil is difficult and sometimes impossible to *disperse* in water.)
26. I (A *comprehensive* test in a course would cover all of the information presented during the entire term.)
27. I (Those who are *modest* do not like to be the center of attention whenever they are out with a crowd of people.)
28. C
29. C
30. I (*Pivotal* decisions usually make a big difference.)
31. C
32. I (The *decimation* of the *ozone* layer presents major problems to our environment because it increases the risk of getting skin cancer.)
33. C
34. C
35. C

Part IV

(Answers for *b* will vary.)

36. a. harmonious
   b. Both have to do with something being deadly.
37. a. tangible
   b. Both have to do with being nice or things working together.
38. a. pesticides
   b. Both have to do with the geochemical view of how earth's temperature is regulated.
39. a. cartel
   b. Both have to do with biological processes.
40. a. diverged
   b. Both have to do with something diminishing or getting smaller.
41. a. brood
   b. Both have to do with helping or assisting.